OULD FIELDS,
NEW CORNE

The Personal Memoirs

of a Twentieth Century Lawyer

By

ERWIN N. GRISWOLD

"Out of ould fields must spring and grow the new Corne"
Sir Edward Coke, Commentaries, Vol. 1, Preface (1600)

WEST PUBLISHING CO.
ST. PAUL, MINN.
1992

Library of Congress Cataloging-in-Publication Data

Griswold, Erwin N. (Erwin Nathaniel), 1904–
    Ould fields, new corne : the personal memoirs of a twentieth
century lawyer / by Erwin N. Griswold.
        p.   cm.
    ISBN 0–314–92951–7
    1. Griswold, Erwin N. (Erwin Nathaniel), 1904–   2. Lawyers—
United States—Biography. I. Title. II. Title: Old fields, new corn.
KF373.G745A3 1992
349.73'092—dc20
[B]
[347.30092]
[B]   91–35927
                                                    CIP

ISBN 0–314–92951–7

Griswold, Memoirs

To
My family,
who have given me warmth and motivation,
and to the legal profession
which, with all its faults,
stands up well against other varieties of mankind.

*

Preface

There is an inevitable brashness in writing a book like this. It is a personal memoir, not a history of the time. It records my pathway as I saw it and remember it—with full recognition, though, that the view of others may have been quite different. It is inherently egocentric—a harsh sort of word. Any hesitation I may have had, though, has been overcome by the encouragement of friends. Michael Boudin, now a judge of the United States District Court for the District of Columbia, was particularly persistent, and I owe thanks to him for getting me started at the task.

Even as a memoir the book is perhaps boldly unusual. Since it is about a lawyer and his work, it is written in what some would call "legalese," with, among other things, footnotes and citations. Those who find this burdensome may read the text and ignore the footnotes. Others may find interesting and useful details in these notes. And they will serve as evidence that I have, to the extent feasible, sought to substantiate my account of the events with which I have been occupied over a period of eighty years, covering every decade of this century.

Acknowledgment has been made in the book to the many people who have helped me along the way, particularly my family, and many members of my staffs. I mention here only my wife, Harriet, who despite "the slings and arrows of outrageous fortune," has played a full role in our joint career. My secretary, Jeanette Moe, has kept my office going for the past eighteen years, with skill and understanding. Particularly with respect to this book, she has provided me with the full benefit of word processors, which are still beyond me.

There are many other acknowldgements I should make—to my colleagues and staff at the Harvard Law School, in the Solicitor General's office, and in the office of Jones, Day, Reavis & Pogue. Many people have given me loyalty and support over the years, and I am grateful to all of them.

In the preparation of this book, Harva Sheeler, the librarian at Jones, Day, and members of her staff, particularly Jill Long, have been constantly helpful. They have produced any book I needed, on short notice. They have provided bibliographical material, and have tracked down quotations. They have, indeed, provided me with anything I asked for, and with amazing speed.

The final part of the dedication, relating to the legal profession, is, of course, based on, though not a quotation from, the well-known remarks of Harrison Tweed in his speech accepting the presidency of the Association of the Bar of the City of New York on May 20, 1945.

Finally, I express my deep appreciation to Jones Day Reavis & Pogue, and the three managing partners under whom I have served, Jack Reavis, Allen Holmes, and Richard Pogue. All have been remarkable men, fine lawyers, with a sense of public service, excellent administrators, with tempered vision, and great energy. During my period with the firm they have planned the "national firm," and have carried it out effectively. It has long been my view that the key to the future of the world will be found in the development of better understanding and greater trust among peoples. That can only be brought about by more substantial and more frequent contacts, and here the international law firm has a promising role. It can facilitate contacts between clients on an international basis, can arrange these contacts in such a way that disputes can be avoided or minimized, and can join with others who are concerned about interchange and harmony on an international and indeed global basis. Though the law is only one angle of approach, lawyers may have a fruitful role to play, not only for their clients, but for the formulation of attitudes and arrangements which will help materially in paving the way for a more peaceful world.

As I was working on this book, my private title for it was "Have fun—and try to do some good." Through the years, with some stress and strain, I have had much fun in my life. If I have been able to do some good, it has been a privilege, and but a small recompense for what my legal life has done for me. I hope that others may find some interest in this overview as I have seen it through my eyes.

ERWIN N. GRISWOLD

Washington, D.C.
October, 1991

Table of Contents

vii

*

OULD FIELDS,
NEW CORNE

THE PERSONAL MEMOIRS
OF A TWENTIETH CENTURY LAWYER

*

CHAPTER I

Introduction

A. BEFORE THE BEGINNING

The Western Reserve was a good place to start.

The thirteen colonies along the Atlantic Seaboard, which joined in the rebellion against Great Britain, were loosely linked together by the Continental Congress and then by the Articles of Confederation. Probably the most important action taken by the government under the Articles of Confederation was the enactment of the Ordinance of 1787, establishing the Northwest Territory. Before this could be accomplished, the Confederation had to obtain the release to the United States of conflicting claims to western lands by the eastern states. Connecticut gave its release in 1786, but it reserved to itself the ownership of all the land north of the forty-first parallel of latitude and extending for one hundred twenty miles west of the Pennsylvania boundary. Thus was set off an area which has since been known as the Western Reserve.

More than a hundred years ago, it was said that "No other five thousand square miles in the United States, lying in a body outside of New England, ever had, to begin with, so pure a New England population." [1] In the 1790s, much of the land was granted to the Connecticut Land Company, which consisted of a group of thirty-five men who purchased a tract of three million acres in the Reserve. Sylvanus Griswold, with a commitment of $1,683, was one of the thirty-five.[2] Another one of the purchas-

---

1. B. N. Hinsdale, The Old Northwest (New York, 1888) 388.

2. Harlan Hatcher, The Western Reserve—The Story of Northwest Connecticut in Ohio (New York, 1949) 25.

1

ers was Moses Cleaveland, of Canterbury, Connecticut, who was made general agent of the company and charged with surveying its lands. Cleaveland arrived at the Cuyahoga River on the south shore of Lake Erie on the fourth of July, 1796, with a party of fifty-two. The town which grew up there was named after Moses Cleaveland. Somehow, about 1830, the spelling of the name changed to Cleveland.

Going west, along the shore of Lake Erie, the Western Reserve begins with Conneaut. Then comes Ashtabula, Geneva, Painesville and Mentor. Just south of Mentor is Kirtland, where the early Mormons, on their way west, established a church which still stands. A number of the towns have names derived from Connecticut, such as Trumbull, Windsor, Hartford and Brookfield. Southwest of Cleveland is Oberlin, where Oberlin College was established in 1833. The western part of the Western Reserve, including the present counties outside the tract sold to the Connecticut Land Company, was known as the Firelands, and was granted by the General Assembly of Connecticut to citizens who had suffered losses brought about by British troops during the Revolutionary War.

The Western Reserve is gently rolling, with slopes down to Lake Erie resulting from the glacial action which created Lake Erie and the other Great Lakes. The recession of the glaciers left several ridges which, because of the drainage they provided, were the early sites of roads. Thus, there remain today the North Ridge Road, and the Center Ridge Road, between Cleveland and Oberlin.

Settlement in the Western Reserve was slow. Books containing details written as late as 1815 show habitations few and far between, and a constant struggle for existence.[3] The towns developed slowly, and they were often much like Connecticut towns, with a central green, or common, often with a modest white church built on one side of the square. There were many trees, maples, elms, oaks, hickory and chestnut, among others. The original survey, by Moses Cleaveland and his group, marked out townships which were five miles square. This, in effect, started the system for the general land surveys of the United States. These began only a few years later at the point where the western boundary of Pennsylvania crosses the Ohio River. For some reason, the townships established by the general land office were six miles square, but this did not affect the townships already surveyed in the Western Reserve.

---

3. See, for example, A Tour to New Connecticut in 1811: The Narrative of Henry Leavitt Ellsworth (Cleveland: 1985).

My father, James Harlen Griswold, was born on January 27, 1873, in Hartsgrove, Ohio, a little town in the western part of Ashtabula County, in the Western Reserve. The day was, he often said, "the coldest day in the history of the Weather Bureau." The town had a few hundred people at that time, farmers and storekeepers, and probably has a smaller population today. Its origin in the New England tradition is readily observable. There is a Village Green, square, with white board fence, and two white painted churches, and several stores, ranged on the outside of the road surrounding the square.

My father never knew why his middle name was chosen. "My folks just liked it," he said. As he was always careful to follow himself, the final vowel was "e" and not "a". Many of his friends knew my father as "Harlen," although he was known about as often as "Jim."

In the Griswold line, his forbears went back to one of three brothers who came from Warwickshire, in England. Their baptism is recorded in the church in Kenilworth. My father's arriving ancestor was Edward Griswold, who, with his two brothers, came to Windsor, Connecticut, in 1639. The reason why they came to America is not definitely known. It is supposed, though, that the three brothers were younger members of the family who had no prospects in England, during those trying times, and that they came to sell lands in Connecticut on behalf of the Earl of Warwick, to whom large grants had been made.

The successive generations of the family lived in Windsor, Connecticut until about 1790, when the third Nathaniel Griswold moved to Enosburg, Vermont. (There were four Nathaniels altogether, which shows where I got my middle name.) How they ever survived the winters of northern Vermont, in those days, I do not know. Transportation was difficult. They were far from a river. It is hard to see how they got their crops out or their supplies in. It must have been a busy time for the women, as well as one of energetic activities for the farmers.

They were in Vermont about thirty-five years. The family story is that Nathaniel Griswold (the sixth generation in this country) endorsed a note or signed a bond for one of his neighbors. There was default, and Nathaniel was wiped out. At any rate, they moved to southern New Hampshire in about 1825, and traces of them are found in New Ipswich and other towns. In 1830, the family went out to Ohio on the Erie Canal. They proceeded by sailing vessel to Cleveland, and then located to the east, in Ashtabula County.

A few days after reaching Ohio, Nathaniel died, on July 26, 1830, probably from typhoid fever. His son, Nathaniel Wells Griswold, born October 24, 1801, in Enosburg, Vermont, was part of the family party, and he carried on, establishing a homestead, and obtaining a farm, located in Windsor, in the southwest corner of Ashtabula County.

Nathaniel Wells was my great grandfather. He had nine children, of whom my grandfather Henry Franklin Griswold, born March 8, 1840, was the youngest. It was he who bought the farm in Hartsgtove where my father was born—probably the poorest land in the Western Reserve. My father was the middle of three sons. My uncle, Wells Laird Griswold, born in 1869, was older, and my uncle Ralph was younger. Thus, my background through my father was New England, with a Western Reserve mid-western accent. In this line, I am in the tenth generation in America.

My mother's forbears, on the Erwin side, came originally from Scotland. (The Erwin name probably shows some connection with the Irvine Clan.) The family proceeded from Scotland to Ireland, and came to America, landing in Baltimore in the 1760s. Shortly thereafter, they were settled in Loudon County, Virginia. They were Quakers, of the Hicksite variety, which meant that their religious beliefs were quite free and liberal. In 1803, when a child was expected, they decided that they did not want to bring up their children where they had slaves. So they moved west. Since the present state of West Virginia was then part of Virginia, they did not reach free territory until they crossed the Ohio River into Ohio. Ohio was the easternmost part of the Northwest Territory, which the Continental Congress had established in 1787, with the provision that "There shall be neither slavery nor involuntary servitude in the said territory." [4] On the west side of the river was Columbiana County, where my great grandfather, Elisha Erwin, was born in 1803.

My grandfather, William Erwin, was born a little farther west, near Alliance, Ohio, on March 3, 1833—a date very easy to remember, since its short numerical form is 3/3/33. About 1848, my grandfather went west, before there was any railroad, driving a flock of sheep. He settled in Bourbon, Indiana, a town in the eastern part of Marshall County. [5] Later, his father, Elisha, came to Indiana, and also a number of his brothers and sisters.

---

4. Ordinance of 1787, Art. VI, printed in 1 Stat. 51, 53.

5. The town was apparently named by a group of settlers who came north from Bourbon County, Kentucky.

In 1875, William Erwin married Jane Cooper, usually known as Jenny. Jane Cooper had been born in a hamlet known as Rosgill, near Shap, in Westmorland County, England in 1848. She came to the United States with her parents by sailing vessel in 1856. The story is told that her father had tickets on one of the new-fangled steam vessels, but was warned by his friends that they often exploded, and were very unsafe. He changed his tickets to a sailing vessel after reaching his departure port. The steamboat took off, and was never seen again. The trip by sailing vessel was successful, but must have been rugged. One time, there was a heavy storm, and little Jenny was found on deck. A sailor picked her up and deposited her inside a coil of rope, where she easily road out the storm.

After reaching the United States, at Philadelphia, the family went west to Ohio, where they had relatives. For several years in the late 1860s, Jane Cooper taught elementary subjects at Mt. Union College in Aliance, Ohio. There are stories of William Erwin meeting Jenny Cooper in the 1850s, when he went to Ohio to visit his family. At any rate, he remembered her, and when his first wife died in the early 1870s, he went back to Ohio, found Jenny, and took her to Bourbon as his bride. Jane Cooper Erwin was well-read. She regularly gave lectures on literature and poetry to ladies' groups at county fairs in many parts of Indiana. She was accompanied in this task by Mrs. Wilkie, the mother of Wendell Wilkie, the Republican candidate for president in 1940.

My mother, Hope Erwin, was born on December 5, 1877, in a house near the center of Bourbon. Her name is said to have come from the fact that her mother kept saying "I hope it is a girl. I hope it is a girl." After a while, the prospective father, William, said: "Well, if it is a girl, I guess we had better name her Hope."

Thus, on my mother's side, my background is a combination of Quaker and Lake Country, England. Through my mother, and her mother, I am a third generation American, with a definitely English outlook. We still have Cooper cousins in England with whom we keep in touch.

Up to this point, all of my direct American ancestors were farmers. They made their living, but they had to work hard to do that, and no fortunes were built up. In the direct line, until my father's generation, none of my ancestors had gone to college, although there were ancestors of some of the women who married into the family who had gone to college, including Harvard. But they were very few. It was, indeed, in nearly all the generations, a typical American rural family, where hard work was the rule, leisure was scarce, and substantial intellectual activities were rare, but not unknown.

My father's oldest brother, my uncle Wells, was the first member of our line of the family who went to college. After going through the local schools, he taught at New Lyme Academy in order to earn some money to enable him to go to college. (One of his students there was Clarence Darrow.) He entered Oberlin College at the age of twenty-one, in the fall of 1890. He graduated from Oberlin in the Class of 1894. My father followed the same route, working on the farm as a youth, and then teaching at New Lyme Academy (where one of his students was Florence Allen, the first woman judge of a federal constitutional court). He entered Oberlin in the fall of 1894, and graduated with the Class of 1898.

My father met my mother at Oberlin, while they were both students there. My mother went first to the Oberlin Academy, to make up for the deficiencies in the education provided by the schools in Bourbon. In due course, she was admitted as a student in the College. However, she spent the year 1900–1901 at DePauw University in Greencastle, Indiana, where she received her degree in 1901.

While at Oberlin, my mother roomed with Stella Taber, who came from Argos, Indiana. Among my father's classmates was Harry A. Ford, of Geneva, Ohio. He married Stella Taber in 1900, and their second child, Harriet Allena Ford, became my wife. We have a picture of the two couples taken while they were students at Oberlin.

On leaving Oberlin, my father moved to Cleveland and entered the Law School of Western Reserve University. While in Cleveland, he roomed at the home of his older brother, Wells Laird Griswold, and his brother's wife, Louise Fitch Griswold. His brother was then principal of the high school in Glenville, an eastern suburb of Cleveland. My father paid his way through law school by tutoring, and also by making Saturday and Sunday addresses for the Anti–Saloon League. He did this through Wayne B. Wheeler, the Director of the Anti–Saloon League, who was a classmate of his brother Wells at Oberlin. My father received his LL.B. degree at Western Reserve in June, 1901, and promptly took, and passed, the Ohio Bar examination, becoming a member of the Bar of Ohio in the summer of 1901.[6] As fortune would have it, my father's first legal assignment was to adminis-

---

6. He and I together have now been members of the Ohio Bar for more than ninety years, or nearly half of the time since Ohio became a state.

ter the estate of his mother, Susanna Laird Griswold. She died in the summer of 1901 of the then scourge, tuberculosis.

One of my father's teachers at Western Reserve had been Alexander Hadden, who was a practicing lawyer in Cleveland, and a part-time teacher at the Western Reserve Law School. My father obtained desk space in Hadden's office. By this time, his brother Wells had moved to Youngstown, Ohio, where he was the principal of Rayen School. We have a bundle of letters written by my father to his older brother during this period, and a few of these have been printed in the Cleveland Bar Journal.[7]

On September 30, 1902, my father and mother were married, in Bourbon, Indiana, at the home of her father and mother, William Erwin and Jane Cooper Erwin, on South Main Street. The bride and groom proceeded at once to East Cleveland, another eastern suburb of Cleveland, where they took up residence at 91 Windermere Street. (At a later time, in order to conform with the system for numbering Cleveland streets, the number of the house was changed to 1889 Windermere Street.) This house had been bought by my grandfather, William Erwin, and given to Harlen and Hope as a wedding present. I have been told that the cost of the house, including an adjacent vacant lot, was five thousand dollars. It was a substantial house, with a long hall on one side, two parlors on the other side, which were soon converted into a single living room with an attractive fireplace, a dining room and kitchen, and a back porch, where the icebox was kept. Upstairs, there were four bedrooms and one good-sized bathroom. Above all this was an attic, which was entered through a trapdoor with the aid of a ladder. It was a comfortable house, though not particularly elaborate. On the back part of the vacant lot was a large barn, with two stories, providing a considerable amount of work and storage space.

---

7. 52 Cleveland Bar J. 188 (1981). One of the letters is reproduced here. It helps to give the flavor of law practice in those days. On November 13, 1901, my father wrote:

"Dear Brother: I am getting along nicely and like it very much. Couldn't be better suited. Yesterday I went with a woman, a defendant in an action in which Hadden is her Att'y, to Rochester a town just beyond Wellington and took a deposition in a divorce case where adultery was charged. I got along all right and got what I went after. Hadden congratulated me heartily on my first piece of work for the firm. It is my opinion he will charge the woman $10.00 for my trip. Today I went into court and got a motion continued. It wasn't much but still was my first appearance in court. Hastily, Jim"

B. The Beginning

I was born at 91 Windermere Street, in the front bedroom, on July 14, 1904. I have no personal recollection of the event, but I feel confident about both the time and the place. Indeed, one's date of birth is one of the oldest and most firmly fixed of the exceptions to the hearsay rule. The attending physician was Dr. Justin M. Waugh, who had only a few months previously been the father of a daughter, Martha Waugh. The Waugh family later moved to Hood River, Oregon, and one of my early recollections is the report of a horrendous encounter Dr. Waugh had with a rattlesnake. He was bitten on the arm while going to visit a patient in rough country, far from town. He realized the seriousness of the situation. He lacerated the wound with his pen-knife, and sucked out the blood. He had a considerable reaction, but survived.

Windermere Street provided a remarkable place for growing up. The neighbors were all hard-working business and professional people, of appropriate success in their endeavors. There were many children on the street, a number of whom were about my age. One of these was James Vermillion, who bestowed on me, for some reason, the name "Ibbie," by which I have always been known by my early East Cleveland friends. In the family, I was "Bow," the result of my younger brother Jim trying to say "brother."

On the southeast corner of Windermere Street and Euclid Avenue stood the Windermere Presbyterian Church.[8] My mother and father had joined that church when they came to East Cleveland, probably because it was conveniently located. My father was for many years an Elder in the church, and it was the church where I was baptized, and went to Sunday school. (My mother thought that she ought to tell her father of this event, since the Quakers, or his branch of the Quakers, did not believe in baptism. My mother reported to me later that her father smiled, and said: "Well, it won't hurt him any.")

Across the street from the church, on the north side of Euclid Avenue, the East Cleveland Public Library was built about 1916. Beyond that, between Euclid Avenue and the Nickel Plate Railroad tracks, was a farm. As our family grew, and milk was

---

8. Next to the church lived Dr. Horton, probably the oldest man I have ever known. He was born in 1820, and I saw him a number of times after he was a hundred years old.

needed for small children, one of my daily chores was to walk to the farm, and carry back a half-gallon jug of fresh milk.

Perhaps my earliest memory goes back to 1907, when I was three years old. During that summer, I was very ill, having measles, pneumonia, and whooping cough in quick succession. For medical reasons, at one stage in these illnesses, my bedroom was kept darkened, with rather terrorizing impact.

Eventually, I overcame the diseases, and there was a considerable period of recuperation. During this period, my mother took me, by train, out to Indiana to visit her father. While there, she had me in a stroller of some sort. She met one of her acquaintances, who said: "Well, Hope, so that's your boy—kind of spindly-looking. Do you think you will raise him?" As things worked out, I was quite free of illnesses, avoiding diphtheria, scarlet fever, infantile paralysis, and other illnesses which were so widespread at the time, and frequently fatal. It was the custom in those days, when there was a contagious disease in a house, to post a brightly colored notice of illness outside the front door. I can remember walking on Windermere Street when three or four houses, out of perhaps twenty, had these warning signs.

When I was about four years old, I began to attend a kindergarten, which was conducted by a widow named Mrs. Ethel B. Gausby. She came originally from Guelph, Ontario. Although Guelph is not actually very far from Cleveland, it was in a foreign country, and this made a considerable impression on me. Mrs. Gausby was a very fine lady. She had one son, a few years younger than me. She ran an excellent school, and I have many pleasant memories of the associations with her and with the other children.

One of my most vivid early recollections goes back to a late evening in 1910, when my father got me up, took me outdoors on his shoulders, and showed me Hally's Comet, very bright and spectacular across the sky. I remember my father saying, "You may be one of those who will see it twice." This was a sound prediction, as I did see it in 1986, but only with the aid of a pair of strong binoculars. It was quite unspectacular at the time of my second view, and not at all visible to the naked eye. This was a great disappointment to me, as I had long looked forward to the reappearance of the comet, and hoped it would be as impressive then as it was in 1910.[9]

9. In the fall of 1987, while on a trip to Moscow, I went, by invitation, to the Soviet space center. We were shown the pictures of the comet taken close-up from a Soviet space craft. These were spectac-

Our house was a long quarter of a mile from Euclid Avenue. In the early days, my father walked to the corner each day and took the streetcar downtown. The fare then was three cents. You dropped the pennies in the box, and the conductor pulled a cord which rang a bell. There were two employees on the car, a conductor and a motorman. The trip downtown took about a half hour, but it was convenient, as well as cheap. My father used to arrive home at about six o'clock, and this was an important event, perhaps because supper soon followed.

Both my father and mother were public-spirited, with a broad interest in the world around them. Though my mother stayed at home, ran the house, brought up the children, and participated in ladies aid at the church, she had many friends, and did not feel personally oppressed. She was active in movements to obtain votes for women, and felt strongly about that, and she was often active in supporting "reform" candidates for political office. One of my first political activities was taking a stack of cards, and going up and down streets, from door to door, handing the cards to whomever answered the doorbell. These were usually women, who by this time had obtained the right to vote in local elections. The cards urged a vote for a young neighboring East Clevelander named Harold H. Burton, who was a candidate for election to the East Cleveland School Board. As I recall, he was elected. He later became a Mayor of Cleveland, Senator from Ohio, and a Justice of the United States Supreme Court. My mother also managed an unsuccessful effort to elect Florence Allen to Congress. But Florence Allen was later elected to the Common Pleas Court in Cleveland, and to the Supreme Court of Ohio. Eventually, she was, as I have indicated, the first woman appointed, in 1934, to a federal court exercising powers under Article III of the Constitution.

Both of my parents were active in the Council of World Affairs in Cleveland. My mother participated in the work of "The Cause and Cure of War," and travelled to Washington each year to attend its meetings. I especially remember one of these meetings while I was in Washington, and we heard an address by General Jan Smuts of South Africa.

Just to the south of us, on Windermere Street, lived the Criley family, with two sons and a daughter. The older son was in the army, in France, in World War I, and we were much concerned about him. Later, the Criley family moved away, and

---

ular (beyond anything we anticipated in 1910), and this helped to make up for the disappointment of the virtual invisibility of the comet from the ground in 1986.

the house was occupied by the Green family. Mr. Green was a professional musician. Among other things, he played in one of the big orchestras which were then used in connection with the silent motion pictures. One of his sons was John G. Green, a year or two younger than me. He became a newspaper man, and was editor of papers in Portsmouth and Akron, Ohio. We have remained friends throughout the years. He now lives in retirement in Sun City, near Phoenix, Arizona, and we still correspond quite regularly. He and his wife are avid travelers and I am never surprised when I receive from them a card from Tibet or Timbuktu, or some other exotic place.

The house to the north of ours was occupied by the Converse family. They had a son, Julius, who was about my age. Among other activities, we rigged up a telegraph line between our bed rooms. It was slow going, as we used Morse Code. I could not remember the appropriate dots and dashes for all the letters, so I kept a copy of the Code beside the key, and referred to it for some of the longer combinations. I remember, too, that sometimes when the signals did not communicate very well, we opened the bedroom windows and shouted to each other.

A little later, I built an arc light out of a maple syrup can, using carbon sticks from dry batteries, and a lens (in a holder) from our lantern slide projector. The power was the ordinary 110 volt current in the house lighting system. The light was bright and could be projected very far. Thinking back, I have never understood why I did not get seriously hurt in this activity. The next step was radio. With my father's help, an antenna was put up between my bedroom and the cupola of the barn. I built a tuning coil by wrapping wire around a rolling pin. The "detector" was a crystal. (This was before the days of vacuum tube detectors.) I did hear a good many signals, but they were all dots and dashes. I did not hear voice or music by radio until several years later.

C. Early Education—School and Other Experiences

In September, 1910, shortly after my sixth birthday, I entered Superior School, located, not surprisingly, on Superior Street, about a mile west of our house. I walked each way, twice a day, coming home for lunch. The walk involved passing the main entrance of the Forest Hills Estate, the Cleveland home of John D. Rockefeller. By this time, the Rockefellers had moved to Pocantico Hills in New York, but the residence still stood. It had been built as a sanitarium on the hills east of Cleveland, but had been extensively rebuilt by the Rockefellers. The entire estate was about a thousand acres, and included a golf course, fine trees, many shrubs, and well-kept grounds. The gateman on Euclid Avenue was Pat, and he always gave us a friendly greeting as we went past on the way to school.

In about 1916, when I was twelve years old, I was waked up by my father one night to see the sky to the west of our house brightly illuminated. Indeed, the sky to the west was always aglow at night, because of the steel mills in the downtown area of Cleveland. But this time the brightness was stronger than usual, and closer. It came from the burning of the Rockefeller house. It was unoccupied at the time, but it did make a spectacular blaze. I can still see in my mind that brightly lit sky, with the silhouettes of many trees in the foreground.

In due course, the Rockefeller Estate became a great playground for the boys of our neighborhood. We were told that we could use the grounds if we behaved ourselves. • Among other things, we used to ski up there in the wintertime. This was a time when skiing was fun, but still relatively simple. You dressed warmly, and had good, heavy shoes. Then you had a pair of skis—any kind would do. The skis had a leather loop across and you put your shoe inside the loop. There was no waxing of the skis, no bindings, and no other paraphernalia. You just found a slope and started down it, being careful to avoid the trees. If you did fall, your shoes simply slipped out of the loops. You might have to trudge through quite a lot of snow before finding your skis. But I do not recall that there were any injuries, or any other serious mishaps. We even built a ski jump, six or eight feet high. It was quite a thrill to go sailing through the air. However, I never yearned to be a real ski jumper.

I attended the Superior School from 1910 to 1917. I had excellent teachers, and I especially remember Miss Sapp in the first grade, who greatly improved my reading, and Miss Leach in the second grade. She led us through a great discussion at the time of the Titanic disaster in 1912, including the first information that I can recall that there could be such a thing as wireless communication. It was hard enough to understand communication by wire, but this introduction to Marconi and wireless—not then called radio—was my first entry into the mysteries of the world of science.

Shortly after starting the third grade, in the fall of 1912, I was told that I should proceed to the fourth grade, under Miss Arndt. I suppose that this was arranged by my parents, and it was a little frightening to me at the time. However, it worked out well, and it may well have been one of the important factors in the career that developed for me, for it put me, all along the way after that, in a different group; and there were times, I think, when the fact that I was in the new group gave me opportunities which would not otherwise have been available.

In the seventh and eighth grades, I began to study Latin. My father had, of course, had Latin in order to get through college, and he used to help me regularly with my work in Latin, including explanations of some of the special quirks in the Latin language. (Indeed, my father knew Greek, too, which he had studied at Oberlin, and he always regarded me as somewhat illiterate since I never studied Greek.) I had a fine teacher in the eighth grade, Miss Alice Williams, who later married our neighbor, Herbert Bailey. As part of our literature instruction, she read extensively from *"Les Miserables,"* where I first heard about Jean Valjean.

For several years, beginning about 1910, I spent a number of weeks each summer with my grandfather at his home in Bourbon, Indiana. At first I went with my mother, but by about 1913 I went by myself on the train. This required going from Cleveland to Orwell, Ohio, which was the junction of the main line of the Pennsylvania Railroad. At Orwell, I caught No. 9. This was the local train on the main line, stopping at every station. It took several hours to get to Bourbon. On one of the early trips, and pursuant to instructions, I sent a telegram to my parents to advise them of my arrival. The message I sent was somewhat self-confident. It said: "I have arrived and am looking around."

The summers with my grandfather, William Erwin, were great events in my life. I had a bicycle, and I used to ride it downtown to get the mail, and to pick up the Chicago Tribune. I also spent a good deal of time in the railroad "Tower," where there were always two men on duty to control the signals and the switches. They would get a telegraphic message from the next town on the line, east or west, announcing that a train had passed that station. They would then set the vertical semaphore signal so that the train could come into, and through, Bourbon. Most of the trains did not stop in Bourbon, and they seemed to me to go very fast. A number of them had mail cars, which would pick up a bag of mail from a standard by the track while the train was roaring through, and the man on the mailcar kicked off a bag destined for Bourbon. On many occasions, I would pick up the bag and carry it to the Post Office. As far as I know, this was my first service for the United States Government. Of course I did not get paid for it. But the employees in the Post Office seemed to welcome it, and appreciate it.

My times at Bourbon taught me a good deal about farms and farming. In the earlier years I was the waterboy for the men in the hayfield, and I was careful to keep the water clean, in a gallon bottle, and as cool as possible. For this, and other work I did, I was usually paid one dollar a day. However, on one occasion, my grandfather said that he would pay me five cents a dozen for potato bugs taken off potato plants in the home garden. Without too much time and effort, I had collected fifty dozen. My grandfather made good on that, but my rate of pay was then renegotiated.

When I was a little older, I led the horse which pulled the hayfork up into the barn, where my Uncle Lewis, my mother's youngest brother, used to do the hot, dusty work in the mow. Later, I helped with thrashing wheat, including driving a box wagon from the thrashing machine to the elevator in town. On other occasions, I went with my grandfather to visit one or another of the farms which he owned in the area. At this time, he was well into his eighties. I remember that he used to hitch the horse to the buggy and hold the reins until he reached the road in front of the house. Then my grandfather would go to sleep, while the horse jogged along, made the necessary turns, and finally arrived, after several miles, at the farm. When the buggy stopped moving, my grandfather would awaken, thoroughly refreshed, and ready to undertake the business at hand.

Those were days, too, when, in the country, "working on the road" was a form of taxation. I can remember my Uncle Lewis digging gravel out of a gravel pit and putting it into a wagon. He then took it out and spread it on one of the roads. His quota for the year was to spread gravel on a set number of rods of road, and he was always very faithful in meeting his requirements.

In 1917, while I was at the farm, my mother and father drove to Bourbon in their new car, a Jordan, made in Cleveland. We then went to stay in the summer house of my Uncle James, my mother's oldest brother, which was at Pretty Lake, a few miles southwest of Plymouth. That was a very pleasant place, where we swam a lot, and did some fishing. One night there was a terrific thunder storm, and I was really frightened. Some of the lightning flashes must have come very close, for there was virtually no interval between the flash and the bang. I had learned that much about science, but I wondered why the light seemed to come instantly, while the noise took a little longer.

My grandmother, Jane Cooper Erwin, died in 1903, before I was born. My grandfather married again. His new wife was Cora Conrick, and she was always Aunt Code to me. I must have been quite a nuisance to her, but she was always very nice to me—though in later years she became quite difficult for my Uncle Lewis. There was a helper in the house, Kate Ladd, and she did most of the cooking. Among other things, she made the most luscious cinnamon rolls that I have ever encountered. She usually had them for Sunday dinner, and I ate, or so it seemed, dozens of them.

In the later years, my grandfather could not see well enough to read, and Aunt Code used to read to him extensively, particularly from the newspapers. My grandfather was much interested in the world news, for World War I was then going on. But one of the items that he was always read was the various prices of wheat and corn on the Chicago Board of Trade. Because of the War, I suppose, these prices were relatively high at the time, and my grandfather was always pleased when the news was good. He also enjoyed the reading of poetry, especially the poems of the Quaker poet, William Cullen Bryant, many of which he knew by heart.

Though I was surely a bother to all concerned, they were very good to me. My Uncle Lewis, who was the active farmer at the time, was always very kind. We shared a double bed in his bedroom. Sometimes, especially on weekends, he would not come in until quite late. When I asked him the next morning what he had been doing, his only response would be: "girlin'". I learned later that he was courting Eleanor Fribley, a daughter of one of the families in town, whom he married in 1921.

One of the important events of my early years came on January 9, 1913, which was the first birthday of my sister Jane. (My brother, James Wells Griswold, was born on June 5, 1909, and my younger sister, Hope Eleanor Griswold, later Mrs. George H. Curfman, was born on June 15, 1918.) I went off to school as usual on the morning of January 9th, but I soon developed a severe pain. There was nothing like a school nurse in those days, but my teacher felt that I had a considerable fever and she sent me home, on foot. When I got home, Dr. Waugh was called. He immediately diagnosed my trouble as appendicitis, and said that an operation was immediately necessary. (In those days, the risk of peritonitis from a broken appendix, without any antibiotics, was extremely serious.) An ambulance was called and I was taken to Charity Hospital in downtown Cleveland. Dr. Waugh had in the meantime made contact with an experienced surgeon. I can remember being given the anesthetic, which was ether. It was several hours later, however, that I woke up, in a hospital bed, attended by a nurse in the garb of a Sister of Charity. I spent nearly two weeks in the hospital. The present regimen of short hospital stays was not the practice then.

After a few days, I felt reasonably well. I had many visitors, including my father and mother and others, who brought books and coloring material. One important consequence of this stay, though, was that it marked my beginning as a stamp collector, an activity which I have pursued, off and on, over the subsequent more than three-quarters of a century, as I discuss in more detail later.[10]

My growing up years were full of new experiences. It must have been in 1912 when my father took me down to the Lake Shore, near downtown Cleveland, where I saw Glenn Curtis come in from Erie, Pennsylvania in his flying machine, landing on the sandy beach of Lake Erie. There was a huge crowd, and there were, of course, delays. But eventually a sound could be heard to the east and then a black spot could be seen over the lake. Before long, it came in, descending slowly, and landed on the sand, with a resultant enormous roar from the crowd.[11]

We were already aware of flying machines. Katherine Wright, sister of the Wright brothers, had been a classmate of my father's at Oberlin College, and had known my mother at Oberlin. After leaving Oberlin, she taught school and kept house and largely supported her brothers in their bicycle shop, where they carried on much of their largely secretive endeavor. On several occasions in the 1915–20 period, Katherine Wright was a guest in our house. In the early years, the Wright brothers were involved in extensive patent litigation. I can remember Katherine Wright saying in our dining room that she "wished the boys had invented a breakfast food." She felt that that would have been less controversial. Wilbur Wright died in 1912. Thereafter, Orville Wright was made an honorary member of the Class of 1898 in Oberlin.

I often attended reunions of my father's class. On one occasion I sat on the porch of one of the Oberlin dormitories and talked with Orville Wright. It was probably in 1928, when the Thirtieth Reunion of the Class of 1898 was held. One of the things that Orville Wright told me was that he and his brother had made two important contributions to heavier-than-air flight.

---

10. See pages 52–56, below.

11. My second sighting of an airplane in flight came in about 1915. This time, the plane was flown by a lady, Ruth Law. She circled over the city, quite low, and flew not far from where a group of boys, including me, were playing football in the family backyard. Needless to say, we stopped our game, and were much impressed. By that time, we had read quite a bit about airplanes in World War I, but it was really impressive to see one flying low in our neighborhood.

The first was the warping of the wings, which provided lateral stability and is now represented by the flaps on the wings of modern planes. The second was understanding the stall, that is, that there was a certain angle (upward or downward) at which an airplane would lose lift, and would start a precipitate fall. I referred to the light Wright engine and the propeller, but he replied that both of those were well known, and would have been developed by anyone in the field. He insisted that the real contributions which he and his brother made were those which I have mentioned, the means to provide for lateral stability, and the need to guard against the stall.

It was in the second decade of the twentieth century that the automobile came into its own. The first gasoline car in our neighborhood was owned by the Smiths, across the street. I believe it was a Pierce Arrow. At any rate, it stood high above the ground, and access to the back seats was through a door in the middle of the back of the car, from which a series of steps could be extended to the ground. This was not an enclosed car, though it must have had some system of curtains for use in the rain.

The first two automobiles in our family were electric. The first one was built rather like a buggy, open in front, with a tiller for steering, and a hand brake. This would go about fifteen miles an hour, and could cover only twenty-five or thirty miles without recharging. The nearest place for a recharge was a garage on Euclid Avenue about a mile to the west. The trip to and from had to be made on the streetcar, or by foot. There was a small rise at the lower end of Windermere Street, and sometimes the car would get that far, and then would not be able to go up the hill. Experience showed, though, that if it was simply left on the street there, for a few hours, the batteries would "accumulate" to such an extent that the car could make it the rest of the way up the street. On several occasions, my mother left the car there, and walked the rest of the way home with us children. When my father came home later from downtown by streetcar, he would see the car there, and often he was able to get it home.

Somewhat later, probably about 1915, there were two great improvements. First, my father bought a Rauch–Lang automobile, made in Cleveland. This was enclosed in glass, but it still had a tiller for steering. At the same time, my father bought a motor-generator converter, which was installed in our barn. This converted the alternating current, supplied by the Cleveland Electric Illuminating Company, to direct current, which would be accepted by the batteries. After this, the car was driven into the barn each night. The motor generator was turned on, with a considerable hum, and for some reason a bright blue light. It was so adjusted that it would turn off when the batteries were fully charged, but often the converter would run most of the night.

Our backyard was a great playground. My father early established a sandbox, and later a horizontal bar and a swing. For several years we played baseball there, but as we grew older, the lot proved too small. Too many times our hits would sail over the barn of the neighbor behind us, and through the backyard there, sometimes hitting the house, with occasional broken windows. This did not prove popular with the neighbor, so we gave up baseball, and played football.

It was during one of these football matches that I heard a newsboy's call. In those days, there was no radio. When there was some major event the newspapers got out an "Extra," and then the newsboys went up and down the streets calling out "extry, extry." My mother went out and bought one of the papers (probably for one cent, though it might have been two cents at that time), with the news about the sinking of the Lusitania.

We were a Republican family, and I wore a button for Taft in 1912. In 1916, I am sure that my father voted for Hughes for President. However, Woodrow Wilson, then President of the United States, came to Cleveland for a campaign speech in October, 1916. The speech was given at the Gray's Armory, and somehow or other my father got two tickets, and took me to hear the President. It was a great thrill to see the President of the United States. I can picture him on the platform, and hear his resonant voice. The theme of his speech was that he should be reelected in order to keep us out of the war. I can still hear him say, several times: "I must solemnly warn you * * *" of this or that danger which lay ahead unless he were elected.

In 1920, both of the presidential candidates were from Ohio, Warren G. Harding for the Republicans, and James M. Cox for the Democrats. I had met Harding when, as a United States Senator, probably in late 1919 or early 1920, he had come to Shaw High School, which I attended, to make a speech. I was responsible for the stage arrangements, and, by inadvertence, at an inappropriate point, I pulled the wrong rope and brought the curtain down between him and his audience. He did not seem to be much bothered, but I was. Later, in the 1920 campaign, I heard former Secretary of State Robert Lansing make a campaign speech, in a tent, in East Cleveland. I did not, of course, realize his relationship with the future Secretary of State, John Foster Dulles, nor with Allen Dulles, who became a graduate of the Harvard Law School, and his sister, Eleanor Dulles, now over ninety, who lives in the same apartment house we do in Washington.

Other schoolboy activities included roller-skating. This was something of an art on the flagstone sidewalks which were standard in East Cleveland at that time. We also raced in coaster wagons, and a little later rode bicycles extensively. Among other things, this included racing around the block—down Windermere Street, along Euclid Avenue, up Knowles Street, and then along Terrace Road back to the point of beginning. We usually did this against the clock—that is, someone held a watch (I do not recall that it was a stopwatch)—and we tried to beat each other's time. In the wintertime, we played hockey. At that time, Terrace Road did not go through, and there was a short stretch to the east of Knowles Street, ending in a dead end. We would pack down the snow there, set up two bricks at each end to indicate the goals, and then play hockey—without skates, but in our regular winter shoes. This provided rather vigorous exercise. At other times, when there had been a heavy snow, we dug into snow drifts, and built igloos. We even had, on a few occasions, an igloo with an opening at the top, and built a fire with kindling and sticks inside the igloo. It was really quite snug.

D. SHAW HIGH SCHOOL

In June, 1917, I finished the eighth grade in Superior School. The following summer was the last time that I made an extensive visit to my grandfather's farm in Indiana. In September, 1917, I entered Shaw High School. The main building of this school was one which had been built for a private academy, but had been taken over, towards the end of the nineteenth century, as the public high school in East Cleveland. This was then a very fine school, where I received an excellent preparatory education. I had four years of Latin there, four years of mathematics, four years of English, three of French, and two years of science, along with a number of other subjects. The students were well behaved—there was little need for discipline. The teachers were able and devoted. I particularly remember Miss Ort, who spoke French as a native, and conducted our French classes. Another fine teacher was Mr. Brown, who taught mathematics. He later went on to teach at the Case School of Applied Science. During my senior year, he gave me, privately, some advanced work in spherical trigonometry. I was able to use this to take a special examination and obtain, through it, advanced standing when I went on to college.

At that time, because of overcrowding, the high school was conducted in two shifts. I remember that our first class began at 8:08 in the morning, and the day's session for us ended at one o'clock. Then there was a second shift, with a different group of students, in the afternoon. Classes were about evenly divided between boys and girls. The girls wore a uniform—middie blouses and dark blue skirts. The boys wore jackets and ties. Beginning in the fall of 1918, the boys wore military-type khaki uniforms—jackets and short pants, with brown shoes, and puttees between the shoes and the knees. The puttees were long strips of khaki wool, which were wound around from the shoe to the knee, and it was something of a trick to put them on—and keep them up. During the fall of 1918, we had to stay several days during the week to drill, in close order drill, following an army instruction book which must have been written during or shortly after the Civil War.

One afternoon we were marched, two or three miles, to the home of a student who had died, probably from the influenza epidemic which was widespread in the fall of 1918. We were required to stand at attention outside of the house. This proved to be very wearing, and some of the boys fainted or collapsed. Finally, we were marched back again to the school. It was probably a good experience, on some basis, but I was not very enthusiastic about it at the time. I was sorry that the student had died, and it was one of my first experiences of the death of a person with whom I had some acquaintance. Nevertheless, I found it difficult to see how we had helped him, or the members of his family, in any way.

I was never an athlete while I was in high school. I did take the regular required gym class, and I also swam in the new swimming pool on a more or less regular basis.

E. Camp Pemigewassett

In the summer of 1918, I started one of the greatest experiences of my early life. I was sent to Camp Pemigewassett, in Wentworth, New Hampshire. This was a boys camp, founded in 1908, so when I went in 1918, it was the eleventh season. The camp had three directors, all of whom were medical doctors, and all of whom had attended Oberlin College. Two of them were twins, Drs. Edwin and Edgar Fauver, of the Class of 1899 at Oberlin. The third director was Dr. Dudley B. Reed, of the Oberlin Class of 1900. All of them had posts as directors of athletics, or as university physicians, at a college. Edgar Fauver was at Wesleyan University, Edwin Fauver was at the University of Rochester, and Dudley Reed was at the University of Chicago. While in medical school, they had been counsellors at Camp Moosilauke, operated in connection with the Horace Mann School in New York City, and they had served there under a Mr. Prettyman. Camp Moosilauke was on upper Baker Pond, and, in the course of time, the three doctors acquired land a few miles away on lower Baker Pond, and, as indicated, started their own camp there in 1908, giving it the name of Camp Pemigewassett. This was a serious activity, where "men were men," but the boys also had a lot of fun, and a wide variety of experience.

The boys kept the buildings and grounds in shape, mowing the grass, rolling and weeding the tennis courts, and doing various other chores. But there was a great deal of time available for athletics and fun. There were swimming periods, both morning and afternoon. Before a boy could go out on the lake in a canoe or boat, he had to "swim his distance," which meant swimming about three-quarters of a mile down the middle of the lake. I got to camp late in June, 1918, and had swum my distance by July 10th. I do remember that it was a real struggle, particularly near the end—but I made it. I have never swum so far or so hard since. However, I have always been glad that I had that experience, as it has given me a confidence, not only when I have been in the water, but when I have been in canoes or boats and have thought about the possibility that I might find myself in the water.

The principal activities at camp, apart from meals, which were hearty and good, were baseball, tennis, and hiking. I did not play tennis very much. It has always been my experience on a tennis court that I could play tennis pretty well if the nets were an inch lower, and the baselines were an inch farther back. I did try hard to play baseball, though I was not very good. At the beginning of my first summer, I played on the fourteen and under team, and was assigned to pitch. Our first game was against Moosilauke, and I was soon driven from the box. After that, my forte was in right field. I could usually catch the ball if it was hit in the general position where I was. If I had to run very far, though, the ball was quite likely to slip through my fingers. I enjoyed it greatly. I became an expert scorer in the senior games, and I kept the score of the "masters" game between Pemigewassett and Moosilauke, conducted later in 1918. This game went for twenty-one innings, with Dr. Reed the pitcher throughout for the Pemigewassett team. The score seesawed back and forth, but, eventually, Pemi won. In later years, I wrote up the score from the scorebook which I had kept. I then had it nicely printed and gave a copy of the box score, together

with the play-by-play account, to the Camp. It was framed, and
it hung in the lodge for many years.

Later I tried my hand at being a catcher. This was hardball,
and, after a few bangs on my fingers, I tended to shy away a bit.
After that, I thought it would be fun to be an umpire. I think
that I was really a rather good umpire, but there was not much
future in being an umpire at camp.

In due course, I found the place where I could do reasonably
well. That was hiking. The camp was located at the edge of the
White Mountains in New Hampshire. The nearest "mountain"
was Mt. Cube, three or four miles away from the camp. The first
mountain trip which new boys took was to climb Mt. Cube,
carrying blankets and other equipment, for an overnight stay on
the top. The climb, though not long, was rather steep and
vigorous. I found that I could do this fairly well, and that I
enjoyed it—not merely the climb, but also the sights of nature,
the trees, wildflowers, other plants, and occasional wildlife, varying from birds to squirrels, and even, occasionally, a porcupine
or a skunk.

In the course of the years, I climbed Mt. Cube more than
forty times. During the first summer, I climbed Mt. Moosilauke,
went through Lost River and the Flume, and then climbed over
the Franconia Range. That first trip was just after the Profile
House had burned. We did, however, have a fine view of the
"Old Man of the Mountain," and camped for the night on the spot
which had been the site of the Profile House.

It was not until the 1919 season that I was first allowed to go
on the trip over the Presidential Range. We were taken to the
Crawford House in mid-August, and went up the Crawford path
to the top of Mt. Liberty. Then we started to go across the top of
the range, soon encountering a snowstorm and high winds. This
was really a very strenuous trip, under the circumstances, and
the counsellors were quite worried. Finally we made it to the
Lakes of the Clouds hut, where we were taken in, though we had
no reservations to stay there. In due course, the hut became very
crowded, but we were all provided for, in one way or another.

This was the occasion where I first met Thomas G. Corcoran,
who later was one of the important aides to President Franklin
Roosevelt. He was then a student at Brown University, and he
had taken a job as hut boy with the Appalachian Mountain Club
for summer employment. True to Tommy's genius in such
matters, he had got himself assigned to the Lakes of the Clouds
Hut. The great benefit here was that the heavy loads were
carried down from the top of Mt. Washington, where they had

been brought up on the cog railroad. The climb up from the hut to the top of the mountain was thus without load. At all of the other huts, the load was picked up at the bottom of the mountain, and had to be carried up to the hut.

Tommy was in his element with the large crowd which was immured within the hut. He had an accordion, and he played songs and sang and led in singing, and otherwise provided a rather happy time for what might have been a bleak occasion. According to the careful plans of the Appalachian Mountain Club, they had reserves of food, so they were able to take care of the double load of campers who had descended upon them.

The next day, about noon, it was decided that we should give up any effort to reach the top of Mt. Washington. We then started down the Ammanoosuc Ravine Trail, and soon were below the snow line. We then continued to the base station, and finally got to a place where we could find a train which would take us back, with a change, to Wentworth. Then we had to make on foot the four-mile walk back to camp.

I did not reach the top of Mt. Washington until the summer of 1920. Altogether, I have climbed Mt. Washington six or seven times, including one climb in 1943, which was my final mountaineering expedition.

In 1923, one of my fellow campers, Bradley Gilman, from Worcester, Massachusetts, and I, after the close of camp, started off on a great hike of our own. We took the train from Wentworth to Warren, and then got off and climbed Mt. Moosilauke for the night. We then walked down to Lost River, and then took the Cannon Mountain Trail and slept, in the rain, near the top of Mt. Cannon. The next morning, we went down and found the site of the "Old Man", and sat on his forehead. After that, we went down the north slope of Mt. Cannon into Franconia Notch. This was before there were any ski lifts or trails there.

On the next day, we climbed Mt. Lincoln, and walked along the ridge to Mt. Lafayette, and then into the wilderness area to the east. That night, we slept in the rain, and continued the next day to the Crawford House, and then up the Crawford path and on to the top of Mt. Washington. We then went down through the Great Gulf, to Pinkham Notch. The next day, we went over the Mahoosic Range, across the road near Gorham, New Hampshire, and then over a mountain path into Maine. We then made our way to Bethel, Maine, where we put up at a modest country hotel, had a shower, and changed to good clothes which we had shipped there. It was at that point that Brad got word about his sister, who was then in Japan. This was the time of the great Tokyo earthquake. He got few details, but he did learn that she was all right.

Brad became a great climber, with many spectacular ascents in the Alps, and a number of first ascents in the Canadian Rockies. He eventually was elected to the prestigious post of president of the American Alpine Club. I never proceeded farther than the modest New England mountains. In 1940, Brad and I, with two others, spent several days in Baxter State Park in Maine. We climbed Mt. Katahdin twice, once by the "knife-edge" trail, and once up the "chimney." On the latter climb, Brad went ahead, and I followed. At Brad's insistence, we were roped together, which was fortunate, for I slipped and fell, but Brad was well based, and stopped the fall. Fortunately for me, he was a skilled and prudent mountain climber.

After our long hike together in 1923, Brad went back to his home in Worcester, but I continued on an expedition of my own. This part of my trip was in furtherance of my long-continued interest in interstate and international boundary lines. I took the train from Bethel to Stratford, New Hampshire, where I changed to another train, and went to Beecher's Falls, Vermont, which is located just south of the Canadian border. There I took a number of pictures of boundary monuments, and spent the night. The next day, I took a train north (on a railroad line which no longer exists) to St. Malo, Quebec. I got off there; it was a tiny place, but I found some local people at the station. It was raining hard, but I was finally able to persuade two of them to take me to the source of Hall's Stream, on the United States–Canada boundary.

The treaty between the United States and Canada had early provided that the boundary between the United States and Canada in these parts should be the Connecticut River. However, there was great dispute and uncertainty as to which of three tributaries in that area was "the Connecticut River." The British contended that it was the one to the east, which is now regarded as the Connecticut River, and is clearly the major branch of the stream. The American claimants said that the branch farthest west, known as Hall's Stream, was the Connecticut River. In the Webster–Ashburton Treaty of 1842, Lord Ashburton, probably in order to mollify the Americans, agreed that Hall's Stream was the Connecticut River, and so it became the international boundary. The boundary follows Hall's Stream to its source, and there is a large iron monument on the hill nearby marking the source of Hall's Stream. I wanted to see it. I got very wet in the process. I took some pictures which did not come out very well, for lack of light, which was important in those days. I finally got back to the station at St. Malo, Quebec, and took the train on to Quebec City, where I stayed at the Chateau Frontenac, and planned to spend two or three days seeing the sights of Quebec.

However, after one night there, I was called to the front desk, and told that they had to have my room "for the Prince of Wales." I thought that my room was rather meager for the Prince of Wales, but it soon developed that better quarters would be provided for the Prince. My room was needed for a member of his very large staff. So I vacated the room, and took a train to Montreal, where I did some sightseeing, and used my French. Then I went on to Toronto. By this time, I was uncomfortable. I had some sort of illness, and appeared to have a fever. So the next day I continued on the train to Buffalo, and then to Cleveland. After I got home, a doctor found that I had pleurisy, and put me to bed for several days. I continued to feel rather miserable for several weeks, but in due course fully recovered.

At Camp Pemigewassett, I started out, in 1918, as a camper. In 1919 and 1920, I was a "waiter," which meant that I waited on the table in the mess hall, and got a reduction in my camp tuition. In 1921, I became head waiter. This meant that I was in charge of the waiter's squad, had to split the wood for the kitchen stove in the mess hall, and also for fireplaces in the homes of the directors "on the hill." It also meant that I had to help Frank Hutchins, who had the job of driving the truck into Wentworth to get the milk in ten-gallon cans. When Frank got back to camp, the ten-gallon cans had to be lifted off the truck, and then into the ice house, and I used to help Frank with this. This was a very vigorous task, and one had to be very careful not to let the ten-gallon can land on his toes. Frank Hutchins—his name was Francis D. Hutchins, was the younger brother of Robert M. Hutchins. He was a very fine person, who was also a fellow student with me at that time at Oberlin College. He did not have the dynamism of his older brother, nor was he so self-centered. He later was, for many years, a very successful president of Berea College in Kentucky, where his father had also served as president.

In my final two years at Camp, 1922 and 1923, I was a counsellor, having charge of a group of seven boys, aged about eleven to thirteen. This was an interesting experience, which I enjoyed. I sometimes thought that they enjoyed me, too.

––––––––––

During the early part of this period, I was a junior and senior at Shaw High School. Particularly, in my senior year, I was very busy. I was chosen to be the founding editor of the monthly magazine, known as the Shaw Shuttle, of which the final issue, in June, was the Annual, with pictures of all of the clubs, and so on, and of the graduating students. This was a very busy job, and I devoted myself to it very vigorously. Among other things, I went downtown to the print shop many afternoons in order to read proof.

In my senior year, I was also the valedictorian of my Class. My speech was on the Colombian Treaty. The spelling of Colombian with a second "o" is, of course, correct, since it was named after the treaty with Colombia, by which the United States made reimbursement to Colombia because of the role of the United States in separating Panama from Colombia. This gave effect to President Theodore Roosevelt's boast that "we took Panama." Finally, the United States had made recompense, and I devoted my talk to this salutary event. I remember my chagrin when I came to the Class Day session, and looked at the program. I was duly billed to give the valedictory address, and the title was listed as "The Columbian Treaty." Someone at the print shop had looked at my spelling, decided that it was an error, and had corrected it by putting in a "u" in place of the final "o". I felt very badly about this, because it made me out to be an ignoramus. Here I was giving the valedictory speech, and I did not even know that it was named after a country, and that the country was Colombia.

In my senior year at Shaw, I was confronted for the first time, in any serious measure, with the problems which come from trying to do too much. I was involved in debating, and had the valedictory speech to write. But most of all, I was committed to the Shuttle, and particularly its final "Annual" issue. This turned out to be a much bigger task than I had anticipated, but it was accomplished, and the Annual appeared on time. In the process, though, I simply could not find time to read all of "Vanity Fair," which was a requirement in the senior English course. This gave me much concern, and I assume that my parents helped in working it out. At any rate, I was allowed to graduate, on my undertaking to read "Vanity Fair" during the course of the ensuing summer. I did read it, but I must say that my enthusiasm for Thackeray has since been rather limited.

CHAPTER II

College, Early Travels, and Other Activities

∽✕∾

A. OBERLIN COLLEGE

In the fall of 1921, I entered Oberlin College as a freshman. Why did I go to Oberlin? Both of my parents had gone to Oberlin, and other relatives, as well. I had frequently visited Oberlin in connection with the reunions of my father's Class of 1898, and on other occasions. And it was relatively inexpensive. I was never under any pressure from my parents to go to Oberlin. Indeed, there was some talk that I might go to Yale, where many Griswolds had studied, over a period of close to two centuries.

In looking back, I suppose that there were two other reasons why I chose Oberlin. In the first place, I never regarded myself as any sort of a brahmin, any sort of an elite. Most of the people who went from Cleveland to the big eastern universities had a superior attitude, which I did not feel. Closely related to this, as I see it now, was that fact that, as I grew up, I was rather shy and bashful. I was not a "mixer," a "backslapper," or, otherwise, a "hail fellow well met." My horizons were somewhat limited, and I found it comfortable to act accordingly. My mother was aware of my shyness, and concerned about it. She tried to help me with it, by putting on an occasional party, and encouraging me to go to other parties where I knew that there would be many people with whom I was not acquainted. I found these difficult. I was a little afraid of the novel and unknown. One consequence of this was that I often underestimated myself, and, indeed, had a trace of what was then called an "inferiority complex." I did not want to get into situations where I would be over my head, and I tended to stand by the sidelines.

With respect to Yale, I know that I was much affected by the club system in operation there. I foresaw, quite rightly, I think, that I would not "make" one of the clubs at Yale, and that I would be disappointed, perhaps bitterly so. I had read "Stover at Yale," and my recollection is that this affected me a good deal. At any rate, I came to the conclusion that I would be happier at Oberlin, where there were no fraternities, and where the people would be "my kind of people." I was a mid-westerner at heart, and I was rather afraid of the east.

Oberlin had a long liberal tradition. It was founded in 1833, and named in honor of John Frederic Oberlin, a far-sighted and innovative pastor in the *Ban de la Roche*, in Alsace. The College admitted Negroes in 1835, and was the first college to admit women, in 1837. It had been an active center of antislavery activity. It was a station on the underground railroad, and many Oberlin students had participated in the Oberlin–Willington Rescue, which led to a famous trial in Cleveland in 1858.[1] Two black residents of Oberlin were a part of John Brown's party at Harpers Ferry in 1859.

The College matured in the latter part of the nineteenth century, but it still maintained its tradition of "doing good." In this period, many Oberlin graduates became missionaries,[2] and a number of the children of missionaries returned to Oberlin for their college work.[3]

Perhaps for reasons like these, though they were never formulated or clearly understood, I went to Oberlin, and have never regretted it. I found it to be congenial, interesting, and stimulating. There was no Scholastic Aptitude Test at that time, and the students at Oberlin probably would not have rated in the heights if there had been. But they were fine people, serious, conscientious, reasonably hard-working, honest and sincere, and I found them a remarkable group with whom to share experiences.

Oberlin was only thirty-five miles southwest of Cleveland. My parents drove me there, following the Center Ridge Road, for the final part of the way. This was one of the slight elevations

---

1. See N. Brandt, The Town that Started the Civil War (Syracuse, N.Y.: 1990).

2. Including a classmate of my father's who became head of the Adams Mission, near Durban, South Africa. At one of the reunions of the Class of 1898, probably in 1923, I heard him give a speech in Zulu.

3. Including Edwin O. Reischauser, a member of my brother's Oberlin class of 1931. Reischauer became a great scholar on Japan, and the Ambassador from the United States to Japan in 1961 to 1966.

left by the receding Lake Erie following the glacial period. Much of the road was unpaved at the time.

In Oberlin I was assigned a room in what was then known as the "Men's Building." (It is now called Wilder Hall, after the Boston man who provided the funds for it about 1915.) My experience with roommates in my freshman year was somewhat rocky. For the first semester my roommate was a pleasant enough fellow who had no idea of working, and he dropped out shortly after Christmas. In the second semester, I was moved to a different room, with a new roommate. He was the son of the President of Tougalou College in Mississippi, which might have been promising. But he had no inhibitions, and often stayed out all night. At other times, he would come back to the room at two or three a.m., turn on the light, and spend an hour in seemingly useless activity. This made sleeping rather difficult for me. My efforts to bring about a change were quite unsuccessful. However, I survived, and I suppose it was a useful experience. Needless to say, he did not return to Oberlin. Thus, I finished off two roommates during my freshman year at Oberlin, which may be some sort of a record.

During my first week at Oberlin, I took a special examination for advanced standing, in mathematics, and also in French. I passed both of these, and thus obtained eight hours of advanced standing. This proved useful a little later, for it enabled me to take a few extra hours during my junior and senior years, and then write a thesis (on the power of the Supreme Court to declare Acts of Congress unconstitutional). Thus I was able to get an A.M. degree along with my A.B. degree in 1925.

My most interesting course during my freshman year was in physics, which I took with Professor S. R. Williams, who later went on to teach physics at Amherst College. At that time, the physics course was almost entirely devoted to mechanics, and electricity. And the electricity was motors, generators, three-phase wiring, and things of that sort. There was virtually nothing about the area which we now know as "electronics," and nothing at all about nuclear physics. Professor Williams did tell us that there were some very interesting things going on at Cambridge, England, which would probably affect the physics of the future, but we did not study it at all.

My work in the physics course during my freshman year enabled me to get employment as an assistant in the physics laboratory during my second year. I do not recall how much I was paid for this, but I think it was something like seventy-five dollars for the semester. I remember that when I received a check in payment, I took it to the local bank, and got gold coins.

I put the gold coins in a cotton bag, tied a label to the bag, and then mailed the bag with the label to my father, by registered mail. At that time, the charge for registration was ten cents. I sent along a letter in which I said that I was making this payment to apply against my costs in going to college.

I had quite a bit of "social life" at Oberlin. When I entered college in 1921, dancing was allowed for the first time, and there was a dance each evening from seven to seven forty-five in "Rec Hall," in the basement of Rice Hall. There was a three-piece orchestra, a piano, violin, and drum, and there was usually a considerable attendance. I kept a graph of my dates, listing the names of six or seven girls, with lines indicating, month by month, the number of dates I had with each. I still have this important record, and it is fun to look at it and to try to recall the causes of the fluctuations from month to month. By the end of the year, all but three had gone down to pretty close to zero.[4]

In addition to Rec Hall, there were a considerable number of social events, house parties, class parties, and other occasions, as well as a fair amount of bridge-playing. Despite these social activities, the general atmosphere was a serious one.

There was a substantial religious background in the College life. The president in those days was a minister, Dr. Henry Churchill King, a remarkable man who provided excellent leadership for the College until his health began to fail, during my junior and senior years. At that time, there was a Graduate School of Theology at the College, of which the Rev. Edward Increase Bosworth, likewise a remarkable man, was Dean. There was required chapel at noon, Monday through Friday, at which President King, Dean Bosworth, and other members of the faculty were speakers. I took freshman Bible, a required course, and senior Bible, taught by President King, was also required.

Many graduates of Oberlin had become missionaries, and a number of my fellow students were missionary children. There were suggestions to current students that they might become missionaries, and there was a Student Volunteers Society which was largely devoted to encouraging this choice of career. I believe that my parents were somewhat concerned that I might

---

4. Among my papers, I have a small booklet called "Oberlin College: Legislation, 1921." Here are a few items: "Freshmen women may not walk with men after dinner until the spring term." "Men and women may not walk together for recreation on Sunday." "Dancing by men and women in boarding houses is forbidden." "All students are required to attend the daily chapel service and the monthly chapel lectures, and to occupy the chapel seats assigned them."

be caught up in this, but I never found the prospect particularly attractive.

Actually, any religious zeal that I might have had waned while I was at Oberlin. My father was a regular church attendant, and active as an elder in the Presbyterian Church. My mother, with her Hicksite Quaker background, was less outward in her religious activities. She attended church with my father, but did not go on Communion Sunday. She was active in the Ladies' Aid Society, but was not committed to doctrine. She had a wide interest in world religions, and frequently read books about comparative religion, the religions of India, China, and Japan, the History of the Jews, and various ecumenical works.

At any rate, while at Oberlin, I rarely went to church, except for the required chapel. I would not say that I became irreligious, but I found myself unwilling to accept any specific doctrines. I particularly dislike the symbolism of the "Body and Blood of Christ," and found, as I learned more about it, that religious strife through the centuries had been useless, inhumane, and essentially irreligious, as I saw it. I remain very much struck by the mystery of it all—what we are, why we are here, the enigma of life and death. However, I found these problems unsolvable, and did not find either answers or solace in religious doctrine.

Despite this, I remained at heart a Christian, though I was always baffled by the Trinity, and particularly by "the Holy Ghost." But I found much of the teaching of Christ encouraging and inspiring. I had no trouble in accepting him as a great historical figure, and wondered why that was not enough. Through the years, I have had many friends who find much solace in religion, in one form of religion or another. I suppose I could be called a humanist or some sort of agnostic. But when I have to fill in a blank stating my religion (as on an Air Liban plane once, where the reason for the question was to designate the sort of meal I would get) I say "Christian".

Looking back on it, with the test of time, I feel that I had an excellent education at Oberlin, probably better than I realized at the time. All of my teachers were competent, many were excellent, and some were outstanding. There were a few original scholars. But many of the faculty had a wide scholarly bent, broad familiarity with their field, and a wise and humanist approach.

Probably the greatest scholarly teacher at Oberlin while I was there was Professor Charles H. A. Wager, in English literature. He taught large classes, and held the students enthralled.

He was easily the most discussed faculty member at the lunch or dinner table. As things worked out, I never had a course with Professor Wager. This was in part because my schedule in other fields did not leave room for it. I think, too, that one of the reasons was that I determined early not to do things just to go along with the crowd. I found it more satisfying to make my own decisions. I would not say that I was very often a leader, but I was definitely not a follower.

I early found myself pursuing two majors, in political science, and in mathematics, and I particularly enjoyed my work in these courses. In political science, my principal teacher was Professor Karl F. Geiser. He had studied in Germany, and made some statements during World War I which were regarded as "pro German." Some college administrators and trustees called for his resignation. I remember this being discussed at our family dinner table—probably about 1918, when I was fourteen years old—because the controversy was reported in the Cleveland newspapers. It is my recollection that my father regarded it as foolish to make a fuss over what Geiser had said, just as it was foolish for Geiser to have made such statements under all of the circumstances. There was a hearing by the faculty which cleared Geiser of any charges, and I have a feeling that there were certain trustees who helped to calm things down. President King was away at the time, on a wartime mission, so that his moderating influence was not directly felt.

Actually, in my recollection, Geiser was not a very exciting classroom teacher. He lectured a good deal, and his lectures were unorganized. Geiser's forte was that he had an extraordinary talent for picking out a half dozen of his students and working closely with them. He had them in his house, often when significant off-campus visitors were his guests. One of these, whom I remember particularly, was Oswald Garrison Villard, then the editor of The Nation. Geiser often stopped individual students on the campus: "Have you read" thus and so? "Well, you'd better read it—best thing that's come out." He had been very stimulating to Ray Hengst and to Robert W. Wheeler, both of whom preceded me at Oberlin, and at the Harvard Law School. He also wrote thoughtful letters to graduate schools on behalf of his chosen students.

My Harvard Law School colleague, Professor Thomas Reed Powell, told me that he got better letters of recommendation from Geiser than he received from anyone else in any college. Powell came to Harvard from Columbia, where he was on the Political Science faculty. I think he was talking in particular about letters that came from Geiser to Columbia supporting candidates for Ph.D.'s in Government. He said Geiser would write: "This man is better than Jones we sent you two years ago but not quite as good as Brown we sent you four years ago. He has this, he has that," and Powell said that these letters were always accurate. Although I never saw it, I have no doubt that Geiser wrote a letter on my behalf supporting a scholarship at Harvard Law School. At that time, there were very few scholarships which were awarded in advance. One of these, the William Cheney Brown, Jr. Scholarship, in the amount, as I recall it, of $200, was awarded to me. William Cheney Brown, Jr. was a student from Rhode Island who left the Law School in 1917 for military service, and died in service in 1919.

The faculty members in the Mathematics Department stand out clearly in my memory. I had at least two courses with Professor William D. Cairns, and a course, and some private work, with Professor Mary Emily Sinclair. The private work was in her field of specialty, known as the Calculus of Variations. I had a somewhat unusual experience with Professor Chester Yeaton. I signed up for a course with him in differential equations. I purchased the textbook, and went to the first two or three classes. By the end of the second week I had written out answers to every problem in the textbook. I took these answers to Professor Yeaton and said, "You know, I do not want to be disrespectful, but I just wonder whether I should continue to take this course." Professor Yeaton replied that he thought it would be fine if I dropped the course, and said that he would give me some individual, more advanced, work along the same line. He added, though, that he had no power to excuse me from attending classes and observed that the rules required that I attend classes. He suggested that we should see the dean, who was, at that time, Charles N. Cole—a fine gentlemen with a very rigid mind. Dean Cole would not relax the rule. He said that I would have to attend the classes. He said that if Professor Yeaton wanted to give me extra work, he could, but that I would have to attend the classes. We left the dean's office, and said very little. But the fact was that my attendance at classes became rather sketchy, and I did regularly meet with Professor Yeaton and do advanced work in differential equations and related areas. Professor Yeaton turned my grade in with the others in the differential equations course. I greatly enjoyed working with him, and was grateful to him for the way he handled it.

I took other government courses, and work in history. I remember, particularly, the course in "Europe Since 1815," given by Professor D.R. Moore. I still remember more than I probably need to know about the Tai Ping Rebellion.

I also took a course in philosophy from Professor Simon MacLennon. This was the only course (other than gym, where I struggled to get a C) in which I did not do very well. I think I was given a B, though otherwise I had A's in all my courses. This was an important lesson to me. I learned from it that though I was quite good in analysis, in seeing how things fitted together and in organizing them with reasonable clarity, I was not very strong on theory. I have been aware of that weakness throughout my subsequent life. The theoretical approach to law is generally known as "jurisprudence." I could probably put together a jurisprudential paragraph today, but certainly not an acceptable article. While a graduate student at the Harvard Law School, I took Dean Pound's course in jurisprudence and received a good grade in it. Dean Pound was a truly great scholar, widely familiar with the authors in many languages. His approach was, however, generally historical and analytical. His own graduate work had been in botany, and his thesis had been on the Botany of Nebraska. He was a great classifier, and that part of his approach I could follow with little difficulty.

Finally, I will mention a course in international law which I had with Professor Harold King, who was the son of President King. This course was given with a regular casebook, and I found fascination in reading and studying the cases.

Two events during my senior year at Oberlin stand out clearly in my mind. A member of the faculty in the field of classics, Professor Leigh Alexander, had been one of the early Rhodes Scholars. He urged me with considerable persistence to apply for a Rhodes Scholarship, but I did not do so. On the whole, I am not sorry. If I could have done the other things I have done, I would have been glad to have done that, too. As I look back, I think that there were two reasons I did not apply. One of these reasons, perhaps the most important, was the feeling of shyness that I have already referred to, the sort of fear of trying and failing and being hurt—perhaps, as I have suggested, an inate kind of inferiority complex. The other reason was that, as of that time in particular, there was a very considerable athletic element in getting a Rhodes Scholarship. And though I was never a bookworm, and I played on class teams, and I went six years to Camp Pemigewassett in New Hampshire, and I climbed all the mountains in that State, including Mount Washington a half dozen times, I was never any good at athletics. I used to say that if the Lord had wanted me to be an athlete, he would have given me a different set of genes. At any rate, I did not apply for a Rhodes Scholarship. I eventually received an Oxford degree by the honorary route, but that is not the same.

The other event which I particularly remember during my senior year was the oral examination which I had to take in connection with my candidacy for the Masters degree. This was held in one of the seminar rooms in the Carnegie Library building. There were several faculty members there. I remember only two, Professor Geiser and Professor Anna Marie Klingenhagen, whom we knew chiefly as Dean of Women, but she was also Professor of History. During the oral examination, Miss Klingenhagen belabored me about Charles and Mary Beard's book entitled "An Economic Interpretation of the Constitution of the United States," published in 1913. Generally speaking, the Beards' thesis was that the Constitution was a structure put together by the high ranks of American society, designed primarily to take care of the rich and hold down the poor.

I vigorously resisted this approach. I said that the Founding Fathers—not only those of the Declaration of Independence who risked their lives, but also those at the Constitutional Convention, and in the ratifying conventions—acted primarily for patriotic motives, and that they had in fact put together a remarkable document for governing a country with all kinds of economic disparities and problems. They were, of course, leading citizens; they were not people picked up off the street. But I stuck to my position that what they did could not properly be written off simply as a scheme to keep everything in the control of the propertied class. Miss Klingenhagen was as persistent in her views as I was in mine. I was told later that she had marked me down heavily. I think that as far as Professor Geiser was concerned, the fact that I did not give in was a plus rather than a minus. Indeed, I think that Geiser probably shared my view.

I have nothing but the warmest feelings for my years at Oberlin. There probably were some unpleasant experiences, but I have learned, to my pleasure, that I have a considerable capacity to forget the details of anything which caused me pain or made me unhappy, and to remember the things which were pleasant. I clearly enjoyed the people I came to know at Oberlin, both faculty and students. I had a very fine group of classmates, and made friendships which have lasted through the years. One of my close friends was Victor Obenhaus, who was my roommate during my senior year. He went on to Union Theological Seminary, and then headed a missionary school in Pleasant Hill, Tennessee. After that, he was assistant minister of a church in Cleveland. Then he taught for a number of years at the Chicago Theological Seminary, and eventually became its President. Another close friend was Ralph Andrews, who came from western New York. He went with me to Harvard Law School, and made his career as a practicing lawyer in Buffalo. My roommate during my junior year at Oberlin was Robert Millikan, nephew of Robert A. Millikan, the Nobel Prize winning physicist. We lived that year at 64 East College Street, the house where Charles Martin Hall had lived when, in the 1880s, in the wood-shed behind the house, he developed the electrolytic method of producing aluminum as a useful and cost-effective metal.

Almost without exception, my fellow students at Oberlin were middle-class Americans from the mid-west. About half of them were from Ohio. There was no one of any particular means there. Many people had board jobs, and other kinds of jobs, and that was regarded as appropriate. Today, many people refer to the 1920s as the "Roaring Twenties," but that aspect of the period never really touched Oberlin very much. During my student days, the women students were subject to a good deal of regulation, though not nearly as much as had been in effect when my mother and father were students in the late 1890s. During my years, the girls had to be in their dormitories by 10 p.m., and the library closed at 9:45. I think we regarded this as a not-too-foolish rule, designed to help people to avoid staying up all night. I think we took ourselves fairly seriously, but we had fun too. We were at college in order to get an education, and in order that we could lead useful, constructive and satisfying lives later on. Most of the older people we knew were educated people who were doing interesting or useful things because they had an education. I do not have any feeling of oppression from the rules while I was there.

Another rule, which I favored (and still do), was that students were not allowed to have cars in Oberlin. My recollection, as of the early 1920s, was that cars were not usually made available to young people, except in the relatively few families which were well off. I would not have had a car, and, on the whole, it seemed nicer to me if other people did not have them either. During my senior year, 1924–1925, my roommate, Victor Obenhaus, had an old, brass-band Model T Ford, a real Model T Ford. I think that it was probably of about 1914 or 1915 vintage. He lived in Oak Park, Illinois and he used the car to drive to and from college, including Christmas and spring vacation. But in Oberlin he kept it in the back yard, with a cloth canopy over it, and did not use it while he was in Oberlin. He tells me that his mother eventually gave the car away. This seems too bad; if he had only kept it, it would probably now be worth a fortune.

This was also the era of prohibition. Oberlin had always been a dry town, and there was a strong tradition. Indeed, the Anti–Saloon League was led by Wayne B. Wheeler, an Oberlin graduate in the Class of 1894. Drinking was essentially a non-issue while I was a student at Oberlin. My recollection is that I understood that one could get alcohol if he looked for it. I never had any desire to look for it. I was not aware of any appreciable number of students who had such a desire. I was quite happy without it; indeed, I always have been. To this day, I do not drink. There are various reasons for this, including family tradition, and my deep-seated tendency not "to go along with the crowd." Incidentally, I think that the absence of pressure with respect to alcohol was one of the reasons that I was glad to be in Oberlin, and not at Harvard, Yale or Princeton, where there were frequent stories of continued high times. We knew of people who did not like such an atmosphere and wished there were some way to avoid it.

There was also, I think a "constructive" atmosphere at Oberlin. The faculty were "good" people, with high standards of conduct and responsibility. The students were pleasant, and had a good time. They were interested in learning how to make a living in an interesting way, with a broad background. But they were interested, too, in finding a way to make their lives useful, so as to make contributions to others, their families, their communities, the nation, and the world.

The 1920s were, indeed, an euphorious time. The "war to end all wars" had just been concluded when I entered college. The League of Nations was beginning to function. The Naval Disarmament Treaty actively promoted by the Secretary of State, Charles Evans Hughes, was concluded in 1921. The economy, for the most part, was good. Fortunately, we could not foresee what the next twenty years would bring. We were excited about the opportunity to serve, to help in the improvement of our country, and of the world.

There were many causes for me to share in this outlook, starting with the interests and vision of my family. But this approach was surely nurtured at Oberlin. It is an approach which I have always valued, and I am grateful to Oberlin for its part in imparting it to me.

My graduation was on June 15, 1925. I remember the date because it was the eighth birthday of my younger sister, Hope, and she sat in the gallery during the ceremony. The Commencement speaker was Newton D. Baker, a prominent citizen of nearby Cleveland, former Mayor of Cleveland, and Secretary of War during World War I. The subject of his address was "The Scholar in Politics." I cannot now remember what he said, but I do remember that the speech made a great impression on me at the time, and the title has continued to provide an impact.

B. Travels with the Bureau of University Travel

There was one important set of experiences which grew out of my Oberlin background. Harry Huntington Powers was Professor of French at Oberlin in 1888–1892. That was, of course, long before my time. After a few years of teaching, he organized University Prints, which provided good pictures (then almost always in black and white) of outstanding European art, both paintings and sculpture. These were widely used in both school and college art classes, and gave students an opportunity to visualize the works of art which they were studying. This business proved to be successful and out of it, under the leadership of Dr. Powers, grew a new activity known as the Bureau of University Travel, with headquarters in Newton, Massachusetts.

The Bureau organized tours, mostly in Europe, but also to Japan, India, and other countries. These tours were mostly patronized by high school and college teachers. It was, however, before the days of easy travel, and many professional people, and others, used the Bureau as a means of taking their first trip to Europe. The Bureau was operated on a comfortable basis, with due regard to economy. It was not simply a "tourist company," because each of the tours was led by well-qualified university lecturers who accompanied the members of the tour when they visited historical sites or art galleries, and also gave evening lectures on the history and significance of the particular place they were then visiting. A number of these lecturers came from the Oberlin faculty, and Professor Louis Lord was especially active. He eventually succeeded Dr. Powers as President of the Bureau.

It was Professor Lord who developed the idea of putting on a minimum expense tour for college men. The leader of the tour was to be Carl C. W. Nicol, a professor at Oberlin, and the Dean of Men. The trip was planned on a strictly third-class basis, except where there was fourth class, and then it was fourth class. Unbelievable as it may be, the entire cost, for ten weeks, from New York back to New York, as far north as Edinburgh and as far south as Salerno, south of Naples, was $458.25.

I had to give up going back to Pemigewassett, which I loved, but it seemed a remarkable opportunity, and the time had come for a change. I talked with my father about it, and he said that he would pay the bill. My parents had been to Europe in 1921, shortly after World War I. They both had world-wide interests, and felt that this trip would be an important part of my education.

COLLEGE MEN'S TOUR

June 21 to September 14

$458.25

ECONOMY
INDEPENDENCE
FELLOWSHIP

College Men's Tour

86 days, $458.25

France, Switzerland, Italy, Germany, Holland, Belgium and England

BUREAU OF UNIVERSITY TRAVEL, INC.
11 BOYD STREET   NEWTON, MASS.

[G7070]

We sailed from New York, steerage class, eight bunks to a room, late in June in 1924, on a very old Cunard ship named the

Saxonia. It took the Saxonia ten days to reach Plymouth. We did not get off there, but continued on board until the ship docked in London. We spent some time in London, and then proceeded to Paris. From Paris, we went to Geneva, and then by boat and train to the Swiss end of the Simplon Pass. We walked over the Simplon Pass, staying at the hospice on top for the night. The next day, we walked down to Airolo on the Italian side. It was a rather strenuous walk, and we felt the need for refreshments. I saw a sign which indicated that milk could be purchased, and I asked for a glass of milk. Eventually, the milk came, and it was hot. This was the custom of the country, but somehow or other hot milk is not particularly refreshing after a long and humid hike.

From Airolo we took the train to Milan, where we saw "The Last Supper," among other things. We then went to Venice, Florence, and to Rome, and then on to Naples. From Naples we went by boat to the Blue Grotto, and then we hiked the full length of the Amalfi Drive, staying for the night in Amalfi. The next day we walked on to Salerno, and then walked up Mt. Vesuvius, a rather strenuous climb, since the ash through which one walks is so soft that each step slips backward and the upward gain is small. Eventually we reached the top, and the view down into the bright and boiling crater was memorable. The next day, we visited Pompeii, including the museum which contains the plaster casts of figures of those who fell during the eruption.

In due course, we made our way north, through Switzerland and Luxembourg to Holland and Belgium, and then back to England, before sailing from Southhampton to New York. The group in the tour was a fine one, coming from a number of other colleges, as well as Oberlin. A number of these people went on to distinction, and remained among my friends through the years.

One other financial matter remains in my mind. In Italy, we stayed at pensions, or *pensione* in Italian. In 1924, the charge for a room and full board was about $2 a day, in American money. These places were all clean, and well run, and we were quite comfortable throughout the trip.

This started a succession of trips to Europe. In 1925, I was employed by the Bureau to be an assistant on a trip for college students. This meant that I was responsible for making the arrangements on the ground, finding pensions and assigning rooms, arranging for transportation and baggage handling, and so on. For this, I got a free trip, but nothing more. It was on this trip that I walked over the St. Gothard Pass on my twenty-first birthday.

In the summer of 1926, I was the tour manager for one of the Bureau's regular parties. Many of the people on the tour were high school teachers, mostly of Latin. I remember that on this trip, while in the Naples area, we visited the site of the Cumaean Sybil and were given a lecture by the Minister of Education of Italy. The minister did not speak English, and the teachers did not speak Italian. This did not prove to be a problem, though, for the minister gave his lecture in Latin. It is the only time that I have ever heard Latin used as a substantial means of current oral communication. Many of the teachers said that they understood it well. I can only say that I understood a word here and there.

In 1927, I did not go to Europe because of my responsibilities as president of the Harvard Law Review.

In 1928, at the close of my third year in Law School, I had a particularly interesting assignment with the Bureau of University Travel. The Bureau had agreed to make the travel arrangements for a party led by Sherwood Eddy, who was a leader of the national organization of the YMCA, and a very influential minister. He organized a party with about fifty members, made up of professional people, ministers, and other leaders from many parts of the country. His plan was to go to several principal cities, where he arranged meetings with locally prominent people.

My task again was to be in charge of the logistics. We spent nearly three weeks in London, then a week in Berlin. We went to Dresden, Prague and Vienna, and then to Paris. In each city, we had a carefully-planned program. In London, we met with Prime Minister Stanley Baldwin at 10 Downing Street. We had tea with Ramsey McDonald on the porch of the House of Commons. We had lectures by Harold Laski, Norman Angell, Philip Snowden, and others. We met the Archbishop of Canterbury at Lambeth Palace, and the Bishop of London at Fulham Palace. We went to Oxford, where we met with the Master of Balliol, and G.D.H. Cole. Although these were all remarkable experiences, perhaps the meeting which stands out most clearly in my mind was with Lady Astor at her London residence, where we had tea with George Bernard Shaw as the guest of honor. This was shortly after he had published "The Intelligent Woman's Guide to Socialism and Capitalism." I wonder what he would say now.

In Berlin, we had a similar program. Like others, we underestimated the importance of Germany in the days ahead. I remember especially meeting with a group of German students about my age. They assured us that things were going well, that Germany was getting back to normal, and would be a leader in a peaceful Europe. Finally, one of them said: "There is, of course, that nut down in Munich, but we will take care of him." I have no doubt that the speaker was sincere, but sometimes things do not work out as we expect. After our week in Berlin (the only time I have ever been in that city), we went to Dresden, Prague and Vienna. This was followed by six days in Geneva, centered on the League of Nations, and then six days in Paris, for meetings with leading French scholars and politicians.

Following the stay in Paris, I returned to England, where I met my father and mother, and my Uncle Wells Griswold, and his wife, Aunt Louise. My father had a client in Cleveland who was a Lincoln dealer. Through the client, my father arranged to hire a Lincoln car in England. This was before the days when rental cars were easy to find. The arrangement was that I would drive the car for the four senior Griswolds, which I did with great pleasure. The car was a very large one, and we occasionally got to English lanes with narrow cuts which we could not get through. We never got actually stuck, but we did on several occasions, have to back out and find another road. Another thing I remember abut the Lincoln is that it had its own air pump, attached to the engine. There was a long, rubber hose, long enough to reach any tire, and the tires could be pumped up by running the engine and flicking a handle on the dashboard, with an air pressure gauge nearby.

Among other places, our trip took us to Askham in the Lake Country, where we visited the birthplace of my mother's mother, Jane Cooper, and had tea with mother's second cousin, Robin Cooper, and his wife. Mr. Cooper gave my mother a small table which had been in the Cooper family for many years, and this was always cherished by my mother. He also gave us a cup and saucer for a "dish of tea," which we still have.

In 1929, I again was an on-the-ground man for the Bureau, with one of their regular parties. I thought that this was probably my last venture of this sort, since I had finished a graduate year at the Harvard Law School in June of that year, and expected to start practicing law in Cleveland in the fall, and to spend my life as a practicing lawyer there.

As things worked out, though, I did go to Europe again in 1930, this time on a rather remarkable assignment. That was the year of the Bimillennium of Virgil, and the Bureau arranged two large and successful Virgilian cruises. These cruises started and ended in Naples, one in July, and the other in August. My assignment was to make the arrangements for the trip through Europe, in July, of the party who would be taking the August cruise, and then, in August, to take the members of the July cruise northward over much the same route. This meant that both parties were in Naples at the close of July, while the ship was being cleaned after the first cruise, and refueled and revictualed for the second cruise. I was responsible for the rooms, transportation, meals and museum visiting of about a thousand persons. A car and driver were assigned to me, and I worked about twenty hours a day. I particularly remember the Bay of Naples at night with Vesuvius in the distance. It was not a time of eruption, but it was a time of considerable activity and the cone of Vesuvius was noisy, with luminescent rocks flying in the air, and continuing bangs and rumbles coming over the water from several miles away.

This was the year of Oberammergau, and we stopped there to see the Passion Play. Since my responsibilities related to the land portion of the trip, I made the trip southward to Naples in July, and then took the members of the first cruise north by land, over the same route. Thus, I was at Oberammergau twice.

On the first visit there, I attended the Passion Play, which, as I recall it, occupied three days. The performance was, of course, in German, which I did not understand very well. But the scenes were largely familiar, and it was a very interesting experience.

On the return trip, I thought that seeing the Passion Play once in one year was enough, so, after getting the party duly established, I took a side trip in southern Bavaria, visiting the fabulous castle Neuschwanstein, and then going on to Garmisch and Partenkirchen. These were already known as ski resorts; but there was, of course, no skiing in August. Garmisch was also to become the mountain hideaway of Adolph Hitler, but that was not foreseen in 1930.

I may observe at this point that one of the nice things about these summer trips for the Bureau of University Travel was the opportunity which it gave me for interesting side trips. I would usually get to new cities ahead of the party, in order to make hotel and bus arrangements, examine rooms, get mail, and so on. After the party arrived, my duties lessened, since the participants were taken in charge by the intellectual leaders, usually college professors, employed by the Bureau. When I could make time available, I often went on short trips of my own. In this way, I visited Palermo in Sicily, and also San Marino in northern Italy. This is a fascinating small mountaintop community, maintaining its independence, though entirely surrounded by Italy. I knew about it through my stamp collection activities, and it turned out to be all that I expected.

All in all, my six summers with the Bureau of University travel gave me important funds of information, and a rich experience which surely contributed materially to the broadening of my horizons.

C. HOBBIES

Boundaries

For some reason that I have never been able to explain, I have long been interested in boundary lines, both international and interstate, though chiefly confined to the United States. How I got started on this, I do not recall, but it began quite early.

At one time, I had the great idea that I would produce the "definitive" work on the boundaries of the United States. I hoped to do this in collaboration with an historian and a geographer, while I would deal with the legal questions and court decisions which have been involved in determining these boundaries. This has never been accomplished. Indeed, it was never really started. I never had the time required. But it would have been fun if I had been able to do it.

While I was a student at Oberlin, I wrote a paper about the eastern boundary of Ohio, running from the Ohio River north to Lake Erie. Actually, when this line was drawn on the ground, in 1785, it was only the western boundary of Pennsylvania, since there was no political entity known as Ohio when the line was surveyed.

Under the grant which King Charles II made in 1681 to William Penn, the Province of Pennsylvania extended "westward five degrees in longitude from the Delaware River." By agreement reached between the Provinces of Pennsylvania and Maryland in 1760, the southern boundary of Pennsylvania was fixed as a parallel of latitude fifteen miles due south of "the southernmost part of the City of Philadelphia." A portion of this line was surveyed by Mason and Dixon from 1763 to 1767. In 1779, Virginia and Pennsylvania agreed that the Mason and Dixon line should be extended due west for five degrees of longitude from the Delaware River, and that a meridian should then be drawn due north to Lake Erie. This line, the western boundary of Pennsylvania, was run from the Ohio River to Lake Erie in 1785.

A number of the original markers on this line can still be found, including one near the shore of Lake Erie, and others farther south, which consisted simply of the letter "P" carved on the east side of convenient rocks which were encountered along the line.

One spring, about 1923, my family took me by automobile to this line, near Conneaut, Ohio, and I took a number of photographs of the markers, and used them in connection with a paper which I wrote for a political science course at Oberlin.

Later in 1923, while I was a counsellor at Camp Pemigewassett, the counsellors had a "day off." I used it to go by train to the southern boundary of Vermont, at the Connecticut River, where Vermont, New Hampshire and Massachusetts meet in a single point. For historical reasons, all of the Connecticut River north of Massachusetts is in New Hampshire, that is, the boundary between the states of New Hampshire and Vermont is at low water mark on the west side of the river. At most times of the year, this point is under water. When I was there, though, the water was only an inch or two above the top of the stone monument, and I was able to get a most unimpressive picture of it. On the bank just to the west, there is a large monument on the Vermont–Massachusetts line.

After this, I continued to visit boundary lines. In 1927, while en route from Cleveland to Cambridge, I travelled through Washington and stopped in Newark, Delaware. My purpose was to locate and photograph the circular boundary line between Delaware and Pennsylvania—the only circular interstate boundary in the country. This was the result of an agreement reached in the seventeenth century. The Duke of York (later King James II) owned Delaware, having conquered it from the Swedes; and William Penn was the Proprietor of Pennsylvania. When it came time to fix the limits of their respective domains, the Duke of York said, in effect, "Give me twelve miles from New Castle, and Penn may have the rest." This was hardly worth the trouble it has caused, as only a year later the Duke conveyed these lands to Penn. Some fifty years after that, the heirs of Penn and the then Lord Baltimore agreed on the western and southern boundaries of Delaware. A line was drawn east and west from Chesapeake Bay to the Atlantic Ocean through Cape Henelopen. The exact middle of this line became the western end of the southern boundary of Delaware. The western boundary of Delaware was fixed as the line through the midpoint which was tangent to the twelve-mile circle around New Castle. This was rather complicated, and finally the Penns brought Lord Baltimore before the English Court of Chancery. This resulted in a decree by the Chancellor, Lord Hardwick, in 1750.[5]

The east-west line was duly surveyed by Americans, but drawing the tangent line on the ground was too much for them. It was for this reason that Mason and Dixon were brought to America from England. They succeeded in their assignment, and

---

5. Penn v. Lord Baltimore, 1 Vesey Sr. 444 (1750).

then spent some time in surveying the east-west line between Maryland and Pennsylvania. It was this latter task that made them famous, though it is clear that their work on the Maryland–Pennsylvania boundary was only incidental to the main purpose of their employment.

The tangent monument set by Mason and Dixon is still standing, about seventy-five yards north of the Amtrak Railroad line between Wilmington and Baltimore. Whenever I take that train trip, I always find a seat on the north side of the train, and catch a glimpse of the monument as the train speeds by.

In later years, I took trips along the boundary of Canada and the United States, between the St. Lawrence River and the Atlantic Ocean, where there are a number of interesting points, including several houses and stores which are partly in Canada and partly in the United States, and an auditorium in Derby Line, Vermont, where the stage is in Canada, and the audience sits in the United States. Thus Americans could see Canadian actors who could appear without troubling to meet the requirements of American immigration laws.

I also located the northwest corner of mainland United States, which is at Point Roberts in the State of Washington, at the western side of a peninsula along the forty-ninth parallel. The land there is accessible only through Canada. The school children of Point Roberts are bussed some thirty miles to get to a school at Blaine, Washington. I have also twice visited the southwest corner of the United States, between Mexico and California.

Once while I was a member of the Civil Rights Commission, a meeting of the Commission was held, through the courtesy of Father Hesburgh, one of its members, at a Notre Dame camp in the northern peninsula of Michigan. The camp was on a lake. It was mid-summer, and we made the most of the swimming opportunities. I must confess, though, that I spent much of my time coming out of the water and climbing on to the diving board, simply fascinated by the fact that when I took off I was in Michigan, and when I hit the water, I was in Wisconsin.

In 1949, Harriet and I, with our children, drove west. One of the places we got to, which proved to be something of an adventure, was the only place in the country where four states meet. These states are Utah, Colorado, Arizona and New Mexico. At that time, there was no road there and this was very much Indian country. The travel was so rough that the oil pan on our car was damaged, and most of the oil leaked away. We finally were towed into an Indian Trading Post at Tees Nos Pas, where the Mormon trader ingeniously drove rags into the break, and we were able to get to Farmington, New Mexico, where we got repairs.

Out of all this, I wrote an article entitled "Hunting Boundaries with Car and Camera in the Northeastern United States," with many illustrations. I tried hard to get the National Geographic Magazine to accept this article, and even made a trip to Washington to aid the effort to bring this about. However, I was unsuccessful. Eventually, the article was published in the Geographical Review for July, 1939.[6]

The United States Geological Survey, of the Department of the Interior, has, since 1885, published a series of reports on the boundaries of the United States. The third edition of this Bulletin was published in 1923, and I used this extensively in many of my boundary searches. After I came to Washington to work in 1929, I got in touch with Edward M. Douglas, the editor of the Bulletin, and made available to him a number of my pictures. Mr. Douglas edited a new edition, which was put out in 1930, using several of my pictures, but giving me no credit for them. I raised question about this, but when the next edition was published in 1966, edited by Franklin K. Van Zandt, the same pictures were used, again without credit. Though I had no copyright protection, I again addressed complaint, this time to Mr. Van Zandt. This led to a friendly exchange of correspondence. Finally, in 1976, another edition was published and I was at last given appropriate credit for my trifling contribution to geographical knowledge.[7]

Another interesting expedition took me to the northwestern corner of Massachusetts, high on the ridge to the west of Williamstown. The southwest corner of Vermont is a quarter of a mile or so due west of this. From this point, the western boundary of Vermont proceeds by a diagonal line to a river crossing. Then, for about a mile, it appears to follow what were the boundaries of individual private land holdings around 1800. It has several angles and jogs which bear no relation to the current lay of the land, running, for the most part, though woodlands.

The western boundary of Massachusetts, between that Commonwealth and the State of New York, was surveyed in 1785 by

---

6. 29 Geograph. Rev. 353 (1939).

7. Boundaries of the United States and the Several States, U.S. Geological Survey Professional Paper 909 (1976), p. 7. The 1966 edition is known as U.S. Geological Survey Bulletin 187. The pictures appear opposite page 13.

the Congress of the United States operating under the Articles of Confederation. This was an extremely accurate survey, and appears to have been one of the major enduring activities under the Articles of Confederation, probably exceeded in importance only by the Ordinance of 1787, establishing the Northwest Territory. This line was a straight line designed to meet the requirement that it be twenty miles east of the Hudson River. It left a triangle at the southwest corner of Massachusetts which was, because of the terrain, inaccessible from Massachusetts. In the 1840s, a railroad line was built north in New York state, close to the Massachusetts boundary. At that time, prizefighting was illegal, but the ever-resourceful promotors put on a fight in this southwest corner of Massachusetts, acting on the premise that neither New York nor Connecticut could prevent it, and that its inaccessibility meant that Massachusetts would not interfere.

This led to a good deal of discussion, and the net result was that a triangular tract was cut off from Massachusetts, and given to New York. This is one of the few instances in which parcels of land have been transferred from one state to another. If you make your way to the hill above the new diagonal line, you can see the remains of the solid stone walls which marked the original southwest corner of Massachusetts, and see, too, the relatively level field where the famous prizefight was held.

One time, in 1942, while travelling in western Massachusetts (this was the first trip that Harriet took after being released from the hospital), I found that the states had built a new highway alongside the Boston and Albany Railroad tracks. The widening of the highway had made it necessary to remove one of the original 1785 monuments, and replace it by another and larger granite monument by the side of the new road. My wife made inquiry as to where the old monument was, and was told that it was in a barn nearby. We were also told that the barn was the property of an elderly lady, Miss Murphy, who then lived in Poughkeepsie, New York. When I returned to our home, I wrote a letter to Miss Murphy, and arranged to buy the monument from her for $25. The monument was then shipped by railroad to me, and I picked it up at the Boston and Maine station in Waverly, Massachusetts. It was very heavy, and it weighed down the back of my car, but I finally got it home. It is now erected in the backyard of my home in Belmont, Massachusetts, reading "Mass." on one side and "N.Y." on the other.[8]

---

8. This boundary stone was actually involved in the case of Blaine v. Murphy, 265 Fed. 324 (D. Mass. 1920), where Miss Murphy was the defendant, and jurisdiction of the federal court depended on her being a

Nearby is another boundary marker which I acquired on one of my trips along the Canadian boundary. This stood on the line surveyed in 1774 between Vermont and Quebec, near Canaan, Vermont. Since it was on the boundary line, it was the place where the snow plow from Vermont stopped and turned around. It was a low monument, rising only a foot or so above the ground. Covered with snow, the snow plow hit it, and broke it off. The International Boundary Commission duly sought to restore it. It drilled holes in the top part of the monument and in the part remaining in the ground, inserted brass rods, and replaced the monument. The next year the snow plow came to this point, turned around, and broke off the restored monument. The International Boundary Commission then gave up. It sawed off the stone monument flush with the ground level and inserted a brass plate at the top of the remnant left in the ground. I found the broken-off top serving as a step to a corncrib of a farmer nearby. Having established the price by my previous contact with the lady from Poughkeepsie, I offered him $25 for the monument and duly acquired it. It now stands in the stone wall at the rear of my house in Belmont.

Some day these two monuments will be found, and they will greatly perplex the archaeologists of the future.

In recent years, many vacations have been spent on the First Connecticut Lake, at the northern tip of New Hampshire. At various times, I have hiked along the international boundary there, going to "the source of Hall's Stream".[9] On one occasion I went to the point along the ridge where New Hampshire, Maine, and Quebec meet. My son accompanied me on this somewhat strenuous hike, and took a picture of me at the boundary monument. I was standing just in Maine. At this time I was Solicitor General of the United States, and I sent a copy of the picture to the Commissioner of Immigration and Naturalization, with a

---

citizen of Massachusetts. Her father owned a hotel built on both sides of the state line, and she continued to live there after his death. They long thought that the hotel was in New York, but a resurvey in 1899, accepted by formal action of both states, showed that the boundary stone in question was about fifty feet east of the true line, and that most of the hotel was actually in Massachusetts. 256 Fed. at 325. Consequently, the court held, Miss Murphy was a citizen of Massachusetts, though she had always thought she was a citizen of New York.

I included this case in several editions of the case book on Conflict of Laws in which I participated, to show that domicile depends on the place where one actually lives, and not on the state where he thought he lived.

9. See p. 24, above.

Monument No. 507—Source of Hall's Stream—July 4, 1975
E.N.G. in New Hampshire, part of hand in Quebec.

note saying that "This is a picture of Griswold entering the United
States without reporting to Customs and Immigration." Within a
few minutes, he came breezing into my office, and said: "How in

E.N.G. at place where New Hampshire, Maine & Quebec meet—September, 1975.

the world did you get there? That's way out in the woods." I
agreed that it was "way out in the woods," and assured him that I
had got there on foot. At least at that time, that part of the
boundary did not present any special problems, and it was

apparently patrolled mostly by a helicopter which flew along the border, in good weather, once or twice a day.

At various times, as I have walked along the border in the woods, I have found myself crossing back and forth across the boundary, thus entering and leaving the United States perhaps a half dozen times within a minute. I have sometimes thought about the statute which provides that "Whoever enters the United States shall forthwith report to Immigration and Customs." I must have violated that statute a thousand times or more in the course of my life. Of course, this has not given me concern. It seems to me quite clear that no court would regard the statute as violated under the circumstances. It is a nice (though relatively unimportant) instance of the fact that absolutely clear and imperious language, with no exceptions or qualifications, still needs to be interpreted in the light of all the circumstances. There is no statute that is so clear that it may not involve interpretation. I recall an argument I heard in the Supreme Court while Justice Holmes was sitting. An eloquent and vigorous lawyer from the south said that "This statute is perfectly clear. There is no way that the Court can decide this case against me." Justice Holmes looked up and smiled, and said: "If this Court's conclusion should be contrary to your position, I expect that a suitable form of words can be devised to state that result."

Stamp Collecting

All my life I have been a stamp collector—at least, it began in January, 1913, when I was in the hospital after my appendix was removed. In those days, one stayed in the hospital for two weeks. After the first distress had passed by, a neighbor brought me a copy of the Scott's Stamp Catalogue for 1908, and a miscellaneous lot of mostly foreign stamps. I still have the catalogue, as well as many others for the intervening years, including the copy I purchased about 1923 of the first edition of the Scott's Specialized Catalogue of United States Stamps. I look at them occasionally to marvel at the low prices which were prevalent at that time.

After I went home from the hospital, I kept on gathering stamps, though, of course, in a very boyish way. However, by the time I got to high school in 1917, I had a considerable collection, mostly of United States stamps. I made many afternoon trips by streetcar downtown to the office of the Cleveland Stamp Company. After a while, they employed me to put stamps on approval sheets, which they sent out by mail. For that, I was paid with a rather battered copy of the first United States stamp, the 5¢ of 1847. Although the stamp's condition was such that it had no appreciable value, I kept that stamp for more than sixty years. I prized it immensely and was very proud of it.

I feel that I learned a great deal from my stamp collecting activities, not only such essential skills as classification and organization of the material, but also a considerable amount about geography, and something about history. The stamps of France, for example, show changes between "Empire Française," and "Repub. Française," and the catalogue shows the dates of these changes. The stamps from the many countries and colonies all over the world led me into geography, locating the countries on the maps, and reading about them in encyclopedias—chiefly, in the early days, "The Book of Knowledge," a set which my mother bought for me and from which I feel that I learned a great deal.

Through stamps, I became familiar with the names of all the countries in the world, and located them in the family Atlas. Most important of all, though, I think, the collecting of stamps gave me a world view, a sense of the importance of communication, and the basic common interest of all the many peoples all over the world. This, together with the broad interests of my mother and father in world peace and order, were important factors in my own later interest in participating as I could in trying to bring about greater trust and better understanding between the peoples of all countries.

At Christmas, 1918, my parents gave me a loose-leaf stamp album, in which I organized my United States stamps, and "wrote up" the various issues, giving information about the printer, the exact dates of issue, the number of stamps issued, and so on. It was in the fall of 1918 that I first subscribed to McKeel's Weekly Stamp News, and I have been a continuous subscriber ever since. I was amused to find in early 1990 that I was the earliest subscriber still on the books of that periodical, more than seventy years after I began. While working in the East Cleveland Public Library, I had the issues for 1919 bound in a sturdy library buckram. I still have that volume, and occasionally look through it, and note the prices of that day, far lower than today. Indeed, there was a time when copies of the Columbian issue of 1893 could be bought for less than face value. Some of them now sell for thousands of dollars.

After I went to Oberlin College, I kept up the collection, though not very actively. I did get copies of many new stamps on "first-day covers," that is, on the envelope, and canceled on the date of issue. After I went to Washington in 1929, I bought many new stamps at the Post Office. These included the Graf Zeppelin stamps of 1934, which I bought at face value. I bought one copy of each for a total of $4.55. I wish I had bought many, many more, for a well-centered set is now worth around a thousand dollars.

I never put the collection completely aside, but I was not very active in developing it until the late 1940s. By that time, I had acquired a considerable amount of background, and skill and understanding of the stamp market, which had shifted somewhat, so that most stamps were bought at public auction sales, for which catalogues were issued. Being a professor of taxation, I noted that older stamps tended to increase in value. Moreover, they produced no current income, and thus no current taxes, while any ultimate gain would be taxable at capital gain rates. By the 1950s, I was buying stamps on an investment basis. In this way, I developed a very substantial collection.

Probably my "gem" was a copy of the 24¢ United States airmail stamp issued in 1918 with the blue airplane in the center printed upside down. A sheet of these stamps was found in a Washington postal station by a man who worked at an office on Fifteenth Street, less than a block away from where my office was in the 1980s. In the 1960s, I bought a copy of this stamp for about $9,200 at auction. When I came to sell my collection in 1979, it bought more than ten times that amount.[10] I also had many other substantial items, including ten or more copies of the large $500 Civil War Revenue Stamp, printed in several colors, and known as the "Persian Rug." Indeed, I think that I nearly "cornered the market" on this item, though, as in the case of all my stamp collecting activities, I always acted quietly, and without publicity.

Another part of my collection was the "Franks of President's Widows." Ever since George Washington died, it has been the custom of Congress to pass a statute granting to the widow of a President the right "to send or receive through the mail, free of postage," by simply writing the word "Free" with her signature in the upper right-hand corner of the envelope. Over the years, I acquired an almost complete collection of these widows' franks. Some of these, such as Mrs. James K. Polk, Mary Lincoln, and Ida G. McKinley are very rare. While we were living in Washington, Harriet had a Stanford friend who was a secretary to Mrs. Hoover. Through her, I acquired a number of widows' franks which were addressed to Mrs. Hoover at the White House.

---

10. A book has been written about the 24¢ inverted center, which includes reference to my copy, which was No. 94 in the sheet. See G. Amick, Inverted Jenney (Sidney, Ohio: 1986) at pp. iv, 121, 221.

These are of no great value, but they served as a very interesting souvenir of my early days in Washington.

In the year 1979, I became seventy-five years old. No one in my family was interested in stamps, and there was no one who knew anything about the intricacies of the stamp market, the best way to sell a collection, and so on. Moreover, my collection had become so valuable that I had to keep most of it in a safe-deposit box in a bank. This meant that I could rarely see it, and this greatly diminished the enjoyment from my collection. I decided that the time had come when I should clear up these difficulties, so I made arrangements to sell my stamps at auction, through Harmer's of New York, one of the leading auction houses. There were a number of sales, but most of them were in New York. Others were in San Francisco and in London. The New York catalogue, in particular, was a very attractive one, with many photographs, including color pictures. The collection was listed as "The Eastern Collection," but my name was not utilized. The sales were very successful. Indeed, my stamp collection was the best investment that I have ever made. The net result, after commissions, was about eight times what I had put into the collection.

One of the inducements to the sale was the fact that my house in Belmont, Massachusetts was broken into in 1971. At that time, my brother and his wife were living in my house, while he worked at the Museum of Fine Arts in Boston. However, they had a home in Exeter, New Hampshire, where they went for the weekends. It was during a weekend that the house was burglarized. It was readily apparent that the thieves must have known about my collecting interests, and were looking for stamps. I did have a number of stamps in the house, though none of any great value. The thieves took my collection of first-day covers, including a number of "first flight" covers from the early days of carrying the mail by air. These were of some value, but they also had sentimental interest to me, and I was very sorry to lose them. Ever since that time, I have watched carefully in stamp auction catalogues, hoping that one of these covers would turn up in a current sale. So far, though, I have never seen one which I could identify as mine.

Another aspect of the collection that I found very valuable, particularly in the years when I was Dean of the Harvard Law School, was the fact that when I was under pressure, as I often was, and felt harassed, as I sometimes did, I could get out the stamp collection and spend an hour or two in an atmosphere which was utterly calm, which involved no tension, which was peaceful and quiet, wholly undemanding, and not very important. Thus, I found the stamp collection a good way to relax, an activity which I enjoyed, even though it had no appreciable practical value. An hour or two with the collection enabled me to shed many cares without any feeling that I was neglecting my duties.

Pen Pal

Another activity which gave me much pleasure, and also helped to broaden my horizons, was an almost life-long friendship with a "pen pal." He was Francis L. Allen. I got his name from an excellent magazine of those times, called "The American Boy." I wrote to him about 1919, and this led to a correspondence and a friendship which lasted until he died in 1987, nearly sixty-eight years later.

When our correspondence began, Francis (who was two or three years older than I was) lived near Cheltenham, in England, where he had gone to school. The years immediately following the War did not offer much promise for a young man in England. I went off to college, and I remember letters from Francis expressing a good deal of discouragement. At any rate, in 1924, he emigrated, as an "assisted immigrant," to New Zealand. He settled in an area near Auckland, and worked on a farm. The opportunities in New Zealand did not prove to be very great, but he started to study, on a part-time basis, at a seminary where he trained to be an Anglican priest. During this period, he was married to a fine New Zealand girl. After his ordination, he was assigned to churches at Pleasant Point, Akaroa, then in a suburb of Christchurch, and eventually in Ashburton, all in the south island of New Zealand.

In the early days, I would write a letter to him which, of course, went by sea. I would then wait about six months for a response. Thus, the correspondence proceeded on a rather leisurely basis. After World War II airmail became available, and the exchange of letters was much more frequent.

I first met Francis in 1951 when my daughter Hope and I stopped in New Zealand on our way to Australia. We visited both the north and south islands, and stayed two or three days with the Allens, at Pleasant Point, in the general vicinity of Mt. Cook. Our effort to visit Mt. Cook, however, was foiled by the weather, for July in New Zealand was mid-winter.

Later, in 1959, Harriet and I visited the Allens when he had the parish near Christchurch. I took a color picture of them outside their church. An enlargement of this picture was submitted in an exhibit of photographs by members at the Association of the Bar of the City of New York. It was called "New Zealand Gothic" and it received an Honorable Mention.

Harriet and I visited the Allens again in 1967, when Francis was assigned to a church in Ashburton, about sixty miles south of Christchurch.

We went again in 1980, once more en route to Australia. The Allens had a son, Ted, who was married, and the younger Allens had a farm on the Pacific Ocean, about fifteen miles south and east of Ashburton. By this time, Francis was retired, and we stayed on Ted's farm, and I had ample opportunity to observe the life and problems of a sheep farmer.

Francis lived into his eighties. He was a kindly, friendly, modest man. (At one point, he was asked by the bishop of Christchurch to be Dean of the Cathedral there. Francis refused, saying that he did not feel worthy of such an important assignment.) His retirement was reasonably active, as he continued to take Vesper services and other duties in the Anglican church is Ashburton.

Although we met for only a few days altogether, we were devoted friends. I learned much from Francis, and feel greatly indebted to him. He had a calm and quiet approach to the world and its problems, and a wise reaction to many of the events of our time. I found him stimulating and satisfying. I was very sorry when his life, and our correspondence, came to an end.

Golf

Finally, I should add my devotion to golf, which I have played badly for sixty-five years, since my college days. I find it pleasant, gentle exercise. I like the people I meet, many of whom are not lawyers. I like the scenery, the trees and shrubs. Despite constant effort, it is a good way to relax.

When I was first in Washington, in the 1930s, I joined the Congressional Country Club, at a time when they were begging for members. There was no initiation fee, and the dues were, as I recall, $200 a year. When I moved to Massachusetts, I joined the Belmont Country Club, and later the Charles River Country Club. When I was appointed Solicitor General, the members at Charles Rivers gave me a solid gold putter, inscribed "Once a dean, now a general—always a golfer." I was much touched by this, and have always regarded it as one of the nicest things that ever happened to me. I still use the putter, though not as well as I did a while ago.

In Washington, I became a member of the Burning Tree Club, a fine institution, which has recently gained some notoriety

October, 1971.

because it has only men as members. Despite my great and real interest in non-discrimination, this has not bothered me. Burning Tree is a golf club. It is not a country club. It has no tennis courts, no swimming pool, and meals are served *al fresco* at long tables. Perhaps it is because of my early experience at a boys' camp, but I do not find invidious discrimination in a place where men can get together for mild physical activity without the restraint which men feel, rightly or wrongly, in mixed company. I have enjoyed my membership in Burning Tree, have benefitted from it in exercise and relaxation, and regret that some people take such a narrowly rigid view of the essence of non-discrimination that they find it objectionable.

CHAPTER III

Entering the Law

A. HARVARD LAW SCHOOL

In September 1925, I entered Harvard Law School. Why did I decide to study law? Why did I decide to go to Harvard? In looking back, I sense that both were inevitable. But I was subject to no pressure. It was always made plain to me by my family that I was free to make my own choice. As a matter of fact, during my senior year at Oberlin, I had two catalogues on my desk. One was the catalogue of the Harvard Law School, and the other was the catalogue of the Department of Astronomy at Harvard. I had long had an interest in physics, and this was the time that the Einstein Theory had been established, even though there was little general understanding of what that theory was. This was also the time of the beginnings of modern cosmology, and I had long been interested in geology, and the age of the earth. I had frequently heard my father discuss work he had in his student days at Oberlin with Professor G. Frederick Wright, who was one of those who wrestled with the problem created by geologic findings with traditional Bible religion. He helped to find a way so that the twain could meet, and I am sure that this had a considerable impact on my father and mother, and thus on me.

Although I toyed with doing graduate work in astrophysics, I finally decided, that the chances of making a living in astrophysics were less than those of making a living in law. In later years, I had a friend on the Harvard faculty, Donald Menzel, who was appointed to the faculty on the same day I was, and who became a very distinguished figure in astrophysics and in cosmology. Among other things, he was the one who developed a means for obscuring the face of the sun when viewed through a telescope,

60

so that, in effect, an eclipse could be seen by blocking out the sun's fiery image locally, without waiting for the brief event of an eclipse in the sky.

In those Harvard years, I often wondered whether I could have been as good an astrophysicist as Donald Menzel was. I had little difficulty in concluding that I would not have made the contributions he did. My observations of myself led me to think that though I was good in traditional mathematics, and in the easier aspects of physics, I was, in those fields, essentially a follower, rather than a leader. I could understand what someone else had worked out, and could follow through the proofs presented, and feel that I understood what had been done. As the problems became more difficult, though I found it harder and harder to work out answers and approaches myself. I doubt very much that I would have made major contributions in mathematics or in astrophysics. I think I would have made a good high school teacher in those fields, and possibly an acceptable teacher in a not-too-demanding college, but that was nothing in which I found any real interest.

As for law school, I had grown up in a lawyer's family, and had heard legal matters discussed at the dinner table. I occasionally worked as a sort of office boy in my father's office, but never for any extended period. I found it all very interesting, and what I saw and heard stimulated the inquiring side of my mind.

Then there were two young lawyers, in Cleveland, John A. Hadden and Jerome Fisher. John Hadden was the son of Judge Alexander Hadden, who had given my father desk room in his office when my father graduated from law school; and my father, in turn, had taken John Hadden into his office when the younger Hadden graduated from Harvard Law School in 1910. Indeed, my father's firm was long known as Griswold, Green, Palmer & Hadden. John Hadden was later in other firms, including a partnership with Harold Burton, who became Senator from Ohio and a Justice of the Supreme Court. Eventually Hadden was one of the founding partners of Arter & Hadden, which has long been one of the prominent Cleveland law firms. Jerome Fisher, who graduated from the Harvard Law School in 1911, became a partner in Thompson, Hine & Flory, another leading Cleveland law firm.

Both John Hadden and Jerome Fisher told me about the Harvard Law School, and urged me to go there. And several professors at Oberlin made references to Harvard Law School faculty members, such as Dean Pound, and Professors Felix Frankfurter and Zechariah Chafee, Jr. After a good deal of

thought, it seemed to me that the wisest thing for me to do, in the
long run, was to follow the law school route.

My father made it plain that he would finance my attendance
at the Harvard Law School. He would have liked to have gone
there himself, but could not afford it, and I think that he took
considerable satisfaction from the fact that his son went to
Harvard, even though he could not study there himself. I may
add that times were different then. My years at Oberlin cost my
father about a thousand dollars for each year, including board,
room and tuition. For my three years in the LL.B course at
Harvard (where the tuition was two hundred fifty dollars for my
class), the aggregate costs, not including transportation, were
about twelve hundred dollars per year.

So, after returning from Europe in 1925, I took the train to
Boston. I went with my Oberlin classmate, Ralph M. Andrews,
whose home was in western New York, and he got on the train at
Westfield. On arrival in Boston, we took the subway to Harvard
Square. I had visited the area in 1919, on my way to Camp, but I
did not have any clear recollection of it. We first sought a place
to live, having our suitcases in our hands. In due course, we
found rooms at 18 Hilliard Street. These consisted of a large
study room in front, a large bedroom in the rear, and a bathroom
on the same floor. It was really designed for three people, so we
set out to find a third. By making inquiries, we located Aaron J.
Palmer, and he joined with me and Ralph in taking the premises
for the year. Palmer was a fine person, and he later became a
much respected judge of the Superior Court in Connecticut.
Alas, he snored vigorously and violently. In the latter part of the
year, when tensions rose as the examinations loomed, I found
that I was missing more sleep than I could afford. By that time,
another room had become available in the house and I took it as
a separate sleeping room, thus solving the problem. My friend
Bradley Gilman, and his roommate, H. Brian Holland, had somewhat more elaborate rooms on Appian Way, which was on the
route from Hilliard Street to the Law School.

After we got settled, we went to the Law School and registered. At that time, all that was required was that you present a
diploma from an "approved" college, and "sign the book." When
the book was put before me, the words "Sign Full Name" were
prominently printed at the top of the page. However, I missed
this, and, acting out of habit, signed my name "Erwin N. Griswold," as I usually do. At this point, the man in the registrar's
office said: "What's the matter with you? Can't you read? You'll
never get anywhere in the Harvard Law School." That may be a

sound statement of what should have happened, but I am glad that it did not work out that way.

In due course, we got our books from the second-hand shop, and settled in to work. My first class was in Civil Procedure, with Professor Austin W. Scott. At that time, I suppose that Professor Samuel Williston was the outstanding teacher at the Law School. However, our class of nearly six hundred students was divided into four sections, and my section was not one of those taught by Professor Williston. My Contracts teacher was a beginner, Robert G. Page, the son of a prominent professor at the Wisconsin Law School. That was the only year that Page taught, but I (and my classmates, too) thought that he did an outstanding job. Page later became Chairman of the Board of the Phelps Dodge Corporation. I occasionally attended some of Professor Williston's classes. They were superb, but I thought that Page was a fine teacher, too.

In Criminal Law, I had Dean Pound for part of the year, and then Francis B. Sayre for the rest of the year. I had Professor Manley O. Hudson, a sort of a showman in the classroom, for Torts, and Edward H. Warren in Property. Professor Warren was known as "the Bull," and he was much admired by students in the first two decades of the century. However, he was very harsh with students. When a student made an answer which he felt was inadequate, he would be likely to shout "You'll never make a lawyer." Even though lawyers were supposed to be able to "take the gaff," this often seemed extreme to most of us. I remember, too, one time when a student brought a young lady to class, sitting in the back of the room. Warren did not see her for the first five or ten minutes. Then he rose, got very red in the face, extended his arm, pointing his finger at the forbidden guest and shouted "Take that woman out."

As a student, I worked hard, thoroughly, and conscientiously. I had some social life, and frequently dated, usually on Saturday evening, an Oberlin classmate who was a student at the Nursing School of the Massachusetts General Hospital. But, by and large, I thought that my role for the time being was to work, and I tried to do so. I did not miss classes, and I was prepared for each class. I found the work intensely interesting, and often exciting. It was really fascinating to see unroll, in the various classes, the ways in which human beings, often acting in good faith, can get into controversy, and the ideas and means which had evolved over the years, through legislation and decision, for resolving those controversies. Analysis went farther and deeper than I had previously experienced. The library was close at hand, and full of resources. I read my Law Review articles and engaged in much discussion with my fellow students, and greatly enjoyed the learning process.

In all of this, I think I was influenced by that lack of confidence in myself which I have called a sort of inferiority complex. I was sure that I had not had as good an education at Oberlin as all those Harvard, Yale and Princeton graduates, and that I could not compete equally with them. But I was determined to do the best I could. I had had a fine experience at Oberlin, and I did not want to let the old school down. As the year progressed, the tension built up considerably. In retrospect, I do not think that this did any harm. I have, indeed, been subject to a good many tensions, of one sort or another, in later years, and the fact that I had shown that I could work through difficult periods has been useful later on.

In April, 1925, in the spring of my first year, I had an experience which did not ease matters. In order to have time for study, I did not go to Cleveland for spring vacation. However, I was invited by my friend Bradley Gilman to come to New Haven, where he was staying during the vacation with his grandfather, Simeon E. Baldwin, a former chief justice and governor of Connecticut, and one of the founders of the American Bar Association. I spent two days in New Haven, and then took a train to begin my journey back to Cambridge. There was a railroad which made a more or less direct trip from Hartford to Boston, and I took this, for the purpose of stopping off and, in pursuit of my developing hobby of state boundaries and markers, locating the point where Connecticut, Massachusetts and Rhode Island meet.

I found the three-state boundary monument all right, near the top of a high hill, in an uninhabited area. There was no trail, and I had to break my way through the brush. In this process, a twig snapped off my arm and one of my eyes was badly scratched. This was quite painful, but I was able to get back to the railroad station, and continue my trip to Boston. I went at once to the Massachusetts Eye and Ear Infirmary, on Charles Street. They gave me emergency treatment, and sent me to the Stillman Infirmary, operated by Harvard University in Cambridge. I was there for about two weeks, during most of which time both of my eyes were bandaged. I was able to telephone to Cleveland, and my mother came to Cambridge to be with me. In due course, I was released from the infirmary, but told not to read for another two weeks. I could, however, attend classes, and my roommates kept notes which they later made available to me. Actually, I think that this period of relative calm and rest was good for me. I think it helped to keep the tension from building up to an undue height. It left me about three weeks in May when I could review intensely all my courses. My recovery from the eye injury was complete, and, as a matter of fact, I cannot now recall which eye it was that was injured.

At any rate, the examination period eventually arrived. My examination papers were written in long-hand in the conventional blue book. I was not "stumped" by any question, but I was quite sure that there were many points that I had overlooked. This concern was, of course, enhanced by post-examination discussions with fellow students who pointed out issues which I had not seen, and so on.

At any rate, on the day of the final examination, I left by train to go to New York in order to take the ship to Europe on my 1926 trip for the Bureau of University Travel. That train trip ·must have been my low point, for I wrote a letter to my parents saying that in all likelihood I had failed at the Harvard Law School, but that I wanted them to know that I had tried very hard, and done my very best, and had not frittered my time away—which was surely true. I guess that they took my letter with a grain of salt. At any rate, there was no way that I could hear from them for some time. And I soon moved into the excitement of the European trip, and fairly well forgot about the law and the Law School.

Finally, when we got to Rome, about the first of August, I received a cablegram from my father. The letter from the Law School had been sent to Cleveland, and then forwarded to Bigwin Inn on the Lake of Bays, north of Toronto in Canada, where my father and mother were vacationing. My father had opened the letter, and then had gone ten miles over a dirt road to Huntsville, Ontario in order to send me the news. As things worked out, I had an A in every course, and an average which made me second in the class. (The man who stood first in the class our first year was Nathan M. Jacobs, who later became a Justice of the Supreme Court of New Jersey.) I could not believe it. I had surely not expected it. I could not foresee what a change this was going to make in my life.

B. 1927–1928

In my second and third years in law school, I lived with three classmates in rooms in Hamilton Hall, at the Business School. This was the year when the new buildings at the Business School, on the Boston side of the Charles River, were completed. At that time, the Business School had more rooms than it needed, and the extra rooms were made available to students in other parts of the University.

My roommate was Malcolm P. Mouat from Janesville, Wisconsin. Adjoining rooms in Hamilton Hall were shared by Bradley B. Gilman and H. Brian Holland. The three others were all members of the Class of 1925 at Yale. I had known Bradley Gilman since 1919 when we were both boys at Camp Pemigewas-

H. Brian Holland, Bradley B. Gilman and E.N.G. outside their dormitory, Hamilton Hall, at Harvard Business School, 1925.

sett. Brad and I had shared the long hike from Mount Moosilauke to Maine in 1923.

The rooms were nearly a mile from the Law School. The
walk across the Lars Anderson Bridge and through Harvard
Square was good exercise. We usually had breakfast in our
rooms, buying grapefruit and cereal in the square, and milk was
delivered at our doors. We had lunches at a small place out
Massachusetts Avenue, and usually had dinner at a nice cafeteria
on Dunster Street. It seems hard to believe, but my meal costs
were just over one dollar a day, about fifteen cents for breakfast,
thirty-five cents for lunch, and fifty cents for dinner.

As a result of my grades, I was invited to be a member of the
editorial board of the Law Review. The invitation was signed by
the new President of the Review for Volume 40, Henry J. Friendly. This marked the beginning of a long friendship with a man
whom I almost immediately recognized to be extraordinary, and
whom I have said was "the ablest lawyer of my generation." [1]

Since I had "made" the Law Review, I had to come to
Cambridge two weeks before classes began. At that time, the
rooms in Hamilton Hall were not yet ready for occupancy. I
found a cheap hotel—too cheap, I fear—on Columbus Avenue in
Boston. We were not able to move into Hamilton Hall until late
in September.

The second year was a busy one for me. I undertook to
attend classes regularly, to do extensive Law Review work, and
also be back in my room no later than midnight. Many of the
students on the Law Review neglected their class work, and
many often worked until the wee hours of the morning, and
sometimes all night long. I early decided that the only way I
could get through the year was to get a reasonable amount of
sleep each night. I also decided that I was under some obligation
to keep up the record I had made in the first year, and that this
could only be done through careful reading of the cases in the
casebook, and regular attendance at classes. Moreover, most of
the classes were interesting, and I found considerable fascination
in learning about the details of the law in new fields, and with
new and stimulating faculty members.

In working on the Law Review, in addition to the regular
work of reading advance sheets and reporting on likely cases, I
wrote a Recent Case on "General Average" in Admiralty, my first
contact with that subject. Although I wrote and rewrote it, under

---

1. "In Memoriam: Henry J. Friendly," 99 Harv.L.Rev. 1709, 1720
(1986).

the guidance of Frederick A.O. Schwarz, the Case Editor, I do not believe that it was ever published. I also wrote a Note, which was published.[2] This must be one of the low points in the history of Law Review Notes. It is only four pages long, though it had twenty-five footnotes. It is hard to follow, and, assuredly, of little importance and not very well written. Of course I was assigned the subject and I recall that I had little enthusiasm for it at the time. It was written under the guidance of Charles S.S. Epstein, Note Editor for Volume 40, who was a very imaginative lawyer, and later became Solicitor General of New York. But even Charles could not put any vitality into the subject matter of the Note.

Late in February, 1927, came the election of officers for Volume 41. All the members of the Board, both second year and third year, met at the Colonial Club, just east of the Harvard Yard, the site of the present Harvard Faculty Club. In previous years, these meetings had often gone on for many hours, sometimes through the night. Nominations were made, and Nathan M. Jacobs, from New Jersey, and I were nominated. Nat Jacobs was a fine person, as well as an excellent student. We were asked to leave the room, and we walked together for several hours through the Harvard Yard and adjacent areas. I have no recollection whatever of the subject matter of our conversation. It was entirely friendly, for we had full mutual respect.

Finally, about 2:00 a.m., one of the members of the Board left the meeting and summoned us to come back. We were then informed that I had been elected president for Volume 41. The president and the treasurer were the two elected officers of the Board, and the treasurer chosen was Carlyle E. Maw, a graduate of the University of Utah, who spent most of his career as a partner in Cravath, Swaine & Moore in New York. In his later years, he became counsel to Henry M. Kissinger, then Under Secretary of State. In this capacity, he travelled extensively with Secretary Kissinger.

I was taken by surprise by the election. I knew I would like to be President of the Review, but I had not allowed myself to think that it would happen. I was probably unduly aware of the fact that I am rather reserved, not a very good mixer, and assuredly not a person of charisma. I had also encountered at Harvard something that had not been a problem at Oberlin, or in my previous life. This was the era of prohibition, a cause for which my grandparents and parents had labored. As I have

---

2. "Transmission of Funds By Indirect Drawing," 40 Harv.L.Rev. 481 (1927).

already observed, my father had paid his way through law school by giving lectures for the Anti–Saloon League under the guidance of the Executive Director, his fellow Oberlinian, Wayne B. Wheeler.

I grew up in a home where there was never any alcohol drinking, and, indeed, where no one smoked. As a consequence, I never felt any interest in, or desire for, either. Moreover, I believed deeply in the cause, particularly with respect to alcohol. There were references to past situations on both sides of my family where alcohol had been a factor, and I had seen people impaired, and lives badly affected, among neighbors on our street and acquaintances of the family. I early came to the conclusion that there was no gain from the use of alcohol which was adequate to offset the dangers to many of the people who used it. I also came to the conclusion that there was no really adequate middle ground. I doubted my ability to keep it under control if I started, and came fairly readily to the conclusion that the only sound solution was to be completely abstemious. I felt this particularly as I grew up in the era of prohibition. Intellectually and emotionally I believed that prohibition was a "noble experiment," and I could not help feeling concern when people I knew, particularly law professors and law students, deliberately violated the law.

Though I always kept these thoughts to myself and tried to be unobtrusive and gracious in declining drinks, this habit or practice of mine made me seem stiff and odd to some of the people I knew, including many of the members of the Law Review, a number of whom came from the east and from eastern universities. They were always friendly with me, but I could not escape the feeling that many of them regarded me as "out of line."

This same practice or rigidity, if it should be called that, has continued throughout my life. I have never taken any alcoholic beverages, and my wife and I have not served them in our home. While I was dean of the Law School, we became aware of the fact that it was the practice of some faculty members who might be invited to dinner at our house to stop at another's home and have their drinks before they came to our house. This bothered me a little bit, not because I felt that we were lacking in hospitality, but because I wished that my views on this subject might be respected, just as I tried to respect the views of those who felt differently.

As I have indicated, I have continued this practice over the years, and have never regretted it. An appreciable amount of my time in the intervening years has been spent in trying to work out problems of people who have become alcoholics, and I have seen a number of people with great minds lose their effectiveness because they could not control their use of alcohol.

In recent years, I have made a number of trips to the Soviet Union. I was told by some people that I could never get away without taking drinks there. However, except for one occasion, I have never had any difficulty. If there was a toast, as there often was, I used a glass of water. Soft drinks are readily available in the Soviet Union, and usually appear in bottles on every dinner table. The one difficulty I had was at the studio of an artist in Leningrad, who was very persistent in forcing a drink on me, and was quite irritated with my response. Finally, one of the Russians present said something to him and everything became calm again. I have no idea what was said, for it was spoken in Russian, but I was glad that it took care of the situation.

After my election as president for Volume 41, it became my responsibility to appoint the other officers. The most important of these offices was that of Note Editor, and I, of course, immediately asked Nat Jacobs to be the Note Editor. He very graciously accepted, and performed with distinction throughout the year. Homer H. Woods, from Iowa, who later became a prominent lawyer in Buffalo, New York, was appointed Case Editor, and Moses S. Huberman was appointed Book Review Editor. We acted as understudies from March to June 1927, and then took full responsibility for Volume 41, in the year 1927–28.

As I examine Volume 41 today, I am struck with how much simpler everything was in 1927–28 than it is now. Life in general was simpler. There was virtually no scheduled airplane travel, and superhighways were unknown. Trips to New York and Washington were by train, and longer trips were rare indeed. Long distance telephone calls required proceeding through an operator, and usually with a call-back. The law was much simpler, too. This was before the great expansion in administrative law which occurred in the first Roosevelt Administration, and before the Securities and Exchange Commission, the National Labor Relations Board, and many other agencies were established. There was no treatment of modern corporation law in the third year corporation course which I took under Professor Edward H. Warren at the Harvard Law School. Indeed, we spent a great deal of time on such matters as "pre-incorporation contracts for shares." On the other hand, the course in constitutional law with Professor Thomas Reed Powell was stimulating, penetrating, and illuminating. I often wished that there was an equally competent and trenchant commentator during the period of the Warren and Burger courts.

I attended classes regularly while I was president. In the summer of 1927, I canceled my arrangements for helping with tours of the Bureau of University Travel in Europe, and stayed in my parent's home in Cleveland through the summer. I used the time to make abstracts of all the cases in the casebooks which were used in my third year courses. Consequently, I did not have to spend much further time in preparation for the courses; but I did profit considerably from the discussion in most of the classes. During the summer, I wrote the usual letters to newly invited members of the editorial board of the Law Review, and I also had considerable correspondence with respect to articles. At the end of the summer, I returned to Cambridge about three weeks early in order to begin the operations of the Review, and to work with the editors and staff before the school year began.

At that time, the president was, in effect, the Articles Editor. He sought such counsel as he thought he needed from the officers and other board members, and received a great deal of help. In the end, though, in accordance with the tradition up to that time, he made the decision as to what articles should be accepted. As I look over the list of articles which were published in Volume 41, I find that they were written by a good mixture of academics and practitioners, such as the article by Charles E. Carpenter, Dean of the Law School at the University of Oregon, on "Interference with Contract Relations," an article by Professor Zechariah Chafee, Jr. on "Equitable Servitudes on Chattels," an important article by Henry J. Friendly on "The Historical Basis of Diversity Jurisdiction," an article by A. A. Berle, Jr. on "Subsidiary Corporations and Credit Manipulations," and a perceptive article by Henry Wolfe Biklé on "The Silence of Congress," dealing with the commerce clause. The volume also included an article by Robert M. Hutchins, the new dean of the Yale Law School, and one by Welch Pogue on "State Determination of State Law and the Judicial Code." Welch Pogue was then an associate in what is now Ropes & Gray in Boston, and he was many years later the managing partner of the Washington Office of Jones, Day, Reavis & Pogue when I became a partner in that firm.

Volume 41 was 1,087 pages long, about average for that period. In recent years, the volumes have been running over two thousand pages. In recent years, too, the articles are very much longer, and sometimes very esoteric. Frequently they seem to me to be examples of one professor talking to a few others, written primarily to support a claim for tenure. There are relatively few articles by practitioners and judges. There are also—unfortunately, as I see it—very few book reviews; and book reviews when published tend to take the form of very long "review-essays," in which the writer of the review takes up much space expressing his own views, and says little about the contents of the book.

The student work in recent issues, indeed for most of the time since World War II, seems to me to have improved enormously in quality and usefulness. In my time, student Notes were usually from five to ten pages long, and were rarely long enough to develop any subject very thoroughly. Since World War II, the "Supreme Court Note" has been developed.[3] Another innovation came a few years later. This was the annual production of a very thorough treatment of some developing area of the law. It became known as the "Developments" Note. It has always been of very high quality. An illustration is the Developments on "Medical Technology and the Law" in the issue for May, 1990.[4] Another change is the size of the editorial board. The board for Volume 104 (1990–1991) has eighty members, some selected on the basis of grades, and others on the basis of a competition, requiring the submission of written work. For Volume 41, there were thirty-one members.[5]

We were a rather tightly-knit group, with free-and-easy interchange. The president usually called on non-officer third-year members for assistance in reviewing manuscripts and editing articles. Other third-year members took primary responsibility

3. Its genesis can be traced to a series of articles written by Professor Frankfurter, usually with participation by a student or recent graduate, on "The Business of the Supreme Court." After Professor Frankfurter's elevation to the bench, and after the School's full activities were restored at the close of World War II, the basic idea was taken over by the Supreme Court Note written by student members of the Review. This has been continued with care, thoroughness and excellent professional skill over the past thirty years.

4. 103 Harv.L.Rev. 1519–1676—158 pages which should be extraordinarily useful to practitioners and scholars in this important and relatively new area of the law. See also "Developments in International Environmental Law," 104 Harv.L.Rev. 1484 (1991).

5. These included, in addition to the officers mentioned above, H. Thomas Austern, long a partner in Covington & Burling in Washington; Abraham H. Feller, later general counsel of the United Nations; Richard H. Field, later a professor at the Harvard Law School; James P. Hart, later Associate Justice of the Supreme Court of Texas; Alger Hiss; Louis L. Jaffe, later, at Harvard Law School, one of the most perceptive professors of administrative law; William Mitchell, later general counsel of the Atomic Energy Commission; and Kingsley A. Taft, later Chief Justice of Ohio.

for Notes under the guidance of the Notes Editor. For the most part, Recent Cases were written by second-year students, and there were usually eight or ten of these in each issue, generally no more than one page long. The Recent Cases were generally of doubtful utility, though they may have been useful at a time when there was no U.S. Law Week, and relatively few general legal periodicals were available. In recent years, they have virtually disappeared, while the other student work has very substantially increased in length and in quality.

As usual, I entered on my year as president with doubts as to my capacity to carry off the job successfully. These doubts were enhanced by the fact that I succeeded Henry J. Friendly, and I knew that he was much superior to me in the requisite abilities. However, with a great deal of work, and fine cooperation from my fellow editors, the year came off successfully. It has always been a source of great satisfaction to me. I learned a great deal, not only about the law and legal writing, but about getting along with people, working effectively with them, meeting deadlines, maintaining a good professional standard, and so on. Much of this work was with students, but some of it was with faculty members at the Harvard Law School and elsewhere, and with others who wrote articles for the Review, or who sent in letters criticizing, sometimes severely, material in the Review.

In particular, I had a series of dealings with Professor Frankfurter, from which I became acquainted with his sometimes mercurial disposition. He had written a series of articles in earlier volumes of the Review on "The Jurisdiction of the Supreme Court." He wanted to arrange to publish these articles, as written, in a book. At that time, the Review was plated, that is, type was set on a linotype machine. After proofreading and correction, it was put into pages, and a copper plate was made of the type as finally set.[6] Professor Frankfurter wanted to use the plates of the Harvard Law Review. This involved some difficulties. Among other things, the running head and the page numbers at the top of the page had to be sawed off, and any cross-references in the text or footnotes had to be punched out, and new cross-references inserted. Then, after the book was printed, the plates had to be restored so that reprints could be made of the issues of the Review. These were somewhat arduous negotiations, but they came off successfully. The book was published in 1928, and is a basic commentary on the history and jurisdiction

---

6. It was at this point that Professor Frankfurter usually began to revise his article in many details. The revisions were usually good, but the process made many complications.

of the Supreme Court up to the passage of the Judiciary Act of 1925.

Another minor problem arose with respect to Dean Pound, who was a very great man and lawyer, and for whom I had great respect. He wrote an article for Volume 41 entitled "The Progress of the Law—Analytical Jurisprudence, 1914–1927." [7] He sent the manuscript to me, and there was no question about its acceptance. It was always the practice that all footnotes in articles to be published were checked by a member of the Review board. (This was then called "cite-checking." For some reason it is now called "subciting.") In the case of Dean Pound's article, I undertook to check the footnotes myself, and for that purpose went to the library. Dean Pound discovered me in this process, and berated me in a loud voice in the main reading room of the library, with many students present. He said that he was paid by the University to be dean of the Law school and that any effort by me to do anything about his footnotes showed not only great disrespect, but a lack of confidence by me in his qualification to be dean. Naturally, I took this in silence. An hour or so later, he summoned me to his office and apologized. As a matter of fact, I did find a few errors in page references, and even in some quotations. I made the corrections, but did not tell him so. The proofs were submitted to him, and promptly returned, with no comment.

During the third year in law school, one had to think of the future. I had always supposed that I would return to Cleveland, and spend my life practicing law there, very likely in my father's office. In those days, there was no placement office at the Law School. The practice was for each aspirant to go to the city or cities of his choice, and "make the rounds," knocking on the doors of several law offices. I did this in New York, early in January of 1928. I received offers from a number of offices, all at the same figure of $1,500 per year. I remember one partner in a well-known New York office who said: "We can offer you"—he reached into a drawer in his desk, pulled out a paper and looked at it, and then said—"$125 a month." I was not particularly concerned by the amount, for that was clearly the "going rate." I rather readily came to the conclusion that life was too short to spend it living in New York, and gave up any thought of going there to practice. (I remember, too, that later in the spring, a former Law Review board member came to Gannett House, where the Law Review offices are, and told us that if we went to New York we could expect that after five years we would be making $5,000 a year.)

---

7.   41 Harv.L.Rev. 174.

There was also the question of Supreme Court clerkships. At that time, each Justice had one clerk, or secretary. Many of these were more or less permanent employees. There were two of the clerkships which were nominated by Professor Felix Frankfurter, for Justices Holmes and Brandeis, respectively. I did not expect to get the Holmes appointment, because I was not the "polished gentleman" who was usually chosen for the post. Moreover, at this time Holmes was rather old, and it was understood that the clerk spent much of his time reading to the Justice. However, I would have liked the appointment with Justice Brandeis, where Henry Friendly was serving following his graduation in 1927, and where Dean Acheson and James M. Landis, among others, had served in earlier years. One day, I was invited to lunch at the Frankfurters, and I knew that I was being looked over. I tried to perform properly, but the appointment went to a man who had graduated two or three years previously.

At about that time, however, a new opportunity developed. Professor Austin W. Scott, whose courses in Civil Procedure and in Trusts I had taken (he was a fine man and a brilliant teacher), was the Reporter on Trusts for the American Law Institute. He asked me whether I would be interested in working as his aide or assistant in this task. He said that the Institute would pay me $125 a month, and he suggested that I should talk with Dean Pound about the possibility of being admitted as a graduate student as a candidate for the S.J.D. degree, while I was working with Professor Scott. I was not sure that I wanted to do this. The advanced degree of S.J.D. was usually taken by people who were teachers of law, or who wanted to be teachers. I had never thought of teaching, and did not think that I wanted to be a teacher. However, when I went to see Dean Pound, he promptly admitted me as a candidate for the graduate degree, and offered me a fellowship of $500 per year, which would cover the tuition. My father was somewhat skeptical about this, but my mother was clearly interested in my spending the fourth year at the Law School. Though she never put it in these terms, I think she saw that I might be fitted to be a teacher, and that it would be a wise move for me to spend a graduate year in Cambridge. At any rate, I accepted the proposal, thinking that I was merely postponing my return to Cleveland for practice.

Having decided to stay in Cambridge, I had to find a place to live. I was able to obtain a room in Walter Hastings Hall, a building adjacent to the Law School which was generally occupied by Law School students. I found that my rent would be free if I was appointed a "proctor" for the dormitory. This appointment was made by Calvert Magruder, then the Vice Dean of the

Law School. I applied for the post, but the appointment went to Alger Hiss. This was entirely appropriate, since Hiss would be a regular third-year student in the fall of 1928, while I would be a graduate student.[8]

            ———

The year 1927–28 was a valuable year for me. I was, in effect, "law clerk" to Professor Scott while he was preparing early drafts of the Restatement of Trusts. I knew, too, that he was planning to write a complete treatise on the Law of Trusts, and that his work on the Restatement was background for the eventual treatise. Professor Scott was forty-five years old at the time, and at the peak of his record fifty-two years of active work on the Harvard Law School faculty.

Professor Scott's arrangement was that we worked together in his office, with Miss Lee, his secretary. He would dictate passages to Miss Lee, and ask me for my comments. I often suggested a different word or phrase, and an addition or deletion. Sometimes Professor Scott would accept my proposal, which pleased me greatly. On other occasions, he would reject it, pointing out its weakness or inaccuracy. From time to time, we would get into a debate about a point, and he would send me out to the library to look up all the cases I could find, and prepare a memorandum. Doing this under highly qualified supervision was a great educational experience.[9]

———

8. In later years, I had a number of contacts with Alger Hiss, though we were not intimate. I never had any personal knowledge of the facts in his case, and I have sometimes said that one of the reasons I would like to go to heaven is so that I could find out what really happened there.

When his trial came up, about 1950, my faculty colleague (and Hiss' classmate) Richard Field undertook to raise funds to help Hiss with his defense. I thought that Hiss was entitled to have support to make the best defense he could, and I made a contribution. This, in due course, showed up in the F.B.I. files. I did attend one day's session of the first trial of Hiss and have learned since that the F.B.I. "monitored" me on this occasion. During a recess in the trial, I spoke to Alger Hiss and his wife and with one of his attorneys. I later learned that this " 'derogatory' information was reported 'to the Truman White House.' " (Kenneth O'Reilly, Hoover and the Unamericans (Temple University Press, 1983) pp. 111–112, with reference to the Truman Library at footnote 25 on p. 332.)

9. On January 2, 1929, I took the Ohio Bar examination, in the Armory, in Columbus, Ohio. In due course, I learned that I had passed. As I was in Cambridge, I missed the general "swearing in," in Cleveland. On April 17, 1929, during the spring vacation at the Law School, I drove

Although I spent most of my time with Professor Scott, I also attended classes as a part of my work as a candidate for the S.J.D. degree. Among other things, I took Dean Pound's course on Jurisprudence, which, I am afraid, did not sink in too deeply. I also had to write a thesis for my S.J.D. candidacy. From the time when I took the course on Trusts during my second year in law school, I had been interested in "spendthrift trusts," and I picked this as the topic for my thesis, since it fitted in with my work for Professor Scott. I undertook to examine all of the cases in every state, and to deal with the various problems which had arisen with respect to the inalienability of the interest of the beneficiary of a trust, including the rights of creditors, and various exceptions to the rule, applicable in most states, that such interests could be made inalienable. Professor Scott's draft of the relevant parts of the Restatement followed my manuscript rather closely. The manuscript was completed in early May, before I, clad in academic dress, took my oral examination for the degree.[10]

In June, 1929, I was awarded the S.J.D. degree. I then left for my summer job, travelling with parties of the Bureau of University Travel in Europe. I was general handyman, and responsible for business arrangements, as in previous years.[11]

---

from Cleveland to Columbus, and was sworn in by Chief Justice Carrington T. Marshall, of the Ohio Supreme Court. Thus I became a lawyer. I was later admitted on motion in the Supreme Court of the United States, in 1932, in Massachusetts in 1935, and in the District of Columbia in 1973.

10. After I became a member of the faculty, I reworked the manuscript, and brought it down to date. It was published as a book by Matthew Bender & Co., in Albany, in 1936. This is one of the few doctoral dissertations in law which have been put out by a commercial publisher. A second edition of the book was published in 1947, by Prentice–Hall.

11. See pp. 40–42, above.

CHAPTER IV

Practice Begins

A. BRIEFLY A BEGINNER IN CLEVELAND

I returned to Cleveland just before the month of September, expecting that I was going to spend my life practicing law in Cleveland, and looking forward to it. My name was duly recorded in the County Clerk's office as a member of the Cuyahoga County Bar. I undertook some assignments for the office, and also carried out a follow-up survey of the report on criminal justice in Cleveland, which had been prepared several years previously.[1] My work was done under the auspices of the Commission on Law Observance and Law Enforcement established by President Hoover, and the follow-up was intended to develop data as to the impact, if any, which the 1922 report had had on the administration of criminal law in Cleveland. I gathered a mass of data, and made my report, but nothing about it came out in the report of the Hoover Commission.

During this period, I also tried two cases in the Municipal Court in Cleveland. These both involved the question whether a furnace was a "fixture." We were representing the Cleveland Builders Supply Company, which could not recover the furnaces if they had become fixtures, and thus a part of the real estate. The cases were assigned to me, I am sure, because the older lawyers in the office regarded them as hopeless. Needless to say, I lost—but it was not for want of trying.

---

1. Cleveland Foundation, Criminal Justice in Cleveland (1922), made under the direction of Dean Roscoe Pound and Professor Felix Frankfurter. The report is comprehensively reviewed by Harlan F. Stone in 35 Harv.L.Rev. 967 (1922).

Then, one day late in October, I received a letter on the impressive stationery of The Solicitor General of the United States. At that time, the Solicitor General was Charles Evans Hughes, Jr. He wrote to ask me if I would be interested in joining the staff of his office. (I later learned that he had written to Professor Scott asking for a recommendation, and that Professor Scott had given my name.) I thought that I probably was not interested. I had just started to do what I had always expected to do, to practice law in Cleveland, in my father's office. I pictured the position in the Solicitor General's office as being part of a great bureaucracy, where I would be the fifth desk in the seventh row in a room which had a hundred desks. However, my father said to me that I should probably go down to Washington and talk with them. So I made the trip by train, round trip in an upper berth. I met Mr. Hughes, and found to my surprise that there were at that time only five lawyers in the Solicitor General's office, two seniors and three juniors, that I would be immediately working with the senior who was actually handling the case, and that I would be writing briefs in cases in the Supreme Court as soon as I demonstrated my capability to do so.

I went back to Cleveland and talked it over with my family. I finally decided that I would take the post for two years, "for experience," and I so advised Mr. Hughes. I received a nice reply from him, telling me to report for duty on the first of December, 1929. When this was decided, my father's partner, David E. Green, called me into his office. He congratulated me and then said: "You will never come back." I replied that of course I would come back, that I was only going to broaden my experience.

B. A Junior in the Solicitor General's Office— Solicitor General Hughes

I reported for duty in Washington on December 2, 1929.[2] The Department of Justice was then located on the north-east corner of Vermont Avenue and K Street, N.W. I was able to get a room at the Racquet Club on Sixteenth Street, now the University Club. (The Club was next door to the closed and boarded-up Russian Embassy.) This was within easy walking distance of the Department of Justice, and the rent was not too high. However, I could not afford meals there, so I took these at various corner

---

2. When I looked at the calendar, I found that December 1, 1929, was a Sunday. Consequently, I reported on December 2. When my first paycheck came, I was docked one day's pay since my term of service did not actually begin until the second day of the month.

restaurants. Later, along with other young lawyers in the Department of Justice, I had my lunches at the new Y.W.C.A. at the corner of Seventeenth and K Streets. My mother was President of the Y.W.C.A. in Cleveland, and she told me about the fine lunch room available only two blocks from the Department of Justice. For the next several years, my lunches cost thirty cents at the Y.W.C.A., ten cents for soup, ten cents for a sandwich, and ten cents for dessert, usually a piece of pie.

The Solicitor General's office then occupied most of the fifth floor in the old Department of Justice building. I was assigned an office on the south side of the building, facing on K Street. There were two lawyers in each room, and we sat on opposite sides of a big square desk, with one telephone in the middle, which was handed back and forth. My office roommate was Paul D. Miller, of the Harvard Law School Class of 1924, who had come from Chicago. He was a fine lawyer, and we got along well together.

I was immediately assigned a number of cases. These came to the Solicitor General's office from the various divisions in the Department of Justice, with a draft of brief in the Supreme Court that had been prepared in the division. With the exception of the antitrust and tax divisions, most of these drafts were quite inadequate, and needed extensive revision. In many cases, we simply put the division's draft aside and started writing a completely new brief. At that time, there was no general practice of bringing young lawyers into the Department of Justice. It was the usual rule that no lawyer would be hired unless he had had at least five years of experience. This meant that, in many cases, lawyers were employed who had not been successful in practice, and who sought a government position because of the security it provided. I was at that time the only lawyer in the Department who was hired directly out of law school.[3]

Before long, I found that all of the tax cases were being assigned to me. I could have gone to the Solicitor General and told him that I knew nothing about taxes, that I had never taken

---

3. I was, of course, a little more than one year out of law school, having had the year with Professor Scott, and a few months in Cleveland. Because of this, I was put on the payroll at a higher grade. My salary was fixed at $3,600 a year after I pointed out the year which had intervened since my graduation. In 1933, shortly after President Franklin D. Roosevelt came into office, all executive branch salaries were reduced by ten percent, pursuant to the Roosevelt Administration's third statute, entitled "An Act to Maintain the Credit of the United States Government," Act of March 20, 1933, 48 Stat. 8.

a course in taxation, and that there was no course on federal taxation at the Harvard Law School at that time. However, I soon found that the senior lawyers knew nothing about the tax law, and did not want to learn. I quickly concluded that it would be wise for me to take myself to the library and dig out what I could about federal tax law.

The questions involved in cases at that time were often quite esoteric, such as the validity of waivers of the statute of limitations filed after the statutory period had expired,[4] or the effect of a change from the cash basis to the installment-sale basis at a time when there was no provision in the statute dealing with such a question.[5] In due course, I slowly became aware that my legal education had given me the tools which enabled me to deal competently with almost any matter after a reasonable period of intensive effort. Of course, in retrospect, this was relatively simple, since there were fewer decided cases to be located, read, and evaluated, and the provisions of the statutes and regulations were less complicated than they are now.[6]

It was not long before I found that I was regarded as an expert in the tax field. Even people in the Tax Division used to come to me and ask for my views and opinion on various cases. In due course, I became fairly well known in the Department, which was much smaller than it is today, and I built up an appreciable status.[7]

---

4. See Stange v. United States, 282 U.S. 270 (1931); Burnet v. Chicago Railway Equipment Co., 282 U.S. 295 (1931).

5. John M. Brant Co. v. United States, 282 U.S. 888 (1930), denying certiorari to review the decision in 40 F.2d 126, 69 Ct.Cl. 516 (1930).

6. An example is United States v. Kirby Lumber Co., 284 U.S. 1 (1931). The question in that case arose when the corporate taxpayer bought property which it paid for by newly issued bonds. Later in the same year, it bought back some of the bonds at less than face value. The issue was whether the difference, or spread, was taxable as income. The definition of "income" in the tax law was completely circular. It simply provided that "income" meant "income derived from any source whatever," and there were then no special provisions dealing with the discharge of indebtedness at a discount. There were, however, regulations going back to 1921. I had never heard of regulations in law school. However, I built the brief around the regulations, and the government prevailed, largely on this ground. The opinion was written by Mr. Justice Holmes, typically concise—indeed it was just two paragraphs long. This has been a leading case in the tax law, and I found it very exciting to have had a small role in it.

7. It was in these days that I first met J. Edgar Hoover, Director of the Federal Bureau of Investigation. This was before he had become a

Shortly after my appointment in Washington, I encountered a problem which gave me considerable concern. Mr. Hughes was a very fine and able lawyer. He was also a very thorough lawyer, and he believed in reading the cases himself, and not simply relying on memoranda prepared by his staff. In addition to the cases in the Supreme Court, the Solicitor General had the responsibility to decide whether any case which the Government lost in any court should be appealed or not. There were several of these cases in the office at all times, and the time for seeking review was fixed by statute or rule, and was fairly short. I found occasionally that Mr. Hughes would be so intently working on a particular case that he was not able to reach other cases which were piled behind his chair. I knew that in some of these other cases the time limit was about to expire. I knew, too, that if the Solicitor General lost a case because he had not acted within the prescribed time limits, he would be subject to serious criticism. Bringing these cases to his attention did not seem to help.

In this situation, in more cases than one, I sent out telegrams to United States Attorneys directing them to take an appeal in a particular case; the telegrams were signed in the Solicitor General's name. I put a copy of the telegram on the pile. I did this to protect Mr. Hughes, but also with the knowledge that if he decided that no appeal should be taken, he could direct the United States Attorney to dismiss the appeal. These are sometimes known as "protective appeals," and were often authorized by the Solicitor General himself as a means of getting more time for study. However, sometimes when Solicitor General Hughes was out of his office, I felt that it was really my duty to protect him against failure to act on them. At this time, I was twenty-five years old, and felt that I was being very brash. I also felt that, under the circumstances, I really had no alternative. I always told Mr. Hughes afterwards. He never thanked me; and he never criticized me either.

From the beginning, the work in the Solicitor General's Office was interesting and stimulating. Almost immediately, I was assigned to make a draft of the brief for the government in the case of *Patton v. United States*.[8] The case involved the constitutional validity of a waiver of trial by jury in a criminal case in the federal courts. The Constitution, in Article III, Section 2 (third paragraph) provides: "The Trial of all Crimes

---

great figure in the public eye. At that time the principal work of the Bureau was investigating bankruptcy fraud, and conducting routine criminal investigations.

8.   281 U.S. 276 (1930).

* * * shall be by Jury." The wording is imperative, and literalists would say that "shall" means "shall". This was, indeed, a view which had been taken in the lower courts over a long period of time.[9] The case before the court did not involve a complete waiver of jury trial. The trial had begun before twelve jurors, when one of the jurors became seriously ill. (This was before the advent of alternate jurors.) Counsel for the accused, with the concurrence of the trial judge, agreed that the trial should continue before the remaining eleven jurors, and this resulted in a conviction. The validity of the waiver of a complete jury was then contested. This was treated by the courts as the equivalent of a general waiver of a jury, since a jury at common law consisted of twelve jurors, no more, no less.

When I started work on the brief, I thought it was important to find out all that could be uncovered as to the practice in the state courts at the time the Constitution was drafted and adopted. In order to conduct this research, I was sent to the Harvard Law School Library where I found quite a bit of material. One case, in Connecticut, was especially interesting. This is *State v. Taylor & Warren*,[10] where two persons were jointly charged with a burglary. They pleaded not guilty. Taylor sought a trial by jury, while Warren chose to be tried by the court. The report continues with the statement that "the evidence being the same in both, the case was ordered to proceed as to both, the jury to be charged with one issue, and the court tried the other." A number of other cases allowing waivers were found in Massachusetts, Vermont, New Jersey, Pennsylvania, and Maryland. The results of this research were incorporated in the government's brief in the *Patton* case, and were later published as a law review article.[11]

The *Patton* case was argued before the Supreme Court in early 1930 by Solicitor General Hughes. The Court upheld the

---

9. See Oppenheim, Waiver of Trial by Jury in Criminal Cases, 25 Mich.L.Rev. 695 (1927). See also Dickinson v. United States, 159 Fed. 801 (C.C.A. 1st, 1908). Cf. Thomspon v. Utah, 170 U.S. 343, 353 (1898).

10. 1 Root 226 (Conn. 1790).

11. Griswold, "The Historical Development of Waiver of Jury Trial in Criminal Cases," 20 Va.L.Rev. 655 (1934).

In working on the brief, I discovered that there had recently been a similar case in Alabama, where Hugo L. Black had been counsel for the defendant. By this time, Black had become a Senator, and was in Washington. I made an appointment to see him in order to get details about the case. This was my first encounter with Hugo Black, who was already a somewhat controversial figure. Needless to say, I did not foresee the distinction of his future career.

validity of the waiver, but included the requirement that the waiver must be approved in all cases not only by the defendant, but also by the prosecution and by the trial judge. I never understood the basis for this qualification, except possibly for the approval of the trial judge where there was room to question the capacity of the defendant to make an intelligent decision as to waiver.

Before long Mr. Hughes, Jr., had to resign as Solicitor General shortly after his father was sworn in as Chief Justice. (The quip was that the younger Hughes was "the extinguished son of a distinguished father.") Stories have been told that the Chief Justiceship was offered to Charles Evans Hughes by President Hoover because he was advised that Hughes would never accept since it would mean the termination of his son's government career.[12] Whatever validity there may be to such stories, Hughes did accept, and his son felt it necessary to resign.

One result of the appointment of the senior Charles Evans Hughes was that he and his family moved to Washington. Shortly thereafter, the Solicitor General, the younger Mr. Hughes, called me into his office. He went straight to the point. He said: "I have a sister." I replied: "Yes, I know. I believe her name is Elizabeth." And his response was: "She is engaged." My answer was: "That's interesting. Who is the lucky man?"

Mr. Hughes, Jr. then said that Elizabeth was engaged to William T. Gossett, who was a third-year student at the Columbia Law School. He added that Elizabeth, having moved to Washington with her parents, was receiving a number of invitations to Embassy and White House receptions, and that Mr. Gossett was unable to get to Washington for these occasions. He asked me whether I would be willing to escort Elizabeth. My response was, of course, affirmative.

I found that some of these affairs would involve wearing white tie and tails, which I did not have. So, I went to Bonds Clothiers, where I acquired a presentable outfit for something like $65. Thereafter, I had the privilege of escorting Elizabeth to a number of receptions, at the White House and Embassies. I remember that I met Andrew W. Mellon at one of the White House receptions, and I also met or saw a number of others among the important people at the time, including President and

---

12. See Pringle, *Chief Justice—III*, The New Yorker, July 13, 1935, pp. 18, 19. See also Wiener, *Justice Hughes' Appointment—The Cotton Story Re-Examined*, Supreme Court Historical Society YEARBOOK 1981, 78. For a response, see Pusey, *The Nomination of Charles Evans Hughes as Chief Justice*, YEARBOOK 1982, 95.

Mrs. Hoover, who were the host and hostess at the White House receptions.

These occasions required me to call at the Hughes home on R Street to pick up Elizabeth, and take her in my second-hand Model-A Ford, newly acquired. On several of these occasions, I met the new Chief Justice, on a very informal basis. Though he was very proper in the courtroom, he was very friendly and kindly at home. Indeed, on one occasion, I saw him down on his knees, playing with one of his grandchildren.

Elizabeth and Bill Gossett were married in 1930. In the summer of 1931, my mother and I went by automobile to California, and, in Los Angeles, stayed with her college room-mate.[13] The daughter of the family, Harriet Ford, and I went to the Huntington Library, in San Marino, California, and to our pleasant surprise, we met Bill and Elizabeth Gossett. Bill was a very prominent lawyer, and became president of the American Bar Association. The Gossetts and the Griswolds remained friends over the years.

C. Solicitor General Thacher

When Solicitor General Hughes resigned, he was succeeded by Judge Thomas D. Thacher, who was, at the time of his appointment, a judge of the United States District Court for the Southern District of New York. He was one of the founding partners in the New York law firm of Simpson, Thacher & Bartlett. He was an able lawyer, careful and thorough, and it was a privilege to work with him. He later went on to be

---

13. I wanted to take a motor trip across the continent, visiting national parks, and other areas. This had only recently become possible, as a practical matter, and there were still virtually no paved roads west of central Iowa. I did not want to take the trip alone, so I asked my mother if she would go with me. My father was a little dubious, but tolerated the plan. When we got to Los Angeles, it seemed natural that we should stay with my mother's one-time roommate and her family. I had known Harriet before, both at Oberlin reunions and in 1928 when she was a graduate student at Columbia and came to visit her grandparents in Geneva, Ohio, at Christmas time, and came to Cleveland by train for a day with us. At any rate, the trip to California led to engagement. (The engagement was not complete until my mother and I arrived at Bryce Canyon in Utah, where a telegram was awaiting me. It developed that telegrams came to the Bryce Canyon Lodge by telephone, and the Bryce Canyon operator, in the lobby of the Lodge, had repeated the telegram as it was communicated to her. When my mother and I arrived at the lodge, we were greeted with cheers from a number of the people who had gathered in the lobby to await our coming.)

Corporation Counsel of the City of New York, and then a judge of the New York Court of Appeals. Judge Thacher ran a "good office." Appropriately, he argued the government's most important cases before the Supreme Court. I often sat beside him, or his deputy Claude Branch, when they argued government cases in Court. In this way, I became very familiar with the atmosphere and the practices of the Court during oral argument.

Work in the Solicitor General's office involved an endless series of cases, sometimes routine, but often of great importance. When I came to Washington, Claude R. Branch, from Providence, Rhode Island, and a graduate of the Harvard Law School in the Class of 1911, was the Deputy Solicitor General, and I worked with him on many cases. I have always regarded him as one of my best teachers. He set very high standards, including the importance of precise accuracy in stating cases, and taught me many lessons.[14] In later years, he was a partner in Choate, Hall & Stewart, in Boston, though he continued to live in Providence. He remained active for many years, and was well in his nineties when he died.

In those days, the rule that a person could not appear before the Supreme Court unless he was admitted to practice there was rigidly enforced. Admission to practice before the Supreme Court required that one had been admitted to practice before a state supreme court for at least three years. As my admission in Ohio occurred on April 17, 1929, that meant that I could not be admitted to the Bar of the Supreme Court until April, 1932.

I had worked very hard on the brief in the *Patton* case, and was disappointed when I learned that my name would not be printed in the United States Reports as one of the counsel on the brief. With boldness, and trepidation, I wrote a letter to new Chief Justice Hughes, and asked whether an exception could not be made in this case. I never received a reply to the letter, but my name was printed in the Report, and this was, of course, its first appearance there. I have never ceased to be grateful to the Chief Justice.

Another important case on which I worked was *Crowell v. Benson.*[15] This involved a rather complex question of constitutional and administrative law. In order to provide for longshoremen and other harbor workers who were not covered by state

---

14. When there was something in a draft where he was uncertain, or where he wanted to read the authority cited, he would put "L.U." in the margin, meaning "Look up." I have found this notation very useful over the past sixty years.

15. 285 U.S. 22 (1932).

workmen's compensation laws, Congress passed the Longshoremen and Harbor Workers Compensation Act. This was, in operation, a workmen's compensation law, effective within the federal admiralty jurisdiction, and (later) in the District of Columbia. Under this law, cases were heard, in the first instance, by administrative officers, appointed by the Executive Branch of the government. This was in contrast to the provision in the Employers' Liability Act, applicable to railroad employees, where trials were then (and still are) held in regular state or federal courts. I spent nearly the whole summer of 1931 working on the brief in this case. The Court, in a lengthy opinion by Chief Justice Hughes, upheld the validity of the Act. The case has remained an important decision in the area involving the validity of a hearing before a tribunal not created under Article III of the Constitution (which provides for judges with life tenure and guaranteed compensation). This is an area which is still the subject, occasionally, of constitutional controversy.

Since I could not then be admitted to practice before the Supreme Court, I thought that I might use the interval to see if I could gain experience by appearing in lower courts. In order to do this, I went to several of the Assistant Attorneys General, and told them that I would be glad to be assigned to argue some of their cases in the courts of appeals.[16] I suggested that this might be useful to them in a situation where the assigned lawyer became ill, or where one of their lawyers was assigned cases which, as things worked out, were set for argument on the same day in two different courts. Very quickly, I had a number of such assignments. I was assigned to argue a series of tax cases in the Court of Appeals for the Ninth Circuit, in San Francisco, in December, 1931. The first of these cases was *Cross v. Commissioner*.[17] This assignment proved fortunate for me, because I then proceeded to Los Angeles, where Harriet Allena Ford and I were married on December 30, 1931. Harriet's father and my father were classmates at Oberlin College in the Class of 1898,

---

16. Attorney General William D. Mitchell had assembled a fine group of division heads in his department. These included, among others, John Lord O'Brien, of Buffalo, one of the wisest lawyers I have every known, who was the Assistant to the Attorney General, handling antitrust and other business-related cases, Charles B. Rugg of Boston, who was Assistant Attorney General for the Claims Division, G. Aaron Youngquist, of Minnesota, head of the Tax Division, and Seth W. Richardson, of North Dakota, head of the Lands Division. It was, of course, a privilege, and a great education, to work for lawyers of this caliber.

17. 54 F.2d 781 (C.C.A. 9th, 1932).

and Harriet's mother and my mother had been students at Oberlin at that time.

One important case that I argued in the Second Circuit was *Porter v. Commissioner.*[18] This involved the effectiveness of a scheme to avoid the operation of the federal estate tax. Lawyers had advised clients that this could be done by transferring property in trust for others, with the grantor reserving the right to amend the trust, but not in such a way as to make himself the beneficiary. It was contended that this amounted to a completed transfer of the property, as far as the grantor was concerned, since he could never get the property back, yet, at the same time he retained effective control over its ultimate disposition. I was then handling the tax cases in the Solicitor General's office, and I had authorized appeals to three different courts of appeals in cases raising this question, all of which were decided against the government. There was then a general practice in the Solicitor General's office that the government would try three times, but would then yield if it was unable to get a decision in its favor. The *Porter* case came to me with a recommendation from the Tax Division that no appeal should be taken. However, I felt strongly that the government's position was sound and I authorized the appeal. The Tax Division then came to me and said "All right. You authorized the appeal, now you argue it."

So I argued the case before the Second Circuit Court of Appeals in New York on May 17, 1932. It was, I think, the best court that I ever appeared before. The judges were Learned Hand, presiding, with his cousin Augustus N. Hand, and Judge Thomas D. Swan.[19] The opinion of the Court, by Judge Learned Hand, supported the government's position. This, of course, produced a conflict of decisions, and led to review by the Supreme Court. By the time the case came up, I had been admitted to practice there, and I argued the case for the government in the Supreme Court on February 9, 1933. The Court's decision, in an opinion written by Justice Butler, without dissent, was announced on March 13, 1933, upholding the position of the gov-

---

18.   60 F.2d 673 (C.C.A.2d, 1932).

19.   During the course of the argument, Judge Learned Hand talked a great deal, as was his wont. I found it hard to stop talking when he interrupted. Finally he said to me, quite sharply, "If you would stop talking when I am talking to you, you could hear what I am saying." At this point, Judge Augustus Hand turned to him and said, *sotto voce,* but it could be heard all over the courtroom, "Aw, give him a chance." For this, and many other reasons, my regard for Judge Augustus Hand has always been very high. Justice Robert H. Jackson was often heard to say: "Quote Learned, follow Gus."

ernment.[20] This was a leading decision in the development of the federal estate tax law and was, I think, an instance where counsel contributed to the sound development of the law.

While I was waiting to argue the *Porter* case in the Second Circuit, I sat through the argument of another important case. This was *Rogers v. American Tobacco Company.*[21] The question presented related to large salary payments made to George Washington Hill, the President of the American Tobacco Company, in excess of one million dollars a year. The plaintiff, William Reid Rogers, a stockholder in the company, challenged these payments, appearing *pro se.* Counsel for the American Tobacco Company was John W. Davis, former Solicitor General of the United States and Ambassador to Great Britain. Counsel for the Bankers Trust Company, trustee of a fund involved, was Nathan I. Miller, former Governor of New York. Mr. Rogers opened his argument. When Mr. Davis then appeared for his client, he said, rather pompously, that Mr. Roger's argument was an example of how unwise it was for a client to appear on his own behalf. He said that Mr. Rogers had referred to many facts—in good faith, he was sure—which did not appear in the record, and he wanted to make it clear to the court that the argument which Davis would present was based solely on the record before the court.

When Mr. Rogers got up to reply, he started out in a most humble and apologetic manner. He said he understood the importance of the record, and that he believed that he had confined his argument to matters appearing in the record. Of course, he added the court would carefully review the matter, and would decide the case only on the basis of the record. He then concluded his apology by saying, in a quiet but clear voice, "Of course, if I had the great resources of these two corporations behind me, I would have aspired to counsel of ambassadorial or gubernatorial rank."

I remember, in particular, the case of *International Paper Co. v. United States.*[22] This involved the use of water power rights in the Niagara River during World War I. The government had issued orders requiring that power be assigned to certain plants which were engaged in war production. The question was whether this was simply a "regulation," or whether it was a "taking" which required the payment of "just compensation."

---

20. Porter v. Commissioner, 288 U.S. 436 (1933).

21. 53 F.2d 395 (C.C.A. 9th 1932), reversed *sub nom.* Rogers v. Hill, 289 U.S. 582 (1933).

22. 282 U.S. 399 (1931). John W. Davis was the advocate for the paper company.

During the argument by Mr. Branch, Senator Robert A. Buckley of Ohio came in, and took a seat beside me at the counsel table. I was there to be of any possible assistance to Mr. Branch. Senator Buckley passed to me a number of notes saying that the facts stated by Mr. Branch were not the way it actually was. He wanted me to pass these notes up to Mr. Branch. It developed that the Senator had been a lawyer in the War Department during World War I, having been brought there from Cleveland by Newton D. Baker, then Secretary of War. I knew, though, that Mr. Branch had stated the record accurately, and that he would be very much bothered and annoyed if I interrupted his oral argument by passing up the notes written by Senator Buckley. There I was, twenty-six years old, acting as a barrier between my senior lawyer and a Senator of the United States. But I knew that the notes would not be helpful to Mr. Branch, and I thought that it was my duty to protect him from that interruption during the course of the argument. After the argument, I showed the notes to Mr. Branch and he assured me that I had done the right thing, saying that he would have been very much disturbed, and thrown off his stride, if I had passed the notes up to him.

In November, 1932, the Tax Division assigned two cases to me in the Eighth Circuit Court of Appeals in St. Louis. The argument was set for November 30, 1932. At that time, my wife was about eight months pregnant, but everything had gone normally. We consulted our physician, and he told us that it would be all right for me to make the trip to St. Louis, but that I should not plan to be away thereafter until the baby came. Accordingly, I went to St. Louis by train. Assistant Attorney General Charles B. Rugg, head of the Claims Division, accompanied me, as he had other cases for argument before the same court.

One of my cases was reached on the morning of November 30th. In the second case, the argument began right after lunch. I was the top side, and thus made the opening argument. I then sat down while my opponent made his argument. While that was going on, the clerk came to me and handed me a note, which said that my daughter had been born that morning in Washington. I am afraid that I did not follow my opponent's argument very closely after that, and I cannot recall whether I undertook to make any rebuttal argument.[23]

---

23. The two cases were Burnet v. Burns, 63 F.2d 313 (C.C.A. 8th, 1933), and Edward P. Allison Co. v. Commissioner, 63 F.2d 553 (C.C.A. 8th, 1933). I lost the first and won the second. At that time, Harry A. Blackmun (whom I did not then know) was law clerk to Judge John B.

I left St. Louis that evening by train, as there was no night flying at that time. My railroad ticket read through to Washington, but I arranged to leave the train at Pittsburgh, and then flew to Washington. The trip was taken in a Ford trimotor plane. In Washington, the plane landed on a dirt runway at the place where the Pentagon building now stands. At that time, this was the Washington airport. It was crisscrossed by two or three roads, and guards stood at each end of these roads to keep cars from travelling across the field while planes were taking off or landing. I took a taxi direct to the Columbia Hospital for Women, where I found both Harriet and the baby well, and surprised that I arrived several hours before I was expected. We named the baby Hope, after my mother and Harriet's sister.

I was admitted to practice as a member of the bar of the Supreme Court on April 18, 1932, one day more than three years after my admission to the bar of Ohio (the previous day was a Sunday). Solicitor General Thacher moved my admission. The first case I argued before the Court did not come for nearly a year, when, on February 9, 1933, I argued *Porter v. Commissioner*, as indicated above.

Over the next fifteen months, I argued all of the government's tax cases, a total of sixteen in 1933 and five in 1934. One of these was *Burnet v. Wells*.[24] The question raised there was the application of the federal income tax to the income of an irrevocable trust in which it was provided that the income should be used to pay the premiums on policies of insurance on the grantor's life. This involved questions of constitutional law, since the statute imposing such a tax, first enacted on June 2, 1924, was explicit in making such income taxable, though the trust was irrevocable so that the grantor could never get the income for himself. When the case first came to my desk, I found that the trusts involved were created in 1922 and 1923, before the statute was enacted, and were applicable to income received during all of 1924, including the period before the statute was passed by Congress. Thus, the case involved not only the validity of imposing an income tax on the grantor of such an irrevocable trust, but also two kinds of retroactivity, namely applying the tax to income of trusts *created* in years before the statute was passed, and also applying the tax on income *received* in 1924 before the statute was passed.

Sanborn, who sat on both cases. It may be that Blackmun, future Justice of the Supreme Court, made drafts of opinions in one or both of these cases. I never asked him.

24. 289 U.S. 670 (1933).

When I was working on the case, I called a man in the then Bureau of Internal Revenue in Washington, and pointed out the problems raised by these questions of retroactivity. His immediate response was, "Oh, it is a test case." I said that I understood that. He then added, "We picked this case because it raises all of the questions. We thought that if we won this case, that would end further litigation in this area." As I saw it, that was fine if we won. However, I feared that raising all of the difficult questions at once considerably lessened chances that the case would be won on all the issues. I regarded this as a very hard case. It was assigned to me for oral argument, and I approached it with considerable trepidation.

In those days, the Supreme Court sat from twelve noon until two in the afternoon. There was a break for lunch for a half hour, and then the Court sat from 2:30 to 4:30 p.m. In all cases before the Court, each side was allotted an hour for oral argument. Some cases took the full time, while others used less time, sometimes considerably less. In some cases, after the petitioner or appellant had finished argument, the Chief Justice, after a quick glance at his fellow judges, would say, "The Court does not care to hear further argument." This meant, of course, that the "bottom side"—the respondent or appellee—had won the case.[25]

If two cases occupied full time, they would fill the day's argument period. However, the Clerk always put four or five cases on the "call list." This meant that counsel in all of those cases should be prepared, and ready to appear in the Court if their case was reached.

On May 9, 1933, there were five cases on the call list, and *Burnet v. Wells* was the fifth case. There seemed to be no likelihood that it would actually be reached. It was a beautiful spring day. I had found it very difficult to do highly concentrated work at the office because of the constant telephone calls and the frequent visits by other lawyers in the Department of Justice to discuss some problem in a case they had. So, I left the

---

25. In one case which I heard, Chief Justice Hughes said that "The Court does not care to hear further argument." Nevertheless, counsel for the respondent arose and started to address the Court. The Chief Justice repeated his statement, in a stronger voice. Respondent's counsel continued his argument, in a very loud voice, apparently having understood the Chief Justice to say that he should speak louder. At this point, the Chief Justice turned to the already defeated counsel for the petitioner, and said: "Won't you please tell counsel that the Court does not care to hear further argument." Counsel for the petitioner rose, turned to counsel for the respondent, and said, in a loud, clear voice, "They say they would rather give you the case than listen to you."

office and went down to Haines Point, in the southern part of
Washington, on the Potomac River. I then walked, and while
walking, rehearsed my oral argument, out loud, and tried to
anticipate questions which I might receive from the bench, and
to formulate and speak my answers to these questions. In due
course, shortly before five o'clock, I returned to the Department
and found members of the staff clearly distressed. It seems that
the first two cases on the call list had taken much less than
normal time, and the next two cases had broken down. One case
was settled, and in another, one of the counsel was ill. At any
rate, *Burnet v. Wells* had been reached for oral argument about
fifteen minutes before the adjournment time and I was not there.
I was representing the "top side," that is, the petitioner, and the
Court could have dismissed the case by default. Instead, though,
the Court adjourned—a wholly unprecedented event, since Chief
Justice Hughes ran the sessions of the Court by the second hand
on the clock.

Of course, I was very much upset. I went up to the Court
early the following day. At that time, the Supreme Court met in
the Old Senate Chamber in the Capitol. There was a rickety
elevator which the Justices took from the ground floor to the
courtroom. They then walked across the hall to the robing
room.

I was standing in the hall, with several of my associates,
when the Chief Justice walked past. He turned to me and said,
somewhat sternly, as it seemed to me: "Well, you kept us waiting
yesterday." I just about collapsed through the marble floor, but
managed to respond: "Yes, Mr. Chief Justice. I am very sorry.
It was not intentional." At this point the Chief Justice broke out
in a broad smile, and said: "Well, we understood. That's quite
all right." The Chief Justice was indeed very kind to me on that
occasion.

Burnet v. Wells was decided in favor of the government in an
opinion by Justice Cardozo. The decision was by a vote of five to
four, with a dissent written by Justice Sutherland, who wrote:
"The powers of taxation are broad, but the distinction between
taxation and confiscation must still be observed." [26]

In *Commissioner v. Duke*,[27] my opponent was John W. Davis.
(During the course of the argument, he passed a note to one of
the other lawyers from the Department of Justice, which was
shown to me later. It read: "Who is this lad?") The government

---

26. 289 U.S. at 683.
27. 290 U.S. 591 (1933).

lost the case by an equally divided Court. The case involved an estate tax on the estate of James B. Duke. As soon as the argument began, Chief Justice Hughes rose and left the bench. We learned later that the Chief Justice, while in private practice, had written a will for Duke. Actually it was not the will which became effective on Duke's death, since he had written subsequent wills. However, the will drafted by lawyer Hughes had referred to the trust which was also involved in the later will, and he felt, rightly, that he was disqualified. This was most unfortunate for the government's cause. We knew in advance that four members of the court—Justices McReynolds, Van Devanter, Butler and Sutherland—would be against us. Thus, the Chief Justice's departure left us with no hope.[28]

My work was by no means confined to tax cases. The responsibilities of the Solicitor General's office cover the full field of law, and I enjoyed working on many different types of problems. I will refer to three cases in which I had responsibility for the Government's briefs, and which I found particularly interesting.

The first of these was *United States v. Smith.*[29] George Otis Smith, who came from Pennsylvania, was nominated by President Hoover to be a member and chairman of the Federal Power Commission. This nomination was confirmed by the Senate on December 20, 1930, and on the same day the Senate ordered that the resolution of confirmation be transmitted to the President. The President received the notification on December 22. Later on that day, the President signed Smith's commission, and delivered it to the State Department. Smith then took the oath of office, and began to discharge his duties.

The Senate adjourned late on Saturday, December 20th, and resumed its session on January 5, 1931. On January 5, a motion to reconsider the confirmation was made, and also a motion to request the return of the resolution of confirmation. Both motions were adopted. On January 10 the President informed the Senate that he had appointed Smith, after receiving formal notice

---

28.   The issue was subsequently decided in favor of the government in Helvering v. Hallock, 309 U.S. 106 (1940). I felt especially bad about the Duke result because I understood at first that the decision produced a windfall for Doris Duke. Later though, I learned that the unpaid tax fell into the residue of Duke's estate, which went to Duke University, and that made me more readily reconciled to the government's defeat.

29.   286 U.S. 6 (1932).

of confirmation, and that, he consequently refused "to accede to the request." The Senate, nevertheless, went ahead with the reconsideration, and a majority of the Senate voted to reject the nomination.

On the following day, the Senate adopted a resolution requesting the District Attorney of the District of Columbia to start proceedings, by a writ of *quo warranto* in the District of Columbia Supreme Court, to test Smith's right to hold office. The proceeding in *quo warranto* was begun on May 4, 1931, with the Senate employing its own counsel. After a trial, the writ of *quo warranto* was denied, and an appeal was taken to the Court of Appeals of the District of Columbia. I was involved as an aide to Attorney General William D. Mitchell in all of the discussions relating to the procedure.

After the decision of the district court, there was great concern about the delay involved. It was suggested that the Court of Appeals should be asked to certify the question to the Supreme Court under section 239 of the then Judicial Code.[30] This was a somewhat ticklish matter, as, understandably, courts do not like to be told by parties how they should handle a case, even on a procedural matter. Attorney General Mitchell felt that he should not make an approach to the court, so he sent me. I made an appointment to see the Chief Justice of the Court of Appeals, William Hitz, and presented the matter to him. Indeed, I had drafted a form of the order, for his consideration, stating the question, and certifying it to the Supreme Court. He was rather stiff about it. However, a few days later, the question was certified to the Supreme Court.

Before the Supreme Court, there was a remarkable array of counsel. John W. Davis was retained to represent the Senate. Former Senator George Wharton Pepper was retained to represent George Otis Smith, and Attorney General Mitchell represented the President of the United States. Working for this trio was a group of three young lawyers: Charles Poletti as junior to Mr. Davis,[31] Ernest Scott as junior to Senator Pepper,[32] and I was

---

30. Now found in 28 U.S.C. § 1254(2), this provision is rarely used. Cases of great public interest are more frequently taken to the Supreme Court under the provisions of 28 U.S.C. § 1254(1), allowing certiorari "before or after rendition of judgment" in the court of appeals.

31. Poletti, a law school classmate of mine, was later elected Lieutenant Governor of New York and served briefly as Governor when a vacancy occurred in the Governor's office.

32. Scott was later a prominent Philadelphia lawyer, becoming Chancellor of the Philadelphia Bar Association.

junior to Attorney General Mitchell. We began working together while the case was being prepared in the district court, and pretty much took charge of it there. We conducted a thorough investigation and produced an elaborate joint memorandum which undertook to summarize every previous instance in which the Senate had reconsidered the confirmation of a nomination after the President had been notified. There were actually a very considerable number of these, and the Supreme Court made reference to this memorandum in its opinion.[33]

The argument in the case was held on March 21 and 22, 1932, with a large attendance. All three of the leading counsel participated, and it was a scintillating performance throughout. Of course, I was especially impressed by the advocacy of Attorney General Mitchell, whose position prevailed when the Court unanimously held that Smith's appointment was valid, affirming the judgment of the Supreme Court of the District of Columbia.

Another case in which I took especial pleasure was *United States ex rel. Greathouse v. Dern, Sec'y of War.*[34] In this case, the relators owned land in Virginia, just north of the Key Bridge. They sought to construct a wharf in the Potomac River adjacent to their Virginia land.[35] Under congressional legislation, in order to protect against obstructions to navigation, the building of any structure in a navigable river required authorization by the Secretary of War. The purpose of the proposed construction was to provide a wharf for oil barges, with oil storage tanks to be built on the property in Virginia. The Secretary of War refused the permit, making it clear that he did not take this action because the wharf would be an obstruction to navigation, but said that he acted solely for aesthetic reasons, relating particularly to the proposed construction of the George Washington Memorial Parkway which had recently been authorized by Congress.

---

33. We examined not only the Senate and White House records, but also records in the Executive Departments. I remember particularly finding a White House memorandum in the Treasury Department files. It was addressed to the Secretary of the Treasury, and read: "We seem to be in hot water in the Plimley matter. Please advise."—signed "T.R." The Plimley matter involved a person who was appointed Assistant Treasurer who apparently got into financial difficulty after his nomination was confirmed. The nomination was withdrawn by the President, though he had signed a commission "at the time he received and acceded to the request for return of the resolution." 286 U.S. at 46.

34. 289 U.S. 352 (1933).

35. Throughout the District of Columbia, the boundary with Virginia is at high water mark on the Virginia shore of the river.

I shared the hope that the tree covered banks north of Key Bridge would not become an oil tank farm, and wrote a brief raising as many questions as I could think of, including a number which turned on jurisdiction, and other questions involving the exact location of the boundary between Virginia and the District.[36] This was before the days when the statute law contained any provisions focused on the environment, but the Court, in an opinion by Justice Stone, unanimously refused to grant the writ of mandamus, relying on the ground that the granting of that writ is largely a matter for the discretion of the Court. I never cross the Key Bridge, looking north to the Virginia shore, and the now-established George Washington Parkway, without thinking about this case.

Another case which I will mention is *Santos Miguel v. McCarl.*[37] Although this was of primary concern to the parties, I found it an especially interesting case to work on.

Santos Miguel was an enlisted man in the Philippine Scouts, beginning on October 1, 1901. By October, 1931, he had served thirty years and he then sought to retire, with the appropriate benefit for a retired enlisted man. A voucher was presented to the Army disbursing officer in Manila. Without making payment, he forwarded it to the Chief of Finance of the Army, who transmitted it to the Comptroller General of the United States, seeking "an advance decision as to the legal authority for payment." The Comptroller General advised the disbursing officer that he was not authorized to pay the voucher, saying that "the retirement of enlisted men of the Philippine Scouts is not authorized even by the remotest implications of the laws."

A suit was then brought on behalf of Santos Miguel in the Supreme Court of the District of Columbia seeking an injunction to prevent the Comptroller General from interfering with the Chief of Finance, or any disbursing officer, in disbursing retirement pay and allowances to the applicant. The Supreme Court of the District decided in favor of Santos Miguel. On appeal, however the Court of Appeals for the District of Columbia reversed the decision and instructed the District Court to dismiss the Complaint. Counsel for Santos Miguel then sought and obtained review by the Supreme Court of the United States, and I was given the responsibility of preparing the government's brief.

---

36. I was aware of the fact that Mrs. Stone, wife of Justice Stone, was an artist of considerable talent and interests, and I felt that Justice Stone and other members of the Court would be concerned about the views of the Potomac River from the District.

37. 291 U.S. 442 (1934).

I got in touch with the office of the Judge Advocate General of the Army, and two lieutenants of the Judge Advocate General's staff came to my office.[38] After talking with them for a while, I became convinced that the Philippine Scouts were a part of the Army, and that Santos Miguel was entitled to retirement pay. However, I asked the Army lieutenants whether the Navy did not have a similar problem, thinking about Filipino mess attendants. They replied that the Navy had the same problem. I then suggested that we ought to get some Navy lawyers to my office for discussion, and asked if they could get in touch with the Navy people. Their immediate reply was: "That would take six weeks." I said, "Why would that be?" Their response was that they would have to make a recommendation to their section chief, who would then endorse it and send it on to the Judge Advocate General of the Army, who would then send it to the Secretary of War, who would transmit it to the Secretary of the Navy, who would send it to the Judge Advocate General of the Navy, who would pass it on to the appropriate section chief in the Navy, who would finally give it to the people in his office who would prepare the response. Then the response would have to come back by the same route.

At this point, I asked the Army lieutenants whether they knew the people in the Navy Judge Advocate General's office who were familiar with the matter. They gave me the names. I said: "What would happen if you called them on the telephone?" They replied: "We would be court-martialed." By this time, I felt rather frustrated. I had made a note of the names of the people in the Navy, and I asked whether I could be court-martialed if I called the Navy people. The immediate response was that I would not be subject to court-martial. I then reached for the telephone, and both of the lieutenants quickly said: "Leave us out of this. Please do not mention our names." I quickly reached the Navy lawyers, and made an appointment to see them, which I did within a day or two, without the presence of the Army people. I found that the Navy was in complete accord with the Army, and, accordingly, the brief was prepared on this basis.

The representatives of the government before the Court were J. R. McCarl, the Comptroller General of the United States, and the Chief of Finance of the Army. In this situation, after consultation with the Solicitor General, I notified the Comptroller General's counsel that we would not support his position, and

---

38. This was in the fall of 1933. The two lieutenants had served for ten to twelve years, but promotions in those days were very scarce, and they had not yet reached the rank of captain.

said that we would authorize him to file a brief, and to appear in Court to represent the Comptroller General, and they did participate on his behalf. The Solicitor General appeared for the Chief of Finance of the Army urging the correctness of the position of Santos Miguel.

The decision of the Supreme Court, written by Justice Sutherland, was unanimous. It held that no injunction could be granted against the Comptroller General, since his only duty was to make a decision, and, having done that, as the Court said, "his function in that regard ceased." [39] He had a duty, and he had complied with it—he had decided. The Court went on to hold, though, that the decision of the Comptroller General was so plainly wrong that the Chief of Finance of the Army was not warranted in following it. The Court said that "the duty of the disbursing officer to pay the voucher in question 'is so plainly prescribed as to be free from doubt and equivalent to a positive command,' and, therefore, is 'so far ministerial that its performance may be compelled by mandamus.' " [40]

I had several assignments during the Hoover Administration to assist Attorney General William D. Mitchell in the preparation of opinions of the Attorney General. Three of these are worthy of mention.

The first related to the question whether the University of California, which was a land grant college, was required to have ROTC training as a compulsory course for all male students. Perhaps influenced by my Quaker background, I made a draft which took the position that the University was required to offer ROTC, but was not required to make it compulsory. I took it to the Attorney General, and, somewhat to my surprise, he approved it. He made a number of changes in my draft, but he did not change the substance. [41]

On another occasion, there came to my desk a request for an opinion of the Attorney General from Ray Lyman Wilbur, the Secretary of the Interior. This related to the Boulder Dam (also known as the Hoover Dam). The request stated that they were about to sign construction contracts for the dam, and it asked that an opinion be given that the contractor would not be bound to comply with the Workmen's Compensation Law of either

---

39. 291 U.S. at 456.

40. 291 U.S. at 454, quoting Wilbur v. United States, 281 U.S. 206, 218–219 (1930).

41. 36 Op. A.G. 197 (1930).

Arizona or Nevada. It also said that the opinion must be rendered promptly, as the bids would be opened in a few days, and it was expected that compliance with the Workmen's Compensation laws would increase the cost of the dam by about $10 million. I was startled by this request, and I called Northcut Ely, a young lawyer friend of mine who was on Secretary Wilbur's legal staff. He assured me that there was no mistake in the request, and that what I feared was what the Secretary wanted. I then took the papers to Attorney General Mitchell's office. I found that he was as startled as I was, and in a better position than I to do something about it. He immediately called Secretary Wilbur on the telephone, and told him that, as chief counsel for the government, he was advising the Secretary that the bid papers for the contract should specifically require compliance with the Workmen's Compensation laws of the two states. There was some talk back and forth, and I gathered that Secretary Wilbur was not pleased. Nevertheless, he complied with the Attorney General's opinion.

There must have been hundreds of injuries in connection with construction of the dam, and very likely a few deaths. On two subsequent occasions I visited the dam, and found some satisfaction in the fact that I had played a role in providing for compensation for the people who had suffered loss as a result of their work on the giant construction project.

Finally, after the elections of 1932, where Franklin Delano Roosevelt prevailed, and during some of the worst days of the depression period, I was summoned to the Attorney General's office, and told to draft Executive Orders which would provide for the closing of the banks. These drafts were made, and delivered to the Attorney General. I understand that President Hoover talked with Mr. Roosevelt, advised him of his view that the banks should be closed, but said that he would take no action without Mr. Roosevelt's approval. Quite understandably, I believe, Mr. Roosevelt refused to give this approval while he had no executive responsibility; and it was equally understandable that President Hoover would not take the action without the approval of the incoming president.

President Roosevelt was inaugurated on March 4, 1933. My wife attended the inauguration ceremonies, having a ticket which she received from Congressman Crail of California. I stayed home and babysat with our three-months old daughter. I listened to the ceremony on the radio. Very soon thereafter, President Roosevelt closed the banks, using Executive Orders which were essentially the same as those which I had drafted. This was the right thing to do, but I did not take much satisfaction from the fact that I had played an incidental role in this necessary action of the new Administration.

Because of the number and significance of these opinions of the Attorney General, and related matters, I became concerned. It seemed to me that the work was both adequate in volume and of such importance that it should not be handled by a young lawyer in the Solicitor General's office. In particular, I felt that these drafts of opinions, and other policy matters, should be the responsibility of an officer appointed by the President after confirmation by the Senate. Since it was clear that the Solicitor General did not have time available to handle these matters himself, I recommended that a new office should be established, and that the new officer should have the title of Assistant Solicitor General, nominated by the President, and confirmed by the Senate. Such a statute was enacted.[42]

When the new Department of Justice building was opened in 1935, the office of the Solicitor General was on the southeast corner of the fifth floor, and the office of the Assistant Solicitor General was adjacent to it, to the west, along Constitution Avenue. This arrangement continued until 1950, when the appointment of a Deputy Attorney General was authorized, thus providing a presidential appointee to take over some of the duties of the Attorney General. At the same time, the office of the Assistant Solicitor General was terminated, and the office of the Assistant Attorney General for the Office of Legal Counsel was established, and has continued to this day.[43] Among other things, this series of events explains why the office of the Assistant Attorney General for the Office of Legal Counsel is now adjacent to the office of the Solicitor General in the Department of Justice building.

Another minor but useful reform that I was instrumental in bringing about is found in section 516 of the Revenue Act of 1934.[44] Until this statute was enacted, all cases on appeal from the Board of Tax Appeals carried the name of the incumbent Commissioner of Internal Revenue as the party on the government side. Thus, many cases were in the courts in the name of *Burnet v. Someone,* or *Someone v. Helvering,* when David Burnet and Guy T. Helvering, respectively, were Commissioners of Internal Revenue. This meant that whenever there was a change in the holder of the office of Commissioner of Internal Revenue, a motion had to be filed in every pending case where the Commis-

---

42. Act of June 16, 1933, § 16, 48 Stat. 283, 307.

43. Reorganization Plan No. 2 of 1950, §§ 3, 4, 64 Stat. 1261.

44. Act of May 10, 1934, 48 Stat. 680, 760.

sioner was a party in the Supreme Court or in any of the lower courts. The motion was needed to substitute the name of the new Commissioner for the previous one. This involved an enormous amount of paper. Such motions had to be filed in hundreds of cases, and if the motion was not filed within a designated time limit, the party who failed to make the substitution lost the case.

The amendment simply provided that when there was a change in the office of the Commissioner, "no substitution of the name of his successor shall be required" in pending proceedings "before any appellate court." The change was basically a good one, and it was eventually made generally applicable by including a provision that "any successor in office is automatically substituted as a party," now found in the rules of the Supreme Court,[45] in the Federal Rules of Civil Procedure,[46] and in the Federal Rules of Appellate Procedure.[47]

In addition to the ever fascinating work in the office, there were many other events which made life interesting in Washington. Although there were some formalities which no longer prevail,[48] life, in general, was much more close, casual and friendly than it is today.

I was early invited to the home of Attorney General and Mrs. William D. Mitchell, for Sunday supper, since their son, William, had been a classmate of mine at Harvard. It was at one of these

---

45. See Rule 35.3 of the Rules of the Supreme Court effective January 1, 1990.

46. Rule 25.

47. Rule 43.

48. For example, it was *de rigueur* in those days when one had received an invitation, either to a dinner or a reception, that cards should be left at the host's house within a few days after the event. If the person leaving the cards called in person, a corner was turned down. The cards could be sent by a messenger or servant, with the corner left unbent.

We were invited to a number of receptions at the White House, helped occasionally by the fact that my wife had been a classmate at Stanford of a young woman who was social secretary to Mrs. Hoover. After each of these receptions, my wife took our Model A Ford (bought secondhand for $360) and drove into the White House grounds, entering off Pennsylvania Avenue. She stopped our car at the portico, and an usher came down the steps. She then handed him the cards, with the corner turned down, separate cards for each of us, and then drove off. That seems a distant day.

suppers, with other guests present, that I first met J. Edgar Hoover, who made a talk about the scientific work of the Federal Bureau of Investigation. Later, I was asked by Assistant Attorneys General to recommend some young lawyers to work in their divisions. I recommended two of my law school classmates, Bradley Gilman and H. Brian Holland, and both soon came to Washington. Mrs. Mitchell had her niece, Gertrude Bancroft, living with the Mitchells as Mrs. Mitchell's social secretary. In early 1931, Brian and Trudy became engaged, and they were married in St. Paul in early August, 1931. Attending the wedding was the first stop on the trip which my mother and I took by automobile to the west coast that summer, where, in Los Angeles, I became engaged to Harriet Ford, the daughter of my mother's college roommate.

The Justices of the Court were very kind to the younger lawyers.[49] On several occasions, I was a guest at the residence of Justice Butler, which was located on Nineteenth Street.[50] Justice Butler, who was very gruff on the bench, was very kindly in his home. The Butlers had two daughters in Washington, Anne and Margaret. Anne moved in the group in which I circulated, though I never dated her. Margaret was seriously disabled by some sort of sleeping sickness. Margaret liked to play bridge. She did this by having the cards arranged on a rack before her and she would nod her head in the direction of a card, and someone sitting with her would put it on the table for her. The group made regular arrangements so that people were available two or three times a week to play cards with Margaret. After our marriage, Harriet and I occasionally joined in these gatherings.

We also were guests at the Roberts' house, partly because their daughter Elizabeth was one of "the group." The Justice talked interestingly about his days in practice, and particularly about events in the Teapot Dome investigation. Both he and Mrs. Roberts were very gracious, and kind to us.

Harriet and I were invited for dinner on two or three occasions by Justice and Mrs. Brandeis. Dinner was served by Poindexter, who was the Justice's messenger. We recall one evening when Harriet was standing before the table, waiting for the Justice and Mrs. Brandeis to sit down. Poindexter shoved the chair forward and said in a clear voice, "sit down." So Harriet

---

49. Further events are described in an article by my wife. See H. Griswold, "Justices of the Supreme Court of the United States I have Known," 8 Sup. Ct. Hist. Soc. Q. No. 4, p. 1 (1987).

50. It had previously been the Dutch Embassy, and it subsequently became the office of Arnold, Fortas & Porter.

sat down. Mrs. Brandeis always kept everything well under control. When the clock in the living room struck at ten o'clock, she rose, and the guests immediately departed. The conversation at the Brandeis's was always very stimulating. I particularly remember his discussions of various matters which arose in connection with the depression of 1893.

We became acquainted with Justice Van Devanter largely because he had come originally from Marion, Indiana, and my wife had been born in that city. One Sunday afternoon in 1932 we called, by invitation, at the Van Devanters' apartment on Connecticut Avenue. As part of the conversation, I remarked that I had the previous summer travelled across Wyoming, where the Justice started his professional career. I said that I remembered particularly a small town called Sundance. His response was: "Yes, I held the first court that was ever held in Sundance." He then added that he made his reputation as a judge in Wyoming because he was the first judge who ever held court there without stepping up to the bench, and pulling two pistols out of holsters on each side, and laying them out on the bench before him. This was a rather graphic reminder of the newness of many parts of our country. Justice Van Devanter had gone to Wyoming in the late 1870s, less than sixty years before the time when we were seeing him.

We also called on Justice Cardozo and found him a remarkably interesting man. After this, we got up our nerve to invite the Justice to dinner at our apartment, which was located at 1750 Harvard Street, near the Washington zoo. For the other guests, we invited Judge D. Lawrence Groner of the District of Columbia Court of Appeals and Charles E. Wyzanski, Jr., who was then the Solicitor of the Department of Labor. The quarters were somewhat cramped, but this gave the Justice no concern. We had fine conversation, and enjoyed the evening very much. In a few days, the Justice duly sent us his card, without the corner turned down.

Other very interesting events for me were invitations which occasionally came to me from Chief Justice Hughes, and from Justice Stone. While I was sitting in the courtroom, late in the afternoon, one of them would send me a note, inviting me to walk home with him. Of course, I always accepted. Chief Justice Hughes would usually walk only part of the way. His car and driver would follow him, a hundred yards or so behind. When the Justice had walked as far as he wanted, he would signal to the driver, who would pick him up. He always offered to take me to my destination, but I usually simply walked to the Department of Justice, which was not far away.

I remember on one of these occasions that the Chief Justice was stopped by a man who said: "Mr. Hughes, you will not remember me, but I was chairman of the Indiana State Speakers Bureau in 1916. I always thought that the American people made a great mistake in that election." I was a little startled, but the Chief Justice broke into a broad smile and replied: "Well, they seem to have survived it."

Justice Stone was especially kind to me, and he and Mrs. Stone were hospitable to my wife and me after she came to Washington. On several occasions, Mrs. Stone called my wife late in the afternoon and said that they were having a formal dinner that evening, and that someone, usually the Ambassador from somewhere, had just called, saying that he and his wife would be unable to be present for the invitation they had accepted. Mrs. Stone would ask if we would be willing to "fill in." Of course, we were delighted to do so, and thus we attended a number of impressive Washington dinners, where we met, on various occasions, Congressmen and Senators, and other distinguished guests. We were, of course, grateful for these opportunities.

In addition to these social events, there was much else going on in Washington at that time. This was the time of the rise of Hitler in Germany, which was duly noted, but no one foresaw how calamitous it would be. It was also the time of the depth of the depression. This was calamitous too, and everyone in Washington was aware of that. One of the events during this period was the Bonus March, where large numbers of veterans of World War I came to Washington demanding assistance. This was regarded as a threat to the government, and President Hoover (unwisely, I think, and thought then) felt that it should be dispersed. General MacArthur was called on to scatter the Bonus Marchers. This was my first encounter with General MacArthur—through the newspapers only. I did not like him then, and never came to admire him thereafter.

There was one final event in the Hoover Administration. In late October, 1931, just before the election, a number of younger staff in the Department of Justice received word that they should go to the Carlton Hotel, on Sixteenth Street, to attend a nationwide radio address by President Hoover. We soon became aware that our role was to provide a claque for the President. Indeed, there were people in the front of the room who held up signs, reading "APPLAUD", or "CHEER," or "STOP". (The "STOP" was necessary so that too much of the radio time would not be consumed.) I cannot remember a word of what the President said in that speech. I do have a vivid picture in my mind of him standing before us. He looked tired and worn. I was, and am, a considerable admirer of President Hoover, and I know how hard he worked to bring about improvement. His approach, though, was too conventional, and I was not surprised that Franklin Roosevelt prevailed in the election. For one reason or another, I always had reservations about President Roosevelt, though he was, in many ways, a great man, and surely a superb politician.

Judge Thacher resigned as Solicitor General shortly after the inauguration. There was some delay in naming his successor. President Roosevelt offered the post to Professor Felix Frankfurter, but Frankfurter declined, possibly because he had accepted appointment as the Eastman Professor at Oxford for the 1933–34 academic year.[51] President Roosevelt had designated Senator Walsh of Montana to be the new Attorney General. Senator Walsh married in February 1933, and went to Florida on his honeymoon. On the return trip, by train, the Senator died of a heart attack. Very soon afterwards, President Roosevelt nominated Homer Cummings of Connecticut to be Attorney General.

Frankfurter strongly recommended that Dean Acheson, then a practicing lawyer with the firm of Covington & Burling in Washington, be named Solicitor General. There was a meeting at the White House, attended by the President, Attorney General Cummings, and Josephus Daniels, a sort of mentor to the President. (Daniels was Secretary of the Navy in World War I, while Roosevelt was Assistant Secretary of the Navy.) The question of Acheson's appointment as Solicitor General came up, and Homer Cummings' reaction "was immediate, violent, and adverse." As Mr. Acheson later learned, the reason was that his father, as the Episcopal Bishop of Connecticut, had refused to allow Cummings to be married, for the third time, in the church.[52] At this point,

---

51. See Phillips, Felix Frankfurter Reminisces (1960) 243–247. In the Phillips "oral history," Justice Frankfurter refers to a memorandum he had made, and quotes from it. In the early 1950s, Justice Frankfurter brought this memorandum to me in my office at the Harvard Law School, and asked me to read it. He then folded it, and put it in a sealed envelope. He then gave it to me, and requested that I keep it securely, and not make it available to anyone as long as he was living. In due course, I noted that he had revealed the contents of the memorandum in his oral history, and I no longer regarded the pledge of security as binding. However, the memorandum remains unopened in my files.

52. See Acheson, Morning and Noon (1965) 161–162. Mr. Acheson records that this was "a crushing blow at the time." President Roosevelt regarded Cumming's conduct on the matter as "petty and unfair" (*id.* at 164). Acheson had later opportunities to fill the office, but he had

the President became exasperated. He threw up his hands and said: "Well, get me somebody." Josephus Daniels, of North Carolina, spoke up saying: "I know just the man." The man turned out to be J. Crawford Biggs of Raleigh, North Carolina, and he was soon nominated, confirmed, and appointed.

D. Solicitor General Biggs—My Final Year

Mr. Biggs was a fine gentleman, honest, kind, friendly, fatherly, thoroughly decent—but he was not very well qualified for the Solicitor General's position. After he was installed in the office, I went to him and said that I understood that, of course, he would want to build up his own staff. I told him that I was prepared to resign whenever he wanted me to do so, but that I would be willing to stay for a short while if he felt that my continuing would be of assistance to him in connection with the transition. Mr. Biggs said that he would want to select his own staff, but that he would greatly appreciate it if I would stay for two or three months.

As things worked out, I remained for a year, and this proved to be an unusual year for me. I stayed as first assistant to the Solicitor General. Many things were left to me for decision. On other matters, my recommendations were overruled. In those days, the Justices and their wives used to have tea at their homes on Monday afternoons, and we young lawyers in the Department of Justice usually attended one or another of these functions. They were also attended by more prominent people, including congressmen and senators, cabinet members and assistant cabinet members, and so on. At these functions I would often be asked: "Why in the world did your office do" such and such in a particular case. I could not respond that I had done everything I could to persuade the Solicitor General to a different conclusion. Sometimes this involved some difficulty, as I was pressed quite hard.

Another problem I had was that Mr. Biggs would, quite properly, assign important cases to himself for oral argument. Then, two or three days before the argument, he would call me into his office and say that he was too busy, and could I take the case. Of course, I always said that I could, as I liked making oral arguments. Getting ready for the argument though, on short notice, required a good deal of concentrated work. After a while, I anticipated this, and picked out particular cases as ones

---

"hardly a twinge of regret" when he found it necessary to decline "these appreciated invitations."

in which I thought it was likely that I would eventually be asked to make the argument.

During the late spring of 1933, when I thought that I would soon be looking for another job, I had conversations with Jerome Frank, who was then General Counsel of the Agricultural Adjustment Administration. Actually, these contacts were originated by Mr. Frank, at the suggestion of Professor Frankfurter. I was not very enthusiastic about working in that office, but I felt that I should keep my options open. This ended during the summer of 1933, though, when I received a brief letter from Mr. Frank saying that he had given careful consideration to my "application," but had decided not to offer me a job.

––––––

During my final year in the Solicitor General's office, there were many legal problems arising from the activities of the New Deal. One of the first New Deal statutes was the Agricultural Adjustment Act, which became law on May 12, 1933.[53] I remember advising friends in the Agricultural Adjustment Administration that it was a mistake to have the Act provide that the processing tax which it imposed should be put into a segregated fund which was to be used to make payments to farmers. I said that there would be little doubt about the validity of a processing tax if it was simply a tax, that is, if the proceeds were paid into the general funds of the Treasury. It would then be up to Congress to make such appropriations out of the general funds as Congress chose. Eventually, the Agricultural Adjustment Act was found to be unconstitutional on essentially the ground which I had indicated.[54] I have always felt that the Act could have been saved, and a lot of trouble for the Administration avoided, if the other route had been followed. At that time though, both with respect to the Agricultural Adjustment Act, and several other new statutes, the general attitude was "push ahead, and don't bother about details."

During the latter part of 1933 and early in 1934, I became involved in a number of matters where there was controversy between the lawyers for the new National Recovery Administration and the Agricultural Adjustment Administration, and the National Labor Relations Board on the one hand, and the Department of Justice, chiefly represented by the new Assistant Attorney General Harold M. Stephens, on the other. This has often been presented as a battle for turf, with the Department of

––––––

53. 48 Stat. 31.
54. United States v. Butler, 297 U.S. 1 (1936).

Justice being very obstructive, by holding out for narrow and technical views.[55] The New Deal lawyers for the agencies had unlimited self-confidence. They felt that they were truly crusaders. I have heard members of this group say, more than once, "The courts won't dare decide against us when the country is in such crisis." Stephens' view was more cautious, and I tended to be on his side, having in mind the basic rule of the Solicitor General's office, "Never risk an important point on a weak case." As for the Court "daring" to make whatever decision its members felt to be correct, we took a more realistic view. We had no doubt that the Court would "dare" to do what they felt the Constitution required.

I left Washington in July, 1934, before these matters were concluded. After my departure, Stanley Reed became Solicitor General, and he added some strong members to the staff of his office, including Paul A. Freund, Charles E. Wyzanski, Jr., Charles Horsky, Warner Gardner, Thomas I. Emerson, and Philip Levy. These matters were then worked out in a fine spirit of professional cooperation.

———

In the spring of 1934 I received a telephone call from Dean Pound of the Harvard Law School. He asked me if I would be interested in an appointment on the faculty of the School as an assistant professor of law for five years. I asked for time to think about it. I had never expected to be a law teacher.[56] I had always looked forward to practicing law in Cleveland, and I kept the position at the Solicitor General's office for so long— nearly five years—because the experience there was so remarkable.

In this situation, I was much perplexed. I recognized that the choice was an important one, though I did not begin to see its full significance. I talked with a number of practitioners, and they all said, in essence, "Don't be a fool, you will disappear if you go into teaching, never to be heard of again. The real active, exciting life is in practice. By all means, you should now

---

55. See, in particular, P. Irons, The New Deal Lawyers (Princeton, New Jersey, 1982) 143–146, 152–155, 221–225. See also Laura Kalman, Abe Fortas (New Haven: 1990) 39–42.

56. My first teaching offer came from Dean Everett Fraser of the University of Minnesota Law School in late 1932. I declined this, as I was then beginning to argue cases in the Supreme Court. I also had an offer from Dean Charles T. McCormick of the University of Texas Law School.

proceed to practice." And then I talked with a number of academics, including Professor Scott, and some other leading teachers with whom I was acquainted. They all said that I should take the teaching position, that I was well-qualified for it, and that I would find greater satisfaction there than in the routines and technicalities of practice.

I tried hard to think of someone who was neutral, someone who had both taught and practiced. I asked for, and received, an appointment to call on Justice Roberts, who had been an outstanding practitioner, and had also had broad experience as a teacher at the University of Pennsylvania Law School. His chambers then were in a small room in the Capitol, which I found with some difficulty. When I put the question to him, his immediate response was: "There is no question there." I thought he was going to come down strongly on the side of practice. On the contrary, he urged me to accept the teaching opportunity. He said, quite emphatically, that if he had it to do over, he would be a full-time teacher. He said that was the place where you could think, and make a real contribution to the law. As a practitioner, he felt he was always harried, always running from pillar to post. He said that most of his briefs were written by others, that he read them while he was in a taxi on the way to the courthouse, and never really felt that he had mastered the case. I rather doubted the last statement, as there was no room to question the fact that Roberts had been a superb lawyer.

At any rate, I left Justice Roberts' chambers with a much more settled mind. I thought that I should at least try teaching. I may, too, have been influenced by the fact—at the bottom of the depression—that there was a salary attached to the teaching position, while positions for young lawyers at that time were scarce and meager.

After a few days, I called Dean Pound and said that I did not know whether I would like teaching, that I did not know whether I would be any good at it, and asked him if I could have an appointment for one year, since I would not want to seem to be under any sort of a commitment to stay longer if things did not work out well. I was asked to come to Cambridge, where I had an interview with recently-appointed President James Bryant Conant. As a result, I was offered an appointment as assistant professor for one year, which I accepted.

It was after this, but not necessarily because of it, that intimations came, I understand, from the Supreme Court to the White House that there should be a replacement in the Office of the Solicitor General.[57]   This was brought about in the summer of 1934.   At that time, the salary of the Solicitor General was $10,000 a year.   In order to induce Mr. Biggs to leave, he was offered two $10,000 positions.   He was made a voting trustee of the Wheeling and Lake Erie Railroad under the Reconstruction Finance Corporation at $10,000 a year.   And, he was appointed special assistant to the Attorney General to conduct important land condemnation cases in Hawaii, also at $10,000 a year. These were the lands which eventually became Hickam Field. So Mr. Biggs went to Hawaii, where I understand that he did very well.   The choice to replace him was Stanley Reed, then General Counsel of the Reconstruction Finance Corporation. Mr. Reed, of course, later became a Justice of the Supreme Court.

During the summer of 1934, I drove my wife and my sister Hope, then sixteen, to the West Coast, visiting national parks in much the same way as on my trip in 1931, but with some variations.   One purpose, of course, was to give my wife a chance to visit her parents.   At that time, our daughter Hope was two-and-a-half years old.   We left her with my mother, and in return took her daughter with us on the trip.   I bought a second-hand Chevrolet to make the trip, turning in the second-hand Model A Ford which I had acquired in 1930.   This was a very pleasant and successful trip, and I have many vivid memories of Yellowstone Park, Crater Lake, Yosemite, Bryce Canyon and Zion National Parks.   On the way east, we came across the Panhandle of Texas, and frequently had to detour through fields because the road was blocked with drifts of sand.

---

57.   Many years later Felix Frankfurter gave me a copy of a letter which Justice Stone had written to him on May 15, 1933.   In it the Justice said: "I feel some concern as to what is happening in the Solicitor General's office.   I wonder if the President realizes how important the efficiency of that office is going to be to his program."   The passage then continues with a complimentary reference to "young Griswold."

Chapter V

A Law Teacher

A. Arrival and First Classes

In early September, 1934, we moved to Massachusetts, where I had rented a house at 65 Horace Road in Belmont. The house had four bedrooms, though two of them were rather small. The rent was $85 a month. We renewed the lease for a second year at $75 a month. The owner of the house was willing to make the reduction since he did not have to pay a real estate commission on the renewal. My salary as assistant professor at the Harvard Law School was $5,000 a year. That was augmented by $125 a month, which I received from the American Law Institute as an adviser and aide to Professor Scott on the Restatement of Trusts. At the close of the academic year I prepared the Index for Volume 48 of the Harvard Law Review, and received $100 for this. A year or two later, I prepared the Index for the first edition of Professor Scott's Treatise on Trusts, and was paid a little more for this, by Little, Brown & Company. I have always been proud of that Index, as I think that I had something of a talent for writing an Index in terms of the way a user would approach his search. What would he look under? If I found an answer to that, I would put it in the Index. Since the Index to the first edition of Scott, however, I have not done any more indexes—it is a painstaking task—except for the casebooks which I prepared for law school use.

Our furniture had been removed from our Washington apartment in July, and it was delivered to us in Belmont the day we arrived. Harriet often drove me into the office, bringing our not yet two-year old daughter Hope with her. I frequently took the streetcar home, out Mt. Auburn Street and Belmont Street. It was a long two-block walk from Cushing Square to the house which we had rented.

Settling in at the Law School was quick and easy. It was familiar territory, and it did not take me long to get acclimated. I was fortunate to be assigned the office of Professor James M. Landis, who was on leave of absence and had gone to Washington. It was made plain to me that my use of the office was at sufferance, and that I would have to give it back when Landis returned. As things worked out, he came back as Dean of the Law School in the fall of 1937, and I kept the office for twelve years, until I moved to the Dean's office in June, 1946.

I was assigned to teach a section of Taxation and to assist Professor Joseph H. Beale in Conflict of Laws, in the Third Year, and also to conduct a seminar on Legislation, which was attended largely by graduate students, and a few third-year students. One of those in the Seminar whom I particularly enjoyed was John W. Wade, a graduate of the University of Mississippi Law School. John was a fine person, and an able student. He later became a professor, and then Dean, of the Vanderbilt University Law School, and did much to build that school up to its present high standard. He also was active in the work of the American Law Institute, and became a Reporter for the Restatement of Torts, Second. Over the years, he has written many valuable articles in the Torts field.[1]

The work in the seminar was very hard going. I did not really know a great deal about legislation. My experience in that area in the Solicitor General's office had been largely limited to questions of interpretation. Dean Pound had prepared and published an Outline of a Course on Legislation, which I utilized, and this was "the book" in the course. It was, of course, very well done, but it was largely based on state statutes and had a sort of late nineteenth century atmosphere. Although I worked hard, I never thought that I was well prepared for the legislation seminar, and I made it plain to the students that we were "learning together"—which may be a fairly good way to teach a somewhat specialized subject. I never felt satisfied with my work, and was glad when the assignment was not renewed the following year.

Everything was much different with respect to the Tax course. I used a casebook prepared by my colleague, Professor John MacArthur Maguire, and by Roswell McGill of the Columbia Law School. My experience with tax cases in the Solicitor

---

1. As a result of his work in the Legislation Seminar, he published an article in the Harvard Law Review. See Wade, "Acquisition of Property by Wilfully Killing Another," 49 Harv. L.Rev. 715 (1936).

General's office was an extraordinary background for teaching. It gave me many illustrations for use in class, and I often departed from the casebook. The casebook included material on state taxation as well as federal, but, after the first two years I confined my course to federal taxation. Thus, in 1936, I became the first teacher in a standard law school in the United States to teach federal taxation alone. It may have been a narrow focus, but it was plain to me at that time that federal taxation had become a special area in its own right, and should be taught that way. I did include federal estate and gift taxation, as well as federal income taxation. In recent years, though, the material has become so voluminous that a separate course in federal income taxation is the standard, and students are usually left to pick up the details of federal estate and gift taxation on the side.

I enjoyed the tax course from the beginning, though I entered upon the task with considerable fear and trepidation. However, I found that I could keep a class lively, producing good discussions, and that the student reaction appeared to be favorable. Many people have criticized the Harvard Law School because of its general use of relatively large classes. My own reaction has been, though, that nearly everything turns on the teacher. There is no doubt, in my mind, that a large class with a well qualified teacher produces far more education than a small class with a teacher who is inarticulate, and lacks the verve, and the ability to project his voice, which helps to communicate his thoughts to his students, and make the thoughts come alive.[2]

My office was on the second floor of the west wing of Langdell Hall, which had been completed in 1930. Across the hall from me was the office of Professor James Angell McLaughlin.[3] Next to him was Professor E. Merrick Dodd. Next to him

---

2. In my days as Dean, I used to say, jokingly, of course, but with a point, that "ninety percent of the qualifications of a really good law teacher was a clear strong voice," adding that "if he has some brains for the other ten percent, that helps."

3. As he then was. A number of years later, after I became Dean, McLaughlin came to me and said that he wanted his name changed for payroll purposes to MacLachlin. I explained to him that he could readily get his name changed by court order, and, if he got such an order, the University would use the new name on the payroll checks sent to him. He applied to the local court, and received an order changing his name. This attracted some attention in the Boston newspapers and he was asked why he had changed his name. Typically MacLachlin, he replied: "I have been masquerading as an Irishman long enough. It seemed to me that the time had come when my name should become honest."

was Professor Felix Frankfurter, and next to him was Professor Austin W. Scott. On my side of the corridor, recently retired Professor Eugene Wambaugh was next to me,[4] and Professor Ralph J. Baker had the office next to him. This was a fine and congenial group.

We did not bother each other very much, but we did have some discussion in the hallways, and occasionally poked our heads in each other's doors to share views on special problems that might arise. I was warmly welcomed and never left to feel that I was a stranger.

B. PUBLICATION OF REGULATIONS, AND THE FEDERAL REGISTER

Almost immediately after my arrival at the Law School, Professor Felix Frankfurter came to my office, and said that he had a topic on which he wanted me to write an article. I had not planned to write anything quite as soon as this, but a suggestion from Professor Frankfurter was, of course, not to be taken lightly. I later learned that the suggestion came to him from Justice Brandeis, but there was no mention of this when Professor Frankfurter talked with me.

The question had to do with the proper publication of administrative regulations, varying from Executive Orders at the highest level through regulations of executive departments, and such things as notices of hearings or of other activities by an already burgeoning federal bureaucracy.

In my work in the Solicitor General's office, I had encountered this problem. One of the cases on which I worked was *United States v. Shreveport Grain and Elevator Co.*[5] This involved a prosecution under a statute for selling feed short-weight. The statute provided that it should be an offense to do this. However, there were practical problems because the amount of moisture absorbed by the feed, under varying atmospheric conditions, could affect its weight. Accordingly, the statute provided that "reasonable variations shall be permitted, and tolerances *   *   *

---

4. Professor Wambaugh had taught constitutional law for many years. He was of the old school. He did not carry on any appreciable activity after retirement. He did, however, have tea in his office quite frequently. He would invite me on most of these occasions, and expect me to stay for thirty or forty minutes. I had considerable difficulty in being polite to him while preserving as much time as I could for my work.

5. 287 U.S. 77 (1932).

shall be established by rules and regulations" made by the Secretary of Agriculture.[6]

When the case came to me, I found that the record was quite unclear as to just what regulations, if any, had been made and what their effect might be. I thought that I must find out whether any such regulations had been made, and, if so, what they were. So I went over to the Department of Agriculture, and located the office of the Assistant Secretary of Agriculture whose duties seemed to cover this particular matter. I entered the office, and found a secretary busily working at her typewriter. I asked her whether there were any regulations under this statute, thinking that they had probably been made, and then published in some sort of a pamphlet, and that I could get a copy of the pamphlet.

In response to my question, she was very thoughtful. She said she was sure that there was no pamphlet available. But she said that she did have "some recollection of something like that." She then went to a file drawer, and, after fingering through several files, she came up with one which related to the "full weight" statute. She opened this, and found a typewritten page stating the "reasonable tolerances." However, there were handwritten interlineations on these pages. There was nothing to indicate who had made these interlineations, or the date when they had been made. The latter was important, because the interlineations would not apply to my case if they were made after the date when the relevant sale of the feed had been made. I felt at the time that this was a "poor way to run a government," and that "something ought to be done about it." I did not see, though, that I could do much. I returned to the Department of Justice with some notes that I made, and completed my brief.

Consequently, when Professor Frankfurter spoke to me, I saw an opportunity. Professor Frankfurter also mentioned that there was in England a Rules Publication Act, under which rules and regulations were published in separate pamphlets as soon as issued, and annually collected into a bound volume.[7] I was further told that this publication of "delegated legislation" was supervised in England by Sir Cecil Carr, that he had written a book about this [8] and that he was currently in the United States, and might be coming to Cambridge.

6. Food and Drugs Act of 1906, as amended by the Act of March 3, 1915, c.117, 37 Stat. 732.

7. Rules Publication Act, 1893, 56 & 57 Vict. c.66. The series of bound volumes is called Statutory Rules and Orders.

8. See C. Carr, Delegated Legislation (London, 1921).

So, I started to work, and after some weeks produced a manuscript which was printed in the December, 1934, issue of the Harvard Law Review.[9]

In the course of my work on the article, I came across a quotation from Jeremy Bentham, which gave me the suggestion for the title of the article. Bentham wrote: "We hear of tyrants, and those cruel ones: but, whatever we may have felt, we have never heard of any tyrant in such sort cruel, as to punish men for disobedience to laws or orders which he had kept them from the knowledge of." [10]

The article summarized the problem, and made a clear statement of the need. It pointed out that "the President alone issued 674 Executive Orders, aggregating approximately 1,400 pages, in the first fifteen months after March 4, 1933"—and added that this was "nearly six times as great as that for the thirty-nine years from 1862 through 1900." It also noted that the National Recovery Administration, during its first year, issued 2,998 administrative orders, and many regulations were "scattered among 5,991 press releases during the same period." The article outlined the actions which had been taken in England, and other British countries, and ended with a draft of a proposed statute.

By a pure coincidence—though it was ultimately inevitable— this question came up in the Supreme Court on December 10, 1934, almost the exact date on which my article was published. The case involved an order of the Railroad Commission of the State of Texas limiting the production of oil in that state.[11] An Executive Order, issued under the National Recovery Act, made it a criminal offense to transport oil in interstate commerce which had been produced in violation of such an order. During the course of the argument before the Supreme Court, it developed that the paragraph of the Executive Order on which the government relied had been stricken out by a new Executive Order on September 13, 1933. The case, however, had proceeded through the district court and the Circuit Court of Appeals without counsel on either side, or the courts, being aware of this repeal. The Department of Justice discovered this [12] and brought it to the Supreme Court's attention in the brief which

---

9. "Government in Ignorance of the Law—A Plea for Better Publication of Executive Legislation," 48 Harv.L.Rev. 198 (1934).

10. 5 Bentham, Works (1843) 547.

11. Panama Refining Co. v. Ryan, 293 U.S. 388 (1935).

12. The discovery was actually made by Moses Huberman, a law school classmate of mine, when he was checking materials for the government's brief. He was on the staff of Harold M. Stephens, the Assistant Attorney General who was in charge of the case for the

the government filed as respondent in the case. When this was disclosed at the oral argument, it received considerable attention in the newspapers. On December 12, 1934, I wrote a letter to Mr. Stephens, with whom I was well acquainted, advising him that my article was about to appear, and seeking his help, through the Attorney General, or otherwise, in advancing the legislation I proposed. The publicity given to this episode in the *Panama Refining* case (popularly known as the "hot oil" case) was undoubtedly an important factor in the eventual enactment of the Federal Register statute.

Having gone so far, I was anxious that some useful result might eventuate. I thought that it was a matter which would move forward if the President supported it, and it seemed to be worthy of the President's attention. I had no way to get his ear, but I went to John Dickinson, then an Assistant Attorney General, since I knew that he saw the President from time to time. Dickinson was much interested, but about six weeks later he reported to me that he had presented the matter to the President, who had vetoed the proposal, saying "I will not have the government in the newspaper business." This was, of course, a misunderstanding—and very disappointing.

I then came in touch with a new young Congressman, Emmanuel Celler, of New York. I was told that he was looking very hard to find a way to make a record, and, in particular, wanted to have a bill which he could sponsor and put his name on. I went to see Mr. Celler, and he was immediately much interested. From then on, the matter was in Celler's skillful hands. There were the usual ups and downs which occur in legislative matters, but, in due course, the Federal Register Act was passed by both Houses of Congress and signed by the President.[13]

Eight months later, the first issue of the Federal Register was published, and it has made its regular appearance on working days ever since. It may well be the dullest publication distributed widely in the United States, but it has been very useful. It is available in all good law libraries, in many law offices, and in large public libraries, all over the country. It enables any citizen, or his lawyer, anywhere in the country, to obtain the precise text of any governmental regulation, very shortly after it is promulgated. In addition to the printed publication, its material is now

government. Letter to E.N.G. from Harold M. Stephens, January 7, 1935.—Harold M. Stephens Papers, Library of Congress, Box 16.

13. Act of July 26, 1935, c. 417, 49 Stat. 501. There was some delay in getting appropriations from Congress, and the first issue appeared on March 14, 1936.

included in LEXIS and WESTLAW, the computer services in the legal field.[14]

The Federal Register was, of course one of those things that had to come. However, it took a long time in materializing. Its contribution to the law, and to lawyers, is hard to evaluate, but it must have saved many mistakes by courts, and enormous amounts of time for lawyers, not to mention the certainty which it provides when the exact text of a regulation can be found in any good law library. Though the need was great when it was established, it has grown enormously in recent years. During 1937, the first full year of publication, the material in the Register filled 3,450 pages. In 1990, even after several years of "deregulation," the total was 53,618 pages.

Another event which occurred during my early days on the faculty caused me considerable concern. Late in the fall of 1934, Dean Pound sent around a circular to the faculty, and others, saying that he was to receive an award from the German Government. He advised us that this award would be presented by the Consul of Germany in Boston, and that the presentation would be made in the main lobby of Langdell Hall. He invited all members of the faculty, and others, to attend.

Dean Pound was brilliant, but he was somewhat rough and ready from his early days in Nebraska, and he was not very sensitive. By this time, Hitler was well in power in Germany, and many sad and disturbing events had occurred in that country. Of course, we could not foresee how much worse the future would prove to be. Nevertheless, accepting a medal from the German government at that time did not seem right. On the other hand, I was a brand new young faculty member, and did not want to insult the dean. I could have stayed away from the presentation, and it is clear to me now that I should have done so. What I did do, though, was to compromise. I did not go to the entrance lobby, where the presentation was made. I did not shake hands with the German Consul, nor did I speak to him. But I did go to the balcony above the entrance lobby, where I could hear and see the presentation. On the whole, this was a rather small matter, but I still feel that Pound should not have accepted the award.[15]

---

14. See O'Connor, "Uncovering Federal Regulations," 62 Wisc. Lawyer 31 (1989).

15. When I took my wife and sister to Europe in 1935, we went to England, Holland, Belgium, France, Switzerland, and Italy, but we did

C. Legal Writing

Following the example of Professor Scott, and some other members of the faculty, I regarded it as my obligation as a faculty member to turn out a substantial piece of writing for publication each year.[16] After completing the article on "Government in Ignorance of the Law," I devoted myself to revising my materials on Spendthrift Trusts, and this was published as a book, with that title, in 1936.[17]

During the spring of 1935, I was recommended by the faculty for a tenured appointment as Professor of Law. This recommendation was approved by the Harvard Corporation, and confirmed by the Board of Overseers, and became effective on September 1, 1935, shortly after my thirty-first birthday. Needless to say, this promotion was a source of satisfaction, and also of challenge. I had developed real enthusiasm for the opportunities offered by an academic career, and I enjoyed the work, the contacts with

not go to Germany, and that was by choice. Indeed, except for stops in airports, I have not been in Germany since 1928.

16. My first published article was "The Pro and Con of Annexation of Suburbs," 14 Nat. Mun. Rev. 86 (1925). This was written as a paper in a seminar under Professor Geiser, at Oberlin, and he encouraged me to seek publication. Similarly, a paper which I wrote with my classmate William Mitchell for a seminar under Professor Felix Frankfurter, on a topic suggested by him (which very likely came from Justice Brandeis) was published as "The Narrative Record in Federal Equity Appeals," 42 Harv.L.Rev. 483 (1929). Thereafter, and before I came to the faculty, two articles were published which were based on the thesis I wrote for the S.J.D. degree. These were "Reaching the Interest of the Beneficiary of A Spendthrift Trust," 43 Harv. L.Rev. 63 (1929), and "Spendthrift Trusts Created in Whole or in Part for the Benefit of the Settlor," 44 Harv.L.Rev. 203 (1930). Reference has already been made to "The Historical Development of Waiver of Jury Trial in Criminal Cases," 20 Va.L.Rev. 655 (1934).

17. In the subsequent years before World War II the following articles were published: "Income Taxation of State Liquor Monopolies," 22 A.B.A.J. 619 (1936), "Res Judicata in Federal Tax Cases," 46 Yale L.J. 1320 (1937), "Renvoi Revisited," 51 Harv.L.Rev. 1165 (1938), "Powers of Appointment and the Federal Estate Tax," 52 Harv.L.Rev. 929 (1939), which made a proposal which was adopted in the Revenue Act of 1942, and "A Plan for the Coordination of the Income, Estate and Gift Taxes with Respect to Trusts, and Other Transfers," 56 Harv.L.Rev. 337 (1942). The latter article forecast a result which was finally reached with the establishment of the "unified transfer tax" by the Tax Reform Act of 1976, Pub. L. 94–455, 90 Stat. 1520. See Bittker, Federal Taxation of Income, Estates and Gifts (1984) ¶ 133.3.

students, faculty members, and alumni, and the occasions which it offered for constructive activity in the law outside the immediate tasks of the Law School.[18]

After the work on the Spendthrift Trusts book had been completed, I gave thought to the preparation of a casebook on Federal Taxation for classroom use—just federal taxation. My experience in the Solicitor General's office was of immense value in this task. I had had close contact with many tax cases, and was thoroughly familiar with the issues that had been decided, and many of those that remained for decision—though I had little, if any, vision of the great complexity and intricate development which would take place in the tax law in the forthcoming years.

D. THE COURT–PACKING PLAN

My work on the new casebook had barely begun when it had to be put aside because of what came to be known as President Roosevelt's "Court Packing" plan. This was announced by the President in early February, 1937. In his message, he said that there was a crisis in the Supreme Court, the Justices were behind in their work, that this was due to the fact that several of them were over seventy years of age, and, as a result, needed help. The plan then proposed that the size of the Court should be enlarged, and that a new justice should be appointed for each member of the Court who was over seventy years of age. At that time there were six justices who were seventy or more, and the Court was often called "the nine old men." The proposal would not directly affect the tenure of any of the older justices, but it obviously would give the President the opportunity to appoint new justices who might hold views more in keeping with those of the administration. The plan further provided that when one of the overage justices died or retired his position should not be filled. Thus, in the long run, the size of the enlarged Court might be reduced back to nine justices—though subject to increase again when members of the Court advanced in years and reached the seventy-year age.

18. In the summer of 1935, I wanted to share my experience in European travelling with my wife. I took her, my sister Jane and two other girls to share expenses, and sailed to Naples on the Italian liner "Rex". When the ship stopped at Gibraltar, I was handed a message from Stanley Reed, the new Solicitor General, inviting me to return to his office. I was much tempted, as I loved the work there, but I finally decided to stay with my newly started academic career.

I was greatly offended by this proposal, primarily for two reasons. In the first place, I thought that the stated basis for the plan was dishonest. The fact was that the Court was not behind in its work.[19] In the second place, I felt that the plan was an attack on the Supreme Court, for which I had developed great respect, even though I disagreed with many of its decisions. In my view, the Supreme Court was sort of an ultimate bulwark which provided essential stability for our political system. If an attack of this sort could be successfully made against the Supreme Court, then further attacks could be made on the Court by later Presidents, or by Congress, and a crucial balance in the operation and stability of the government under the Constitution would be lost.[20]

Holding these views, I soon found myself involved in making speeches to groups in the Boston area. There was intense public interest in the plan, and a considerable amount of support for it, both from politicians, and from the general public. I made speeches before Rotary Clubs, church groups, and the like.

At about this time, the announcement was made that James M. Landis would be the new Dean of the Harvard Law School. I thought that this was an excellent choice, because there was no doubt that Landis was a very able and productive person.[21]

19. After the Judiciary Act of 1925, the Court had broad power to select most of the cases which it would hear, and, thus, it could control, to a considerable extent, its intake. After the appointment of Chief Justice Hughes in 1930, the Court had regularly decided, by the end of the Term each June, every case in which it had heard oral argument, with a very few exceptions, where, for one reason or another, the case was set down for re-argument in the following Term.

20. The origins of the specific plan advanced by the President were long in doubt. It became clear that Felix Frankfurter had had no part in it, that Thomas G. Corcoran and Benjamin Cohen, two of the President's advisors and go-betweens on legal matters had not been consulted, and that James M. Landis may have heard about it, but was not consulted. A careful study reaches the conclusion that the motive power came from the Attorney General, Homer Cummings, aided by Carl McFarland of his staff, and by the Solicitor General, Stanley Reed. Much assistance came from articles written by Professor Edward S. Corwin, of Princeton University, who was in touch with Attorney General Cummings throughout the development of the plan. See Leuchtenberg, "The Origins of Franklin D. Roosevelt's 'Court Packing' Plan," 1966 Supreme Court Review 347.

21. I had known him when he came to the faculty in 1926, and became Professor of Legislation in 1928. I had been particularly impressed by his essay on "Statutes and the Sources of Law," in Harvard Legal Essays (Cambridge, Mass.: 1934) 213.

Shortly after the announcement of his appointment was made, though, Landis came out in favor of the President's plan. This caused a considerable amount of controversy among prominent Harvard Law School alumni, and this appeared, to some extent, in the news. I expect that this is what brought me to the attention of the Senators on the Judiciary Committee of the Senate who were apparently seeking another Harvard professor to oppose the plan. At any rate, I received an invitation to appear before the Committee, and I did so on March 30, 1937.

When I arrived in Washington, on the morning of March 30th, I called, as instructed, at the office of Senator Homer Ferguson of Michigan, who was one of the leaders of the opposition to the plan. He told me that the outlook was not good, and that the best that they might hope for was probably some sort of compromise. Consequently, he asked me to include a compromise proposal in my testimony. I asked him what the compromise was and he said that it would involve a constitutional amendment fixing the number of justices at nine and providing that their terms of office should be eighteen years. Any justice who had served eighteen years or more when the amendment took effect would cease to be a member of the Court. Thereafter, the appointments would be for eighteen-year terms, spaced at two-year intervals, so that it would follow that at least two vacancies would occur in each presidential term. There might be other vacancies as a result of death or resignation, but these would be filled only for the unexpired residue of the terms.

I was not very happy with this proposal. However, it did appear that those leading the opposition thought that this was the best that could be obtained, and I included it in my testimony. I appeared before the Senate Judiciary Committee on the morning of Tuesday, March 30, 1937, and was before the Committee for about three hours.[22] After my original statement, which occupied about a half-hour, nearly every member of the committee questioned me. As I read the transcript now, more than fifty years later, I am impressed by the way I handled the questions, and, in particular, by the fact that I appear to have "kept my cool." Senator Logan asked me my age, and when I replied that I was thirty-two, he said:[23]

22. Hearings before Committee on the Judiciary, United States Senate, March 30, 1937, on "Reorganization of the Federal Judiciary," Part 4, 75th Cong. 1st Sess., pp. 760–808.

23. Senate Committee Hearing, *supra,* p. 771. I was well defended by Senator Connally, see *id.,* p. 805.

Senator Logan. Thirty-two. Do you regard yourself as better qualified than any other youngster who has graduated from a good law school within the last 6 or 7 years, to discuss this important question?

Mr. Griswold. Certainly not, Senator.

Senator Logan. Did you ever practice law any?

Mr. Griswold. I did, Senator.

Senator Logan. How long?

Mr. Griswold. Five years.

When I was further pressed, I conceded that I had had "very little experience in the private practice of law."

As a matter of fact, though we did not realize it at the time, the case for the President's plan had already started to crumble. This began with the letter prepared by Chief Justice Hughes and delivered to Senator Wheeler on March 21, 1937, refuting many of the grounds advanced by President Roosevelt. Then, by happy coincidence, the Supreme Court on Monday, March 29, 1937, decided the case of *West Coast Hotel Company v. Parrish*,[24] in which, by a five to four majority, the Court upheld the validity of a statute of the State of Washington providing for minimum wages for women. At the time I appeared before the Senate Judiciary Committee the following day, I knew about this decision only from the newspapers, and had not read the opinions of the Court. The decision was, however, referred to by a number of the Senators at the hearing. The change in result between this case and the recent decision in *Morehead v. New York ex rel. Tipaldo*,[25] came about because Justice Roberts found a way to distinguish the two cases, and voted for the majority in *West Coast Hotel*, though he had voted against the validity of the New York statute involved in *Tipaldo*. It was widely suggested that he did this because of pressure from the Court Packing Plan, and the quip was that "A switch in time saved nine." I do not think that this was a fair appraisal, as I have tried to develop in an article entitled "Owen J. Roberts as a Judge." [26]

_____

24. 300 U.S. 379 (1937).

25. 298 U.S. 587 (1936).

26. 104 U. of Pa. L.Rev. 332 (1955). In reaching this conclusion, I wrote (pp. 343–344):

Roberts did not switch his vote to save the Court. He voted in favor of the validity of a minimum wage statute in the *West Coast Hotel* case because that was his judicial view when, in his opinion, that question first came before him. The only criticism that can be made, I think, is that he did not sufficiently make his position known in the *Tipaldo*

During the months following the hearing, I continued to make speeches in opposition to the Court Packing Plan. On April 29, 1937, I wrote to Harold Stephens:

> I seem to have got myself embroiled in making a number of speeches on the Supreme Court issue. It keeps me very busy, and I doubt if it does any good. But my feelings on the subject are such that I want to do anything that anybody thinks may be of some use.[27]

As is well known, the strength of the opposition continued to develop, and the Senate Judiciary Committee finally reported against the Plan.[28] The opposition finally prevailed in dramatic fashion when Senator Robinson, one of the Plan's chief sponsors, collapsed and died while making a speech on the floor of the Senate, in June, 1937.

E.   RETURN TO CASEBOOK—AND MORE ARTICLES

The manuscript for my casebook on Federal Taxation was finally completed in the late spring of 1938, and I submitted it in succession to several publishers of law school books. None of them would take it. They said that there was no market for a casebook limited to federal taxation. I talked with my colleague, Professor Edmund M. Morgan, about this. He was the general editor of the casebook series published by the Foundation Press, a subsidiary of West Publishing Company. Professor Morgan said little to me, but about two weeks later I received a letter from Foundation Press saying that they would like to publish the book. I had no doubt that Professor Morgan had intervened, and brought about this happy result. The casebook was published in 1939—at a time when the total enrollment in approved law schools was about thirty thousand students, and the number taking classes in taxation was quite small. The war came a year and a half later, and there were very few students in law schools

---

case, although the ground on which he acted is written all over that opinion for those who choose to look for it. [The ground was that the constitutional question was not properly raised in the *Tipaldo* case.] It is undoubtedly true, though, that this procedural ground was somewhat subtle, and he did not take the steps to identify it with himself. This may have been an error in opinion writing. It was not a switch of vote under political pressure.

See also Frankfurter, "Mr. Justice Roberts," 104 U. of Pa. Rev. 311 (1935); Sutherland, Constitutionalism in America (1965) 481–501.

27. Harold M. Stephens Papers, Library of Congress, Box 16.

28. Senate Rep. No. 7111, 75th Congress, 1st Session (1937).

for several years after that. The first edition was well received, but its total sales amounted to only 2,140 copies.[29]

During these years I was also teaching conflict of laws, and became deeply interested in that important, often neglected, fascinating, difficult field. As indicated above, I published an article called "Renvoi Revisited" in 1938.[30] Conflict of laws is the area of the law which deals with questions which arise when a transaction has elements in more than one state. In England, it is often called "Private International Law," since conflicts which arise in English courts ordinarily involve two or more wholly independent countries. In the United States, though, there are fifty states, each with a sphere of the law in which it can make its own decisions. Thus, in the United States, most conflicts are interstate. With the growing expansion of commercial activity, and the ease of shipment and travel, these conflicts arise frequently, and present great difficulty.

My teacher in the field, Professor Joseph H. Beale, had a rather mechanical view of the problems, often called the "territorial" or the "vested rights" theory—and sometimes called "the checkerboard theory."[31]

In my work in the field, I felt that there should be some greater flexibility, and that this could be achieved, in some cases,

---

29. Eventually six editions were published under my editorship, and total sales of all editions were about 200,000 copies. A new edition was published in 1976, with Professor Michael Graetz of the University of Virginia Law School as a joint editor. At this point, I withdrew entirely, and Professor Graetz was the sole editor of the "successor edition," dealing with income taxes only, published in 1985.

30. 51 Harv.L.Rev. 1165.

31. At a dinner during my student days, an irreverent student made a speech where, though expressing affectionate regard for Professor Beale, he characterized his approach in these words: "All the world's a checkerboard, and every square has its own law, and everything that happens there is governed by the law of that square because that is the only law there is there."

While I was a student in Professor Beale's class, I once asked him a question. I referred to then Chief Justice Taft who had a summer house in Murray Bay, Quebec. It was well known that the Chief Justice signed various orders (extending time, granting stays, and so on) while he was in Canada. In a classroom interchange, I asked Professor Beale whether these orders were valid. His immediate response was: "Obviously not. Chief Justice Taft derives his authority from the law of the United States. That law does not apply in Canada. Thus the Chief Justice is without legal authority when he acts in Canada." I pursued the discussion no further.

by regarding the reference by a state court to "the law" of another state as "the law of that state, including its rules of conflict of laws." This is sometimes called "the whole law" of that state. Thus, there might be a "reference back" or a "reference to a third state," according to the conflict rules of the state to which the first reference was made. This has been referred to by conflict of laws scholars as the "renvoi," and I wrote in support of that view. This greatly annoyed Professor Beale, who was much my senior, and I soon understood that he was upset because I, a colleague, had "attacked" him. I had not looked at it that way. I felt that I was essentially taking Professor Beale's approach, and enlarging on it, or refining it. But Professor Beale, as Reporter for the first Restatement of Conflict of Laws, had stated categorically that a reference to "the law" of another state always meant "the internal law" of that state, without any regard to its conflict of laws rules.

By this time Professor Beale had retired from the Law School faculty, having reached the ultimate retirement age of seventy-five years in 1936. I was sorry that I had offended him, but I still felt that the article was a contribution. Indeed, I have long regarded it as one of my best efforts at legal writing.

F. Conflict of Laws Casebook—and Professor Sachs

One consequence of the article was that I was asked to join a distinguished group in the production of a casebook on conflict of laws. Professors Elliott Cheatham and Noel Dowling of the Columbia Law School, and Dean Herbert Goodrich of the Law School of the University of Pennsylvania had published a casebook on conflict of laws in 1934. They asked me to join with them in putting out the second edition of the book, and I gladly accepted. This casebook continues to this day in a succession of editions, with a shifting group of editors. The ninth edition was published in 1990. When I became Solicitor General, I dropped out of the group, and the last edition in which I participated was the sixth edition, published in 1966.

Another outgrowth of my work in Conflict of Laws was a task that I took on in 1939 on behalf of Professor Alexander N. Sachs of the Law School faculty at New York University. He was the author of a very fine article entitled "The Conflict of Laws in the History of the English Law," which was published in a three-volume set of scholarly articles put out by the New York Univer-

sity Law School on the occasion of its centennial.[32] We exchanged several letters about this article.

Following this correspondence, Professor Sachs came to me,
and asked for my assistance. It developed that he was being
dismissed from the faculty at New York University on the ground
of antisemitism. This seemed to me to be unlikely, since Professor Sachs was himself a refugee who came to the United States in
the early 1930s. He told me that he was charged with having
made racial remarks about Frank H. Sommer, the recently retired dean of the New York University Law School. Professor
Sachs wanted me to represent him in academic freedom proceedings before the Association of American Law Schools and, perhaps, the American Association of University Professors.

I agreed to undertake the representation, but with the understanding that I would accept no compensation for my work,
though I would accept reimbursement for actual expenses incurred. The matter was a rather delicate one, not only because
of the subject matter, but because the dismissal had come from
Arthur T. Vanderbilt, then dean of the Law School, former
president of the American Bar Association, and the future prestigious Chief Justice of the Supreme Court of New Jersey. He
was known to be a man of great self-confidence and determination.

I aided Professor Sachs in filing a complaint with the Association of American Law Schools, and it was referred to the
Committee on Academic Freedom and Tenure. A committee to
hear the complaint was promptly appointed, of which Professor
James William Moore of the Yale Law School faculty was the
chairman. Hearings were held in New Haven and in New York.
The evidence appeared to show that Professor Sachs had recently
suffered a substantial loss of hearing, and I felt that this was the
primary cause of his difficulties, and that retirement with suitable financial provision, rather than dismissal, was appropriate.
The hearings were handled with promptness by Professor Moore
and his colleagues, who eventually suggested that a settlement
would be appropriate.

As a result, a meeting was arranged at the University in New
York at which both the president of the university and Dean
Vanderbilt were present. The dean strongly opposed a settle-
ment, and nothing was accomplished. About two weeks later, I
received a telephone call asking me to come to New York again.
I wondered whether this would be useful, but when I was told

32. 3 New York University, Law—A Century of Progress (New York:
1937) 342–454.

that the meeting would be in the office of the counsel for New York University, I agreed to attend. When I got to the meeting, I found that only counsel were present. Neither the president of the university (who had said little at the earlier meeting) nor Dean Vanderbilt was there. It was suggested by the university's counsel that they would pay one year's salary. I said that I thought it ought to be three years, and this produced a counter offer of two years' salary, from which they would not budge. I consulted Professor Sachs, and on my recommendation, he agreed to accept two years' salary and seemed very much pleased. Accordingly, the matter was settled on that basis.

After this was completed, Professor Sachs gave me a handsome electric clock, mounted in onyx, with a brass plate underneath the dial expressing his thanks for the help which I had given him. I was very much pleased with this, and I still have the clock in my office. During the ensuing years, I had a number of contacts with then Chief Justice Vanderbilt in connection with American Bar Association matters. He was always very cold on the occasions when our paths crossed. It is still my view that he handled the matter very badly.

G. The Littauer School

An important participation in University affairs came late in the 1930s. At that time, an alumnus of Harvard College, Lucius N. Littauer gave a substantial sum to the University. This was to be used for a building, and to establish the Littauer School of Public Administration. The old Hemmingway Gymnasium was torn down, and a substantial granite building, viewing Harvard Square, was built on land in front of Austin Hall.

A faculty was appointed for the Littauer School of Public Administration before the building was completed, and it was assigned the task of plans for the new school. My colleague, Professor Henry M. Hart, Jr. and I were appointed members of this faculty, and regular meetings were held at a round table in University Hall, with all the comment and discussion being preserved on wax cylinders. These were, I suppose, duly transcribed, but I never saw a transcript.

The other members of the faculty appointed for the Littauer School came chiefly from the Departments of Economics and Government in the faculty of Arts and Sciences. They were all quite senior, and most had already achieved distinction. Henry Hart and I were the youngest members of the faculty, but because we were lawyers, I suppose, perhaps the most articulate.

Henry developed a proposed curriculum for the Littauer School, based to a considerable extent on methods used in the Law School and the Business School. He sought to deal with actual practical problems in administration. In order to do this, "cases" and other materials would be developed through which students might consider actual problems which had arisen in public administration, and examine and consider these, with guidance by a qualified instructor, as a means which might be used in developing skills for the resolution of future problems. Most of the work on these plans was done by Henry Hart, but I made some contributions, and I supported him in the planning sessions of the Littauer faculty.

We soon found, though, that Henry's proposals were not looked on with favor by the other members of the faculty. We also found that, for the most part, they regarded the Littauer School as a source of new space and additional funds, with a convenient library, for the Departments of Economics and Government. To us, they appeared to have no interest in anything which could, in any practical sense, be called a School of Public Administration. Their interests in public administration appeared to us to be extremely theoretical, perhaps designed to give more theoretical training to teachers in the field, but with minimal scope for training for prospective careers in actual governmental administration.

At times, the differences of opinion became somewhat tense. I think I should have seen sooner the hopelessness of our proposals among other members of the faculty, and I doubtless spoke too much and too warmly.

Professor Arthur N. Holcomb, a fine person, and a distinguished member of the Government Department, complained to President Conant about me. Nothing came of that, but, in due course, Henry Hart and I resigned from the Littauer faculty. For the next twenty years or so, the Littauer building was used by the Economics and Government Departments. A rather theoretical journal was published called "Public Policy." But there was nothing, in my view, which could fairly be called a graduate school of public administration, in anything like the structure of the Medical School, the Business School, and the Law School.

One thing that I learned from this experience was that non-lawyers, at least in the academic field, are more reticent than lawyers are. In the Law School faculty, it was, I think, the general practice to speak frankly, and to put our cards on the table. Arguments were met by counter-arguments, and often a consensus could be reached. In the Littauer faculty meeting, though, discussion was much less frank. On one occasion, a faculty member from the Economics Department spoke to me as we were leaving the committee room, and said that he agreed with me almost entirely, but did not think it appropriate to speak up. In other cases, agreement was less specific, as the observation that I had made a "good presentation," and others to that effect. Of course, I wished that faculty members had been willing to state their views at the meeting. Instead, the atmosphere appeared to be that "harmony should prevail."

We had, in 1936, bought a new house in the nearby suburb of Belmont, at 36 Kenmore Road. This house is on the edge of a hill, with a fine view of Boston. It is in a considerable grove of pine trees, with a beautiful Norway Maple in front. We paid $12,500 for this house, and I did it with great trepidation, feeling that I was unduly extending myself.

By using all of my resources, I was able to pay $3,500 down, and the Cambridge Trust Company lent me the remaining $9,000 on a mortgage, at five percent interest. We "passed papers," as they say in Massachusetts, and moved into the house on June 1, 1936. Within a few days, the builder of the house came to me and offered to sell me the adjoining lot, with two beautiful maple trees, for $6,000. I had no money, but I went to my neighbor, on the other side of the vacant lot. He had no money either, but he was a veteran of World War I. Congress had just passed, over President Roosevelt's veto, a Veteran's Bonus bill. We agreed that if I could raise my share of the money, he would use his bonus payment for his share, and we would divide the lot into equal parts so that neither of us could build on it.

I then went to Professor Warren A. Seavey of the Law School faculty, a graduate of the Law School in the Class of 1904 who had offered to be of assistance to me. He immediately made a loan to me of $3,000, without security. I gave him my note for this amount, and thus my side of the lot was acquired.

About three years later, I went to Professor Seavey with my check for $3,000 plus an amount for interest during the life of the loan. He looked at the check, and threw it back to me, saying: "It's the wrong amount." So I went back to my office and made out a new check for $3,000, and handed it to him with my great thanks. His only comments was: "Glad to do it." This was, indeed, very generous on his part, and typical of his approach to the younger members of the faculty.

We greatly enjoyed the house. It was in a quiet neighborhood in Belmont, about four miles from the Law School. We still own the house, and use it on the rather rare occasions when we can get back to Massachusetts, with house sitters, usually a Harvard Law School couple, in occupancy. When we bought the house, the real estate taxes were about $450 a year. Now they are more than ten times that amount.

In October 1937, our son was born. We named him William Erwin Griswold, after my grandfather, and were very happy to have him arrive.

H. Polio

In August 1939, a disaster hit my wife, which we have all since shared, a period of over fifty years. In July 1939, I took my family by train to California in order that Harriet might visit her parents, and in order that they might see their grandchildren. After a week or so in Los Angeles, including several trips to the beach, Harriet and I went by train to San Francisco, where we visited the World's Fair. From San Francisco, she returned to Los Angeles, and I left by train to go to New York for a meeting with the American Chicle Company tax people. The last time that I ever saw Harriet walk normally was when I was on the ferry leaving for Oakland (there was no Bay Bridge at that time), and she was walking away to go by train back to Los Angeles.

When Harriet reached Los Angeles, our daughter Hope had a high fever, and was very lethargic. A doctor was called in, but he thought that it was some sort of "flu." A few days later, Hope was much better, and Harriet started back by train. The arrangement was that she would go to Chicago, that I would meet her and the children in Chicago, and take them back to Cleveland, where we would spend a few days with my parents. When I met the train in Chicago, about July 30th, she was obviously unwell. We had some time between trains, and I suggested that we take a short walk to see the city. This was more than Harriet could do, so we went by taxi to the LaSalle Street station, and waited for the New York Central train to Cleveland. When we arrived in Cleveland, Harriet had to be helped off the train. We got Harriet and the children to my parents' home in Shaker Heights. When a doctor arrived, he said that she must immediately go to the hospital. She had a lumbar puncture there, which led to a diagnosis of infantile paralysis. She was immediately transferred to the contagious wing of the Cleveland City Hospital. Her temperature was 105 degrees for five days. She was in the charge of Dr. Toomey, who handled the infantile paralysis cases in Cleveland. This was the week that World War II started in Europe. It seemed to me then that my whole world was collapsing.

Harriet was very ill for many days, and there was a short period when her vision was blurred and her speech was slurred. These impairments gave grave concern; they soon abated, but the paralysis from the waist down was complete and proved to be permanent. In due course, Harriet received massage, and was lifted in and out of a tub, in an effort to restore motion to her legs.

My mother took care of our two children, and this was a blessing. Hope went to the elementary school in Shaker Heights. Bill was just two years old, a handful for my mother. By the middle of September, I had to return to Cambridge in order to teach classes, not only to meet my Harvard obligations but so that I might provide for my family. All through the fall, I came every two weeks to Cleveland for a long weekend, travelling on a special rate which the railroads then had for a "round trip in an upper berth." On Monday morning, my train was due at South Station at 9:40 a.m. and my class would begin at 10:10 a.m. My trip out to the Law School was necessarily a hasty one, and I was usually out of breath when I entered the classroom.

During the fall, I learned that there were two schools of thought about treating poliomyelitis. The treatment advanced by the doctors at Johns Hopkins University involved complete immobility. The affected limbs were put in a cast for several months, and all motion was inhibited. On the other hand, the treatment which Harvard favored required massage and gentle movement. Thus, the people who were "expert" and experienced in the field took completely divergent views, and there was no choice for me, a layman, except to make the decision. Recognizing my total inexperience, the treatment by "complete immobility" did not appeal to me, and I decided to adopt the other approach.

In November 1939, Harriet was examined by a specialist in Cleveland. After he had seen her, I asked him what he thought,and he replied: "She will be permanently crippled for life." This was a searing experience, though the doctor was surely correct in telling me. I did not really believe it at the time, but that is the way it has been.

If it had to happen, I have always been grateful that it happened as it did. If Harriet's severe disability had been the result of an automobile accident for which I was responsible, I would never have overcome my feeling of guilt, and it would have been a heavy burden for life. If it had been the result of an accident for which she was responsible, I would have found it very hard to accept. But, as it was, it was no one's fault. Some people would find comfort by saying that it was the will of God.

But, to me, a God who would inflict such a burden on a person without fault would not be worth having. It just happened. It has been a challenge, and Harriet has met that challenge with surpassing grace and unwavering courage.

In early January 1940, I took Harriet and the children by train to Boston, and, under the supervision of Dr. William T. Green, she became a patient at the Peter Bent Brigham Hospital. She stayed there for the next sixteen months. She had massage and exercises in a Hubbard tub. The long stay was, of course, very hard on Harriet; and it was a very busy time for me. Fortunately, we had a good housekeeper who lived in our house, and watched out for the children while I was gone. I would dash home from the Law School to have dinner with the children at six o'clock each evening, and I would then drive several miles to the hospital, arriving at about 7:30, to be with Harriet. At nine o'clock, I would leave the hospital, and drive back to Belmont, and then start the task of getting ready for my next day's classes.

In due course, Harriet began the process of learning to walk again. This began with exercises in the pool at nearby Children's Hospital, since there was much less weight to move when her legs were under water.[33] After several months, braces were made for her at the Children's Hospital brace shop, and she then began to walk with two long braces and crutches. Eventually she learned how to get in and out of an armchair, and even to go up and down a short flight of steps, if there was a stair rail.

In April 1941, we brought Harriet home. In order to make things more convenient for her, we made substantial changes in the house, including a breakfast room and laundry downstairs, an elevator, and a drive to the porch at the rear of the house, so that Harriet might have a level entrance. Without a level en-

---

33. At first, the doctor who managed Peter Bent Brigham Hospital told us that Harriet could not cross the street to get to Children's Hospital unless I paid for an attendant to take her. This was because of his concern that his hospital might be liable if there was an accident on the street. I could not afford the attendant. After a few days, though, it occurred to me that there were a number of Harvard Law School graduates, prominent Boston lawyers, who were trustees of Peter Bent Brigham Hospital. I spoke to one of them, and shortly thereafter the doctor-manager of the hospital called me and said that the difficulties had been worked out and that Harriet could be taken to the Children's Hospital pool without the extra expense of a special attendant. I suppose that this was "using influence." But I think it was fully justified—just as I frequently was able to work out things in the government's interest by contacts with former students in other government offices.

trance, we would not have been able to stay in the house. This driveway ran over land which belonged to our neighbors, Mr. and Mrs. McCreary, who lived in a large house in substantial acreage to the south of our house.[34] It is hard to express adequate appreciation to the McCrearys for their generous grant to us of an easement for a driveway over a bit of this land, and refusing to accept any payment for it.

In 1946, we found a man who equipped our car with hand controls. Later in 1946, Harriet took the drivers' test and got her license as a handicapped driver. She continued to drive for the next thirty-five years, but finally let her license expire in the early 1980s.

Polio has inevitably had an impact on all of us.[35] The heaviest burden has, of course, been borne by Harriet, and she has handled it superbly. She has, within the limits of her handicap, led a normal life. She has always been a great asset for me, and has helped me constantly and in many ways. I think of the leadership she provided at the Law School, both with the wives of students, and with women students when they came in 1950, as well as in our own social life, and our life together. In the immediate post-war years, when the Law School had a large number of more than ordinarily mature students, many of them married, she was instrumental in organizing a day care center on Law School premises, so that wives of students might hold daytime jobs, and thus contribute to family support—"putting the husband through by the sweat of his frau," as the saying went.

But more than that, and over the now more than fifty years, she has carried her burden cheerfully and without complaint. Her smile is often the subject of comment. It has been my effort to help her to have as normal a life as possible. For many years, she has been responsible for the operation of our household, wherever we might be. She has made many friends, and she has given me constant support in all my various activities. We have

---

34. I made an appointment to call on Mr. McCreary at his house, in the evening. I told him that I had asked to see him so that I could ask him to sell us an easement over his property. His immediate response was negative, and I was much concerned. Then he said: "I won't sell you an easement, but I will give you one for as long as you need it." He then had a formal grant of an easement drawn up, and this was duly recorded in the Middlesex County land records.

35. We have long felt that Hope, then in her seventh year, had infantile paralysis in Los Angeles. The fever she had went away, but slowly. She had a limp in one foot thereafter, but it is no longer noticeable, and has not been a handicap.

been able to travel extensively both within and outside the United States, including trips to Australia and New Zealand, to Japan, Korea and Taiwan, to Africa, to the Soviet Union, and many trips to England. These involve a good deal of planning and some special effort, but they have all worked out well. Wherever Harriet has been, she has been a great asset.

Some of the burden has been borne, too, by our children, more than we anticipated or realized at the time. What we did was what we thought we ought to do when it was done, but, in retrospect, I think we should have done more to provide backing for the children in our unusual family circumstances. But they have come through very well. We are proud of them, and love them dearly. They have given us five grandchildren, and one great-grandchild, who will see much of the twenty-first century. I envy them. Though challenging, indeed, it is a wonderful world, full of opportunities for fun and satisfaction, even though there are, too, times of difficulty and even of despair. When times are hard, we can all think of Harriet and how well she has met the handicap which she has conquered with such determination and courage.

I. THE COMING OF THE WAR—SUMMER AT THE TREASURY

The year 1939–1940 was, of course, an unusual one at all American universities. War had been declared in Europe and a number of ships had been sunk, notably the *Athenia.* But the first several months were a "cold war." Then, in the early spring of 1940, came the invasion of the Scandinavian countries, with the participation of "Quislings." There was much talk among Americans about staying out of the war, as there was in the 1916 Presidential Campaign by Woodrow Wilson. However, many persons spoke on the other side. "Protect America by Aiding the Allies" was one of the slogans. President Conant of Harvard was active in this movement.

For the most part, though, classes went on more or less normally at the Law School. After January, 1940, I had my family back in Massachusetts. It was a busy and difficult time for me, but there was less strain than there was in the fall of 1939, when I was commuting to Cleveland every other weekend. I bought a new car in this period, a Buick, for which I paid less than a thousand dollars, with no expectation that I would be keeping it for nearly ten years.

Everything changed in the early summer of 1940. The Germans broke through the Maginot Line, and reached Paris.

They also drove the British out of northern Europe, and we heard detailed reports about the miracle at Dunkerque. This was followed by the Battle of Britain, one of the first turning points in the War.

These developments, of course, had a great impact on the Law School and, generally, all over the country.[36] In the fall of 1940, Congress enacted the Selective Service Act for one year, and then extended it in 1941 by a margin of only one vote. There were still many who felt that we could stay out of the War and that our chances for staying out would be better if we did not take major steps for preparedness. When Congress enacted the Selective Service Act, there was a general registration at the Law School, and faculty members were asked to be registrars. It is my recollection that Joseph P. Kennedy, Jr. was one of the students whom I registered. This was not, however, a step in his being a casualty of the War. He was not drafted, but entered the Marines, and lost his life while piloting a Marine plane.

After the attack on Pearl Harbor, on December 7, 1941, the situation, of course, changed. Like many other persons, I well remember when I heard the news of Pearl Harbor. It was a Sunday afternoon, about 2:30 p.m. and I was listening, as I usually did on Sunday afternoons, to the broadcast of the concert of the New York Philharmonic. The broadcast was interrupted by an announcement of the attack on Pearl Harbor, with few details at that time. I knew, though, that the world had changed, that it was the end of an era, and I was greatly troubled as to what my role could and should be, particularly in view of my family circumstances.

The Law School continued in operation, but minds and thoughts were elsewhere. Numerous students left to join the Armed Services. It was possible, in some instances, for law school students to get a commission, and many took steps to bring that about—while others waited to be drafted. My two faculty colleagues, W. Barton Leach and A. James Casner, sought to get commissions in the Navy. Both were turned down, Leach because he was too tall, and Casner because he was too short. Both eventually did receive commissions in the Air Corps, and

---

36. During 1940, I kept on working more or less normally. I wrote a substantial article dealing with the effect which should be given to Treasury Regulations in the interpretation and application of tax statutes. This was published under the title of "Summary of the Regulations Problem," 54 Harv.L.Rev. 398 (1941). The article was cited a number of times by the courts, and made, I believe, an appreciable contribution towards solving some difficult problems.

had distinguished careers in military service. Both became colonels in the Air Corps, with extensive foreign service, and Leach stayed on in the Air Corps Reserve after the close of the War, and became a brigadier general.

The faculty held many meetings to determine what should be done with students who left the School before the final examinations in June. All of those in good standing were given credit for the full year regardless of the time when they left, and all were guaranteed reentry to the School when they should be free from military service. Perhaps one-fourth of the students left during the spring of 1942. The rest concluded that they should get as much of their education as possible, and await their call in due course.

In the summer of 1942, I went to Washington to work as an aide to Randolph Paul, who was then General Counsel of the Treasury Department. I returned to Belmont each weekend, and Harriet got along with the aid of Myrtle Saunders, who lived in the house with her, and kept house. Our daughter Hope was nine-and-a-half years old that summer. She went to a day camp, five days a week. Our son Bill was approaching five years of age, and was very active. In the summer of 1943, Hope went by train to the Bourbon farm for a month, and in 1944 she took her brother Bill with her by train to Bourbon. It was very good of my uncle Lewis and Aunt Eleanor to take them in and to give them some of the same experience I had as a boy.

In Washington, I was first assigned an office in the Washington Building at the northeast corner of Fifteenth and G Streets, N.W., diagonally across from the old Treasury Building. (This was, in fact, about fifty yards from where my office has been in the latter years of my work with Jones, Day, Reavis & Pogue in Washington.) I had to cross Fifteenth Street several times a day in getting back and forth between my office and the Treasury Building. The traffic then was heavy, with streetcars in addition to automobiles. As usual, it was hot in Washington and most of the offices had no air conditioning. After a few weeks, an office in the Treasury Building was found for me.

At first, my work consisted largely of handling Mr. Paul's mail, which was voluminous. I drafted answers to numerous letters which came in for him. He accepted about nine out of ten of my drafts, and in the remaining cases he had information or ideas which he noted in longhand on the drafts, and I prepared new drafts.

Before long, I became accepted as part of the group of younger lawyers in the Office of the Tax Legislative Counsel and the Office of Tax Analysis. It was here that I first met Roger Traynor, Stanley Surrey,[37] Louis Eisenstein, and others.[38] Before long, I was working rather intensively on various aspects of the bill then before Congress, which later became the Revenue Act of 1942—the greatly enlarged wartime Revenue Act. I was regularly assigned to attend hearings before the Senate Finance Committee, where the bill was then pending, and to participate with members of the staff of the Joint Committee on Internal Revenue Taxation, and others, on the drafting of various provisions of the bill, reporting back, of course, to Mr. Paul and other officers of the Treasury.[39]

One of the provisions which was enacted into the law was the allowance, for the first time, of a deduction for extraordinary medical expenses.[40] This was not my proposal. It was Mr. Paul's idea, though he knew about the problem I had encountered in connection with medical expenses for my wife.[41] Mr. Paul had another thought—a thoroughly sound one—in which he had reason to be interested. This was the allowance of a deduction

---

37. My first awareness of Stanley Surrey came in 1933, when he published an article shortly after his graduation from Columbia Law School. See Surrey, "Assignments of Income and Related Devices," 33 Col.L.Rev. 791 (1933). I was then in the Solicitor General's Office working on these problems, and I was much impressed by Surrey's analysis. That was the beginning of a long professional friendship and association. Surrey was, in my opinion, the leading tax scholar of our generation.

38. It was some member of this group who first gave me a guarded warning about Harry Dexter White, and suggested that I avoid any close contact with him. This proved easy to do, as our respective areas of work did not appreciably overlap.

39. My duties involved the preparation of memoranda for Mr. Paul to present to Secretary Morgenthau. The rule imposed by Mr. Morgenthau was that no memorandum prepared for his eyes could be more than one page long. Most tax problems are inherently complex, and meeting the Morgenthau requirement took a bit of doing and the preparation of numerous drafts, each of which had to be completely retyped, as there were no word-processors in those days.

40. Section 23(x) of the Internal Revenue Code of 1934, added by the Revenue Act of 1942, section 127. It is now found, somewhat limited, in section 213 of the Internal Revenue Code.

41. After my wife came home from the hospital in 1941, our medical expenses were not very high. Consequently, I received no benefit from the medical expense deduction (which did not become effective until 1942) except in connection with the estate of my father, who died in 1960, when his final medical expense reached an amount which allowed a deduction to his estate.

for alimony paid. He felt that the proposal with respect to alimony would be better received if it was accompanied by a proposal for a deduction for medical expenses. The two were recommended to Congress and were enacted as part of the Revenue Act of 1942.[42] These deductions were especially appropriate at this time as a means of preventing undue burden from the very large increase in tax rates provided by the 1942 Act.

I also worked on a section of the Revenue Act of 1942 which subjected to the Federal Estate Tax all community property over which the decedent had power of control.[43] The taxation of community property had long been a source of difficulty. The Supreme Court decided in *Poe v. Seaborn*,[44] that community property income was taxable half to the husband and half to the wife, regardless of who actually earned the income. Because the income tax rates were progressive, this provided a substantial advantage to taxpayers in the eight community property States, who could divide the husband's earned income and pay tax on each half at the relatively lower rates. As a result, a number of other States, including Oklahoma, Oregon, Nebraska, Michigan, and Pennsylvania, adopted community property laws.

Efforts to change the rules with respect to the taxation of community property were generally unsuccessful, as the Representatives and Senators from the community property States, including the Chairman of the Senate Finance Committee, stood four-square in support of their benefit. However, they overlooked the significance of the Estate Tax provision which was enacted in 1942. This subjected community property to the Estate Tax on a basis which was analogous to the tax applied to jointly held property in the States following the common law system.[45]

This Estate Tax provision proved to be the means by which the income tax problem was finally resolved. In 1948, Congress repealed the provision of the 1942 law which treated community property like jointly held property for Estate Tax purposes, and, at the same time, adopted the "split income" solution to the

---

42. The alimony provision was added by section 120 of the Revenue Act of 1942. It is now found in section 215 of the Internal Revenue Code.

43. This was section 402(b) of the Revenue Act of 1942, which added section 811(e)(2) to the Internal Revenue Code.

44. 282 U.S. 101 (1930).

45. This provision of the Estate Tax was held to be constitutional in Fernandez v. Wiener, 326 U.S. 340 (1945) (Louisiana), and United States v. Rompel, 326 U.S. 367 (1945) (Texas).

family income problem, which is still, in substance, in effect. Under this provision, husbands and wives in all States may elect to file a joint return on which the tax is computed essentially as twice the tax on half the income. The tax benefits of the community property system were extended to married persons in the entire country, thus ending the discrimination which existed for many years in favor of residents of the community property States.[46] Thus, in the long run, the problems in our tax laws with respect to family income and property were eventually worked out.[47]

During the summer of 1942, I also made speeches on behalf of the Treasury before lawyers' groups, discussing current developments in the tax law. In particular, I spoke in Detroit in August, 1942 before the Tax Section of the American Bar Association.[48]

During the latter part of the summer of 1942, I was considerably concerned about what I should do. I wanted to make some contribution to the war effort, and felt that my experience at the Treasury had been useful. On the other hand, I could not disregard my responsibilities in Belmont, and it became clear that there was more that I should be doing there. I thought a good deal about moving the family to Washington, but could not find a way to work this out. For example, Harriet was not able to do shopping. We would have needed housing and well-qualified help, which was hard to find in Washington in 1942. Harriet put no pressure on me by word or action, and always made it clear that the decision was for me, and that I should do whatever I felt I should do. With much misgiving, I decided that I should return to Belmont, and continue with my work on the Harvard Law School faculty.[49]

---

46. For a full discussion, see Surrey, "Federal Taxation of the Family—the Revenue Act of 1948," 61 Harv.L.Rev. 1097 (1948).

47. Another provision added to the Estate Tax law in 1942 broadened the tax on property over which the decedent had a general power of appointment, whether the power was exercised or not. Section 403 of the Revenue Act of 1942, adding section 811(f) to the Internal Revenue Code. This followed the general lines proposed in my article on "Powers of Appointment and the Federal Estate Tax," 52 Harv.L.Rev. 929 (1939).

48. Later in the year, in early December, 1942 after my return to Harvard, I spoke at a tax gathering in Los Angeles, by special request of Mr. Paul.

49. Based largely on my work in Washington, I wrote an article which was published in the November, 1942 issue of the Harvard Law

J. *Betts v. Brady*—and *Gideon*

One event which occurred during the summer of 1942 is worthy of mention. On June 1, 1942, the Supreme Court decided the case of *Betts v. Brady*.[50] This case involved a man who had been convicted of robbery in a Maryland state court. He requested counsel at his trial, but was advised by the judge that it was not the practice "to appoint counsel for indigent defendants save in prosecutions for murder and rape." The defendant received an eight-year sentence. While serving this sentence, he sought *habeas corpus* from a Maryland judge, contending that the refusal to give him counsel had violated the Fourteenth Amendment of the Federal Constitution. *Habeas corpus* was denied, and he sought review from the Supreme Court.

This case raised the question of the interrelation between the Fourteenth Amendment and the Federal Bill of Rights found in the first ten Amendments. The Supreme Court, in an opinion by Justice Roberts, held that "appointment of counsel is not a fundamental right, essential to a fair trial."[51] Many persons, including myself, were surprised at this decision, which was reached over the dissent of three members of the Court.

During the summer, I was approached by Benjamin V. Cohen (of Corcoran–Cohen fame) and asked if I would join with him in a letter to the New York Times, contending that the *Betts* case was wrong. I readily agreed. Mr. Cohen drafted most of the letter, but I participated, making suggestions as to phraseology, and adding what I felt to be a strong conclusion, which read as follows:

> Yet at a critical period in world history, Betts v. Brady dangerously tilts the scales against the safeguarding of one of the most precious rights of man. For in a free world no man should be condemned to penal servitude for years without having the right to counsel to defend him. The right to counsel, for the poor as well as the rich, is an indispensable safeguard of freedom and justice under law.

This letter was printed in the Sunday edition of the New York Times for August 2, 1942,[52] and a number of people made

Review. This was "A Plan for the Coordination of the Income, Estate and Gift Tax Provisions With Respect to Trusts and Other Transfers," 56 Harv.L.Rev. 337 (1942).

50. 316 U.S. 455 (1942).

51. 316 U.S. at 471.

52. Section 5, page 6.

favorable comments on it. The sequel did not come for more than twenty years, when the case of *Gideon v. Wainwright*,[53] came before the Court. This, too, involved a conviction in a state court for breaking and entering a poolroom, which was a felony under Florida law. At the beginning of the trial, the defendant applied for counsel, but this was refused, and the Florida Supreme Court denied review in *habeas corpus*.

The defendant, Gideon, then wrote his own petition for certiorari in the Supreme Court of the United States, in longhand. The petition was granted, and the Court appointed attorney Abe Fortas to represent the petitioner. Mr. Fortas made reference to the Cohen–Griswold letter at the conclusion of his brief.[54] In addition, to the surprise of many, Attorneys General from twenty-three states joined in a brief supporting Gideon's petition. This group was led by Edward J. McCormack, Jr., the Attorney General of Massachusetts. Two of my colleagues at Harvard, Professors Mark DeWolfe Howe and Roger Fisher, worked with me in helping with the drafting of this brief, which was then joined by the other Attorneys General.[55]

This brief called for the overruling of *Betts v. Brady*, and this is what the Court did in its opinion in *Gideon v. Wainwright*, decided March 18, 1963. This was a unanimous decision, with three concurring opinions. The *Gideon* case is surely a landmark in our law of criminal procedure. It was helped by the development of thought with the passage of time, but I know of no one who now thinks that the ultimate result is unsound, either as a matter of "justice," or, in the more technical sense of the proper construction of the Constitution.

K. Return to Cambridge

The number of students at the School had dropped drastically. At the same time, though, the number of faculty members remaining in Cambridge was also reduced. Several, like Professors Leach and Casner had entered military services. Professor Lon L. Fuller was working in labor law at the firm of Ropes, Gray, Best, Coolidge & Rugg in Boston. Professsor Henry Hart was working for the Office of Price Administration in Washington, and Dean James M. Landis was in Washington, first as head of the Office of Civilian Defense, and later as a special representative in the Middle East. Professor Milton Katz was with the

---

53. 372 U.S. 335 (1963).

54. See A. Lewis, Gideon's Trumpet (New York: 1969) 144.

55. See Lewis, *supra*, at 154–55.

Office of Strategic Services. Professor Edmund M. Morgan was the Acting Dean of the Law School, and he urged me to return to Cambridge.

Throughout the war years, I never communicated with my Draft Board, and they never communicated with me. I never asked for an exemption. I have assumed that it was very likely that Acting Dean Morgan communicated with them, and told them the facts of my situation. However, I never had any knowledge of such intervention, if it did occur.

I was always prepared to do whatever I was assigned to do. I would not have claimed to be a conscientious objector, because I was not, especially with respect to that particular war, which seemed to me to have been brought on by as evil a figure as we have known in modern history. I do not think that I was influenced appreciably by my Quaker background, particularly as exemplified by my mother and her father. I honored those who went to war, and was grateful for their contribution.

In the early fall of 1944, I was summoned to Washington by a New York lawyer of my acquaintance, who was then in uniform, heading up a group which was engaged in government contract work. By this time, the Government had begun to terminate contracts, and there were many difficult legal and practical questions involved.

I was asked to join the staff of that office, and I was told that I would be a lieutenant commander in the Navy. I went so far as to go to an office in downtown Washington for a preliminary physical examination. Then I returned to Cambridge, and, within a few days, wrote that I did not feel that I should accept the appointment. I did not want to be in uniform when I was performing essentially civilian work. It seemed to me that this would be, in a sense, acting under false pretenses. So, I continued in Cambridge, as I had done since I returned there in 1942. As a consequence, I have never been in military service, and, in a very real sense, I have not carried my share of the burden. As a matter of fact, as far as I know, no one of my forbears has served in the military for the past 200 years, back to the time of Ensign Nathaniel Griswold, who drove a mule team carrying ammunition during the French and Indian War. It is nothing to be proud of. It is a fact. It has troubled me, but the decisions were difficult. They seemed right to me when I made them, and I still feel that the circumstances which confronted me made any other decision hard to sustain.

During the war years, it was quite a problem to keep the Harvard Law Review in operation. There was a fairly good supply of Articles, but there were few students available for the production of student work. As a result, faculty members wrote a number of Notes, and I wrote several of these.[56] I also wrote a substantial article on "The Need for a Court of Tax Appeals." [57] This raised an important question whose time had come, but it still has not been dealt with. If the proposal had been adopted, it would have made an important contribution towards speed and certainty in the resolution of tax problems. Generally speaking, the tax bar does not like the plan, because the bar thrives on uncertainty. The question has been raised again a number of times over the intervening period, now approaching fifty years. Eventually, something along the lines proposed will have to come as it makes no sense to have tax cases decided by thirteen different courts of appeals, with no effective guidance on most questions from the Supreme Court. And the Supreme Court simply cannot resolve all of the tax controversies in a country of 250 million people. But I think it is unlikely that I will see the day when what obviously should be done (as I see it) will actually be adopted into our court structure.

Thus, I spent the war years in Cambridge and Belmont, teaching very small classes, often in fields which I had never taught before, such as Administrative Law. The total enrollment of the School fell to less than one hundred students, while the pre-war enrollment had been around sixteen hundred. By 1944, a few students came back who, for some reason or another, had been released from military service.[58]

---

56. These included "The Statute of Limitations in Gift Tax Cases," 57 Harv.L.Rev. 906 (1944); "Finality of Administrative Settlements in Tax Cases," 57 Harv.L.Rev. 912 (1944); "The Tax Treatment of Employers' Contribution to Pension Funds," 57 Harv.L.Rev. 247 (1944).

57. 57 Harv.L.Rev. 1153 (1944).

58. One interesting assignment which came to me during the War years was my election, as a policyholder-trustee, to the Board of Trustees of the Teachers Insurance and Annuity Association. This is a descendent of the pension system which was established by Andrew Carnegie early in the twentieth century, and it has performed a very important service in providing "portable" deferred annuities (or future pensions) for college teachers throughout the United States and Canada. I was on the Board for four years, from 1941 to 1945, and was a member of the Board when its total funds reached $100 million. Now, the total assets of TIAA and of its affiliate CREF (College Retirement Equity Fund) are around $80 billion.

In 1940, as a policyholder, I had written to Henry James, the President of TIAA, and questioned whether policyholder trustees had any real

The buildings of the Law School were largely taken over by war-related activities. The north end of the reading room in Langdell Hall Library was completely blacked out, and was used, with the aid of projectors, in training military aviators for night flying. The gymnasium (which belonged to the Faculty of Arts and Sciences rather than the Law School) was completely turned over to the "Underwater Sound Laboratory," though we understood that the activity actually carried on related to radar. The building was connected by a bridge to Austin Hall, a portion of which was used in this activity.

The war years were tense ones, even for those who stayed at home. For a long time, each day's news made things seem worse and worse. There was the relentless progress of the Germans through the Balkans and Greece and into Africa. The German attack on the Soviet Union raised some hopes, but as the Nazi troops proceeded further and further east, and reached the outskirts of Leningrad and Moscow, these hopes seemed doomed to failure. The steadfastness and oratory of Churchill, and the wily but effective leadership of Franklin Roosevelt were inspiring, and the unity of the nation in support of the war was striking. Things began to get better in the Pacific.

There were many rumors about some sort of activity in Tennessee. I remember going to Nashville to make a commencement speech at Vanderbilt University. I was asked if I knew what was going on at Knoxville. The questioner said: "Great trainloads of material go into the huge plant there, and nothing ever comes out." In addition, I had heard something about the Manhattan Project, by name only, since my brother, who was then working at Fenn College in Cleveland, was engaged in recruiting large numbers of secretarial and other people for work there, but he had no idea what the project was. Similarly, I heard about activities at Los Alamos in New Mexico. And I had some correspondence where the return address was a post-office box in Santa Fe, which I assumed was the address used for the Los Alamos project. I had known something about Los Alamos

---

influence. Mr. James graciously replied that policyholder-trustees played an important role in TIAA. A recently-published history of TIAA–CREF, written by William C. Greenough (who joined the staff of TIAA while I was a trustee, and later became President and Chairman, as well as historian), includes the following passage:

Dr. Griswold was subsequently selected by the policyholders for the Board. I can testify that there was no lack of effective participation on his part in the Board deliberations.

Greenough, It's My Retirement Money (Homewood, Il.: 1990) 266.

before, since a second cousin of mine had gone in the 1930s to the ranch school which was located there, and we had driven past the hill there on the return trip from Colorado in 1936. I had heard something theoretically about fission, but I never supposed that it could be done on a large scale. I thought that if it was done, it would be on a laboratory basis. I had no idea that the work would involve a huge plant, such as the one at Oak Ridge near Knoxville.

In the early summer of 1945, there was a forthcoming vacancy in the Presidency of Oberlin College. I was appointed Chairman of the Committee of the Board of Trustees to make a recommendation for filling this vacancy. I asked the members of the Committee to consult people, and to seek suggestions for the Committee's consideration. As a part of this process, I made an appointment to see President Conant of Harvard University. A few days before the date fixed, I was called by President Conant's secretary and told that he would be unable to keep the appointment. She asked me to call again to fix a new date. I later learned that the reason why he was away from Cambridge was because he was an observer at the first atomic explosion in New Mexico. We did not know the significance of any of these things until the bomb was dropped on Hiroshima in August, 1945.

In the meantime, D Day had occurred in Europe, and the Allied Forces proceeded to cross France and into Germany, with the eventual surrender of the German armies. On the day of the armistice, there was a large but quiet celebration in Harvard Yard. Thousands of people connected with the University walked there, and for the most part, simply gathered. There was some speaking, but I do not remember now who spoke, or what was said. The war in Europe had lasted for six years, and the United States had been directly involved for three-and-a-half years. Never, I suppose, had so many people worked so effectively to bring about a result as that which culminated in May and September, 1945.

By January, 1946, substantial numbers of students had been released from the Armed Forces, and were returning to the Law School. The faculty voted to adopt a new program for the immediate post-war years. Under this program, the School operated through the year, without break. There were three terms of four months each, beginning in February, and students were required to attend for a total of seven terms, with appropriate allowance for studies completed prior to military service.

Dean Landis returned to the School late in 1945. He had some responsibilities with respect to the Civil Aeronautics Board, and it was not clear that the School was his primary interest. Nevertheless, we expected that he would soon be devoting full-time to his decanal duties and that he would lead the School during the important and somewhat difficult post-war period.

During this time, I received two offers of deanships. One was at the University of Pittsburgh Law School, made at the suggestion of John G. Buchanan, a graduate of the Harvard Law School, who was a trustee at Pittsburgh. I had no particular desire to be a dean, and I was not tempted by this invitation. Another offer came from Stanford University. I gave this serious consideration, not only because of the reputation of the school, but also because my wife was a Stanford graduate. My chief interest, though, was that the climate at Palo Alto, and the one-story houses common there would make things easier for her. As usual, she said it was up to me, and after a week or so of thinking about it, I decided to stay at Harvard.

CHAPTER VI

Now A Dean

A. ENTRY ON NEW TASKS

Late in April or early May, 1946, we heard the news that Dean Landis had resigned in order to devote full-time to his work in Washington. We speculated a good deal about who his successor might be. President Conant chose to act promptly. In a few days, I received a request to come to the president's office. President Conant was a great scholar, a fine person, and an able administrator. Without much preliminary, he said to me: "I have asked you to come here in order to see whether you would accept an appointment as Dean of the Harvard Law School for five years."

Of course I heard the last three words. I did not want to seem abrupt, so I asked if I might think about it overnight. This was agreeable. I returned the next day, and said: "I greatly appreciate the suggestion, and I understand why you have put it that way. However, in my view, the best job in American legal education is being a professor at the Harvard Law School. I would rather do that than break my career by a five-year interval as Dean." I had in mind the fact that both Professor Williston and Professor Scott, two great teachers, had declined the opportunity to be Dean, and also the fact that being Dean for five years meant that you started out as a "lame duck," and that you would be viewed as an errand boy and doer of odd jobs during the five-year period. I regarded being Dean of the Harvard Law School as a career—always at the pleasure of the Harvard Corporation—but with time for planning and exercising effective leadership, which could not really be done on a short-term basis.

President Conant thanked me, and I departed. I was not sure whether the five-year concept came from him, or whether it had been advanced by one or more members of the Harvard Corporation, and he had thought it wise to proceed on that basis. About a week later, I was visited by a distinguished retired member of the Harvard economics faculty with connection at the Business School, and urged to accept the five-year appointment. But I was content with my position, and indicated that I would not change.

After another week, I was called again to the president's office. President Conant said: "Would you accept appointment as Dean of the Harvard Law School?" I replied that I would accept, and would look on the opportunity with enthusiasm. I then left the president's office. I knew that the actual appointment could only be made by the Harvard Corporation, and that this would have to be confirmed by the Board of Overseers, which would meet on Commencement Day. In the meantime, I was not free to make any disclosure.

On the morning of Commencement Day, in early June, I was advised that the appointment had been confirmed. Harriet and I were asked to lunch that day at the Harvard Club in Boston by the lawyer whom I admired perhaps most of all, John Lord O'Brien, who was in Cambridge for the Fiftieth Reunion of his Harvard College Class of 1896. The lunch was a quiet one, but it was a great satisfaction to have Mr. O'Brien's clear endorsement.

After the newspapers got the word, reporters and photographers came to our house in Belmont. Our son Bill was then eight years old, and he advised The Globe reporter: "You will not like my father. He doesn't read The Globe." Nevertheless, The Globe published a nice article, with a family picture.

Jim Landis had left Cambridge about the 10th of May, so there was little opportunity for interchange with him. I knew nothing about the details of Harvard's administrative operations. I did know that we had a summer term beginning early in July. After my appointment was announced, I moved to the Dean's office, even though my appointment was actually effective only on July 1, 1946. As things turned out, the Dean's office was not in chaos; it was simply empty. There was no staff there, no one who could provide any transitional advice. Moreover, I found that virtually no arrangements had been made for visiting faculty for the summer term, which was going to begin in about three weeks.

I hastily brought together the appointments committee of the faculty, and we canvassed possible people to be invited to come

to Cambridge as visitors for the summer. We soon compiled a
list of ten or more possibilities. I then got on the telephone and
began giving invitations. In many cases, the persons consulted
had already made commitments for the summer. After a great
many calls, I was able to put together a very fine group. These
included Merton L. Ferson, of the University of Cincinnati Law
School, Merrill I. Schnebley, of the University of Illinois Law
School, and (a fine idea of my own) Murray L. Seasongood, of
Cincinnati, former mayor of that city, and active in the Good
Government movement there. He was then about seventy years
old, but he agreed to come and give a course in Municipal
Corporations. With the assistance of these people, and others,
and with the participation of several members of the regular
Harvard Law School faculty, we organized an excellent program.

In the course of this work, I found that I badly needed an
administrative assistant. Jim Landis had told me one time when
he came back to Cambridge for a weekend that "There is only
one good girl on the staff." This turned out to be Mary Conlan, a
graduate of Boston University, who was then working in the
Admissions Office. I asked her to be Administrative Assistant to
the Dean. With some hesitation, she accepted,[1] and she thus
became the first of a remarkable group of women who contributed mightily to my administration as Dean. The second of these
was Janet Murphy, who came, after graduation from Radcliffe
College, to be my second secretary, in February, 1947.[2] I soon
found that Julie Grenier, who was working in the Office of the
Secretary of the Law School, was an extraordinary person, and I
unloaded many things on her, including general oversight of Law
School publications, and, eventually, of the *Harvard Law Bulletin,* which I established as the Law School magazine.

Later, Mrs. Elisabeth Wahlen joined the staff, and she proved
to be invaluable in many ways. She was first brought to my
attention by Antonia Chayes, the wife of Professor Abraham

---

1. She had previously worked as secretary to Dumas Malone, at that
time director of the Harvard University Press, and as a faculty secretary
at the Law School. She continued to hold the demanding post of
Administrative Assistant to the Dean (which meant Business Manager
and Staff Director) through my twenty-one years as dean, and through
the deanships of Derek Bok and Albert M. Sacks, until she retired in
1978.

2. Barbara Livingston became my principal secretary in 1946. She
later married a Law School graduate, John Hally, and resigned in 1952
when her child was coming. At that time, Janet Murphy became my
principal secretary. The second position was then filled by a succession
of fine women, mostly student wives.

Chayes. Mrs. Wahlen wanted only a half-time job, since she wanted to have freedom for her responsibilities at home. However, I soon found that she was working on virtually a full-time basis. I said to her that I wanted to change the arrangement, and that it was unfair to her to have her working full-time and yet being paid for only half-time work. She insisted that she only wanted a half-time job and she would not accept more than half-time pay. In due course, though, this arrangement was changed, so that she received full-time pay (which was not very much in those days) in return for which she worked as a general manager, largely in the fund-raising area, and regularly devoted more than full-time to the job.

During the course of the summer Harriet and I took a two weeks' vacation, spending it at the Crawford House in Crawford Notch, New Hampshire, a location which I had first visited in 1919 when I was on a mountain-climbing trip as a boy at Camp Pemigewassett. I played golf there, on its easy nine-hole course. And I did some climbing in the nearby mountains there, including one trip up the Crawford Path to the top of Mount Washington, my last time there.

We later returned to the Crawford House several times in following years. It was a fine old place, with a rich local history, but the times passed it by. It was torn down about 1975, and its beautiful notch area now seems somewhat despoiled.

During the summer of 1946, President Conant was away on vacation. Because of the needs of returning veterans, the Law School was extremely busy. There were a number of appointments which had to be made, including the ones to which I have referred above, and also new appointments to become effective in the fall. The routine at Harvard was that appointments were made by the Corporation. The deans had no authority except to recommend, and I found that the Comptroller would not pay a salary until there was a Corporation vote. I inquired of the Secretary to the Corporation and was advised that the Corporation would not meet again until September. When I consulted the Comptroller to see if some sort of arrangement could be made, I was advised to tell our summer appointees that they could expect to receive their salaries early in October. This did not strike me as a good way to handle the situation, so I wrote a letter to President Conant asking him "if some sort of *modus vivendi*" could be made to help us get through the summer. The reply came by telephone from the president's secretary, and it showed no sympathy for my predicament. I was not ready to give up though. I found some discretionary accounts which had balances in them in favor of the Law School, and I finally persuaded the Comptroller to make the salary payments, charging them against these discretionary accounts, to be reimbursed when the Corporation actually voted the appointments.

I undertook the task as dean with some apprehension. I had a rather exalted idea of the role and responsibility of the Harvard Law School, and wondered if I had the scholarly competence, the managerial skill, and personality to be an effective leader. I was aware of the fact that the job had, in one way or another, broken the last three persons who held it. Dean Ezra Ripley Thayer had committed suicide by throwing himself into the Charles River in 1915. Dean Roscoe Pound had brought about a bitter division in the faculty during his final years. And Dean James M. Landis, though of great ability, had personality problems which brought about his resignation.

I was quite sure that my scholarly ability did not measure up to the standard reached by Dean Pound. I knew that I had an analytical mind which could divide and subdivide problems into their component parts. But I knew, too, that I had no great theoretical or philosophical capacity. My lowest marks in college were in Professor McClennen's philosophy course, and my experience in mathematics led me to think that my imagination and capability to synthesize were not too great. As I saw myself, I was a pragmatist and not a theoretician.[3]

I had another concern, too. I did not feel confident in my ability to "get along" with people, to work with them smoothly and effectively, and without raising unintended but adverse reactions. I have never been gregarious, or a "good mixer." I tend to be reserved, and some people think me distant and aloof. I tend, too, to "speak my mind," and to speak in words which are sometimes perceived to be stronger than I intend. I am often too quick in my responses, and this may be taken as a form of arrogance. I have worked with these things all my life, but have never been able to get them under a full measure of control.

As Dean, I knew that I would constantly be working with people—faculty, students, staff, alumni, and general public—and these contacts would provide plenty of opportunities for misunderstanding. As a matter of fact, things worked out fairly well—

---

3. It has been said that the English legal profession glories in its aversion to theory. P. Atiyah, Pragmatism and Theory (London: 1987) 3. This is true, too, of American lawyers, with few exceptions. Indeed, it can perhaps be said to be true of America, where the "make do" approach of the immigrant and pioneer still has great impact. See also R. Posner, "What Has Pragmatism to Offer Law?" 63 So. Calif.L.Rev. 1653 (1990).

or, to put it another way, people were very tolerant of me. I adopted certain practices that I hoped would help. For example, I never summoned a faculty member to come to my office. I always went to the office of any faculty member with whom I wanted to talk. If he was not there, I left a note saying, in summary form, that I had been there, with the date and time, and asking him to let me know when he was available. Similarly, I never had office hours. I would always see anyone, faculty, student, or anyone else, if I was in my office and did not have anyone with me at the time.[4]

I tried, too, to recognize accomplishments of the faculty. If a member published an article, or made a speech which appeared in the paper, I would send a note to him; and this would be more than a formal note. It would undertake to discuss some of the points made, or give my reaction to the article. I also undertook to answer my correspondence promptly. I did this partly in self-defense, since I found that the volume of mail was so heavy that I would be overwhelmed if I let it accumulate on my desk.

All of these things proved worthwhile. At any rate, and considerably to my surprise, I had good relations with most of the faculty and alumni, and where I fell down the default was not too great. As far as I could tell, there was no schism in the faculty about me during the twenty-one years I was dean, though the level of enthusiasm for me differed from one member to another. I also enjoyed my contacts with faculty members, and was proud of their achievements—though concerned about the failure of some of them to produce scholarly writing. Failure to produce scholarly work is, indeed, one of the significant problems of the academic world. But the overall production at the Harvard Law School remained high.[5]

---

4. I must say that I am rather shocked when I go to Cambridge in recent years, and see notices outside faculty doors which read: "Office hours: Tuesdays from 2-3 p.m."

5. There was one situation, in particular, which gave me great concern. In the late 1950s, Professors Henry M. Hart, Jr. and Albert M. Sacks worked together on a very fine book for classroom use which was called "The Legal Process." I thought that it was probably the most significant contribution to legal education in the twentieth century. However, it never got beyond mimeographed sheets. The production of this material had to be done at the Law School. The materials came to be used at some other law schools, and the Harvard Law School had to take care of running off the mimeographed sheets, packing, shipping, and billing. I urged my colleagues to seek a regular publisher, telling them that any one of several publishers would be delighted to put out the book. However, they said: "We are not yet ready. The work is not

One of the things that I learned at Camp Pemigewassett was "Never turn back after you start to steal second base." So I turned to the tasks at hand, and tried not to be overwhelmed by the multiplicity of daily details. The immediate tasks were immense, and there was little opportunity for detailed planning.[6] A new term opened in early July, a few days after my appointment became effective, and I spoke to the entering first-year group. We soon had over 2,200 students in the School, and were operating twelve months a year. Some temporary housing structures—formerly a military barracks in Maine—were moved down to Cambridge and placed on the former tennis courts of Jarvis Field, adjacent to the Law School, in order to provide some housing for the large number of married couples who, in the post-war period, were at the School. I knew that this meant the end of the tennis courts, and it gave me an idea for future permanent housing for students, an idea which I put in the back of my mind for future use.

At that time, the School had no dining facilities and virtually no housing for students except for the temporary structures which had been moved to Cambridge. We did have a residence on Massachusetts Avenue, known as Kendall House, with a few rooms for students upstairs. With my wife's assistance, we opened up a dining facility in the ground floor of Kendall House. I use the word "facility" because this was in no real sense a dining room. The students brought their lunches in a paper bag.

---

finished. There are many details which we have not resolved." I said, in response: "Why don't you put it out as a Tentative Edition? Then let people use it and criticize it, while you continue to work on it. This will give you useful comments and new ideas, and you can then incorporate what you learn into a finally published book." However, this was to no avail. Both Professor Hart and Professor Sacks have died, and the book has never been published. This has, in my view, been a great loss to legal education.

6. When I became dean, we were confronted by a flood of applications for admission from returning veterans. During the war, Professor Warren A. Seavey, a veteran of World War I, had been appointed "Advisor for Veterans." Many letters came in from men serving in the armed forces all over the world, and Seavey would write individual responses, usually in long-hand. Someone would write in saying that he was in a foxhole at Iwo Jima, that things were quiet, and he was whiling away the time by thinking of his future in a more rational world. Seavey would send a kindly response, saying "You are just the sort of man we are looking for. When you are released from the service, come to Cambridge, and we will admit you." There were several hundred letters of this generous tone. We honored all of them. We called them "Seavey estoppels."

Eventually, soup, sandwiches, coffee and milk were made available at a small charge. Student wives, one of whom was Marrietta Hansen, were hired to take charge of the operation. At this time, too, I found that there were rooms in the basement of Walter Hastings Hall—half above ground, with windows opening outdoors—which were stacked full of broken furniture. I arranged to have the furniture removed, to have the rooms cleaned up, and rudimentary plumbing facilities provided. This was the place where my wife established the day-care center for small children of students, with the assistance of students' wives, and a few wives of faculty members.

In the spring of 1946, a weekly newspaper for the Law School was begun by a group of students. It was called the Harvard Law School Record, now the Harvard Law Record, and has been in operation continually for forty-five years. When the first issue was available, the students wanted to send it to all of the alumni of the School, as a means of seeking support. They used the addressograph plates which the School had compiled before the war. After the mailing, copies were returned from the Post Office by the truckload, because, with the war, and the passage of time, many of the addresses were no longer valid. Among other things, this involved a substantial charge for the return postage. Thus, it became clear to me that we would have to compile a complete new list of names and addresses of Law School graduates and former students.

For many years, the School had published an alumni directory at intervals of five years. This was known as the "Quinquennial Catalogue," or the "Quin," for short. The series had been interrupted by the war. It was obviously important to get out a new edition of the Quinquennial as soon as possible. This could then be used as a means of compiling a complete list of our graduates and former students in a way which was suitable, with the technology then available, for mailing purposes. One result was the establishment of an alumni office, which, among other things, was charged with keeping files of alumni records. The new Quinquennial was published in 1948, with the aid of the Harvard Law School Association. Publication of the Quinquennial has been continued since, with wide distribution among Harvard Law School alumni. The most recent edition was published in 1990.

When I entered the Dean's office in June, 1946, I could find no list of the numbers of the accounts held by the Comptroller of the University for the Law School. It was at this point that I transferred Mary Conlan to be my administrative assistant, and her first assignment was to go to Lehmann Hall, where the

Comptroller's office was located, first to get a complete list of our accounts, with their numbers, and, second, to get instructions in the steps we should take to see that our bills were paid and that our employees received their salaries. She had no background in this area, but she went at the task vigorously, and soon was able to instruct me so that I could begin to feel that I understood the School's financial affairs, and had them under some control.

One matter which gave me concern when I entered the dean's office was the extent of my responsibilities. The Law School then had several buildings, the greatest private law library in the English-speaking world, and a considerable art collection. I called Paul Cabot, the Treasurer of the University and thus a member of the Harvard Corporation, and asked him what responsibilities I had for insurance. He immediately advised me that I had no responsibility, and that the University was self-insured. Some years later, the University took out "catastrophe" insurance, and made an annual charge to each of the departments in order to build up a reserve to cover "ordinary" losses. After about ten years, the income on the reserve was regarded as adequate, and the annual charge was discontinued.

In 1946, the School still had an outstanding indebtedness owed to the University, resulting from the building of the extensions to Langdell Hall in 1929–30. Some say that this shortfall resulted from Professor Frankfurter's activities in the Sacco–Vanzetti case, which led many prospective donors to refuse to make gifts to the Law School. I never knew the facts about this, nor did I care. I was, though, concerned by the fact that the School had an outstanding debt of $300,000 when I took over. With the School's total annual income at that time only a little over $1 million dollars, a debt of $300,000, drawing interest at the University rate, was necessarily a matter of concern.[7]

A deliberate decision was made not to increase the tuition charge during the period of the "G.I. Bill of Rights." It was felt that it would not be appropriate to increase the tuition from government sources simply to fill the coffers of the Law School. In retrospect, I think that this was probably a mistake, but it

---

7. At that time the tuition was $400 per year, and the number of students in the immediate post-war years was about two thousand. This produced a total of about $800,000 in tuition income. The total endowment held for the Law School then was about $5 million. The interest allowed on this was at the rate of five percent, or $250,000. Thus, the total income available was just over $1 million. It may be added that in the year 1946–47, the total amount received by the School through the Harvard Fund was just over $5,000.

seemed to be the right thing to do when it was done. Somehow or other, we paid the $300,000 debt during the next three or four years, and I remember my relief when that event occurred as being even stronger than my relief in finally paying off the $9,000 mortgage on my house some ten years earlier.

One of the immediate problems facing the School in the post-War period was the rebuilding of the faculty. There were some retirements, actual or impending, and there were some vacancies arising from the fact that a few pre-War faculty members who left for other employment during the war years had decided not to return.

B.   The Formulation of Policies

In the fall of 1945, President Conant had established a committee to locate prospects for invitations to the faculty. I was a member of that committee, so that I was familiar with the situation when I became dean. One of the likely sources for prospects was a legal office in the War Department, operating under Assistant Secretary of War Robert P. Patterson. From that source, we added Benjamin Kaplan and Robert Bowie to the faculty. Robert Braucher and Robert Amory, who had been in active military service during the war, were two other additions.[8] David Cavers was brought from the Duke University Law School. Mark Howe and Ernest Brown were brought from the Law School of the University of Buffalo and Arthur E. Sutherland, Jr., was brought from the Cornell University Law School. An appointment in which I took a special interest was that of Harold Berman who was asked to come to the School to start teaching and research in the field of Soviet law.

As I saw it, one of the functions of a university is to develop and transmit knowledge. At that time, we had virtually no knowledge of Soviet law. The University was establishing a Russian Research Center. A friend of mine, Donald McKay, a professor of history, was active in the Center, and he suggested to me that we ought to get a faculty member to do research and teaching in the field of Soviet law. After inquiry, we learned that Harold Berman, a graduate of the Yale Law School who had studied Russian while in military service, was then doing research at Stanford. Somewhat fearfully, I proposed him to the Harvard Law School faculty. I expected that there would be

---

8. In due course, after about twenty five years of distinguished service on the faculty, Braucher and Kaplan were appointed Justices of the Supreme Judicial Court of Massachusetts.

opposition on the ground that the teaching of Russian law was "too far out." However, the appointment was approved, and Professor Berman served ably for thirty-five years.[9]

Ever since the 1920s, the Harvard Law School had been quite large, over fifteen hundred regular students. This was in part due to the fact that Dean Pound wanted to take in as many students as he could in order to get funds to cover expenses, notably the cost of building the addition to Langdell Hall which was constructed in 1929–30. The School had long had a reputation for being a very "tough" institution. During the early part of the twentieth century, one of the most highly regarded members of the faculty was Professor Edward H. Warren, who may have been the basis for Professor Kingsman in the book, motion picture and, later, television program called "Paper Chase." [10] Professor Warren was known to the students as "the Bull" and customarily referred to as "Bull Warren." Students were expected to do their work, to be prepared for classes, and to defend positions they might take in the classroom. Nearly all of the classes were large, frequently with a hundred twenty-five students, or more. There was little feedback from the faculty, and

---

9. One time, about 1960, Professor Berman came to me and said that though he had been to Russia, he really knew very little about Russian law. He said that he would have to find a way to get to the Soviet Union for at least a year, and, hopefully, to have an opportunity to do some teaching at the University of Moscow Law faculty. I fully agreed with him, but it was difficult to find a useful point of contact, and travel, and arranging for a substantial stay in the Soviet Union, presented problems.

It was just at that time that General Secretary Khrushchev appeared before the United Nations in New York. I found that there was going to be a reception for Khrushchev hosted by Cyrus Eaton of Cleveland. I had a slight acquaintance with Mr. Eaton, based principally on the fact that his second wife knew my wife, because each had rather severe cases of polio. Taking advantage of this connection, I called Mr. Eaton's secretary in Cleveland and asked if it might be possible for Professor Berman to receive an invitation to attend the reception. This was arranged. When Professor Berman, in the receiving line, came to Khrushchev, he said, in Russian: "I am an American law professor. I want to arrange to spend a year at the University of Moscow." Khrushchev immediately turned and spoke over his shoulder to one of his aides, saying "Take care of him." As a result, Professor Berman, with his wife and four children, did spend the year of 1961–1962 in Moscow. All that I had to do was to find a way to finance six people in Moscow for a year. This was not only a great opportunity for Professor Berman, but it also opened up contacts which were useful in ensuing years.

10. Professor Warren wrote a book discussing his methods. It was entitled "Spartan Education" (Boston: 1942).

the students' grades depended entirely on the results of one final four-hour examination in each course at the end of the year.

Much turned on the examinations. The highest ranking students "made" the Law Review. The next highest became members of the Board of Student Advisers, which operated the School's moot court system, known as the "Ames Competition," named after one of the School's greatest teachers and scholars, James Barr Ames. Ames was dean of the School from 1895 to 1910. The third ranking group of students were elected to the Harvard Legal Aid Bureau, which had been established in 1914.

These choices took care of the top ten percent of the class. Of equal importance was the fact that the examinations at the end of the first year, for practical purposes, constituted the School's admissions system. Any graduate of an approved school would be admitted. On the other hand, students who failed two courses in the annual examination at the end of the first year were excluded from the School. For a long period, from about 1912 to close to 1940, the students so excluded constituted about thirty percent of the entering class. This gave rise to the story, sometimes attributed to Bull Warren, that he opened his class by saying: "Gentlemen, welcome to the Harvard Law School. Look to the man on your right. Look to the man on your left. One of you three won't be here next year."

I thought that the basic rigor of the Harvard Law School was good. It led the students to work hard, while many of them had coasted through college, having a good time, and without too much effort on their studies. It represented an appropriate transition between the general undergraduate attitude, and the "real world" which law students would face on graduation. Their success as lawyers and their contributions to society would then depend upon their ability to work hard and thoroughly on often difficult problems of their clients. In my own case as a student, the stimulus to do careful and thorough work showed me that I could do better than I had thought I was capable of doing. Nevertheless, I thought that some things about the Harvard Law School were unduly grim, and I wanted to find ways to eliminate unnecessarily severe atmosphere and practices.

Dean Pound, who had been born in Lincoln, Nebraska in 1870, two years after the city was founded, was a supporter of the vigorous approach, particularly with respect to admissions. After Dean Pound retired in 1936, the faculty, largely as a result of the efforts of Professor James A. MacLachlin, began steps to develop an admissions system which would do more to keep out of the school in the first place those who were likely to fail at the end of the first year. I supported this approach, and worked to make it effective. In particular, in the years just after the War, I joined with the deans of the Yale and Columbia Law Schools in seeking help from the Educational Testing Service in developing what has now become the Law School Admission Test. This, together with the great increase in the number of applicants, has virtually eliminated failure at the end of the first year, which is a great step forward.

I also undertook a few "cosmetic" changes. The great building of the school, Langdell Hall, started in 1903 and completed in 1929–30, rose starkly out of the ground. I had a considerable amount of planting put in to soften the appearance of the building. This consisted of hedges on both sides of the walkway in front of Langdell Hall, and flowering shrubs between the inner hedge and the building. During much of Dean Pound's time, the main entrance to Langdell Hall was kept permanently locked. Thus, students could only get into the building through the library, and it was hard to locate faculty offices.

Dean Pound had a large round desk built for his office. He sat in the center of the desk, where he could reach his papers in every direction. Dean Landis had this desk removed, and placed in the reception area. One of the first things I did as dean was to replace the receptionist. She was a somewhat grim old lady who had a genius for giving gruff answers over the telephone, and to callers at the building. I found another place where she could be usefully employed, without having contact with the public. Then, with the aid of my administrative assistant, Mary Conlan, I found a personable young lady who could handle the reception desk in a helpful and agreeable manner. Among other unimportant things, I introduced the practice of having Christmas decorations installed after the first of December, and I tried to encourage the faculty to be more accessible to students, and to try not to be quite so frightening in class. These things had some impact on the atmosphere of the School. But I still believed in the efficacy of hard work and careful thinking, and their usefulness in the proper training of a lawyer.

In my opening address to new law students each fall, I called attention to the fact that going to Law School was a serious matter, the last stage before the actual practice of a learned and important profession. I noted that the Law School had no Glee Club, and very little in the way of athletic facilities. I ended these remarks by saying, with a smile on my face, that we really had no objection if they went to the movies once a month. That was sometimes thrown back at me in later years. I did not expect it to be taken seriously.

One of my plans when I became dean was to do what I could to keep the School from becoming any larger. Because of financial considerations, I did not feel that we could reduce its size. But I thought that the time had come to keep it from growing. In that, I was successful, and I take considerable satisfaction from that. At the end of the post-War bulge in 1950, the School had about fifteen hundred and fifty LL.B. students. In 1990, it had fifteen hundred and fifty J.D. students.[11] In the meantime, though, the number of applicants enormously increased. When I left the dean's office in 1967, we had about seventeen hundred applicants for five hundred and fifty places in the first-year class, and I thought that was intolerable. In 1990, the number of applicants was over eight thousand, with the same number of students. The result, of course, is that a large number of well-qualified applicants cannot be offered admission.

Another goal that I early set for myself was to double the size of the faculty while keeping the number of students unchanged. I deliberately refrained from advising the faculty that this was my objective, for I knew that if I told them that I wanted to double the size of the faculty there would be substantial opposition and that would be a continuing source of division within the faculty. What happened was that we had an appointments committee, of which I was the chairman, and played an active role, while at the same time seeking all the help that I could get from the other members of the committee. Each year, we would come up with one or two or three very likely candidates. They would, indeed, be so good that the faculty had no difficulty in supporting the proposals for appointment. As a result, the size of the faculty grew slowly, year by year. The new faculty members were fine additions, and the size of the faculty increased with a minimum of friction. The basic problem was where to put them, as we soon developed a severe shortage of faculty office space. I am still chagrined by the fact that when we added Derek Bok to the Law School faculty in 1958, he was assigned a library carrel, about six feet by six feet, with a temporary partition. There was a door in the partition, separating the space from the adjoining library stacks. Adding a telephone made an office; and this was

---

11. The law degree had always been Bachelor of Laws, and I am proud of my LL.B. In the 1960s, however, pressure arose to change the degree to J.D., for Juris Doctor, since some Universities discriminated against LL.B.'s on the ground that they were not doctor's degrees, and thus did not rank with the M.D. or Ph.D. Shortly after I left the School in 1967, the faculty yielded to the pressure and adopted the J.D. as the law degree, giving holders of the LL.B. the option to receive the new degree. I did not elect to make the change.

where the future dean, and president of the University, did his work for his first two years. Similar arrangements were made perforce for other new members of the faculty.

One of my concerns was to stimulate the scholarly production of the faculty, as well as emphasizing teaching ability. Some of the new young teachers, like their older predecessors, were not very productive of scholarly work. A problem which gave me great concern arose from an experienced, able and productive faculty member of middle age, who was also an extraordinarily fine teacher. He was appropriately highly admired by the new faculty members, and had great influence with them. He used to tell them: "Don't do any writing during your first five years. Let your thoughts mature. When you have really thought something through, try to put it down on paper. Then put it aside for a year or two, and reexamine it. By that time, you should know enough about the subject matter so that what you publish will be worthwhile." My experience was that if a new teacher did not publish anything during his first five years, the odds were that he would never publish much of any particular importance. I avoided any direct confrontation with the senior and respected teacher, but he was very influential—and productive himself. I still think that, considering the substantial selectivity of choosing younger faculty members, his advice was wrong, and I was pleased in the cases when it was not followed.

One of the things which contributed to the somewhat grim atmosphere of the Law School was the fact that it had never had any appreciable living and dining facilities. Walter Hastings Hall, a fine old dormitory building, was on Massachusetts Avenue, adjacent to the Law School. Although it was a Faculty of Arts and Sciences building, it had long been occupied by Law School students. Indeed, I had a room there in 1928–29, my fourth year at the Law School. In the early post-War years, we were able to have the building transferred to the Law School. However, this took care of only five or six percent of the Law School enrollment. And we had no dining facilities whatever.

I knew that it would be hard for the Law School alone to do much about this, so I joined forces with Professor Paul A. Buck, the Dean of the Faculty of Arts and Sciences, and Provost of the University. Our plan was to seek authorization to raise funds for dormitory buildings and a dining hall, to go on Jarvis Field, just north of the Law School, replacing the temporary barracks which had been moved there in 1946. Paul and I arranged a meeting with President Conant. He was not very enthusiastic about our proposal, and wanted detailed information as to just how we expected to pay for new buildings. Near the end of our conversation, Paul threw a ten-strike—which he had not previously discussed with me. He said to President Conant, "Jim, in your first annual report, in 1933, you said that the greatest need of the University was for adequate dormitory and dining facilities for graduate students." And he added: "Are you going to come to the end of your time as President without having met the greatest need of the University?"

Shortly after that, we were told that the Harvard Corporation had assigned the old Jarvis Field for use for dormitories and a dining room for graduate students and law students, and we were asked to start to formulate plans for raising the money. I got in touch with Robert P. Patterson, who was then President of the Harvard Law School Association, our general alumni body. With his guidance, we first sought a professional fundraiser to look at our situation and tell us how much money we could raise. The report was that the outside limit of our fundraising capacity was $1.5 million. At this point, the University authorized us to go ahead. It retained Walter Gropius to be architect of the project, and, most important, informed us that the University would provide the funds to build the dining and meeting room facility. The funds for this building came from a Harkness bequest to the University, and the building was appropriately named Harkness Commons. J. Edward Lumbard, then a New York lawyer, agreed to be chairman of the fundraising effort, and he got us off to a good start. However, he became a justice of the Supreme Court of New York later in 1947, and had to withdraw. His place was taken by John B. Marsh, another prominent New York lawyer, who devoted much time and thought to the effort.

Eventually, we raised $1,520,000. When I discussed our situation with Walter Gropius, the architect, before any appreciable amount of funds had been raised, I told him that the outside limit of our funds would be $1.5 million. I think it is much to his credit that he delivered the buildings to us, completed (and on time) at a total cost of $1,487,000, from the Law School. He never came to me and said that his art would be ruined unless he could spend a further sum on a tower here or a decoration there. He accepted the assignment, and carried it through, including some interesting art work, and, in particular, the so-called "World Tree," a "sculpture" which stands outside of Harkness Commons. A dedication ceremony was held on October 27, 1950, which happened to be Dean Pound's eightieth birthday.

One of the things I had in mind in joining with Paul Buck in the effort for these new facilities was the desirability of encouraging more contact between law students and graduate students in

Six deans of the Harvard Law School (left to right)—back row: James Vorenberg, Dean 1981–89, Robert C. Clark, Dean 1989–   , Derek C. Bok, Dean 1968–71, Albert M. Sacks, Dean 1971–81. Front row: A. James Casner, Acting Dean, 1967–68, Erwin N. Griswold, Dean, 1946–67.

Arts and Sciences. The dormitory buildings were separate, but all grouped together, and the dining facilities were joint, so there was good opportunity for law students and Ph.D. candidates to meet around the dining table. Although this did happen to some extent, it was never a very great success.

In retrospect, it is clear that the dormitory buildings are too spartan. Although the exteriors are attractive in the Bauhaus style, the rooms are quite small, and the walls are of cinder block, without plaster, or other permanent covering. It would have been better if we had spent, say, fifty percent more on the buildings, to make the rooms larger and more comfortable. As things worked out, we could have financed it. However, at the time the buildings were built, we simply did not have the money. We spent everything we had—indeed, we did not have it until the fundraising campaign was completed, shortly after the buildings were finished—and we got what we paid for. I have long wished, though, that we might have provided more generous quarters for our students.

With the success of the fundraising effort for the dormitory buildings, we began to look ahead. The School had an alumni organization, known as the Harvard Law School Association. This had been founded at the time of the University's Two Hundred and Fiftieth Anniversary, in 1886, and the active mover then was a recent graduate, Louis D. Brandeis. The Association sponsored the founding of the Harvard Law Review in 1887, and it had played a useful role in holding alumni meetings, and in giving counsel and advice to the School, over the years. Membership in the Association involved the payment of modest dues, and the Association did not play an important role in general fundraising for the School.

One result of the fundraising effort for the new buildings was that we built up a small fundraising staff at the School. This was headed by Wesley E. Bevins, Jr., who, after military service, had received his LL.B. degree in 1948. At that time, the only ongoing fundraising effort for the University was the Harvard Fund. The rule was that gifts to the Harvard Fund should be credited to Harvard College, the undergraduate school, even though the donor had also been a student in one of the graduate schools. In other words, the Law School was credited with gifts only when the donor was a graduate of the Law School, and *not* a graduate of Harvard College. I joined with Dean Donald David of the Business School in recommending to President Conant that we should be authorized to establish separate funds for each graduate school, that the Law School should be authorized to solicit gifts from the graduates of the Law School even though they were also graduates of Harvard College—and similarly for the Business School, the Medical School, and the other graduate schools of the University. This was stoutly resisted by President Conant, who felt that it would impair the resources of Harvard College.

We told the President that we thought the authorization of separate Funds would at least triple the resources available from annual giving to the overall university. Finally, we were authorized to go ahead, and the Harvard Law School Fund, usually known as "Annual Giving," was inaugurated in 1950, covering the year from July 1, 1950 through June 30, 1951. I told several of my faculty colleagues that I would settle for $50,000 from the Law School Fund, to be used, essentially, for financial aid to students. As things worked out, the amount raised during the 1950–51 year was $64,055.

The Fund has now completed more than forty years. In the year 1990–91, the forty-first year, the total amount received by the School through the Fund was over $7.3 million. The aggregate amount received over the first forty years was over $80 million. The largest part of this was used for financial aid to students. Thus do the active graduates of the Law School contribute to the needs of the current generation of students. The American legal profession is extremely generous in helping out its younger and neophyte members. This has been in sharp contrast to the long-established English practice—now fortunately abandoned—under which students and recent graduates had to pay a fee for the privilege of working in senior lawyers' offices and chambers.

In 1946, the amount available for financial aid to students was very small, not much over $100,000 per year, with a few small loan funds. As a result, there were few entering scholarships, and only students who made an A or B average were eligible for scholarship aid during the second and third years. Under the strict grading system then in effect, this meant that about twenty percent of the students were eligible for scholarship aid. In any event, the scholarship was limited to the amount of tuition. Of course, expenses then were far less than they are now.

One of my reasons for seeking to develop the Harvard Law School Fund was to see if we could produce the means to offer to any student in the school whatever financial assistance he needed in order to stay in school, on a part grant, part loan basis. This came about slowly, but by 1960 it had been largely achieved, primarily through gifts received through the Harvard Law School Fund, with some assistance from the Harvard Law School Association. In recent years, the cost of attending the School has greatly increased, and it has required continued effort, and great generosity from the School's alumni, to keep the financial aid available up to the amount required. Much of the assistance is provided through loans. These, together with college loans, are often a substantial burden on those entering into law practice. Fortunately, the salaries available to new graduates in recent years have, in most cases, been sufficient to take care of the loans over a reasonable period of time.

As a step in making contact with alumni and evoking their interest in the School, I took a trip to the west coast in January 1947. I spoke to the alumni in St. Paul, Seattle, Portland, San Francisco, and Los Angeles. In 1947, I received my first honorary degree, from Tufts College, as it then was, and later from the University of British Columbia. The Law School there was newly founded in 1945, and I had been helpful to George F. Curtis, its founding dean, in recommendations for faculty positions, and in his relations with the practicing profession in Vancouver and elsewhere in British Columbia. He was anxious to avoid a situation like that which had existed in Toronto, where the practicing profession dominated the Law School. Indeed, the only avenue to first admission to the Bar in Ontario for many years was through attendance at the Osgoode Hall Law School, which was operated by the Law Society of Upper Canada.[12] Fortunately, there were several graduates of the Harvard Law School who were practicing in Vancouver. Due to the careful work and fine personality of George Curtis, the Law School there established excellent relations with the practicing profession and this has worked out very well—as it eventually did, at a later time, in Toronto. The Osgoode Hall Law School was eventually transferred to York University, and graduates of other law schools in Ontario were made eligible for admission to the Ontario Bar on the same basis as those of Osgoode Hall.

C. The Admission of Women

There was another important matter which occupied my time and thought in 1948 and 1949. The Harvard Law School had always been an all-male institution, like Harvard College, and the Medical School and the Business School. Radcliffe College had been organized in the nineteenth century as a separate but related institution to provide collegiate education to women. The students there, for the most part, were taught by members of the Harvard faculty, but always in separate classes. The Harvard Law School was all male in the 1920s, while I was a student, and I took it for granted. That was the way it was, and

---

12. For some of the details of the situation in Ontario at that time, see B. Laskin, "Cecil A. Wright: A Personal Memoir," 33 U. of Toronto L.Rev. 148 (1983). See also J. Bichenbach and C. Kyer, "The Harvardization of Caesar Wright," 33 U. of Toronto L.Rev. 162 (1983).

it gave me no concern. There were men's schools, and women's schools, and coeducational schools, and at the time that seemed a reasonable and satisfactory arrangement, particularly since the number of women who wanted to go to law school was very small.

As far back as the 1890s, the Harvard Law School faculty had recommended to the Harvard Corporation that women should be admitted to the Law School.[13] This recommendation apparently was motivated in part by the fact that some members of the faculty had daughters for whom they would like to have the opportunity of attending the Law School. All suggestions to this effect were, however, refused by the Harvard Corporation.

After the close of World War II, it was clear that the atmosphere had changed, to some extent. By that time, and largely because of a shortage of male students at Harvard College during the war years, Radcliffe and Harvard classes had been combined. But this was rather short of a complete merger. The men were all enrolled in Harvard College, and the women continued to be enrolled in Radcliffe College. The women received a Radcliffe degree, which was countersigned by the President of Harvard University in order to certify that it was the equivalent of a Harvard College degree. Of greater significance was the fact that the Corporation had admitted women to the Medical School. It became reasonably apparent that the time had come when the Harvard Corporation would act favorably on a recommendation from the Law School faculty for the admission of women.

After talking with several members of the faculty about this, I found, as expected, that there was sharply divided opinion. Edward H. Warren was strongly in opposition, saying: "I would have to revise all my notes." Others, including some of the younger members of the faculty, did not think well of the proposal. On the other hand, there were a number, apparently a majority, who thought that the time had come. I worked particularly with Professor Mark Howe to do a little proselytizing. Mark was a Harvard College graduate, of an old-line family. He had many friends on the faculty, and a fine personality. I had told him that I did not think that we could move before the fall of 1948, because of the large number of returning veterans who sought admission to the School. It did not seem fair to the young men who had lost their normal opportunity to go to Law School because they were in the Armed Services to cut down the

---

13. See A. Sutherland, The Law at Harvard (Cambridge, Mass.: 1967) 319–320. See also Centennial History of the Harvard Law School (Cambridge, Mass.: 1918) 55.

number of places available for them in the Law School. Mark, and others, agreed with this.

Finally, in the spring of 1949, Mark Howe and I, and a few other members of the faculty, recommended to the faculty that we should ask the Corporation to allow us to admit women students. As part of our preparation for this, the deans of a number of other law schools that did admit women—Yale, Columbia, Pennsylvania, Chicago and Stanford—were consulted. They all replied favorably. They also said that we would never get as many as five percent women students. In urging the change on the faculty, this was reported and the information was advanced to show that the change would not be very important. From my experience as a student in a co-educational college, I told the faculty that the women would be just as good and just as bad as the men.

The discussion of the matter by the faculty showed some tension. Feelings varied from mild to strong on both sides. Although it seemed clear that there was a majority in favor of the change, it was suggested that we put the matter over for the next meeting so that people could have a further opportunity to think about it and to discuss it in the hallways. When the next meeting came, there was still opposition, tempered somewhat. We took a vote. I do not remember the exact figure, but it was about three to one in favor of the proposal. There was some sputtering from some of the opponents, but it soon dropped into the background.

The recommendation was made, and approved by the Harvard Corporation. It called for an announcement in the summer of 1949 that applications would be received from women to come as students in the fall of 1950, and that is when the first class of women entered the school.

For the next eighteen years, the women students were never more than five percent of the total enrollment in the School. This was not because of any discrimination against women applicants, but was simply the result of the fact that few women applied. Many of those who did come were very fine students, and have had distinguished records—as judges, such as Sylvia Bacon, LL.B. 1956, Zita L. Weinshienk, J.D. 1958, and Judith Rogers, LL.B. 1964, public servants, such as Elizabeth Dole, J.D. 1965, who became a member of the Federal Trade Commission, and Secretary, successively, of two government departments, and Pat Schroeder, LL.B. 1964, long-time member of Congress, and practitioners, such as Judith Hope, J.D. 1964, who is the first woman to be a member of the Harvard Corporation.

The great increase in the numbers of women students came after 1968. At the present time, about forty percent of the

students at the Harvard Law School are women. Fifteen percent
of the students come from minority groups. This means that it is
much harder for a white male to obtain admission to the Harvard Law School than it was before World War II. In my
student days, there were close to six hundred students in the
entering class. All of these were male, and there were only a
handful of black students.[14]

At the present time, however, the total first-year class is
about five hundred fifty students, and only about forty-five percent of the places, or about two hundred seventy five, are filled
by white males. I do not say this in any sense by way of
complaint. I merely state it as a fact. The change was overdue
and desirable, offering opportunity to a wider group, and more
fairly. Sometimes I worry about the extreme selectivity of the
Harvard Law School, and other institutions, but the development
has been a generally sound one.[15]

---

14. These included persons who became very distinguished lawyers,
including Charles Houston, LL.B. 1922, S.J.D. 1923, who planned and
led the legal assault against discrimination in voting, housing and
education, and William H. Hastie, Jr., LL.B. 1930, S.J.D. 1933, who
became a judge of the United States Court of Appeals for the Third
Circuit, after serving as a district judge in the Virgin Islands. There
were many others. The first black graduate of the Harvard Law School
was apparently George Lewis Ruffin, LL.B. 1869. He was later a judge
of the Boston Municipal Court. The School did have a good record of
non-discrimination in the case of Jewish students. These included,
among many others, such persons as Louis D. Brandeis, LL.B. 1877,
Felix Frankfurter, LL.B. 1906, and Henry J. Friendly, LL.B. 1927.

15. In my Annual Report for the year 1963–64, quoted in A. Sutherland, The Law At Harvard (Cambridge, Mass.: 1967) 320, I wrote:

Although the increased volume of applications has changed the
whole character of the admissions situation, our methods of selection
have remained essentially the same. These methods were developed
when we were trying to separate those whom we thought could do our
work from those who were not really qualified. * * * I believe that
our methods of selection have been inadequate and unrealistic. Too
many able and interesting students fail to survive the first cut, which
is now made in terms of college records and admission test scores.
The final choice now is made essentially on the basis of the most
refined discrimination in terms of marks and scores. It may well be
that in the zone in which we are operating, reliance on marks and
scores, though having the appearance of objectivity, is in fact quite
arbitrary * * *.

Our new students are a very fine group, with a high level of
academic ability. It is possible, though, that this ability is more
limited in range and type than it should be. We may be overlooking

When, later, I was in private practice, one of my roles was to interview applicants for positions in the office. Some of these were women students from Harvard Law School. I used to say, with some pride, that I was the dean who brought about the admission of women to the Harvard Law School. The reaction, though, was, in a firm, clear voice, "Well, why didn't you do it sooner?" So I stopped patting myself on my back.

The development has been an interesting one, the consequence, of course, of basic changes in society and in the general outlook as to the opportunities for women. We now have many women in our law office, and, as I said, they are just as good, and just as bad, as the men.

For several years after women students first came to the Law School in September, 1950, my wife and I used to invite all of the new women students to our house for buffet supper early in the fall. This was possible, since there were only about fifteen women in the class. We were afraid that they might feel some pressure from the fact that they were so greatly outnumbered by the men. We thought that it would be useful for them to get to know each other better, thus helping to develop solidarity and support among them. After dinner, we had a general conversation about the law, the Law School, and other matters. I used to ask the women what it was that had led them to choose to come to law school. I found the answers interesting and encouraging. I said on a number of these occasions that one of the things that had been considered in connection with the admission of women was whether they would really practice law, or, in some way, would use their legal training effectively for the benefit of the community. I said, among other things, that there was concern that there might be a number of women students who did not use their legal training to any considerable extent, and that they might be taking the places of men students who would devote their careers to the active practice of law. I was assured that this was not the case, and experience has shown that the women graduates did find ways to utilize their legal training effectively, either in practice, or in public service activities of one sort or another.

To my regret, I now find that these questions—though purely factual in intent—were resented, and that they are now recalled by some women graduates as examples of sexism on my part.

_____

qualities and virtues which are not adequately reflected in the college records and test scores which we receive.

I ended by observing, somewhat tongue-in-cheek, that we might do better if we "drew by lot * * * for places in the class."

That was really far from my intention. I was trying, if anything, to encourage the women to make full use of their legal training, in practice or in service, of varying kinds, to the public. Now it is more than forty years later, and I have seen a great many women lawyers, and I am enthusiastic about them. It is obvious, though, that they have a very difficult assignment, particularly in the childbearing years. They face this, and meet it with great determination, and very effectively. And they receive, in most cases, great help and cooperation from their husbands. I am proud of them. If to say that is sex-discrimination, I can only respond by saying that it is intended to be a sincere expression of appreciation and approval for some very remarkable lawyers who would not have entered the profession a couple of generations ago.

D. The Work of Sheldon and Eleanor Glueck

In one way or another, the Law School kept in the public eye. The work of Professor and Mrs. Sheldon Glueck in Criminology was outstanding, and they carried out innovative research, and wrote many books on the causes of crime, particularly with respect to juvenile delinquency.[16] For some reason which was not clear to me, they never developed any "disciples," and their fine work had minimal impact. This may have been due in part to the fact that it was done in a law school, and the sociologists and criminologists looked down their noses at it. Another reason may have been that they worked so closely together that they would never let others participate in their

---

16. Sheldon Glueck's first book was published in 1925. He later wrote an article, "Principles of a Rational Penal Code", 41 Harv.L.Rev. 453 (1928), and a book, Law and Psychiatry (Baltimore: 1962). Most of his work was done in joint authorship with his wife, Eleanor Turow Glueck, and included the following important and path-breaking books:

Five Hundred Criminal Careers (New York: 1930); One Thousand Juvenile Delinquents (New York: 1934); Five Hundred Delinquent Women (New York: 1934); Later Criminal Careers (New York: 1937); Juvenile Delinquents Grown Up (New York: 1940); Criminal Careers in Retrospect (New York: 1943); After Conduct of Discharged Offenders (London: 1945); Unravelling Juvenile Delinquency (New York: 1950); Physique and Delinquency (New York: 1956); Delinquents and Non–Delinquents in Perspective (Cambridge: 1968).

In addition, the Gluecks collaborated in editing several volumes of essays: Probation and Criminal Justice (New York: 1933) Crime & Justice (Boston: 1936); Preventing Crime (New York: 1936) The Problem of Delinquency (Boston: 1959). Their career of original and significant contributions to criminology extended over a period of forty years.

work. As I look back, I do not think that I gave them adequate encouragement and moral support. The consequence has been, though, that after their departure, their great work is largely forgotten, and their contribution to the resolution of what has become one of our most intractable problems has not had the impact it deserved.

E. The Case of Dr. Miriam Van Waters

My own small opportunity in this area came early in 1949. Massachusetts had a reformatory for women, located in Framingham. A distinguished woman criminologist, Dr. Miriam Van Waters, had recently been appointed as Superintendent of this institution. Dr. Van Waters was a fine and able lady, an Episcopalian, perhaps a little on the "prim" side. Her approach was "forward looking," and she had developed a practice of "work release," under which selected inmates were allowed to work outside the institution during the daytime, returning to custody each afternoon. The Director of the Department of Corrections was of the old school. He and many of his constituents believed that prisons were for "punishment," and he disapproved of many of Dr. Van Waters' practices. Some of these, indeed, had stretched the Department's rules quite far.[17]

After a period of charges and counter-charges, followed by an extended hearing, the Director removed Dr. Van Waters from her position. He made some rather wide-ranging charges against her, as well as some very narrow ones. He was perhaps surprised at the outcry which followed his action. The result was that the Governor of the Commonwealth, Paul A. Dever, decided to appoint a Commission to hold hearings, and to make a report to him.

On a Sunday morning in February, 1949, I received a telephone call from an aide, asking whether the Governor might call at my home, specifically asking me whether I would object to such a meeting on a Sunday. I had no objection, and soon the Governor arrived in a big black car, accompanied by three State Police cars, causing some consternation among our neighbors. The purpose of his call was to ask me if I would accept appointment as Chairman of his advisory commission. I asked who the other members of the commission would be. He replied that he

---

17. A careful and thoughtful discussion of the Van Waters case was written by Thomas H. Eliot (later President of Washington University in St. Louis), as Number 22 in the Inter–University Case Program of Cases in Public Administration and Policy Formation. See T. Eliot, The Van Waters Case (U. of Alabama Press, 1954).

had not approached anyone else as yet, but he gave me the names of five or six persons he had under consideration. They were all satisfactory to me, and I so advised him. The other members of the Commission finally chosen were Mrs. Carolyn Putnam, a well-known civic leader in Springfield, and Robert Clark, an Assistant District Attorney of Norfolk County. Thomas H. Eliot has written that "this trio was impartial. They had not prejudged the case." [18]

When I undertook this assignment, I thought that the underlying cause of the controversy might be religious, or at least ethnic. But that did not prove to be the case. The problem was simply one of a very conservative Commissioner, of the old school, who was honestly convinced that the Superintendent of the Reformatory, Dr. Van Waters, was violating the laws and regulations with her more modern views of penology. The atmosphere is revealed by the concluding words of a report prepared for Commissioner McDowell by his Deputy Commissioner, Frank A. Dwyer, Jr. Mr. Dwyer wrote that a "Handbook for the Newcomer to Framingham" was given to each inmate when she arrived, and that on its first page was written: "Here you are a student, not a prisoner." Dwyer then said: "I find that * * * the statement 'You are a student, not a prisoner,' is a misstatement of fact, in that the official name of the institution is the Reformatory for Women at Framingham, and the legal status of a person sentenced by the courts of the commonwealth is that of a prisoner." [19]

The Commission moved quickly into action, and it began to hold hearings in an auditorium in the State House in Boston. A considerable number of persons attended, and it was not easy to keep the proceedings orderly. I remember in particular a woman of formidable mien, who sat in the second or third row and frequently interrupted witnesses in a loud voice. Though we were a Commission appointed by the Governor, we had no powers, no sergeant at arms or other officer subject to our direction. I thought, though, that I should try to keep things under control. I said, in a strong clear authoritative voice: "Madame, you will take your seat, and not interrupt proceedings any further." Rather to my surprise, and much to my relief, she did. I don't know what I would have done if she had continued her interruptions.

After a day or so, the auditorium in the State House was no longer available, and we moved the hearings to the Court Room,

---

18. See Eliot, above, at 44.
19. See Eliot, above, at 19.

then in Langdell Hall, at Harvard Law School. This meant walking up three flights of stairs—there were no elevators at that time—which may have held down the attendance somewhat.

Dr. Van Waters was represented by a Boston attorney, Claude Cross. His style was quiet, thorough, persistent. I thought he made a very effective presentation.[20] The hearings lasted several more days, and included a visit to the institution at Framingham, which gave every appearance of being well-run. The Commission then deliberated, and drafted and reached unanimous agreement on a report. This report upheld Dr. Van Waters' actions, and the Governor duly reinstated her in her position.

F. Work in Practice

From the beginning of my tenure at the Law School, I had a small amount of consultation with private lawyers, chiefly in the tax field. One of the lawyers who called me was Haskell Cohn, of the Harvard Law School Class of 1925. He was then practicing with a small firm in downtown Boston, and I worked with him on several tax matters. Another assignment came to me through one of my colleagues on the Law School faculty, Professor Livingston Hall. He was the son-in-law of Thomas H. Blodgett, who was involved in a number of business activities. At his request, I did tax consultation for a number of years for the American Chicle Company, the American Writing Paper Corporation, and several other companies. Generally speaking, each of these companies had its own tax department, and my assignment was to be available for consultation by the company's people when any special problem developed. I also did tax work for the Massachusetts Indemnity Insurance Company, through my friend Jarvis Farley.[21] I later had a small retainer from his company

---

20. Shortly thereafter, the second trial of Alger Hiss was about to begin. (The jury had disagreed at his first trial, where his counsel was a criminal lawyer of the hard-driving and outspoken type.) After the Van Waters Commission had made its report, friends of Alger Hiss came to me, and asked me for my opinion of Claude Cross, and specifically whether he would be a good lawyer for Hiss at his second trial. I gave a favorable report on Cross, as I was impressed by his quiet, thoughtful, persistent style. Cross was chosen, and was Hiss' counsel at his second trial, where Hiss was convicted. Though I did not in any sense "select" Cross, I have always been bothered that my reaction may have been a mistake, and that, in the particular circumstances of the case, Hiss might have fared better with a more "slam bang" approach in his representation.

21. At his request, I briefed and argued the case of Massachusetts Protective Assn. v. United States, 114 F.2d 304 (1st Cir. 1940), involving a

and provided frequent tax advice. In addition, I had a certain amount of consultation in specific cases. One of the assignments I particularly liked was when counsel would send me the semi-final draft of their brief in a tax case. I was told: "We think your reaction will be much like that of a judge. Will you please review this draft, and tell us where you think there are weaknesses, unanswered questions, or anything else which might cause a judge to become dubious about our case?"

Out of this work in practice, I received many ideas which were directly helpful in my teaching. Not only did I learn a great deal myself, but I got many of my examination questions from this work. Often the problems which came to me from practitioners were ones I had never thought of before, and they frequently provided opportunities for effective classroom discussion.

During my time on the faculty, I argued seven cases before the Supreme Court.[22] One of these cases—*Granville-Smith* v. *Granville-Smith*—warrants special mention. Throughout the twentieth century, the law of divorce in the United States has gone through gradual but steady change. The underlying law of divorce is a matter of state law, and the states have varied widely in their grounds of divorce, and in their practices in granting divorces. The accepted rule was that jurisdiction to grant a divorce rested on the "domicile" of the parties.[23] Some states with "easy" grounds for divorce became "divorce havens."[24]

---

novel and interesting question concerning the taxation of companies writing non-cancellable accident and health insurance.

22. Warren v. Palmer, 310 U.S. 132 (1940); Helvering v. Reynolds, 313 U.S. 428 (1941); American Chicle Company v. United States, 316 U.S. 450 (1942); Commissioner v. Estate of Bedford, 325 U.S. 283 (1945); National Carbide Company v. Commissioner, 336 U.S. 422 (1949); Granville–Smith v. Granville–Smith, 349 U.S. 1 (1955); Bank of America v. Parnell, 352 U.S. 29 (1956); United States v. Cannelton Sewer Pipe Company, 364 U.S. 76 (1960). In addition, I presented the oral argument in one case in the Board of Tax Appeals, four cases in the Second Circuit Court of Appeals, one case in the Sixth Circuit, and one case in the Court of Claims.

23. This is exemplified by the decision of the Supreme Court in Haddock v. Haddock, 201 U.S. 562 (1906), holding that the full faith and credit clause of the Constitution did not require recognition of a divorce in the absence of domicile of at least one of the parties in the state granting the divorce. See also E. Griswold, "Divorce Jurisdiction and Recognition of Divorce Decrees—A Comparative Study," 65 Harv.L.Rev. 193 (1951).

24. See Blake, The Road to Reno: History of Divorce in the United States (New York: 1962).

Where the divorce was unopposed, one of the parties could go to
such a state and testify that he or she was domiciled there, that is,
that his or her "home" was in the state. In many cases, this
involved perjury, but since the divorce was in substance consen-
sual, and the state was interested in attracting visitors to the
state, nothing was done about it.

In 1953, the legislative assembly of the Virgin Islands, a
territory of the United States with a population at that time of
less than 50,000, changed its law to provide that where the
plaintiff in a divorce case was "within" the Virgin Islands "continuously for the six weeks immediately prior" to filing the complaint "this shall be prima facie evidence of domicile" and "if the
defendant has been personally served in the Virgin Islands" or
"enters a general appearance in the action, then the Court shall
have jurisdiction of the action and of the parties thereto without
further reference to domicile * * *" The purpose of this, of
course, was to establish domicile by "presumption." Since both
parties wanted the divorce, no questions would be asked with
respect to "domicile" and, in the absence of any dispute on this
matter, domicile would be presumed. Thus perjury as to domicile would no longer be required, and, in substance, where there
was mutual consent, domicile ceased to be relevant in the granting of a Virgin Islands divorce.

When the matter came before the district court in the
Virgin Islands, however, the divorce was denied "because of
the insufficiency of [the procedure authorized by the Virgin
Islands law] to prove a *prima facie* case of domicile." The
case then went to the United States Court of Appeals for the
Third Circuit, which has appellate jurisdiction over the Virgin
Islands court. The Third Circuit, sitting *en banc,* upheld the
district court, by a four to three vote.[25] The case then went to
the Supreme Court, where it was argued before the Court in
early April, 1954. In the Supreme Court, the petitioner wife
was represented by attorney Abe Fortas.[26] No one appeared
for the defendant.

---

25. Alton v. Alton, 207 F.2d 667 (3d Cir. 1953). The opinion for
the majority was written by Judge Herbert Goodrich. Judge William
Hastie, who had been Governor and then U.S. District Judge in the
Virgin Islands, wrote a dissenting opinion in which two other judges
concurred.

26. Mr. Fortas had served in the Interior Department, where he
had special responsibilities with respect to Puerto Rico and the Virgin
Islands. Though his client was Mrs. Alton, the Virgin Islands Government was much concerned, and they brought him into the case.

We now know that the *Alton* case was decided by the Supreme Court on April 12, 1954, in conference.[27] An opinion was written by Justice Clark, reversing the decision of the Third Circuit, and upholding the validity of the Virgin Islands statute. Chief Justice Warren wrote a dissenting memorandum.[28] Justice Frankfurter concurred in this dissent. Then, an unexpected and fortuitous event occurred. Mr. Alton became impatient with the delay in the Virgin Islands proceeding, and he obtained a divorce in Connecticut, where he was undoubtedly domiciled. In fulfillment of his responsibility, Mr. Fortas advised the Clerk of the Supreme Court of this event, since the valid Connecticut divorce made the Virgin Islands proceeding "moot." Justice Frankfurter wrote to Chief Justice Warren on May 1, 1954, "about the changed aspect of Alton v. Alton," and suggested that "a reargument is called for on the question of mootness." [29] The Court did not find reargument to be necessary, and it dismissed the case as moot on June 1, 1954.[30] Thus, as Professor Schwartz says, "no one outside the Court knew how close the Justices had come to upholding the Virgin Islands divorce law." [31]

However, another case—*Granville-Smith v. Granville-Smith*—soon arrived in the Supreme Court, with facts similar to those in *Alton v. Alton*. This followed the same route as the *Alton* case, and the Third Circuit held that its earlier opinion invalidating the Virgin Islands statute was controlling.[32] This case then proceeded to the Supreme Court.[33] A motion to submit the case without oral argument was denied. Obviously, the Court was concerned because there had not been any genuine adversary proceeding at any stage in either the *Alton* or the *Granville–Smith* cases, since both sides in each case wanted the divorce, and wanted to have the validity of the statute sustained.

On November 20, 1954, as I stopped by my office after the Harvard–Yale football game, I received a telephone call from

---

27. The story is told in Chapter 1 of B. Schwartz, The Unpublished Opinions of the Warren Court (New York: 1985) 22–44.

28. The full text of these opinions appears in B. Schwartz, above, at 28–38.

29. Schwartz, above, p. 39.

30. Alton v. Alton, 347 U.S. 610 (1954).

31. B. Schwartz, above, at 40. I knew nothing about this until after the publication of the Schwartz book.

32. Granville–Smith v. Granville–Smith, 214 F.2d 820 (3d Cir. 1954).

33. Certiorari was granted in the Granville–Smith case on October 14, 1954, 348 U.S. 810.

Chief Justice Warren. He said that the Court wanted to invite me "to help it out" by appearing to "present oral argument, as *amicus curiae*" against the Virgin Islands statute.[34] Of course, I accepted this invitation.

I immediately went to work on the brief, with the assistance of a third-year student who made major contributions. I quickly saw that the ground taken by the court of appeals, namely that the Virgin Islands statute violated the due process clause, was hard to support, since nothing was being taken from anyone without his consent. Indeed, the husband was the petitioner who was seeking to have the decision denying the divorce overturned. On examining the issues, it occurred to me that some question might be raised about the authority of the Legislative Assembly of the Virgin Islands to pass such a statute. That Assembly had only such powers as were given to it by the Act of Congress establishing the Virgin Islands as a territory of the United States. That provided that the legislature had power to enact laws on "all subjects of local application." [35]

Relying on this statute, I urged the Court to decide the case on statutory construction grounds, and thus "to avoid grave constitutional questions." I contended that the statute which the Virgin Islands had adopted was not "of local application," but was "designed for export." To put it another way, the statute was of no use to persons who really lived in the Virgin Islands. They were domiciled there and had no need to invoke the statute. The statute was obviously designed only to be used by persons *not* domiciled in the Virgin Islands.

The argument was held on February 3 and 4, 1955, with Abe Fortas again acting as counsel for the petitioner. The decision was announced on April 11, 1955, in an opinion written by Justice Frankfurter, with Justice Clark writing a dissent in which Justices Black and Reed joined.[36] The Frankfurter opinion added much to the materials I had developed, but it turned on the extent of the power given to the Virgin Islands Legislative Assembly. In sum, the opinion said that "We cannot conclude that if Congress had consciously been asked to give the Virgin Islands Legislative Assembly power to do what no state has ever at-

---

34. The Court's order is reported in Granville–Smith v. Granville–Smith, 348 U.S. 885 (1954).

35. See Act of June 22, 1936, 49 Stat. 1811, 48 U.S.C.A. § 1405r.

36. Thus, Justices Burton, Douglas, and Minton changed sides from the earlier opinion. Justice Harlan did not participate in the decision.

tempted, it would have done so." [37]   Thus, perhaps it may be said that this was a case where the soundness of the adversary process was sustained.   Whether domicile is a prerequisite to jurisdiction to grant a divorce has not yet been decided.

G. RACIAL DISCRIMINATION

As I have indicated, I had long been concerned about the "Negro question," as it was then called.   I had not done much about it, except in a minor way, in personal relations.   William H. Hastie was a second-year student at the Law School in 1928–1929, the year I remained as a graduate student.   Because of his fine academic work, he was elected to the Board of Editors of the Harvard Law Review.   The Review held its annual dinner in April of each year, a rather formal black-tie affair.   Some members of the Board objected to Hastie's attendance.   When he heard about this, he let it be known that he would not attend. This seemed to many of us to be wrong.   He was a member of the Board and ought to be welcomed.   A considerable number of members of the Board, with whom I joined as an alumnus member, let it be known that we would not attend the dinner unless Hastie was welcomed and did attend, and the matter was worked out on this basis.

Later, when I went to Washington, Hastie was a member of the faculty of the Howard University Law School, and in practice in the firm of Houston and Houston, active in civil rights cases. Harriet and I had him to dinner with others at our apartment at 1750 Harvard Street.   As is well known, Hastie had a great career, finally becoming a judge of the United States Court of Appeals for the Third Circuit.   He was the first black lawyer to become an appeals court judge.   He filled the post with great distinction, and in due course became the Chief Judge of the Third Circuit. [38]

During my early years in Washington, I heard one of the important voting rights cases argued before the Supreme Court, [39] and thus became aware of the work of Charles H. Houston, and the group which he organized and led at Howard University Law

---

37.   349 U.S. at 16.

38.   See Gilbert Ware, William Hastie: Grace under Pressure (New York: 1984).

39.   Nixon v. Condon, 286 U.S. 73 (1932).

Another case I heard argued was the Scottsboro case (Powell v. Alabama, 287 U.S. 45 (1932)), which was decided in a great civil rights opinion by Justice Sutherland.

School. Houston was the first black member of the Board of the Harvard Law Review, and, in terms of his ability and achievement, is surely entitled to be included in any list of truly great American lawyers.[40] It was his vision, energy, and skill which underlay the great legal developments in race relations around the middle of the twentieth century.

Thurgood Marshall was a member of Houston's "team" and it was because of this that I first became aware of Marshall. Marshall had earlier played an important role in representing Negro defendants under difficult conditions, in criminal cases in southern courts.[41]

In the spring of 1948, Marshall came to Cambridge and talked with a number of members of the Law School faculty. He wanted to get their views on the question whether the time had come for a frontal attack in the courts on the constitutional basis for segregated education, that is, whether the time had come when the courts would hold that enforced segregation in public schools violated the constitutional requirement of "equal protection of the laws." At that time the prevailing view, going back to *Plessy v. Ferguson,*[42] was that "separate but equal" met the constitutional requirement. It was well known that throughout the south, public schools were "separate," but they were never "equal." Already cases had been started—and sometimes won— to enforce equality in school facilities and expenditures, without a direct attack on segregation. Most of the group of faculty members, and I was one, joined in saying that it was too soon for a frontal attack on segregation, that it would be wise to build up a group of decisions, if possible on the "inequality" issue, and any other indirect attack that could be developed. The Supreme Court had as recently as 1927 upheld segregated education in state public schools.[43] We feared that if a direct attack on segregation was launched, and was unsuccessful, the cause would be set back for a great many years.

40. See Smith, Book Review, in 98 Harv.L.Rev. 482 (1984); Segal, Blacks in the Law (1983) 210.

41. *Cf.* G. Myrdal, The American Dilemma (New York: 1944), reviewed by Charles E. Wyzanski, Jr., in 58 Harv.L.Rev. 285 (1944).

42. 163 U.S. 537 (1896).

43. Gong Lum v. Rice, 275 U.S. 78 (1927). This case involved a student of Chinese ancestry, but it was clear that it would be applied to black students. The opinion treated the matter as routine, and though Justices Holmes, Brandeis and Stone were then on the Court, no dissenting vote was expressed. See also Vol. IX, Bickel and Schmidt, History of the Supreme Court (1984) 759–760.

By this time Thurgood Marshall was the Legal Director of the National Association for the Advancement of Colored People. He had successfully carried one case to the Supreme Court, involving a black student who was a resident of Missouri. He was refused admission to the law school at the University of Missouri, but he was told that his expenses would be paid by Missouri if he went to a law school in some other state. The Supreme Court held that this denied him equal protection.[44]

Marshall was also successful in another case involving a graduate student who was admitted to the University of Oklahoma, but was required to sit at special seats and tables in the classroom, in the cafeteria, and in the library.[45]

It was in this period that Thurgood Marshall asked me to appear as an expert witness in cases involving legal education. I had no problem about doing this, though I learned later that President Conant was not pleased. The first case where I appeared was in the Federal district court in Durham, North Carolina. The well-known law school of the University of North Carolina was located in Chapel Hill, and it did not then admit Negro students. The North Carolina College for Negroes was located in Durham, and the State authorities decided to open a law school for Negroes there. At the time I appeared it had about twenty-five students and a rudimentary law library.

When the time came, I went to Durham by overnight train from New York. I was met at the Durham railroad station by Thurgood Marshall, his chief aide, Spottswood W. Robinson, and two other Negroes. They had an automobile, and we drove to downtown Durham. In due course, they stopped by an alley. They asked me to get out and walk down the alley to the third gate on the right, and to go through the kitchen into the restaurant. It turned out that we were to have breakfast in a Negro restaurant—the only way that we could eat together, and plan the day's work—and that I could not be seen entering the restaurant through the street door. So I followed directions, and we had a fine breakfast.

After breakfast, we went to the federal court house, and in due course I was called as a witness. I appeared as an expert on legal education—a designation for which I thought I was qualified. I testified, in short, that a segregated legal education *could not* be equal. I referred to the fact that legal education is in large

---

44. Missouri ex rel. Gaines v. Canada, 305 U.S. 337 (1938).

45. McLaurin v. Oklahoma State Regents for Higher Education, 339 U.S. 637 (1950).

part self-education, that the basic role of classes is to provide materials for discussion, and that a large part of the education comes from interchanges and debate among the students outside of the classroom. I said that the success of this operation depended in large measure on the capacity of the students who took part in the discussions, and, in particular, on their representing a cross-section of the community, with its varying viewpoints, which would introduce and educate the students into the atmosphere in which they would be practicing as lawyers. I believed this and stated it as effectively as I could.

A short time later, I made a similar appearance in the federal court in Oklahoma City. At that time the law school of the University of Oklahoma, at Norman, was not open to Negro students. The state officers had opened a law school for Negroes, which occupied two small rooms in the state capitol. This school had two students, no full-time faculty, and no library. It was said that the library need was met by the well-equipped state law library, also located in the capitol building. My testimony here was essentially the same as that given in North Carolina—a separate law school *could not* be equal.

After my testimony in Oklahoma City, I was invited to visit the State University Law School at Norman. At that time, Page Keeton was the dean there. He later became dean at the University of Texas Law School and a preeminent authority on the law of torts. When I arrived in Norman, I was very cordially received by a large group of faculty members. I also met a considerable group of students. All comments were favorable, and appreciative of my effort. (Those who felt differently, I supposed, did not appear at the meetings which I attended.) It was clear that there was wide support for the end of segregation at the law school at Norman, and that they were appreciative of my expression of that view, since they did not feel free then to take a public position on this question.

During this period, I had been active in discussions about segregated legal education in the Association of American Law Schools. The only power of the Association was that of membership, and there were those who thought that the requirements for membership of a school in the Association should be changed so that a segregated school could not be a member, and would be dropped from the rolls unless it admitted Negro students without discrimination. That position was understandable, but it was not clear that it was wise to make it immediately effective. We all knew many fine teachers in southern law schools who felt that segregation was wrong and were working to change it, but were subject to the power of state Boards of Regents, often elected, and usually of an older generation. The Governing Boards were not ready to make the change, and would not be induced to do so by such a matter as membership in the Association of American Law Schools. To force the issue in that way would produce much heat and might well hold back a solution for some time. A compromise was reached, establishing the new requirement but making it applicable some years in the future.

The final case involving legal education was *Sweatt v. Painter.*[46] This was a suit by a black Texan seeking admission to the law school of the University of Texas at Austin. My role in this case was a different one. I did not appear as a witness in the case—indeed I did not know about the case until it came before the Supreme Court. This was after the discussions in the Association of American Law Schools, and a group of law school professors[47] was quickly formed to prepare and file an amici brief in the Supreme Court in support of the position that a state which segregated its students in law schools denied the equal protection of the laws to the black applicants. This position was adopted by the Supreme Court. The *Sweatt* case, along with *Gaines* and *McLaurin,* were important parts of the background when *Brown v. Board of Education* came before the Supreme Court in 1953 and 1954.[48]

H. A White House Assignment—Declined

In March 1952, I received a telephone call from Justice Felix Frankfurter. He told me to report to the White House the next morning at 10:00 a.m. He said he was not free to give me any details. It was late in the afternoon, and I did not have enough cash in my pocket to cover rail fare (trips to Washington were regularly made by train in those days). So I went up and down

---

46.   339 U.S. 629 (1950).

47.   The members of the Association who joined in the amici brief included Thomas I. Emerson (Yale), Erwin N. Griswold (Harvard), Robert Hale (Columbia), Harold Havighurst (Northwestern), and Edward Levi (Chicago). The text of the brief is printed in 34 Minn.L.Rev. 289 (1950).

48.   Many years later, in 1988, I was invited to attend the eightieth birthday party for Justice Thurgood Marshall, held at the residence of William T. Coleman, Jr., distinguished lawyer and cabinet officer, who had been a student of mine in the Class of 1943. In his after dinner remarks, Justice Marshall very generously referred to me, saying that I had been willing to come to his aid at a time of need, and that this had been of great assistance in his work.

the corridors and borrowed from faculty colleagues enough to cover expenses for the trip.

At that time, J. Howard McGrath, of Rhode Island, was Attorney General, after previous service as Solicitor General. Some problems had arisen in his administration in the Department of Justice, and some serious charges were being made. When I arrived at the White House the next morning, I learned that this was the basis of my summons to Washington. I was ushered into the oval office. It was the first time I had met President Truman. He immediately told me that he was setting up a two-man commission to investigate the Department of Justice and report to him. The other member of the commission was to be Judge Thomas J. Murphy, of the Southern District of New York. Before appointment to the bench, he had been one of the United States attorneys who had prosecuted the Hiss case.

All of this raised serious questions in my mind. In the first place, I wondered whether it was appropriate for a sitting federal judge to engage in such an investigative activity. The President responded that there was no problem about that, and that the propriety of Judge Murphy to be a member of the commission had been "cleared." [49]

I also raised the question of what powers and facilities we would have. I referred to the investigation of the Teapot Dome situation in the 1920s. There Congress, at the request of President Coolidge, had enacted legislation which made an appropriation and gave subpoena power. Under this legislation, the President had appointed former Senator Atlee Pomerene of Ohio, and Owen J. Roberts of Pennsylvania, and they had successfully carried out the assignment. In response to this, President Truman waved his hand and said, a bit impatiently, I thought: "You will have all the resources of the F.B.I. behind you." I responded that this might present some difficulties, that it might be hard to investigate the Department of Justice through the F.B.I. when the Attorney General was in charge of the F.B.I.

All of this left me with much concern. I was well aware of the customary rule that when the President of the United States asks you to do something, you do it. On the other hand, I saw

---

49. Judge Murphy was supposed to be at the White House when I was. However, he planned to fly to Washington and his flight was canceled because of fog in New York. I later learned that when the proposed commission assignment came to the attention of Chief Judge Learned Hand, of the Second Circuit, he exploded, as only Learned Hand could do. That terminated Judge Murphy's participation in the proposed investigation.

very serious problems, and I felt that the President (who was not a lawyer) was not fully aware of the difficulties. I felt the need of time for consideration, and asked the President if I could have a few hours to think it over, and then to return to see him at some convenient time in the afternoon. The President graciously responded that that was agreeable to him. He suggested that I discuss the matter with his counsel, Clark Clifford, and I did so. This was the first time I met Mr. Clifford, whom I have known and admired as a great public servant over the ensuing forty years.

When I left the White House, I went at once to the Supreme Court, where I sought a meeting with Justice Frankfurter, who made himself immediately available. As I recall our conversation now, he made it clear that the decision was up to me, but I had the feeling that he felt that I was being unduly fussy. He felt that the commission would have the backing of the President, and that would be enough.

All in all, though, I found myself more and more in doubt about the wisdom of undertaking the assignment. After lunch I went back to the White House, and soon found myself once more in the oval office. I summoned up my courage, and said that I did not feel that I could undertake the assignment. The President's reaction was one of impatience—he was not pleased. I then blurted out: "Mr. President, you do not need an investigating commission. You need a new Attorney General." That was the end of the meeting, and I soon found myself leaving by the west wing door and out on the White House lawn. There were no locked gates and guard houses in those days.

Ten days or so later, there was an announcement in the newspapers that President Truman had appointed a New York lawyer, Newbold Morris, to investigate the Department of Justice. There were subsequent accounts of problems and difficulties, and the Morris investigation became something of a fiasco. After several weeks, he resigned, without any report. I never knew the details. A few weeks after that, President Truman dismissed Attorney General McGrath. I was told that there was no personal communication, that McGrath heard about it over a loudspeaker in the Washington airport, as he was walking to take a plane to keep a speaking engagement. Whether he made the speech and what he said, I do not know.

I. The McCarthy Period and the Privilege Against Self–Incrimination

The early 1950s brought a new experience to the American people, and to academic communities. This was the massive upsurge of concern about communism. It was blown into a sort of firestorm by the activities of Senator Joseph McCarthy of Wisconsin. In retrospect, it is hard to explain why the reaction was so extreme. At the time, though, it was very real, and was the cause of great distress to thoughtful people, particularly those in academic communities who were accustomed to, and deeply believed in, broad views of academic freedom.

In addition to Senator McCarthy, there were the activities of J. Edgar Hoover, the head of the Federal Bureau of Investigation. Hoover was firmly convinced that internal communism was a serious threat to the United States. He developed, within the Bureau, a "Communist Intelligence Program" which was abbreviated to "COMINTELPRO." The activities of the FBI, under Hoover's leadership, were of great importance because he was a skillful publicist, and an undoubtedly dedicated American, as he saw it. He had developed a large and vigorous following among many of his countrymen. His influence was great, and this was fired into white heat by some of Senator McCarthy's activities.

It is very hard to reconstruct the atmosphere of those days. Today's young lawyers were not born until nearly ten years after that time. They sometimes ask me: "What was so bad about McCarthy?" It is not easy to respond, because it is very difficult to describe today the intensity of feelings during the early 1950s.

The problems became intensified with the case of Alger Hiss, who, as indicated above, was a graduate of the Harvard Law School in the Class of 1929. He served in the State Department during the War, and was active in planning the charter of the United Nations, and was Secretary General of the San Francisco Conference where the United Nations was inaugurated. Shortly after the War, he was elected President of the Carnegie Endowment for International Peace, where he was sponsored by John W. Davis, the prominent New York lawyer who had been Solicitor General in the Wilson administration, Ambassador to the United Kingdom, and the Democratic candidate for President in 1924. I mention these well-known facts simply by way of background, for the blow to public confidence was understandable when Hiss was indicted for perjury before a congressional committee where a new young congressman, Richard Nixon, was in the chair. I had known Hiss fairly well, and had no reason to doubt his loyalty or integrity. (Indeed, his brother, Donald Hiss, had been a boy at Camp Pemigewassett with me as far back as 1921.) My faculty colleague, Richard H. Field, was a classmate of Hiss, and he organized a committee to raise funds to help finance Hiss's defense. I made a gift for this purpose, since I felt strongly that Hiss was entitled to make the best defense possible, and I knew that the investigatory facilities of the FBI were virtually unlimited.

At the first trial of Hiss, the jury was unable to agree. There was then a second trial, where Hiss was convicted in January, 1950. I was in New York at the time of the first trial, and I attended the trial for a part of a day. During a recess, I went up to Hiss and spoke to him. We shook hands, and had a brief and general conversation. I later learned that "The FBI kept contributors to the Hiss Defense Fund under surveillance," and that "In 1951 they forwarded 'derogatory information to the Truman White House about Harvard Dean Erwin N. Griswold's allegedly close association with Hiss.'" According to the FBI, "at the first Hiss trial Griswold conferred during an intermission with Alger and Priscilla Hiss, with one of Hiss's attorneys, and with another unidentified individual." [50]

Similarly, "FBI Reports * * * on Erwin N. Griswold of the Harvard Law School noted such facts as the refusal to disband the [National Lawyers] Guild's Harvard chapter and then identified the National Lawyers Guild as subversive by citing the Dies Committee's Appendix IX and HUAC's more recent characterization." [51] A student chapter of the National Lawyers Guild had been formed at the Harvard Law School, and "was preparing an article on FBI wiretapping." The Boston Field Office was immediately alerted, and three days later the President of the Massachusetts Bar Association, Samuel Sears, publicly blasted the Law School for harboring the subversive NLG Chapter. "In an open letter to Harvard Law School Dean Erwin N. Griswold, Sears condemned Harvard for 'playing host to the Communist Party' and demanded the disbandment of the student group and the cancellation of a scheduled appearance by NLG Vice President Osmond K. Fraenkel, a well-known attorney for the American Civil Liberties Union." [52] I received this letter after I had read

---

50. K. O'Reilly, Hoover and the Un–Americans (Philadelphia: 1983) 111, 112.

51. The memorandum to the White House is in the Harry S. Truman Library, designated as "LHM re Erwin N. Griswold, 12/14/51, PSF–FBI F, HST." K. O'Reilly, above, p. 139.

52. Beyond the Hiss Case (A. Theoharis ed.: Philadelphia: 1982), p. 148.

about it in the newspaper. The Boston FBI office reported to the Director on March 5, 1951, and again on March 10 and 13.[53]

Another event occurred soon after the National Lawyers Guild episode. In March 1953, two members of the Harvard chapter of the National Lawyers Guild were subpoenaed before a hearing in Boston of the Senate Internal Security Committee. They were twin brothers, Jonathan and David Lubell. They had done their undergraduate work at Cornell. They were asked questions about their activities at Cornell and specifically whether they were members of the Communist Party. They refused to answer the question on Fifth Amendment grounds. "Samuel Sears and the Boston newspapers demanded their expulsion from the Harvard Law School."[54] Under the circumstances then existing, this presented a very difficult problem. I discussed the matter with the Vice Dean of the Law School, Professor Livingston Hall, who was a wise source of advice. We recommended to the faculty that the students should not be expelled. Our general position was that the school was an educational institution, and that this experience would be an important part of the education of these students. This recommendation was approved by the faculty, with some vigorous dissents.

There arose then the question of their membership in student organizations. One of the two brothers had been elected to the board of editors of the Harvard Law Review, and the other was a member of the Harvard Legal Aid Bureau. Rightly or wrongly, we concluded that these two student organizations were, by the tradition of the Law School, "basically independent" in the conduct of their affairs, and that we should leave the question to the students. The Law Review voted to expel Jonathan Lubell, but the Legal Aid Bureau retained David Lubell as one of its members. Whether this was the right decision may be questioned by some, though allowing the student boards to resolve the issue without faculty intervention seemed at the time to be what we should do, on the ground that this would be an educational experience for the student members of the organizations.

Thereafter, when the students had graduated from the Law School, Vice Dean Hall and I joined in recommending to the Character Committee of the New York Bar that they should be

---

53. Theoharis, above, at 148. The account in the Theoharis book continues with the information that "The Boston Field Office soon reported the recruitment of a member of the Harvard chapter as a 'confidential informant' of the Bureau with the assigned symbol number 'BOS–627.'" Ibid.

54. Beyond the Hiss Case, above, at 170, n. 49.

admitted to the Bar of New York, and they were admitted.[55]
They did have a somewhat difficult time for a while,[56] but they
are now practicing law together in New York in the firm of
Lubell & Lubell.[57]

———

During the early 1950s, and especially after the conviction of
Alger Hiss, Senator McCarthy and his supporters continued to
make speeches which were widely circulated, and he made new
sweeping charges almost daily. This had considerable impact in
the academic world, particularly when witnesses before the various committees refused to answer questions on the ground of
the privilege against self-incrimination provided by the Fifth
Amendment to the Constitution. They were called "Fifth Amendment Communists," reliance on the privilege being regarded as
an admission of guilt.

Few voices were heard in the academic world in opposition
to the charges which were being made. It is hard to reconstruct
the atmosphere now, but a deep sense of fear was widespread.
At first, I was simply annoyed that no one in the law school
world throughout the country was speaking out against the
tactics of the McCarthyites. But then I asked myself if I was
doing anything myself.

It was at this point that I received an invitation from Robert
W. Bodfish, of Springfield, Massachusetts, a Harvard Law School
graduate who had just succeeded Samuel Sears as president of
the Massachusetts Bar Association. He asked me to be the
speaker at the annual dinner of the Association, to be held in
Springfield on February 5, 1954. I sensed that this invitation
came because Mr. Bodfish did not fully share the views of Mr.
Sears. I asked him what he thought about my speaking on the

———

55. Both received their Harvard Law School degrees *magna cum
laude.*

56. See J. Seligman and P. Rosenberg, "Jonathan Lubell and the Law
Review: How Harvard Reclaimed Its Nerve," Nation 226 (March 18,
1978) 197–300.

57. Twenty-five years later, the Board of the Harvard Law Review
(most of whom were not born in 1953) voted to reinstate Jonathan
Lubell. See 91 Harv.L.Rev. 1003 (1978). This was a kind and generous
act, though taken with minimal responsibility and without a full awareness of the depth of feelings which permeated the atmosphere at the
time of the prior decision. A subsequent generation can properly make
its own judgment on issues which arise during its own period of
responsibility, but whether it is warranted in "rewriting history" may
sometimes be open to question.

subject of "The Fifth Amendment," in an effort to explain the background of that provision, and its role in our society. He said that that would be fine, and that he was sure the audience would be interested in my views. I then told him that I would accept his invitation, but only on condition that time would be allowed for a question period after my speech, and that the audience would be advised of this when I was introduced. I did not want anyone to say or think that I could "dish it out," but that I "could not take it." I anticipated that there would be substantial opposition to my remarks.

I spent much time preparing the speech, trying to keep it professional, but understandable to an audience which, though made up of lawyers, probably did not have much knowledge of the background of the privilege. In due course, the evening came, and, with some trepidation, I started on my speech. Before long, I sensed that there was great interest in the audience. There was complete silence and attention to my remarks. In due course, I finished the speech, and I was astounded when the audience stood up and cheered. I have never before, or since, had such a reaction to any speech I have made. There was little discernible opposition. The question period was called for, but there were no real questions. Those who rose did so to express approval of my speech.

The reaction in Springfield led me to seek a wider audience. The Harvard Law School Record had been established as a student newspaper in 1946, but it was financed by our alumni body, the Harvard Law School Association, and was circulated to all the members of the Association (about 10,000 in number) all over the country. I offered the speech to the editors of the Record and they printed it, and thus distributed it to our students and many of our alumni. This produced a good many reactions, not all of which, by any means, were favorable.[58]

Later that spring I was invited to give two further lectures. One was the Phi Beta Kappa address at Mt. Holyoke College and the other was before the Connecticut Bar Association in Hartford. These speeches, too, were printed by the Record and circulated to students, and alumni members of the Harvard Law School Association. At this point, someone suggested that the

---

58. A sequel was an invitation from Edward R. Murrow to appear on one of his television programs. This was produced in one of the classrooms in Landgell Hall, at the Law School. It reached a wide audience, and produced many letters. For some time afterwards, I was stopped on the street in various cities of the country, and told "I saw you on television."

speeches ought to be gathered together and published as a book. This was done by the Harvard University Press.[59] The book sold modestly and it has occasionally been cited and quoted by courts, including the Supreme Court. It has long since been out of print, and copies are now hard to find and expensive when they can be located, for interest in the Fifth Amendment has continued to surface in such matters as Watergate and the Iran–Contra affair.

J. The Bricker Amendment

After President Eisenhower came into office, one of the burning issues was "The Bricker Amendment." This was a proposed constitutional amendment sponsored by Senator Bricker of Ohio which was designed to eliminate "treaty law." It was contended that provisions were included in treaties (thus becoming a part of "the Supreme Law of the Land," pursuant to the Constitution), which could not validly have been enacted into law by Congress in the absence of the treaty.[60] Some of the concern arose from the agreements made with the Soviet Union at the time President Roosevelt recognized the Soviet Union in 1933. The adoption of such an amendment would have limited the President's powers in the field of foreign relations. President Eisenhower was opposed to the Bricker Amendment, but Senator Bricker was a prominent Republican, and the President, as he often did, kept his opposition at low key.

The issue came up before the American Bar Association, where I joined with others in opposing the Amendment. And I appeared on national television—taped at my desk in my office in Cambridge—stating my views in opposition to the Amendment. In due course, the Amendment was defeated in the Senate, failing by a few votes to reach the required two-thirds vote. I supposed that was the end of my participation. However, a short time later I received an invitation to attend a dinner at the White House. The guests were all men, and they were all persons who had been active in opposing the Amendment. To my great surprise, I was seated on the President's right. At each place, there was a small pocket knife, and also a shiny new copper cent, designed to negative any inference from giving a cutting instrument. I still have the knife. The copper penny, though, is lost, maybe spent.

---

59. E. Griswold, The Fifth Amendment Today (Cambridge 1954). Later a paperback edition was printed and distributed by The Fund for the Republic.

60. *Cf.* Missouri v. Holland, 252 U.S. 416 (1920); United States v. Belmont, 301 U.S. 324 (1937); United States v. Pink, 315 U.S. 203 (1942).

K. OTHER OPPORTUNITIES

Over the years while I was in Cambridge I was sounded out from time to time about becoming a college or university president. I never had any interest in becoming a president of a state university.[61] I knew that I would not be good at dealing with the "political" problems in such a post, particularly in working with the committees of state legislatures for appropriations, and on all of the other sorts of petty matters, including athletics, which inevitably occupy a large proportion of the time of the president of a state university. It was even more clear that I would not enjoy such tasks.

As for college presidencies, I had some opportunities. One was at my alma mater, Oberlin College. I was, indeed, Chairman of the Committee of the Board of Trustees to recommend a new president, both in 1945–46, and in 1959. In both cases, the committee asked me to leave the room, and when I returned, they asked me to resign from the committee so that they could recommend me for the post. But I had foreseen this and would never have accepted election to the committee if I was interested in the position. My reason was simple and clear. I regarded myself as being a lawyer. I wanted to be a lawyer. Being dean of the Harvard Law School was, I felt, one form of lawyers' work, and indeed a very interesting and challenging one, even though a considerable measure of administration was involved. Moreover, being dean of the Harvard Law School provided almost unlimited opportunities for making contributions to the profession, both in teaching and in various forms of public activity and scholarly work.

But being a college president, though important, and challenging, too, was not being a lawyer. I was pleased when people felt that I might be qualified, but I was never tempted. I felt that being dean of the Harvard Law School was the best legal job in the country, save one. I had undertaken the post as a career, and as long as I felt I was meeting my responsibilities, I had no desire to give it up, unless the other post became available, which I did

---

61. One of the universities about which I was consulted was Ohio State University, of which Senator Bricker was a trustee. I was told later that the Senator had vetoed me because I was "too radical." That was all right with me since I would never have accepted an invitation if it had been made. The basis of Senator Bricker's opposition always amused me, as I was generally regarded by most of my faculty colleagues as much too conservative.

not regard as a realistic possibility.[62] I have never regretted that
conclusion. Ever since my law school days, I have been sure
that I wanted to be a lawyer, that the law is a great profession of
basic importance to the country. It has problems, of course, but
one of the lawyer's opportunities is to contribute to the resolution
of those problems if he can, and he can rightly find great
satisfaction in feeling that he has played a meaningful role in the
task.

Opportunities for judicial appointment came to me on a few
occasions. One came from Governor Herter, to serve on the
Supreme Judicial Court of Massachusetts. I was pleased to have
the offer, and I gave it much thought. I finally concluded that I
would chafe at the sedentary and somewhat isolated nature of
the work. So I declined the opportunity with sincere thanks.
Through Senator Saltonstall, I also received requests about my
willingness to accept appointment to the United States District
Court in Massachusetts. As to this, I concluded that I was not
tempermentally suited to be a trial judge. I could be too impatient, and unwilling to accept the slow pace of activity of many
trial lawyers. I think I probably would have accepted an opportunity to become a judge of the United States Court of Appeals.
But that never came. And, as things have worked out, I have no
regrets.

One of the privileges of being dean of Harvard Law School is
the fine class of people with whom you have contact—students,
faculty colleagues, alumni, judges, other lawyers. Almost without exception, they are stimulating. Many of them make important contributions in widely varying ways. It has been fun to
know them. Many of them are gone now, of course, but I find
great encouragement in the new generation of lawyers. They are
at least as good as my generation was, not only in energy and
ability, but in zeal for the contributions they can make as lawyers. I am glad that my life has been devoted to the legal
profession and I have never regretted that I made that choice or
that I have stayed with it over a period of sixty-five years.

---

62. In the spring of 1953, after President Eisenhower had come to
office, I received a telephone call from his newly appointed Attorney
General, Herbert Brownell. For the moment available, I thought to
myself, "Well, maybe this is it." But Brownell's question was whether I
knew H. Brian Holland, and whether I felt that he would be qualified to
be Assistant Attorney General for the Tax Division. I replied that I knew
Holland well, and was sure he was well qualified. Shortly thereafter,
Holland was appointed to the post.

CHAPTER VII

Travels

⟨⟨~⟩⟩

A. NEW ZEALAND AND AUSTRALIA

In the spring of 1951, I received an invitation to attend the meeting of the Law Council of Australia, which was held in Sydney, Australia, in August, 1951. This was in connection with the fiftieth anniversary of the founding of Australia, which was established by the Commonwealth of Australia Constitution Act, enacted by the British Parliament, and effective on January 1, 1901. Judges from British areas all over the world were invited, and also a large number of practicing lawyers. Cody Fowler, of Florida, then President of the American Bar Association, was invited to represent the American Bar; I was invited to represent American law teachers. I was also asked to deliver a paper at one of the sessions of the convention.

My wife and I were both invited to make the trip, and it was suggested that the Carnegie Corporation, through its "British Dominions and Colonies Fund", might provide the necessary finances. At that time, though it was more than ten years after the onset of Harriet's illness, we had not found out what problems she might encounter in extensive travel. We decided that she should not undertake this trip. In essence, the feeling was that I should first go to a place, and get a feel for the situation, and that she might later have an opportunity to go with me. The Carnegie Corporation kindly said that I could take our daughter Hope, who was then a student at Oberlin College. Harriet's mother came to be with her during the summer, and Hope and I set off for Australia early in July.

We first spent a few days in Hawaii, my first trip there. We visited Pearl Harbor to the west of Honolulu, and Diamond Head to the east. Our host in Hawaii was Norman Smith, a classmate of mine at Oberlin, who was then principal of the Honolulu Community School for Adults. We drove around Oahu, saw the other sights, and met with a number of Harvard Law School alumni.

Our transocean travel was by Boeing Strato–Cruiser, a two-level propeller plane. From Honolulu we went on to New Zealand, stopping at Canton Island and Fiji on the way. Visiting the law schools in New Zealand and Australia and finding out what might be done to assist them was part of my assignment from the Carnegie Corporation.[1] While in New Zealand, I visited the Law Schools at Auckland, Wellington (Victoria University), Christchurch and Dunedin. Particularly in the South Island, these schools were then operated on an essentially part-time basis. Classes were held before nine in the morning, and after five in the afternoon, and the students were expected to spend virtually all of the daytime working in a law office, with little or no compensation. I met with practicing lawyers in all of the cities, but there was no suggestion that they were contemplating any change in the law school arrangement. Some of the schools were badly in need of more extensive library facilities.

While in the South Island, after our stay at Christchurch, we were met by my long-time pen pal, the Reverend Francis Allen, whom I had never met before. He drove us to his home in Pleasant Point, on the road to Mt. Cook, where we met his wife and son. This was a very happy meeting.

Hope and I then flew back to Wellington, where we took a flying boat to Sydney. This was my only trip on such a plane. People were packed into it on two levels, and there was not much room to walk around. The flight was delayed by weather, but it was quite uneventful when it eventually took off. We spent a week in Sydney attending the convention, and greatly enjoyed the people we met. Among those in attendance were Lord Jowett, the Lord Chancellor of England, Sir Raymond Evershed, later Lord Evershed, the Master of the Rolls, Sir Thomas Denning, later Lord Denning, Chief Justice Centlivers, of the Appellate Division of the Supreme Court of South Africa, Chief Justice Rinfret, of Canada, and Chief Justice Kania, of India, and many others. In addition, I met a number of Australian judges, including Chief Justice Latham of the High Court of Australia, and Sir Owen Dixon, later Chief Justice of the High Court.

---

1. After my return home, I wrote "Observations on Legal Education in Australia," which was published in 5 J. of Legal Ed. 139 (1952), and in 2 Univ. of West. Aust. Ann. L.Rev. 197 (1952).

For some reason, Lord Jowett took a special interest in me. He almost immediately asked me if I would go for walks with him before breakfast, and I did for several days, though it involved my getting up earlier than my usual custom. During these walks, we discussed a number of matters. After several days of quite frank discussion, I said to him: "You have been Labour Lord Chancellor in England now for three years. How many members of the Labour Party have been appointed to the bench during your term of office?" His response was almost vehement. He said: "That is a very improper question. It is wholly irrelevant. We never take into account politics or anything like that in making judicial selections. It is simply a matter of character, ability and standing at the bar." I waited for an appreciable period of time, and said: "Yes, I understand that. But my question is simply a factual one: how many members of the Labour Party have been appointed during your tenure?" He waited a little longer, and responded: "None."

About three months later, when the participants had returned to their homes, I learned that a member of the Labour Party had been appointed to the High Court in England. I do not now recall the name of the judge. I never met him. However, on at least two subsequent trips to England, I visited the Royal Courts of Justice on the Strand and went into his courtroom, and sat for a while, looking at *my* judge.

The paper I wrote for the Sydney meeting was entitled "Divorce Jurisdiction and Recognition of Divorce Decrees—A Comparative Study." [2] I chose this subject because the Australian Constitution establishes a federal government, with some provisions derived from the Constitution of the United States. One of these is the "Full Faith and Credit" clause. I thought, therefore, that my discussion would be of interest to the Australians. I found out, though, that the Australians pay little attention to the Full Faith and Credit clause—or have little need for it—and that my reference to it was not of any particular interest to Australian lawyers.

The commentator on my paper was Herbert Vere Evatt, the Deputy Prime Minister of Australia, and formerly a Justice of the High Court of Australia, and President of the General Assembly of the United Nations. Mr. Evatt had been a guest in our home in Belmont when he came to Harvard to deliver the Holmes Lectures in 1948. I felt honored that he was to discuss my paper. However, it soon became apparent that he was doing it "off the

---

2. 65 Harv.L.Rev. 193 (1951). The paper was also published in the Australian Law Journal.

cuff," and I could find nothing to indicate that he had read the paper. A number of the Australian lawyers apologized to me after the meeting. Mr. Evatt was in many ways a great man. But he was also erratic, with downs as well as ups.[3] Lord Denning was also a discussant at one of the sessions. He was very popular among American law teachers and American law students as a judge who was relatively free of the rather rigid British judicial ways. In the chit chat at various social gatherings, I heard him sharply criticized by some of the Australian judges, notably Chief Justice Latham.

After the session in Sydney, there was a further meeting in Canberra. The hotel there had two wings, one of which was heated, and the other was not. We were assigned to the unheated wing. It was not terribly cold, but August in Australia is winter. Our side of the hotel was known among the delegates as Siberia.

We next went to Melbourne, where there was, among other things, an elaborate dinner at Government House, hosted by the Lieutenant (pronounced Leftenant there) Governor. The invitations read "White Tie and Decorations." Cody Fowler and I had neither. But we were told that it would be all right to come in black tie, which we did. Music was provided by the equivalent of what we would call the Marine Band, and someone had taken pains to select a tune representing each one of the delegates. They were played during the progress of the dinner. When they got to me, they played "Yankee Doodle." This did not particularly please me, but it did not seem inappropriate. The next tune played was in honor of Cody Fowler, and it was "Marching Through Georgia." Someone had tried very hard to make the appropriate selection. I looked at Cody, and he looked at me. We succeeded in our efforts to refrain from outright laughing, but we did smile very broadly, and did not mention it to any of our hosts.

In Melbourne, we saw the sights, and were entertained by Chief Justice Herring of the Supreme Court of Victoria. We then went on to Hobart, in Tasmania, and finally to Brisbane in Queensland. It was, all in all, a most interesting and productive trip. During the course of it, I met a number of Australian law teachers, including Norval Morris of the Law School in Adelaide, South Australia, who later became dean of the faculty of the University of Chicago Law School, and Zelman Cowen, now Sir

---

3. See the excellent and appreciative discussion in Michael Kirby, "H.V. Evatt, The Anti–Communist Referendum and Liberty in Australia," 7 Australian Bar Rev. 93 (1991).

Zelman, who later became Dean of the Melbourne Law School, President of the University of Queensland, Governor General of Australia, and, more recently, Provost of Oriel College, Oxford, where he had been a student as a Rhodes Scholar at the close of World War II.[4]

In April 1953, Harriet and I made a trip to England. We had both been to England before, and knew the lay of the land, and what the problems might be. We flew in a propeller plane, of course, and, with some weather delay, it was a very long trip. We had learned that we could take her wheelchair with us, and this solved many of the problems.

My purpose was to establish contact with the law faculty at the Institute of Advanced Legal Studies in London, and then to visit law faculties at Oxford and Cambridge, and other universities, including the University of Nottingham, where I wanted to talk with Professor Harry Street, who was thereafter a Visiting Professor at Harvard in 1957–1958, and the University of Edinburgh, where I was anxious to meet Thomas B. Smith (later Sir Thomas), whom we eventually had as a Visiting Professor at Harvard in 1962–63. Ronald H. Graveson, S.J.D. 1936, Dean of the Faculty of Law of Kings College, University of London, was a Visiting Professor in 1958–59. We made the trip in a rented automobile, and eventually visited distant relatives in northern England on the way to Glasgow airport, where we departed on our return home.

B. SOUTH AFRICA

When I went to Australia in 1951, I met and was much impressed by Chief Justice Centlivres of the Appellate Division of the Supreme Court of South Africa, and we kept in touch through correspondence after we had returned to our respective countries.

Almost immediately, there was a considerable confrontation in South Africa when the government enacted a statute eliminating the right of coloured persons—that is, persons of mixed race—to vote in the Cape of Good Hope, despite the fact that

---

4. Norval Morris had visiting appointments at the Harvard Law School in 1955–56, and in 1961–62. Zelman Cowen had visiting appointments in 1953–54 and 1963–64. In addition, Julius Stone, then of the Sydney Law School, had visiting appointments in 1949 and in 1956–57. Other Australian law teachers paid extended visits at Harvard, including David Derham, later Vice-Chancellor at the University of Melbourne, and Peter Brett, of the Faculty of Law at the University of Western Australia.

their status as voters was entrenched in the South Africa Act, 1909. This was the United Kingdom statute which established the Union of South Africa.[5] The Appellate Division unanimously held that the statute was invalid.[6] I wrote a short piece about the opinion in the Harvard Law Review.[7] The "Entrenchment Clause" provided that the right of coloured persons to vote could be barred if the bill was passed "by both Houses of Parliament sitting together," and "agreed to by no less than two-thirds of the total number of members of both Houses." After the decision in the *Harris* case, the government enacted "The High Court of Parliament Act."[8] The Appellate Division held that this statute, too, was invalid.[9] Again the court was unanimous, though several separate opinions were written by members of the court.

Still, the government did not relent. A statute was now enacted giving the government power to appoint additional senators, so as, in our terms, to "pack" the Senate, and thus to give the Government a "two-thirds majority of the total number of members of both Houses," as provided by the Entrenchment Clause.[10] The Appellate Division concluded that it had no alternative but to accept this result, and thus the coloured vote was eliminated in the Cape of Good Hope.[11]

Perhaps it was because of my articles on this important but basically legal subject that I was asked in 1958 by the South Africa Fund in New York to go to South Africa to be an observer

---

5. 9 Edw. 7, c. 9.

6. Harris v. Minister of the Interior, [1952] 2 So. Afr. L. Rep. 428.

7. "The 'Coloured Vote Case' in South Africa," 65 Harv.L.Rev. 1361 (1952).

8. Act No. 35 of 1952 (South Africa), which made "Every senator and every member of the House of Assembly" a member of the court, and gave it appellate jurisdiction over the Appellate Division of the Supreme Court of South Africa.

9. Minister of the Interior v. Harris, [1952] 4 So. Afr. L. Rep. 769. See also Griswold "The Demise of the High Court of Parliament in South Africa," 66 Harv.L.Rev. 864 (1953); Hahlo and Kahn, The Union of South Africa: The Development of Its Laws and Constitution (London and Cape Town: 1960) 151–153.

10. Act No. 53 of 1955.

11. Collins v. Minister of the Interior, [1957] 1 So. Afr. 552. I did not write a piece about this third decision, though a tribute to Chief Justice Centlivres and his colleagues would have been in order. But there was not much more to say about "the law." The defeat was political, not legal. See E. McWhinney, "Law and Politics and the Limits of the Judicial Process," 35 Can. Bar Rev. 203 (1957).

in a treason trial in that country. When I went to South Africa, I put myself in the hands of Arthur Suzman, who had spent a year at Harvard in 1930–31. Arthur Suzman was the brother of Dr. Moses Suzman, who was the husband of Helen Suzman, the leading liberal (and long the only liberal member) of the South African Parliament. Arthur's help was invaluable, as he arranged my contacts, and helped greatly in filling me in as to the background of many of the problems.

During the course of my stay in South Africa, I visited several of the native townships, Soweto, Orlando, Alexandria and Sophiatown. I met many people, including Issi Maisels, the lead advocate for the defense in the treason trial, and his junior, Sydney Kentridge.[12] Sydney's wife, Felicia Kentridge, is also an advocate. The friendship of these three persons, thus started, has continued ever since, with great admiration on my part for the important and courageous work which these lawyers have performed.[13]

The Treason Trial of 1958 was held in Pretoria, in a former synagogue which had been refurbished to be a large courtroom. There were ninety-two accused at this trial, charged, in a four hundred page indictment, with serious offenses under the sweeping "Suppression of Communism Act." In the courtroom, the accused sat in rows of chairs. Each had a sign with a large number fastened around his neck, and all references were made to them by number, as "accused number eighteen," or "accused number ninety-one," and so on.

Before I went to South Africa, Gerald Gardiner, a British barrister, later Lord Gardiner as Lord Chancellor of England, had been an observer at the trial. After he had been there about ten days, he was denounced in a public statement by Mr. Louw, the Minister of External Affairs, who said that South Africa could run its own business, and that they did not need any interference from troublemakers from England. Mr. Gardiner then left the country. When I went to South Africa, I told my sponsor that if there was a similar blow-up with respect to me, I would probably leave. I said that I did not think that I could be useful if I was simply the occasion of controversy.

---

12. The bar in South Africa is divided, as in England. The lawyers who are known in England as barristers are called advocates in South Africa, and those who are solicitors in England are known as attorneys in South Africa.

13. Arthur Suzman had been made a Queen's Counsel ("Q.C.") before South Africa separated from the British Commonwealth, and he always used Q.C. after his name. After the separation, the term for new appointees was State's Advocate (S.A.).

As things worked out, I was received very cordially. A chair and small table were provided for me in the courtroom, and I was given a full set of papers, with an attendant being instructed to see that I got any additional papers that might be involved. The leading advocate for the prosecution was Oswald Pirow, an Afrikaner who had opposed South Africa's participation in World War II. I came to know Mr. Pirow somewhat, and I asked him one day why it was that I was treated so well, when Gerald Gardiner had been denounced by the Foreign Minister. To which Mr. Pirow responded, in his heavy Afrikaner accent, "Because he is a fool"—referring to the Foreign Minister. During the course of the trial, I met the judges, and thus became acquainted with Judge F. Rumpf, who later became Chief Justice of the Appellate Division of the Supreme Court of South Africa.

I left home on July 13, 1958, and did not return to the United States until August 21st. This gave me a considerable period in which to meet people in South Africa, and to travel to various parts of that country. I spent several days in Cape Town, met with people at the University of Cape Town, and at the University of Stellenbosch, nearby. I spent several days in Durban, meeting lawyers there, and visiting the branch of the University of Natal located there. I also had a long weekend at a game reserve some two hundred miles northeast of Johannesburg. I saw some fourteen different animals—everything but elephants—and fourteen different birds.

As for the trial itself, I was only able to attend the first week, and this was entirely devoted to a motion for recusal of one of the judges—who did recuse himself, because of a prior connection, in practice, with a case with related facts—and a motion to quash the indictment. Everything was very leisurely. Counsel showed high ability, but there was no time limitation on their presentations. The accused were all out on bail—£100 for Europeans—as all white people are known in South Africa [14]—and £25 for Africans. Except for the seating of the accused themselves, everything was strictly segregated. There was even a wooden barrier between the white section of the spectator's gallery and the section reserved for non-whites. [15]

14. Thus, I was a European during my stay there.

15. At my hotel in Johannesburg, when I gave my bag to a porter, I went out a door labeled "Whites" or "Blankes Only". The porter had to go out a separate door, labeled "Non–White" or "Nie Blankes." The customary separation was so complete that all personal contact was avoided. When I gave a tip to the porter, he did not hold out his hand to take it from my hand. Instead, he bowed quite low, and extended his

The noon lunch was provided for the accused at the Anglican Mission located near the Synagogue. I there met many of the accused, including Walter Sisulu and Nelson Mandela. The trial went on for weeks after I left. Eventually, though, the case resulted in an acquittal of all of the accused. As is well known, there were subsequent treason trials with different outcomes.

While I was in South Africa, I kept a rather extensive journal. When I visited Soweto, under the guidance of Mr. W.J.P. Carr, the Manager of the Non–European Affairs Department of the City of Johannesburg, I recorded that he was "obviously a dedicated social worker." I added: "He is doing what he can as an officer of the City of Johannesburg to improve things as much as possible. Given the rigid legal structure, with living in locations required, he and his people are working hard to improve conditions, and have obviously done much to that end. Things are clearly much better on average now than they were five, ten, twenty years ago. I did not see anything as bad today as I have seen in various places in the United States. But there was a greater concentration here, a greater monotony and sameness, and a clearly perceptible pall arising from the fact that these places are virtually prisons, not economic prisons, but legal prisons. Probably I am affected by my preconceptions, but it seems to me that there is a real and fundamental difference. These rigidly controlled and segregated people are cheerful on the exterior, but there is much to indicate that they are seething inside. Of course there are all varieties of them, some not long off the reserves. But others have been born here, have seen the city, have natural hopes and ambitions. And the situation, of which the housing is the ear-mark, so to speak, gives them little opportunity to accomplish anything to improve themselves, or their families and children."

After my trip to the Kruger Park, I observed "I get the impression that the country native is on the whole better off than the one who goes to the city. There may be more wages in the city, but there seems to be much more of something approaching freedom in the country. As we drove in to the city, I looked at the native faces on the street corners, lounging in front of the shops on a Sunday afternoon. Most of them were just sitting or standing, doing nothing. Perhaps it is evidence of my preconceptions, but it did seem that almost without exception the older ones—that is, seventeen or eighteen or older—looked sullen and bitter, and resigned and hopeless."

---

two hands cuplike. I then dropped the tip into the bowl made by his extended hands.

The bizarre way in which the restrictive laws operated are shown by the following passage:

"In the Johannesburg paper yesterday morning was this item: An African woman is a housemaid in Johannesburg. She has recently had a baby. She has just been served with an order to remove the baby. An African is an African, and the baby does not have a work permit, the official said. She can either give up her job and leave, or else send the baby away, perhaps to her parents, or other relatives, who live on the reserve, away from the city. But the baby cannot stay in white premises, though the mother can because she has a work permit."

With respect to the Afrikaners, I made this observation:

"It is hard to find out what these people really think. They are all very cordial, but few people really talk about issues. There have been tensions all through their lives, and they have learned, I think, to keep them in the background, for the most part. There is, first, the tension between the people of English descent and the Afrikaners. The English really had little, if any, justification for the Boer War. It was about the last stand of British Imperialism. The Afrikaners, who lost their independence then, have not forgotten it, even down to their grandchildren. Then there is commercial rivalry, with the English-speaking people controlling most of the industry. And finally, there is the race question, or rather all the race questions. On this the Afrikaner is more emotional than the English-speaking South African. He has built his rural economy on the labor of Natives. He has a deeply Calvinistic theology, which not only says that the Natives have their place, but that it is the duty of the white man to keep them in their place. He is intransigent, inflexible in all this, seemingly almost unthinking about it."

When Arthur Suzman arranged a luncheon for me with a group of Afrikaner businessmen, I put down this observation about one of those present, Mr. Jooste, business manager of Dagbreek, an Afrikaans Sunday newspaper:

"Mr. Jooste was most articulate. He is not a very profound man, but he did talk freely and frankly, and it was very helpful to get his views. We started out on the matter of a Republic. He said that it was important and that it would come. He said that it was important chiefly for psychological or sentimental reasons. He then went on to add that his father was in the Boer army, and that his mother was herded into a concentration camp fifty-eight years ago. He says these things are not forgotten by the present generation. Then we went on to apartheid. Mr. Jooste started by saying that there were two questions that he did not know the answer to: Why does a man want to be in control of things? Why does he not want his descendants to be coffee colored? He said there was no clear answer to these questions, that there might well not be much sense in them, but they were very deep-seated, and they were what really lay behind apartheid. He said that the liberal way (which would let each man reach whatever level he could, regardless of color) might work well for ten years, but that down that way lay the vote for coloured peoples, and that meant an eventual colored majority, and then colored control, and eventually intermingling of the races. He said that the only way to keep the white race white, and to retain white control, was through apartheid, and that was why he and nearly all Afrikaners are for it. It is a question of eventual destination, and not of immediate answers."

When I was in South Africa on this trip, the natives were always called "boys," both in the mines, and elsewhere. There were "police boys," uniformed, in the compounds. There were "boss boys," who were sort of foremen. There were many other kinds of "boys"; but they were all "boys" no matter how old they were. There were "house boys" and "boys" who work in the garden, and so on. Similarly, the white man is always called "baas," pronounced the same as "boss." Thus, when I said "good night" to the elevator boy in the hotel in Johannesburg, who wore a fine uniform and a red fez, he always replied "good night, baas."

I summarized the trial in these terms:

"Observation: Everything about this trial is a little absurd. It should not have been started in the first place. If started, the evidence should have been carefully sifted and digested, and it should have been confined to ten or twelve persons at the most. Apparently they had little idea what evidence they had when they started. If started, the charge should not have been High Treason, and 156 persons should not have been arrested at four o'clock in the morning on the Minister of Justice's birthday, and taken by military plane to a military field quite a distance from Johannesburg, and then locked up in the Fort, with large numbers of special guards. If these people are really dangerous, really guilty of High Treason, it is hard to think of them being out on bail of £100 down to £25. There should not have been a preliminary examination of thirteen months. There should not be a system of 'Special Courts.' If there is, the Minister of Justice should not go to great lengths to get through an amending statute under which he names the members of the court. If he does, he should not name a judge who is as vulnerable as Justice Ludorf was. (It is hard to conceive how this could have been overlooked, but Justice Ludorf told Mr. Maisels after the hearing yesterday that he (Ludorf) had not thought of the connection until Mr. Maisels pointed it out in his argument.) And the Minister of Justice should not have been making speeches in Parliament about how he had consulted Justice Rumpf in connection with the personnel of the court. If it were not all so serious for the people involved, and a symptom of such a difficult and indeed tragic situation, it would be material for a great legal comic opera. The trial itself is, and will be, exemplary. It is the general setting, and the moves leading up to it, which puzzles one."

When I visited the City Deep Mine, I met the Chief Compound Manager, and the Assistant Manager, Mr. King. The manager gave me no propaganda at all, but the assistant manager, Mr. King, gave me the full treatment. He came and sat beside me, and his talk went like this: "They are better off than we are. They don't have to worry about their food or shelter, and they get paid besides. They come and go just like we do, and they can go home whenever they want to do so [not saying that they had to pay their own transportation costs if they left before the end of their contract, and that they were subject to criminal prosecution if they did not work as they agreed to do in their labor contract]. They complain about passes, but we have to do the same thing; we have to carry our identity card [not saying that the pass is wholly different, must be constantly signed and validated, and that the white man is not thrown into jail if he forgets his identity card]. See how happy the Natives are. They are a very primitive people, and they are happy if they stay primitive. But when they get some education, they don't want to do any work. They just sit around and become agitators. They talk about strikes and things like that, why we never used to have any talk about strikes. It's a shame what has been happening in the mines. All this talk about the mines you hear in America—there's nothing to that. It's just a lot of propaganda put out by the communists to make people misunderstand South Africa." Well, that's the substance of it, though there was much more. I just sat and listened and didn't say a thing.

Later, I added this observation:

"A part of the problem in this country is a lack of any libertarian tradition. Another part may be a sort of insensitiveness, which is apparently congenital or at least deep-seated on the part of the Afrikaners. Mr. Jooste referred to the hullabulloo in America about Sophiatown. He was in America at that time, and said that he felt that South Africa must have been pulled to pieces. But then he came back and found that it was just about moving some people out of the west end, and nobody in Johannesburg really had known much about it. They put the locations far away and over the hill so they won't see them, and make it a point not to see them. They uproot people who have worked in a place for many years, and say they must leave. This often means going back to a tribal reserve, with which the people have no connection. But there is no outcry. Most of the people do not think anything about it. I do not mean that there are not people who are deeply concerned, but they are in a small minority; they have learned that there is not much that they can effectively do. They do what they can, but it is not much.

"At the time I was in South Africa, non-European medical students at the University of Witwatersrand were not allowed to attend an autopsy on a white body, or even to examine organs removed from a white body. This was a governmental regulation, not anything imposed by the University itself. But Africans wheeled the body into the operating room."

I summed up my views in these words:

"There is fascination and promise, and somewhere somehow hope for this country. But as one reads the legislation and sees how every little point is picked off one by one, without any effective or even vocal protest, with some exceptions, one has the feeling that the place is going slowly, steadily, remorselessly, and deliberately to hell. The present Afrikaners say that their troubles today are due to the fact that their predecessors did not provide sufficiently for racial separation, so they are going to do the job now that ought to have been done before. Having taken that position, no step that increases separation while keeping the African's labor is too extreme. There is no libertarian tradition at all, and most of what is done is done more or less as a matter of course. Some people say, 'It really is rather rough for them, isn't it?'—but that is about as far as the general reaction goes. Of course this does not apply to the small group of liberals, but they are without any effect on action, and without appreciable effect on general public thinking."

C. New Zealand and Australia Again

In 1959, I had my one and only Sabbatical leave during my thirty-three years as a member of the faculty at Harvard. This was not due to any lack of generosity on Harvard's part. The War was on when my first leave had been due, and at the close of the War I became dean of the School, with many administrative responsibilities. In early 1958, I went to President Pusey and said: "What would happen if I asked for leave during the spring semester in 1959?" His quick response was: "You would get it."

Again, the Carnegie Corporation offered to assist me with expenses, and encouraged me to visit the Law Schools in New Zealand and in Australia. This time, Harriet went with me. We left, early in January, 1959, immediately after the close of my term as President of the Association of American Law Schools. I found a cruise which left from New York on the Kungsholm of the Swedish–American line. We went through the Panama Canal, and then on to the Galapagos Islands. We did not go ashore there, but went out in small boats, and saw the lizards and other fauna on the rocks. Then we proceeded to American Samoa, where we had a day ashore. Harriet attracted a great deal of attention, mostly from children, as I pushed her in her wheelchair. Our next stop was at the island of Moorea, where we had a beautiful day enjoying the tropical scenery. Again the wheelchair was a center of attraction. We then went on to Suva, in Fiji, and then to Auckland, New Zealand, where we left the ship.

We hired a car at both islands of New Zealand, and saw many friends, including a visit with my "pen pal" the Reverend Francis Allen, who then had a parish in a southern suburb of Christchurch. We went on to Dunedin, then to Invercargill, at the south end of the South Island. On the way back, we went to Queenstown, and through the tunnel that leads to Milford Sound.

From New Zealand, we went on to Australia, where we visited law schools in Brisbane, Sydney, Melbourne, Hobart, Adelaide, and Perth. This was my first visit to Western Australia, which I found to be thriving and most attractive, though rather isolated.[16] We saw many old friends, including Julius Stone in Sydney, and Zelman Cowen in Melbourne, who were particularly kind and helpful.

We came back by plane in June, and attended our son's Commencement when he graduated from Oberlin College.

D. Soviet Union

In 1961, I was invited to participated in a "Dartmouth Conference" in the Soviet Union. These meetings were largely organized by Grenville Clark, a prominent Harvard Law School graduate, and the first session was held in Dartmouth College in 1960. I was invited to attend the 1960 Conference, but could not do so

---

16. The American Consul in Perth told me that his post was the most distant from any other American post in the Foreign Service.

because of conflicting engagements. I was much pleased to be asked to attend the meeting in 1961.

I left earlier than the other members of the group, in order to visit my son, who was in the City of Tunis, in Tunisia. He was working there for the American Friends Service Committee, providing assistance to Algerian refugees. From Tunisia, I flew to Amsterdam, and then to Moscow on a Soviet plane. The first few days of the meeting were held in Moscow, where we visited with people at the University of Moscow, and at the Institute of State and Law. Then we flew to Simferopol, in the Crimea, and went on a bus to an elegant guest house (which they called a sanitarium), on the Black Sea at Lower Oreandra, near Yalta, where the remaining days of the Conference were held. Along with the others, I had an elegant suite, including entrance hall, sitting room with balcony overlooking the Black Sea, bedroom, and a large bathroom. I took a shower, and used the large towel which was on a rack. After using it, I wadded it up and threw it in the corner, since there did not seem to be any receptacle for it. Later, though, I found that that was my towel for the week. So I was more careful with it thereafter.

The discussion, with simultaneous interpretation, continued for several days. Our delegation was a remarkable one, including Marian Anderson, Margaret Mead, Norman Cousins, and William Benton (who was then the owner of the Encyclopedia Britannica) among others. One of the unforgettable moments came one evening when we visited a camp of the Consomol, the Soviet Youth Organization. This was a clear, warm night, lighted by a full moon, on the shores of the Black Sea. Marian Anderson had then retired from concert singing, but she sang several songs to the boys and girls—without accompaniment—and we were all enthralled.

The Soviet members of the Conference were friendly and courteous, but they showed no signs of yielding. I had some talks with one of their economists. I was rather critical of some of their practices, and particularly the rigidity which results from central planning. But he said, they were working on these things, and would bring about improvements.

On leaving the Soviet Union, I flew to England on a British plane. I can remember the feeling of relief when the wheels left the ground. No longer did I have to look over my shoulder, or see that nothing was slipped into my pockets.

E. Nigeria

In the summer of 1960, I went to Nigeria, just before its independence. I was a member of a group, including persons from England, Canada and Australia, who were assembled to talk with Nigerian government people about problems relating to federalism. We went first to Accra in Ghana, where we had a fascinating interview with Kwamie Nkrumah, and then to Kano in northern Nigeria. We also visited Zaria, and Kaduna, the capital of Northern Nigeria, and then Lagos, where most of our meetings were held.

While in Lagos, I stayed in the guest house of the Chief Justice of Nigeria, Sir Adetokunbo Ademola and Lady Ademola. Sharing the guest house with me was Kenneth Diplock, then a Justice of the High Court in England, who later became Sir Kenneth and then Lord Diplock, one of the leading English judges of this half century.

We met many people in Nigeria. But I paid little attention to the military. There were only about five thousand of them altogether, and there did not seem to be any reason to think that they would play an important role. This was, of course, a wrong assessment on my part. Despite the finding of large deposits of oil, Nigeria has had a troubled existence since its independence.

In the summer of 1965, the Harvard Law School put on a program in London, in association with the University of London. Several Harvard faculty members gave short courses, over a period of two weeks, in what might be called "the Harvard Law School style." I participated, giving lectures on conflict of laws. I was honored that Lord Scarman, then one of the leading English judges, faithfully attended nearly all of my lectures.

On the whole, this venture did not work out too well, and it was not repeated. There was a reasonably good attendance. However, it was not possible to get those attending the lectures to participate very much. There was little "give and take." Consequently, the sessions tended to be literally "lectures," without the vitality of a case method class.

It was during these sessions, on July 14, 1965, that Adlai Stevenson died, while walking on a street in London. I had been an admirer of Stevenson, and particularly of his public addresses. I remember the date of his death since it was my birthday.

F. East Africa

After the London session, Harriet and I went on to Africa, at the invitation of the Rockefeller Brothers Fund. We flew from London to Nairobi in Kenya, stopping at Khartoum on the way. As we took off from Khartoum, our plane was struck by lightening, and one engine, out of four, was disabled. But we continued on our way, and arrived eventually in Nairobi, a couple of hours late. We visited lawyers and law schools in Nairobi. We were taken on a day's trip by automobile to the north of Nairobi, crossing the equator, seeing the Great Rift, and the lake at Nakura, which was largely covered by the spectacular crimson of Scarlet Ibis.

From Nairobi we went to Uganda, where we stayed in Kampala. There we had the privilege of an audience with the Kabaka of Buganda. When the Kabaka arrived at the audience chamber, all of the local people immediately dropped to the ground, with their foreheads touching the floor. This was, of course, impossible for Harriet to do, and I did not try it. Later we told the American Ambassador that we had had an audience with the Kabaka. He was quite incredulous. He said that he had been unable to arrange such an audience for any visitor for a period of two years. We then explained that the arrangement had been made for us by Andrew Frederick Mpanga, who was the Attorney General of Buganda, and had been awarded the LL.M. degree at the Harvard Law School in 1965.

When we were in Uganda, it was the most promising place in Africa. Though located on the equator, it is fairly high, so that the climate is mild. Both business and agriculture seemed to be thriving. We did not at all foresee the disaster which would soon be occurring in that country.

Over the weekend, while we were in Uganda, we were taken by automobile to Murchison Falls Park on the Nile River. We saw the Falls both from the top, and later from a boat which we took up the river, from which we saw many alligators, rhinoceroses, and other animals and birds. On our drive to the park, we saw dozens of elephants.

While we were at the place where we boarded the boat for the trip up the Nile to the Murchison Falls, we found special difficulties. The ground leading to the launching pier was rather soft, and it was filled with elephant footprints, eight to ten inches across, and four inches or so deep. It was impossible for Harriet to walk over this with her crutches, and it was extremely difficult to take her wheelchair. Finally, we got several people together and carried the wheelchair, though this had to be done very carefully, for the footing for the carriers was precarious.

From Uganda we flew to Dar es Salaam in Tanzania. There we visited the law school which was established for the three countries of Kenya, Tanzania and Uganda. We also spent a very interesting day in Zanzibar. We travelled from Dar es Salaam in a small plane. This involved getting Harriet up on the wing of the plane. Then she slid along the wing to the window, and was hauled through the window to her seat.

While in Zanzibar, we had lunch with the judges of the East Africa Court of Appeals. We saw many cloves drying in the sun, and the odor of cloves was pervasive. We met with the American Consul in Zanzibar. His wife was teaching their small children out of textbooks provided by the State Department.

G. Far East

In 1966, Harriet and I went at the request of the State Department to the Far East. We went first to the Philippines, then to Singapore, Kuala Lumpur in Malaysia, Taiwan, Korea, and Japan. In Japan we were several times the guests of my long-time friend Edwin Reischauer, then Ambassador to Japan, and his wife Haru.

H. South Africa Again

In 1967, we went first to South Africa, where I had been invited to give the Day of Affirmation Lecture at the University of Natal, in Pietermaritzburg. This lecture had been given the previous year by Robert Kennedy. When I wrote the lecture, I entitled it "We Hold These Truths * * * ." However, the National Union of South African Students, who sponsored the lecture, printed it, and I found that it was entitled "Academic Freedom and Human Freedom." I could understand the reason for this change.

Harriet's and my movements were under observation throughout our stay in South Africa. We were photographed as we entered airports, and as we left. While we were in Johannesburg, I gave a lecture one evening at the University of the Witwatersrand. I noticed that there was a man in the front row industriously taking notes. I judged, correctly as it turned out, that he was one of the internal police, and that he was taking notes of my lecture. I also realized that he was undoubtedly an Afrikaner, whose primary language was Afrikaans, and that the notes were probably in Afrikaans. I was worried that there might be some sort of mis-translation, not because of any dishonesty in the person making the notes, but simply because of the nuances of translation. So, when my lecture was over, I walked down to the man. I had a copy of my speech in English, and I gave this to him, saying that perhaps this would help him in making his report.

After giving the lecture in Pietermaritzburg, we drove to Durban, stopping on the way to pay a call on Alan Paton (whose home was nearby). This was a memorable experience for us. Unfortunately, his wife was then very seriously ill. He seemed anxious to talk to us, though he was several times interrupted in order to pay attention to her. We then visited Durban and Cape Town, where we saw many friends.

From South Africa, we flew to Lusaka in Zambia, and I visited the law school there, where Kwamena Bentsi–Enchill, who had studied at the Harvard Law School in 1961, was the dean. He was a very promising man. Unfortunately, he died a few years later in an automobile accident. While in Lusaka, we took a trip by automobile to Ndola in the northern part of Zambia. The Chinese, who were then building the railroad from Zambia to Dar es Salaam, had a large exhibit there. Because of my interest in boundary lines, I took a short trip out of the city to the place where Zambia joins with Zaire. We then returned to Lusaka, where we paid a visit to the National Capitol building. This is an imposing structure, entirely encased in copper, on which the economy of the country largely depends.

From Lusaka we flew back to England. This was fortunate, because one of Harriet's braces broke in Lusaka and there were no facilities there for repairs. Nevertheless, our journey was delayed. Because of the six-day war, overflight of Moslem areas in Africa by British planes was forbidden. As a result, we had to fly to Teheran. Then we flew non-stop to London, arriving about eight hours late.

After arriving in London, we went to Oxford, where Harriet was planning to visit a rehabilitation hospital, and where we hoped her brace could be repaired, as turned out to be the case. I then continued to a conference at Ditchley Park, near Oxford.

In due course, we took off again, this time for the very long flight from London to Sydney, and then back to Adelaide, where we were to attend a conference of the Law Council of Australia. On the way, we landed at Singapore, which is where I completed my one and only trip around the world, since I had been in Singapore from the east, in 1966.

After attending the meeting of the Law Council in Adelaide, we went to New Zealand, and then to Honolulu for a meeting of the American Bar Association. Eventually, we returned to Boston after another eventful trip.

CHAPTER VIII

Other Activities

A. OBERLIN COLLEGE

For many years, I was a trustee of Oberlin College, and devoted much time, thought, and effort to that task. I was elected to the Board in June, 1936, probably at the suggestion of President Ernest H. Wilkins, and I was then continuously a trustee until January 1, 1980. Having then passed my 75th birthday, I elected to become an "honorary trustee."

Early in my trusteeship, President Wilkins asked me to draft an amendment to the bylaws providing for the retirement of trustees. He was concerned by the fact that the members of the Board were regularly reelected, and there were many in the older age group. I prepared a bylaw providing that any trustee could elect to become an honorary trustee on reaching the age of seventy, and that all trustees became honorary trustees no later than the close of the year in which they reached the age of seventy-five. President Wilkins sounded out several member of the Board, and came to the conclusion that there would not be a majority vote to support this proposal. Each of the trustees consulted said that he was willing to abide by the proposal, but that he did not wish to impose it on his fellow trustees. I then suggested that we provide that the change in the bylaws should not be applicable to any present member of the Board of Trustees. Though this did not resolve the immediate problem, it did take care of the matter in the long-run.

The amendment was then adopted by the Board, without difficulty. Under it, I was not required to retire at the end of the year in which I reached the age of seventy-five, since I was in the excepted class, that is, I was a member of the Board of Trustees

217

when the amendment was adopted—the last remaining member of that group. However, when that year came, I felt that I was morally bound—or that, at least as a matter of taste, I ought to accept the rule which had become established for all other trustees. This means that I can attend meetings of the Board, receive copies of various papers, and can even be a member of committees of the Board, but I have no vote.

I was an active member of the Board for forty-three and a half years. On two occasions, I was chairman of the committee assigned the task of recommending to the Board a person for election as president of the College. The first time was in 1946, when William E. Stevenson was elected president. The second time was in 1959, when Robert Carr was elected to succeed Stevenson.[1]

The presidency of Oberlin College is, in my view, a particularly difficult assignment. This goes back to a position held strongly by a considerable (and vocal) group of faculty members that all decisions with respect to the College must be made by the faculty, and the president's responsibility is, primarily, to see that the faculty decisions are carried out—and also to raise money. It is said, on behalf of the faculty, that this arrangement goes back to 1836 when it was agreed by the trustees that the faculty should have full "internal control." I do not think that there is any foundation for this position. In my view, it goes back to the early 1920s, when the president was not well, and there were some strong members of the faculty who took over responsibility, and then inculcated newly arriving members of the faculty with this "long-standing tradition."

Be that as it may, for many years, at least back to the early 1930s, the life of an Oberlin president has often been extremely difficult. Among other things, a number of members of the faculty have shown little compunction about disagreement with the president, and have, indeed, sharply criticized him in public statements, so that his life has sometimes been quite unpleasant.

Over the years, I have worked at this problem. I felt particularly responsible because of my academic background, though in an institution with a very different outlook and traditions. Unfortunately, my efforts have not been fruitful. I have tried to help the Board of Trustees to be more aware of this problem, and to take stronger positions in support of the president. One aspect

---

1. On both of these occasions, I reached the conclusion that I did not want to be president of a college, and particularly that I did not want to be President at Oberlin, for reasons which will be indicated shortly. See also p. 195, above.

of the problem stood out clearly in the 1970s, when a large group of faculty sought to establish a labor union, and lost an NLRB election for that purpose by only a few votes.

Despite these problems, the College has played a substantial role in American collegiate education. When I was a student there, in the 1920s, a high proportion of the students came from Ohio, and most of the rest came from the mid-west, with a considerable concentration in the Chicago area. In recent years, the College has grown considerably in size, and a much higher proportion of its students come from the eastern seaboard, the far west, and from foreign countries.

In the post-War years, the average academic caliber of the student body has increased. The faculty includes many fine teachers and scholars, many buildings have been added to the physical resources, and the endowment has substantially increased.

If only the matter of the relation between the President and the faculty could be worked out, I think that Oberlin should be a nearly perfect undergraduate institution. It has a long tradition of service. In origin, this tradition was essentially religious. Over the past fifty years, there is less religious emphasis, but there continues to be a strong desire to make contributions to the public weal.

In 1982, after my retirement, the College awarded me the honorary degree of LL.D. And in 1990, one of the large dining halls in the Stevenson Building was named Griswold Commons. I am grateful for this recognition. I am also glad that I had the opportunity over the years to work with successive presidents of the College, members of the faculty, and of the Board of Trustees, to try to support the college in its important role in American education. I am only sorry that, for some reason which I have never been able to understand, it has not been possible to work out a more satisfactory relation between the faculty and the President.[2]

B. FUND FOR THE REPUBLIC

These activities are part of the background of another venture on which I spent considerable time and energy over a period of several years. This was the Fund for the Republic, sometimes

2. At the request of the College, I have done an "Oral History," with the aid of Professor Geoffrey Blodgett, which deals primarily with my Oberlin experiences. A copy of this is on file at the Oberlin College Library.

known as "a wholly disowned subsidiary of the Ford Foundation." The Fund was established in October, 1951, but for a while it existed only on paper.[3] In due course, a Board of Trustees was set up, and I was asked to be a member of the Board.[4] Paul Hoffman had been president of the Ford Foundation. However, he resigned, and shortly thereafter became president of the Fund for the Republic.

The stated objectives of the Fund were "to advance understanding of civil liberties, to eliminate restrictions on freedom of thought and inquiry and to promote the principles of individual liberty expressed in the Declaration of Independence and the Constitution." In February, 1953, a group of trustees of the Fund for the Republic appeared before the trustees of the Ford Foundation and requested a grant of fifteen million dollars to be expended over a period of years for these purposes. The grant requested was approved by the Ford Foundation. A few days later, on February 26, 1953, Robert Hutchins wrote me, saying "I want you to know that in my opinion you single-handed and alone got fifteen million dollars for the Fund for the Republic."[5] Others have told me since that this was a considerable exaggeration, and that, indeed, the grant had been "programmed" before our committee arrived in Pasadena.

Shortly thereafter, the Fund for the Republic was actively organized with headquarters in New York. Hoffman had intended to be only an interim president. In September 1953, he was succeeded by Clifford Case, than a congressman from New Jersey. However, in March, 1954, Case resigned in order to run for the Senate from New Jersey, where his race was successful. On April 15, 1954, the trustees of the Fund unanimously elected Robert Hutchins to be its president. Not a great deal had been accomplished up to this time, but Hutchins provided imaginative and active leadership.[6] The Fund soon sponsored the publication

---

3. The story is fully told in Thomas Reeves, Freedom and the Foundation: The Fund for the Republic in the Era of McCarthyism (New York: 1969). See also F. Kelly, Court of Reason—Robert Hutchins and the Fund for the Republic (New York, 1981).

4. Other members of the Board included Chester Bowles, Paul G. Hoffman, William H. Joyce, Jr., Meyer Kestnbaum, Jubal R. Parten, Elmo Roper, George N. Shuster and Eleanor B. Stevenson.

5. Reeves, above, p. 305, fn. 13.

6. My first contact with Robert Hutchins came in 1927, when I was president of the Harvard Law Review. We published an article by Robert M. Hutchins and Donald Slesinger, "Some Observations on the Law of Evidence—Memory," 41 Harv.L.Rev. 860 (1928). This was, I

of a number of books.[7] The Fund financed a study by a committee of the Association of the Bar of the City of New York on the Loyalty–Security Program, a study of Communist influence in American life, under the direction of Professor Clinton Rossiter of Cornell, a study of Fear in Education by Paul F. Lagarsfeld of Columbia University, and a series of case studies in personnel security. It also granted fellowships and made grants in aid. It distributed many books and articles, including twenty-five thousand copies of the special issue on loyalty-security of the Bulletin of the Atomic Scientists, twenty-five thousand copies of an article that Harpers Magazine published by Richard H. Rovere entitled, "The Kept Witnesses," twenty-five thousand copies of an article in the American Scholar by Richard Hofstadter entitled "The Pseudo–Conservative Revolt," and thirty-five thousand paperback copies of my book of speeches on "The Fifth Amendment Today."[8]

The work on the board of the Fund for the Republic was interesting, intensive, and eventually distressing. Two events

---

believe, Hutchins' only venture into legal writing. Hutchins was then Dean of the Yale Law School, but he was soon called to the University of Chicago, as president, at the age of thirty.

I was well acquainted with Hutchins' younger brother Francis. We had been students together at Oberlin, and we also worked together several summers at Camp Pemigewassett. Frank had the job of driving the camp truck into Wentworth to get the mail and the milk. The milk came in ten gallon cans, and one of my duties was to meet Frank when he arrived and to help him get the milk off the truck and into the ice house. I still remember with some intensity that a ten gallon can of milk is very heavy and that it is a challenging task to get it off the nearly shoulder-high platform of a truck without having it drop down on your toes.

Frank taught at Yale–in–China for a while and then had a distinguished career of service as president of Berea College in Kentucky for many years, following the footsteps of his father in that task.

7. Including Samuel A. Stouffer, Communism, Conformity and Civil Liberties (Garden City, New York: 1955).

8. In Harry S. Ashmore's biography of Robert M. Hutchins, entitled "Unseasonable Truths," the author suggests that the distribution of my book brought about financial return to me and that "the board had approved an expenditure of fifteen thousand dollars to provide widespread distribution of the paperback edition of the book." Actually, though, I took care to make special arrangements so that no royalties were paid to me on account of the paperback edition, and the price was reduced accordingly. I also "refused financial remuneration for my services on the board" of the Fund. Reeves, Freedom and the Foundation, above, at p. 235.

stand out particularly in my memory. The activity of the Fund
soon led to "an orchestrated campaign" being directed against
Henry Ford II and the Ford Motor Company "from the right." [9]
As a result, the trustees of the Fund were summoned to the New
York residence of Mr. Ford for a meeting in early 1956. This
was, of course, a rather tense affair. Mr. Ford disclosed some of
the pressures to which he was subject, but he never sought to
issue any orders, nor made any threats. I left the meeting with a
considerable feeling of understanding for his concern, and with
real appreciation for the approach he had taken.

The other meeting was when the lawyer members of the
trustees of the Fund were requested to meet with Fred C.
Scribner, Jr., the Under Secretary of the Treasury. We knew that
the Treasury had been subjected to a considerable amount of
pressure from the Unamerican Activities Committee of the House
and the Internal Security Committee of the Senate to remove the
tax exemption of the Fund for the Republic. We felt that the
summons we had received might indicate a weakening on the
part of the Treasury, and that we might have a difficult time at
the meeting. Various matters were discussed at the meeting in a
temperate way. Such was my concern in advance, though, that it
took me quite a while to realize that the Treasury was not
presently disposed to take any action, and that the meeting was
being held primarily so that the Treasury could report the fact of
the meeting, and that the matter was receiving careful consideration there.[10] President Eisenhower never appeared in the picture, but I have always assumed that he had been consulted, and
that, in his usual quiet way in such matters, he had intimated that
no adverse action should be taken.

In due course, after the Fund for the Republic had achieved
a measure of success in restoring balance to the general atmosphere, Hutchins began to lose interest. At this point, about half
of the Fund's original grant had been expended or committed.
Hutchins began talking about the "Great Issues." He had always
preferred to live in California, and he and his wife bought a
residence in Santa Barbara. He proposed that the balance of the
funds held by the Fund for the Republic should be transferred to
a new activity to be known as the Center for the Study of
Democratic Institutions. I opposed this from the beginning (and
still think that I was right in my opposition). I felt that the Fund

---

9. Ashmore, Unseasonable Truths, above, at 361.

10. This conference with Under Secretary Scribner is discussed, but
without detail, in F. Kelly, Court of Reason—Robert Hutchins and The
Fund for the Republic (New York: 1981), at pp. 56–57, 65–71.

for the Republic had done good and useful work in the field of civil liberties, but that its task was really little more than started. Among other things, it had shown almost no interest in any aspect of the racial problems in the United States—segregation, voting rights, job discrimination, and so on.

I started out as an admirer of Robert Hutchins, and he surely was an unusual and able person. As time went on, though, I came to have a rather different view of him—that he was, in essence, a very self-centered person, whose basic interest was to promote himself and to advance his own projects. Often, though not always, these were quite good projects; but they were always centered on Hutchins. He mesmerized many good people with his charm and ability, I thought. But we were responsible for charitable money, not Hutchins' money. Overall, I feel that Hutchins was a great figure in our time, with more innovative ideas than any other person I can recall in the field of education, and with a remarkable personality, which gave him great influence over many persons. My view came to be, though, that his basic interest was not education nor freedom. It was Bob Hutchins, and looking out for Bob Hutchins seriously affected his judgment. He was, perhaps, one of the authentic geniuses I have known, and all of them had serious flaws in one respect or another.[11]

Eventually the Board of the Fund for the Republic approved the shift and a Center for the Study of Democratic Institutions was established with Fund for the Republic money in Santa Barbara, California. In a letter to Thornton Wilder, written in 1954, Hutchins had told his long-time friend that he was "spending fifteen million dollars stolen from the Ford Foundation on civil liberties and racial & religious indiscrimination, if you know what I mean."[12] I felt that he had "stolen" the money again when he took half of the Fund to support his essentially personal venture in Santa Barbara. I had worked hard to get the money for civil liberties, and I felt that any action taken to divert the remaining half of the funds to another and wholly unrelated—and very nebulous—idea, centering on Hutchins, was in reality a failure to use the money for the purpose for which it was given and was very badly needed, and was simply immoral, or a breach of trust.

---

11. Much of the above paragraph comes from a letter which I wrote to Harry Ashmore on September 12, 1987. The letter is cited in Ashmore's Unseasonable Truths, above at p. 359, fn. 10, and at 377–378, fn. 7 (where the letter is misdated as September 12, 1981).

12. Quoted in Ashmore, Unseasonable Truths, above, at p. 343.

Harry Ashmore says that "money was never an active concern of Hutchins's" [13] I agree with this statement, after a nice comfortable minimum amount was available and assured. He never had any desire, in my view, to be a wealthy man, or to make any particular show. But he was always careful to see that he was comfortably provided for, and this was surely one of the motivations in the move to Santa Barbara. What he really seemed to me to want was not money, but a field of activity where he could continue to be a "key" figure and could have a very pleasant and stimulating life, without very much regard for its social or intellectual utility. My feeling was that Hutchins had the basic ability to be a really great man, and that he is indeed one of the disappointing figures of my time. He did not really effectively utilize the abilities he had—in the sense of making an impact on society, in developing and contributing ideas which were truly effective, and in obtaining acceptance for his ideas.[14]

All in all, I have felt over the years that my participation in the Fund for the Republic was a valuable experience which was moderately effective. I was sorry when its efforts were terminated at a time when there was so much more that needed to be done. As for the Center for the Study of Democratic Institutions, I doubt that it had any appreciable general impact.

C. Teaching, Faculty and Related Developments

Despite these other activities, my basic task always remained doing what I could to see that the Harvard Law School ran smoothly and constructively. I continued to teach throughout my deaning days, although I undertook only about a half of a normal classroom schedule. This consisted of two sections, two hours a week each, of the introductory Tax course. At the beginning, this course was offered in the third year on an elective basis. However, the faculty yielded to the pleas of the tax teachers that an understanding of taxation was an essential background for a number of other courses, and the course was, about 1960, transferred to the second year and made a required course. My classes were scheduled from ten to twelve on Monday and Tuesday mornings.[15] This meant that I was free on the

---

13. Ashmore, Unseasonable Truths, above, at p. 378.

14. For another evaluation, see Edward Shil's "Robert Maynard Hutchins," 59 American Scholar 211 (1990).

15. In the immediately post-war years, the class sessions were given complete in one term, and the courses were doubled up. Thus, for three

other days of the week, including Saturday, for meetings and travel. It also meant that I had to give up teaching Conflict of Laws, a subject which I greatly enjoyed, and where I think I might have made some contribution.[16]

I had had no particular "management" experience, but, as dean, I was in a field which required a great deal of planning, organization, and contact with people. From the beginning, I tried to dispose of things promptly when that could be soundly done, in order to keep them from piling up. In particular, I tried to answer letters within a day or two from the time when they were received. The correspondence—from alumni, from other law schools, from faculty members all over the country (and, indeed, from many foreign countries), from government agencies and officers, and from lawyers generally—was voluminous. I delegated the admissions correspondence to the admissions office, except that I often sampled the incoming mail on Saturdays, in an effort to keep my finger on the pulse.

There were many meetings of faculty committees. The appointments committee was the most important, and I always designated myself as chairman of that committee. The Administrative Board served as a sort of advisory committee, and handled various administrative matters, and also disciplinary problems. There were few of these, but when they arose, they were often quite difficult. In this connection I remember two contacts with Bishop Wright, of the Boston Catholic Diocese, later Cardinal Wright, resident in Rome, and sometimes, until his untimely death, spoken of as likely to be "the first American Pope."

When we brought Harold Berman to the faculty, in 1948, and he started teaching Soviet law, he put out a list of books, which the students were supposed to read. Almost immediately, a group of

---

years, I had one section for two hours on Monday, and the same section for two hours on Tuesday. Faculty members were free to teach from 10:10 a.m. until 11:00 a.m., and then from 11:10 a.m. to 12 noon. However, along with a number of my colleagues, I chose to teach the course continually, that is, from 10:10 a.m. to 12 noon, without a break. This was a bit strenuous, for teacher and students alike, but it worked out very well, and there were no complaints from the students.

16. This would have included dealing with some of the question-begging heresies of Professor Brainerd Currie, who had great impact on judges and scholars in the field of Conflict of Laws during the years just after the middle of the century. Conflict of Laws is a full-time and demanding field; and Professor Currie was a vigorous and resourceful advocate. I have long regretted that I was not able to devote myself to the field, and to do what I could to ameliorate some of the unfortunate consequences he helped to bring about.

students came to my office—directed there by Professor Berman—and told me that they could not read most of the books, since they were on the Index, and thus proscribed by the Church. I had done some legal work with Bartholomew A. Brickley, a Boston attorney who was Chancellor of the Diocese of Massachusetts. I asked him if he had any suggestions as to what I might do. He immediately advised me that he thought this was a matter for Bishop Wright, and said that he would introduce me to the Bishop. So, I called Bishop Wright on the telephone, and told him what my problem was. He chuckled, and said "I can take care of that. Can you send me a list of the books involved, and also a list of the students. Unless there is some problem that I do not now see, I will be glad to issue a dispensation which will enable the students to read these items without breaking any church laws." This was quickly done, and the problem was resolved.

The other matter related to a chapel which had been built, after much planning, at the Massachusetts Institute of Technology. This was known as "the Chapel of the Three Faiths," since it was so constructed that it could be readily converted for use in Catholic, Protestant, and Jewish services, with a chaplain for each of these groups. One evening, a group of students, including two who were students at the Harvard Law School, broke into this chapel, and conducted a "black Mass" there. The Catholic chaplain told the MIT authorities that the chapel had been desecrated, and that it could never be used again for a Catholic service. Understandably, the M.I.T. people were greatly concerned, and since Harvard Law School students were involved, they called me. Having in mind the understanding experience I had already had with Bishop Wright, I called him again on the telephone, quite fearful that the problem would prove to be very difficult. But, again, the Bishop chuckled, and said: "We have a special service to deal with such matters, and I have never conducted such a service. It would be a fine experience for me to do so, and I will advise the MIT authorities in order to arrange a convenient date." [17]

---

17. Later, I had another occasion to approach Bishop Wright, which did not involve the Law School. My brother was the Treasurer of the Congregational Church in Exeter, New Hampshire. This building was close to two hundred years old, and the meeting room was on the second floor. This caused problems for elderly people and handicapped, and also in connection with funerals. The governing board of the church wanted to make renovations, including the installation of an elevator. This required more money than the church had immediately available, so my brother went to the local bank, which, without difficulty, arranged a loan. The matter was then referred to the bank's lawyer to

As I had more experience in the dean's office, I became more familiar with the capacities and interests of members of the faculty. Professor David F. Cavers had long impressed me as imaginative, constructive, and energetic, and after obtaining his approval, I recommended to the Harvard Corporation that he should be appointed Associate Dean of the faculty, with special responsibilities in the development of research in law. This appointment was made in 1951, and he held the post of Associate Dean until 1959. He developed substantial work in the field of Atomic Energy Law. With active participation by Professor Mark Howe, he encouraged the production of the Adams Legal Papers, ably edited by two recent graduates of the Law School, Hiller Zobel (now a judge of the Massachusetts Superior Court) and L. Kinvin Wroth, later Dean of the Law School at the University of Maine. He encouraged and facilitated the ideas and plans of Professor Stanley S. Surrey in organizing and then developing the International Program in Taxation. This program produced a number of books, including several volumes of a Foreign Tax Series, and two large volumes by Elizabeth A. Owens on the foreign tax credit.[18] The International Program in Taxa-

---

examine the title. He found that the title to the church was still in the Town of Exeter.

When the church was built, it was the parish church, owned by the town; and the minister was supported out of taxes. Town support of the minister fell away in the early nineteenth century, although "establishment" of the church did not end until about 1830. At that time, the congregation was responsible, the church was there, and nothing was done about the title in the land records.

Under New Hampshire law, the town could convey title to real properly only by a two-thirds vote of the town meeting. My brother prepared an article for the warrant at the next town meeting, providing for this transfer. At this point, though, the local Catholic priest advised the members of his church to vote against the transfer, saying that it would violate separation of church and state. My brother brought the question to me, and I, of course, consulted Bishop Wright.

Bishop Wright responded pleasantly: "That is in New Hampshire, and I have no authority in New Hampshire. However, it just happens that the Bishop of New Hampshire and I went to seminary together. I will see what I can do." I never heard further from Bishop Wright, but about three weeks later the local priest announced that the matter had been discussed by "higher authorities," and it had been decided that it would be appropriate for the town to transfer the church to the Congregational congregation.

18. Owens, The Foreign Tax Credit (Cambridge: 1961); Owens (and Gerald T. Ball), The Indirect Credit (same publisher, two volumes, vol. I in 1975, vol. II in 1979).

tion also brought to Cambridge each year a number of tax officials from foreign countries, usually less developed countries, and thus had a considerable impact on the development of sound tax procedures in many parts of the world. Dave Cavers, Professor Surrey, and other members of the faculty, including Professor Arthur von Mehren, made a number of trips to Japan and to India, learning much about practices in those countries, while bringing some of our ideas to them. Professor Milton Katz, who was appointed Director of International Legal Studies, undertook special responsibility for South America and made a number of trips there, establishing contacts with lawyers and law schools in that continent.

Developing research in a law school is not altogether easy, as we found out. Things can be done in a law school only through people, and, generally speaking, faculty members who are first-class know what they want to do, and are not interested in doing other things. If an outsider comes to the school and says "Here is some money, and I want you to do research on so and so," it may be very difficult to find a person, on or off the faculty, who is interested in doing that particular kind of research. On the other hand, if a faculty member says that he wants to do research on this or that topic, it may be very difficult to find a donor or grantor who is interested in funding such research. It became clear to me that, somehow or other, we needed to develop more funds within the Law School in order to facilitate the research ventures which appealed to members of the faculty.

In one instance, this worked out. Professor Robert E. Keeton, who taught both Torts and Insurance, came to me with an idea which has come to be known as "no-fault" insurance. He was well qualified to develop this novel proposal, and I was able to find some seed money in Law School funds. Professor Keeton later found outside support. Thereafter, he associated Professor Jeffrey O'Connell with him, and they produced a fundamental work in this field.[19] Professor Keeton became a United States

---

Another publication of the International Program in Taxation was Donald R. Ravenscroft, Taxation and Foreign Currency (Cambridge: 1973).

19. The original work was Robert E. Keeton and Jeffrey O'Connell, Basic Protection for the Traffic Victim (Boston: 1965). See also Keeton and O'Connell, After Cars Crash (1967), and R. E. Keeton and J. O'Connell "Basic Protection—A Proposal for Improving Automobile Claims Systems," 78 Harv.L.Rev. 329 (1964); R. E. Keeton, "Is There a Place for Negligence in Modern Tort Law," 53 Va. L.Rev. 886 (1967); R. E. Keeton and J. O'Connell, "Basic Protection Plan for Traffic Accident Losses," 48 Notre Dame Lawyer 184 (1967); R. E. Keeton, "Compensat-

District Judge in Boston, but Professor O'Connell continues to do extensive research and writing in the field.

Their plan calls for the development of a system under which compensation for traffic accidents will be made available on a workmen's compensation basis, without regard to ordinary fault. There is no doubt in my mind that, eventually, a system of this sort will have to be adopted.[20] When the time comes, people will wonder why it took so long before it was effectively adopted. The reason is a simple one. Legislative bodies in this country, state and federal, are heavily influenced by trial lawyers. I do not impugn these lawyers; I simply think that they are wrong. They may be subject to "the distortions of reason because of self-interest."[21] The trial system has some virtues, but it is very expensive and time-consuming. The workmen's compensation system must handle hundreds of thousands of cases each year, and it does so promptly, and with reasonable satisfaction. The trial system for automobile accidents involves frequent jury trials—and badly overcrowds our courts with factual disputes. And it is needlessly expensive. As I see it, we must find a better way to proceed in this area.

Even before he became Associate Dean, David Cavers had been very helpful. He, together with Professor Lon Fuller, and several members of the faculty, had been discussing for some time the problem which arose from the large classes in the Harvard Law School (averaging about one hundred thirty-five students in each section in the first year). They proposed that we adopt a system of Teaching Fellows, to work with first-year students. These would be recent graduates of law schools—not

ing the Injured Claimant: The Keeton–O'Connell Plan," 44 Fed. Rules Dec. 122 (1968); R. E. Keeton and J. O'Connell, "Alternative Paths toward Nonfault Automobile Insurance," 71 Col. L.Rev. 241 (1971); R. E. Keeton, "Compensation Systems and Utah's No–Fault Statute," 1973 Utah L.Rev. 383.

See also Keeton, Venturing to do Justice (Cambridge: 1969) pp. 101–146.

20. In New Zealand, "no fault" has been made applicable to nearly all tort liability. See N.Z.P.D. McKenzie, "Report of the Select Committee on Compensation for Personal Injury in New Zealand," 34 Modern L.Rev. 542 (1971); G. W. R. Palmer, "Compensation for Personal Injury: A Requiem for the Common Law in New Zealand," 21 Am. J. Comp. L. 1 (1973); C. Brown, "Deterrence in Tort and No–Fault: The New Zealand Experience," 73 Calif.L.Rev. 976 (1985); J. O'Connell, "Reforming New Zealand's Reform: Accident Compensation Revisited," 1988 New Zealand L.J. 399.

21. Miller, The First Liberty (New York: 1986) p. 351.

limited to Harvard by any means—some of whom might have some interest in going into careers of law teaching. There were usually about six Teaching Fellows each year, and they were ordinarily appointed for one year only.

This program began in the fall of 1949, and was very success-ful, for many years. The Teaching Fellows met with first-year students in relatively small groups. They supervised written work, with substantial "feedback" to the students. They did beginning work in pleading and procedure. Through their con-tacts with students, they did much to reduce the impersonality of the Law School, and to provide a place where students felt free to come with their questions.

A number of the Teaching Fellows went on to distinguished careers in law teaching, including Paul D. Carrington, who be-came Dean of the Duke University Law School, Clarence Clyde Ferguson, who was Ambassador to Uganda and became the first black member of the Harvard Law School faculty, David R. Herwitz, who became a member of the Harvard Law School faculty, and Kenneth Karst, who became a professor at the University of California at Los Angeles, among many others. David H. Gambrell was briefly a United States Senator. Much may also be said of Charles R. Simpson, who was blind, and performed exceptionally well as a Teaching Fellow. He became a judge of the United States Tax Court, where he served with distinction for many years.

One of the things that I sought to do was to encourage the activities of student organizations, particularly if they had some intellectual or professional content. Since 1914, the School had had an effective Legal Aid Bureau. This was housed on the ground floor of Gannett House, near Harvard Square, with the Law Review occupying the second and third floors of the vener-able building. The Legal Aid Bureau was limited to civil cases. The School provided a practicing attorney as an adviser, but we tried to follow the practice of giving the students virtually com-plete control of this activity. We felt that this was a part of their training in accepting responsibility.

Few problems ever arose from the Bureau's activities. I recall one occasion when a prominent Cambridge politician called me on the telephone. He was much annoyed. He said that the Legal Aid Bureau was representing a landlord, and that this was outrageous. I asked the President of the Bureau to come to my office. When I put the problem before him, he said: "Yes, we are representing a landlord. She is a widow with four children, and she is trying to keep her family together by operat-ing a rooming house. She has few other resources. Some of the tenants do not pay, or are way behind in their payments. She came to us and we looked into the situation carefully. We felt that she qualified for legal aid assistance, and we have started suits to collect back rents, and to evict some of the tenants who do not pay." He then handed me materials they had compiled showing the amount of her aggregate income from rent (if paid), and her expenses. It was obvious that the amount available to her for living expenses was very small.

I then called the Cambridge lawyer who had made the complaint, and outlined the situation to him. To my pleasure, his response was: "Well, that's different. Obviously she needs help. Tell the boys that if they need any assistance, they can call on me."

As an outgrowth of the activities of the Legal Aid Bureau, the Harvard Voluntary Deffenders was established, in 1949, chiefly as a result of the careful work and planning done by Samuel Dash, of the Law School Class of 1950. The Voluntary Defenders undertook the defense of criminal cases, particularly in the District Court, the lowest of the Massachusetts courts, from which there was an absolute right of appeal for a trial *de novo*. As a part of this enterprise, I made application to the Supreme Judicial Court of Massachusetts for an amendment of their rules which would allow students in the third year, at all Massachusetts law schools, whose names were on a list certified by their dean, to appear in the District Courts on behalf of indigent defendants.[22]

The new rule was duly adopted, and the Legal Aid Bureau was included in it. Thus, we soon had a considerable number of students authorized to appear in the Massachusetts District Courts. The result was excellent practical training for students, and a considerable service to the community. The only adverse comments we had came from the police. Although they were not members of the bar, they prosecuted minor crimes in the District Court. Before the new practice was adopted, they had a relatively easy time in presenting their cases. The students, however, had much energy, and could devote whatever time was necessary to their cases. As a result, the police had to work much harder than they had done before—but they soon got used to it.

A similar group was organized to assist prisoners in the eastern part of Massachusetts, both with personal problems, and with questions with respect to sentences, and other such matters.

---

22. I felt some confidence in making this application, since Raymond S. Wilkins, then Chief Justice of the Supreme Judicial Court, had, as a member of the Class of 1914, been one of the organizers of the Legal Aid Bureau.

A related organization was fostered by Vice Dean Livingston Hall in the late 1950s. This was the Harvard District Attorneys. Through this organization, a number of Law School students were placed as interns in the offices of the District Attorneys for Suffolk and Middlesex counties, Massachusetts, and of the United States Attorney in Boston. These students participated in the preparation of cases, and in assisting the trial lawyers at trials.

The Harvard Law Review was established in 1887, and had quickly developed as a leading legal periodical in the country, soon copied at other law schools. Though there was an alumni board of trustees to give continuity, the student editors were given virtually complete control. They were free to consult with faculty, and often did so. But they were not subject to faculty direction. As I have indicated, we believed in maintaining student responsibility as an important part of the education provided to the editors.

For many years, about thirty-five students, in the second and third years at the School, were members of the editorial board. This was little more than three percent of the students in those years. Thus, the great educational benefits of working on the Review were available only to a very small segment of the student body. This had long troubled me. I did not want to weaken the Review in any way, because I felt that its caliber and leadership were important to the Law School, and, indeed, to legal education generally. On the other hand, I wished that we could make the benefit of work of the Law Review type available to a larger number of students. Students came to me with plans to establish new journals, and I encouraged them.

To a considerable extent, the problems were financial. At that time, the School had very little money available for innovations. However, in due course, a number of these journals were established. These were the Harvard International Law Journal, the Harvard Journal on Legislation, and the Harvard Civil Rights—Civil Liberties Law Review. In more recent years, a number of additional journals have been added to the list. This means that it is now possible for virtually any student in the School who wants to undertake work of this sort to find a place where he can do it. The caliber of these journals has remained high, and they do contribute substantially to the overall educational process, as well as making available to lawyers and academics a body of thought and research.

Another organization which contributed substantially to the life of the Law School was the Harvard Law School Forum. This was established in 1947, primarily through the efforts of Jerome Rappaport, who received the LL.B degree in 1949, and was later a real estate developer in Boston. The Forum usually arranged eight or ten programs a year, bringing prominent speakers, some distinguished, and some more or less notorious, to Cambridge.

At one of those programs, Harry S. Truman was the speaker, after his presidential term had ended. I introduced him as the "junior ex-President of the United States." Another program of the Forum was a debate between Paul Blanshard and Father George H. Dunne, S.J., on Catholicism. I feared that there might be some untoward event at this program, and some repercussions after it, so I felt that I should attend. As things worked out, it was a tense session, but, generally speaking, kept on a relatively high plane. A good account of it has been given in the Memoirs of Father Dunne.[23] Father Dunne records that after the debate I came up to shake his hand, and made pleasant conversation about his presentation.

Another program of the Forum caused more difficult problems. This was when the officers of the Forum, without consulting the dean, invited Fidel Castro to speak, in 1959. The public interest in the program was very great, and it was finally moved to the Harvard Stadium, where some twelve to fifteen thousand people attended. There were no untoward events, but the size of the crowd, and the possibility of disturbance, made substantial police protection necessary. This cost the University about $20,000, and was a serious problem for the dean. I then made a rule that the Forum could not invite a foreign head of state without advance approval from the dean.

At a later program, I met former Senator Claude Pepper for the first time. He was a graduate of the Law School in the Class of 1924, and had been a somewhat controversial member of Congress. I attended, because I wanted to have a better understanding of the man. Actually, he made a very fine speech, completely attuned to the caliber of his audience, thoughtful and constructive. I was very favorably impressed. In later Washington years, we became well-acquainted and good friends.

Finally, I will mention Benjamin O. Davis, who was a classmate of mine in the Class of 1928. He was a black man of considerable ability. After graduation, he finally obtained a position with a law firm in Atlanta, but he was subject to considerable discrimination, including the fact that he was not allowed to enter the building and proceed to his office except by way of the freight elevator. In due course, largely impelled by the discrimination to which he was subjected, he became a

---

23. See G. Dunne, King's Pawn (Chicago: 1990) 196–207.

Communist, and he was one of those who were convicted, and his conviction was sustained in *Dennis v. United States*.[24] After he had served his sentence, the Harvard Law School Forum invited him to speak at the Law School. There was a considerable amount of complaint about this, but I saw no reason to interfere, and I attended the program. He spoke very well and frankly, and quite impressively, I thought.

On one occasion, when Harold Laski was in the United States, the Forum invited him to speak. There was no auditorium at the Law School which was big enough for the expected crowd, and the Forum had made arrangements to lease the auditorium of the Cambridge High and Latin School, controlled by the Cambridge School Committee. When there was some publicity about the forthcoming speech, the School Committee yielded to pressure and revoked the lease. This resulted in considerable publicity in the newspapers throughout the country. The officers of the Forum came to see me. There was no question in my mind about allowing the program. The problem was simply to find an adequate auditorium. I finally made arrangements to hold the meeting at the auditorium of the Music building, near the Law School.

A short time later, Laski flew in from Los Angeles. He came storming into my office and said "What is this about your barring me from speaking at the Law School?" With some difficulty, I finally got it across to him that I had nothing to do with barring him, and that I had worked very hard to find an auditorium for him on University premises, and that the program was going ahead. The meeting was held, and there were no repercussions.[25]

D. INTERNATIONAL LEGAL STUDIES

Another area in which a substantial number of faculty members were interested was international law. We soon broadened this concept by renaming it "International Legal Studies." My own experience in foreign travel, and my inherited deep interest in working towards better understanding among nations, were powerful motivations, and this was moved forward by a substan-

---

24. 341 U.S. 494 (1951).

25. During his stay in Cambridge, Laski entered my outer office while I was not there. He pushed his way right through into my office, and sat in the chair behind my desk. My secretary, Janet Murphy, followed him, and asked if there was anything she could do to be of assistance. His response was "Who would have thought that I would one day be sitting in the chair of the Dean of the Harvard Law School?"

tial participation from a number of faculty members, notably Professors Cavers, Katz, Surrey and von Mehren.

Milton Katz had been on the faculty since 1938, with absence during the War years, where he had a distinguished record of service in the O.S.S. He returned to the School after the War as Byrne Professor of Administrative Law, but he was soon on leave in order to serve as a deputy to Paul Hoffman in the operation of the Marshall Plan in Europe, with the rank of Ambassador. He was also the chief U.S. delegate for the Economic Commission for Europe in 1950 and 1951. He became Vice President of the Ford Foundation in 1951. In 1954, we persuaded him to return to Cambridge as Director of International Legal Studies, a post which he held until his retirement in 1978. He was also Henry L. Stimson Professor of Law from 1955 to 1978.

The School had long had an appreciable number of foreign students, chiefly graduate students, that is, students who had received the basic law degree in their own countries. They came to Harvard for an advanced degree, usually LL.M., but in many cases, particularly where they looked forward to a teaching career, they were candidates for the S.J.D. degree (Doctor of Juridical Science). During the 1950s, the number of foreign students considerably increased, so that, eventually, about half of the graduate students came to us from other countries, all over the world. I regarded this as a very important part of the role and mission of the Harvard Law School, I looked upon these students as future leaders in their countries, and I felt that the development of able people in various parts of the world, who had a common tie, would contribute materially to world progress and peace.[26]

When I became Dean of the Law School in 1946, and had to make many talks to alumni, I used to say that there was no city in the United States where I might walk down the main street at noon and not be invited to lunch. Thanks to the achievements of

---

26. One of the early foreign students during my deanship was J. Rudolph Grimes, of Liberia. I had trouble getting the Admissions Committee to admit him to our regular LL.B. program, because, they said, his college education was inadequate. I pointed out that it was the best that was available in his country, and I finally persuaded them to admit him as a special student. He worked very hard, and passed the first year examinations successfully. He received the law degree in 1949. Within about six years, he was Secretary of State of Liberia, and he was the President of the Bandung Conference held in Indonesia in the late 1950s. As so often happens, though, the political situation in his country proved to be unstable. The latest I heard of him he was living in the United States, after a precarious time in Monrovia.

our predecessors, it really was a remarkable body of students and alumni, with graduates in every state in the Union, and a truly national constituency. After the development of our International Legal Studies program, when I would go abroad, I broadened my statement. One evening, in 1966, I was asked to speak at the Abraham Lincoln Library of the United States Information Service in Kuala Lumpur, Malaysia. I said that: "There is almost no city in the world where I can walk down the main street at noon and not be invited to lunch. But, alas, that is not true in Kuala Lumpur. I checked our records just before I left Cambridge, and found that we have no graduate in Kuala Lumpur." At that point a man of East Indian background arose in the back of the room and said: "I want you to know that I am taking care of that. Just last week I put my son on a plane to go to Cambridge and study at the Harvard Law School." [27]

As a result of the development in International Legal Studies, it became necessary to increase our facilities. With the approval of the Harvard Corporation, an effort was begun to raise funds for a new building. At first, this aroused little enthusiasm among some of our alumni. They did not then feel that there was much of practical concern in the international field. I told them, though, that we had all these books on international law, and they took up a great deal of space. I said that if we could find a new building for the international law books, we could then move those books out of the main building, and have more room for "real law." This proved encouraging to some.

The first chairman of the fundraising committee was Henry J. Friendly, then practicing in New York, just before he began his distinguished career as a federal judge. With great effort and help from alumni, the necessary funds were raised, and the new International Legal Studies building was opened in 1960. It is connected with the main building of the Law School, Langdell Hall, by arcades and a tunnel, and it is a most attractive building. I feel much indebted to Mr. Henry R. Shepley, of the architectural firm of Bulfinch, Coolidge, Shepley and Adams, who produced the design.[28]

---

27. The student was Herbert V. Morais, LL.B.1967, S.J.D.1972, now Assistant General Counsel of the World Bank. There are now six persons in Malaysia who have studied at the Harvard Law School, all since 1966. There are thirty-one former students of the School in Singapore.

28. I made one small contribution. As Mr. Shepley planned the building, the east wall was blank, that is, it had no windows. This left some staff offices on the ground floor which would have only artificial

E. Continuing Legal Education

Another area which was developed over these years was in the field of what is now known as Continuing Legal Education. During the War years, I gave a series of lectures on federal taxation to members of the Rhode Island Bar Association, in Providence. These were quite successful, as there were few practicing lawyers then who had much background in the tax field—an area which took on new importance during the high tax period of the War years. After the War, I spoke at a number of programs sponsored by the Practicing Law Institute of New York, whose director, Harold Seligson, was one of the pioneers in the continuing legal education field. In the spring of 1949, I became one of the founders of the Federal Tax Institute of New England, Inc.[29] That Institute has continued in effective existence now for more than forty years. It puts on two programs, of one or two days each, each year, and has a consistently large attendance, with generous participation from government officials, who help to make the programs seem very "real." I am still president, and have presided at nearly all of the meeting sessions over the years.

In addition to this "outside" activity, it seemed to me that it would be a useful service, and good for the School, if the Law School put on programs in Cambridge which were of interest to practicing lawyers. This was easier said than done. The faculty were all busy people, and many of them did not share my interest in lectures for practicing lawyers. About 1950, we put on a program on "Government Contracts," organized and led by Professor Robert Braucher. But there was no pressure from the faculty to do this on a regular basis. In due course, though, and with the active help of Professor A. James Casner, a program was organized to be given in the summer. This came to be known as the Program of Instruction for Lawyers, and developed rapidly

---

light. I was concerned about this, and told Mr. Shepley that I thought we ought to have a window. He said that this would spoil his design. Then, a few days later, he came to me and said that there was a similar wall in the Bargello in Florence, and that it had a window, placed just right, and that he thought that such a window in our building would improve the design. Thus, the building was built with the window, which is, as far as I know, my only contribution to Cambridge architecture.

29. The real motive power for this came from Kenneth W. Bergen, of the Boston bar, a graduate of the Harvard Law School in the Class of 1937.

under the direction of the tireless Professor Casner. The program was designed to occupy two weeks, and lawyers were free to attend one week or the other, or both. Faculty members received extra compensation for this work. At the beginning, the programs were put on only every other year. However, in the 1960s they became a regular annual feature at the School. These programs have been very successful, attracting five or six hundred participants. And similar programs have been developed at a number of other law schools.

During my time, we had two formal reviews of the Law School curriculum. The first was conducted by a committee under the chairmanship of Professor Lon L. Fuller. With much effort, and appreciable delay, these committees produced reports which were then discussed by the faculty.

Revising law school curricula is not an easy task. The subject matter is reasonably well laid out, though it has been expanding enormously over the past forty years. The teaching of the basic fields of law, like contracts, torts, property, and so on, and the development of legal concepts, can, with the right instructors, be done with primary emphasis on the decisions of appellate courts. Harvard drew its students from all over the country, so there was no particular emphasis on the law of any one state. The law taught was "the common law" as administered by the courts in the United States. This, though, was not all "the law," and many teachers had other means and methods for bringing in other materials. Professor Fuller's committee, made its report in 1948. It laid considerable stress on developing "forward looking" teaching—that is, less emphasis on the decisions of the past, and more consideration by the students of current problems arising in advising clients with respect to future actions. This emphasis was, I think, welcomed by many on the Law School faculty, who developed it in their subsequent teaching.

One important recommendation made in the Fuller Committee report, sponsored particularly by Professor Henry M. Hart Jr., was the establishment of a requirement that each student, as a prerequisite for graduation, must produce "a satisfactory piece of written work," under the supervision of a member of the faculty. The standard for a "satisfactory piece" was that met by a good law review article. This requirement was adopted, and is still in effect. It has been, in my view, a major factor in the overall quality of legal education at the Law School.

For a hundred years or more, the Harvard Law School had had black students, though not very many. The number increased slightly in the 1920s and thereafter, but did not become very large. As far as I can tell, or know, there was no discrimination by the School itself. There were simply few black applicants who met the academic requirements and could afford to attend the School, even with the relatively low costs of those days.

In the late 1950s and early 1960s, we noticed that the number of black students was declining considerably. We discussed this, and reached the conclusion that black students who had been applying to us in the past were now in some demand, and were receiving substantial scholarships in other fields, particularly the sciences. We were still working to develop our financial aid resources.[30] In recent years, the number of black applicants has risen substantially, and currently more than ten percent of the students are black.

Early in 1966, a group of faculty approached a foundation and received a grant which was designed to encourage students in black colleges to study law—not necessarily at Harvard, but at a law school of their choice. Under the plan, students who had finished the junior year in college were invited to spend six weeks at Harvard, where a group of faculty would give "pre-law" instruction. The purpose was to encourage these students to think of going to law school, and to give them background which would help them in that undertaking if they chose to follow it. The students received all of their expenses in connection with the time in Cambridge and travel to and from Cambridge. In addition, a stipend was paid to their college, applicable against their tuition fees there. The purpose of this was to give the students essentially the same financial benefit as they would have received through employment during the summer.

This program went fairly well, largely due to the devoted work of the faculty members who conducted it. As the end of the period drew near, we planned a final dinner. I invited the then Solicitor General, Thurgood Marshall, to attend the dinner, and to speak to the students. He accepted, and made a very fine talk. I attended the dinner, and was much pleased. After the talk, he invited questions and comments. I was startled by the nature of the remarks made by a number of the students. They

---

30. We had an offer (from a faculty member) of a gift for scholarship aid limited to black students. We referred this to the Massachusetts Commission on Discrimination, and they advised us that it would be illegal to accept it.

said to Mr. Marshall, with considerable vehemence, "Why have you sold us out?" And, "You are a tool of the white power structure." [31] Mr. Marshall handled the situation very well, and refused my apologies when I offered them. He was more understanding than I was. He said to me: "I think they are taking the wrong approach, but I know what they have been through."

Two further episodes with respect to black students are worthy of mention.

About 1960, we had a black student who was also blind. With considerable help, he passed the examinations and received his LL.B. degree. He then applied for admission to the bar of Pennsylvania, which, in those days, had to be made through the county of his residence. The county character committee turned him down, saying, in effect, that a black applicant who was blind, and who wanted to practice law in Pennsylvania, could not be of good moral character. Vice Dean Livingston Hall and I helped him to prepare an application to the Pennsylvania Supreme Court, and we both appeared in support of the student before a committee appointed by that court. Before long, the applicant was admitted to the bar of Pennsylvania, and, shortly thereafter, the rules were changed so as to put admissions on a state-wide basis. Previously, in some of the smaller counties, the requirements had been administered so as to limit admission, to a considerable extent, to sons and other close relatives of already admitted lawyers, much as was done by some of the trade unions at the time.

In another case, we had a black student who, in the summer following his second year, obtained employment in the office of a black lawyer in Farmville, Prince Edward County, Virginia. One day the lawyer gave the student a paper, and told him to deliver it to the office of the judge at the courthouse, and to take care that it was not delivered to any other place. The student went to the courthouse. As he knew the judge's office was on the second floor, he started to walk up the stairway. His progress was stopped by two or three deputies. He told them where he was going, and said that he was instructed to deliver the paper to the judge's chambers. He was told that he could not do so. There was a scuffle, in the course of which one of the deputies was kicked on the shin, which drew blood. At that time, it was the

---

31. Other comments were: "Why don't you get rid of all the whites in the NAACP?" Marshall replied that they were only a small percentage of members, and they had been very helpful, referring to me. Another of the students said "If a policeman does anything to me, I will kill him." Marshall's response was "I thought we got rid of lynching."

law of Virginia that an assault which drew blood could be prosecuted as a felony. He was arrested, and charged with felonious assault. It was a short time later that we heard about the case.

This was soon after the establishment by President Kennedy of the Lawyers' Committee for Civil Rights Under Law, and Bernard G. Segal, of Philadelphia, was one of the first two co-chairmen of that committee. I got in touch with him, and he was much interested. He first called Dean Ribble, at the University of Virginia Law School, who gave him several names. Mr. Segal then approached a prominent Richmond law firm, which refused to undertake the case. Eventually Mr. Segal found his way to a remarkable Richmond lawyer, George E. Allen, Sr., then nearly eighty years old, who practiced with his three sons in the firm of Allen, Allen, Allen & Allen.[32] He took the case on a pro bono basis, and handled it very carefully and effectively. Of course, we were concerned about the felony charge. If the student was convicted of a felony, that might bar his admission, not only in Virginia, but elsewhere. After much negotiation, Mr. Allen was able to obtain an agreement that if the student would plead guilty to a misdemeanor of unaggravated assault, with a $50 fine, the felony charge would be dropped.

Under all the circumstances, we felt that obtaining this agreement, at that time, at that place, was a very considerable achievement. But then we had further trouble, because the student absolutely refused to plead guilty to anything. He said that he had committed no assault, that, indeed, he was himself the one who was assaulted. This was all very reasonable and I could readily sympathize with the student. But it seemed wise to take a long-range view of the situation. We provided the money to pay the fine, and eventually he accepted the plea. It is always hard to evaluate such things, but the hazards of litigation are often considerable, particularly on an uneven playing field, and it seemed to me to be prudent—and still does—that the guilty plea was made. I felt much indebted to Mr. Allen for his effective handling of the case.

F. American Bar Association Activities

Another aspect of my work in these years should be mentioned. I felt strongly that it was important that better relations be established between the Law School and the practicing bar.

32. The senior Mr. Allen died in 1972. According to Martindale-Hubble, there are now ten Allens in the firm.

Indeed, it was my view, not fully shared by all of my colleagues, that the basic purpose of the Harvard Law School was to train lawyers for the practice of law in the United States. There were other purposes, such as training law teachers, providing background training for judges, administrators, and other public servants, and training students from foreign countries so as to give them a better understanding of the United States, and thus to enable them to contribute as they could to better relations among the nations of the world.

I early discussed the matter of relations with practitioners with Vice Dean Livingston Hall, who shared my views. We agreed that he would devote himself to the Massachusetts Bar Association, of which he eventually became president, and that I would develop my Bar activities in the American Bar Association, which I had joined in 1932. We proceeded on that basis.

At that time, the American Bar Association was extremely conservative, and it had, in many ways, a negative outlook. Many of my fellow faculty members would have nothing to do with the American Bar Association. They would not join it, and they expressed themselves quite freely. I urged them to join, saying that the only way to make things better was to have people with broad points of view get in and participate as members, and vote, at crucial places, for less conservative measures. Carping on the outside produced little result. But my arguments were persuasive to few, if any, new members.

Following this plan, I was one of the founding members of the Section of Taxation in the American Bar Association, which was established at the Philadelphia meeting in 1949, under the leadership of Robert N. Miller, a prominent Harvard Law School graduate of the Class of 1906. I was active in the Tax Section, and, in 1954, I was elected a member of the Council of the Tax Section.[33] I continued to work with the American Bar Association, serving on committees, and finding many kindred spirits who were looking for help in bringing about improvements.[34]

In December, 1957, I became President of the Association of American Law Schools, which is the organization of the law

---

33. I believe that I was the first academic elected to the Council of a Section, other than the Section of Legal Education and Admission to the Bar.

34. One of the most conservative members of the Association was Frank C. Holman, of Seattle, Washington, who was President of the Association in 1948–1949. He opposed me regularly in the Association. But, at every annual meeting of the Association, he sent flowers to my wife. I appreciated this greatly, and took pleasure in telling him so.

teachers of the country. The President of that Association is a member of the House of Delegates of the American Bar Association, and it was in this capacity that I first became a member of the House—at the mid-winter meeting of the Association, held in Atlanta in February, 1958. I continued to be a member of the House of Delegates, in one capacity or another, for twenty-seven years. After my term as President of the Law Teachers Association ended, I was elected as a State Delegate from Massachusetts. In 1966, I was elected a member of the Board of Governors for the First District, for a term of three years, and this continued my membership in the House of Delegates. While on the Board of Governors, I played an appreciable role in the establishment of the Section of Individual Rights and Responsibilities.[35] I also played a role in the establishment of what eventfully became the Law Student Division of the Association, providing a natural channel for law students to proceed to full membership in the Association. When my term on the Board expired, I held the office of Solicitor General, which, at that time, gave me a seat in the House of Delegates. Thereafter, I was elected Assembly Delegate for three terms of three years each.[36] In 1985, when the last of these terms expired, I reluctantly came to the conclusion that I should yield my place to a younger member.[37]

I was also active in the related organization known as the American Bar Foundation. Although this is called a Foundation, it is actually a grant-receiving rather than a grant-making body. Much of its financing comes from the American Bar Endowment, which receives benefits from life and health insurance policies written on many of the more than three hundred thousand members of the American Bar Association. The actual role of the Foundation is to conduct research for agencies of the Association and to contribute to better understanding of, and improve-

---

35. There was considerable opposition in the Board to the authorization of this Section. It was said that it would just attract "trouble makers." My special contribution was adding the words "and Responsibilities" to the title of the Section. I contended, too, that the Section would be a place where concerned members could "let off steam," and where other members could emphasize the "Responsibilities."

36. The Assembly Delegates are elected by the members who attend the annual meeting, many of whom come from the area where the annual meeting is held. As there are alumni of the Harvard Law School all over the country, I had a sort of built-in claque for this particular office. My political base was fairly secure.

37. In 1978, I was awarded the gold Medal of the American Bar Association for "conspicuous service to the cause of American Jurisprudence."

ment in, the law generally. I was President of the Foundation from 1971 to 1974, but have not been active in it since.

I greatly enjoyed participating in the many activities of the American Bar Association. In the House of Delegates, I took part in many hard-fought battles, sometimes successfully and sometimes not. In the Board of Governors, I played some role in the leadership of the Association at a time when the Association had become considerably less conservative than it had formerly been. In the American Bar Foundation, I tried, not too successfully, to help develop useful and effective research activities devoted to improvement in the law. In all of this work, I had great respect for my fellow members, even in disagreement.[38]

G. American Law Institute

Another activity in which I have participated for many years is the work of the American Law Institute.[39] My first direct contact with that organization came in 1928, when, during my graduate year at Harvard Law School, I was employed by the Institute to work as an assistant to Professor Austin W. Scott in his role as Reporter for the first Restatement on Trusts. Thereafter, I was, from time to time, an Advisor on other Restatements, including the Restatement on Judgments. In due course, I was elected a member of the Council of the Institute, where I have now served for most of thirty-seven years. During that time, I have attended nearly all of the meetings of the Council, and have tried to participate actively in advancing its work. I fear that, at times, I have been too argumentative, but the other members of the Council have tolerated me. I have found this association a particularly pleasant one, bringing me into contact with such people as Judge Learned Hand, my old friend, Judge Henry

---

38. In 1969, when I thought that my tenure as Solicitor General might expire with the beginning of President Nixon's term, I toyed with the idea of running for President of the Association. The idea of being the first academic elected to that office appealed to me, and I thought it would help to solidify relations between the practitioners and the legal educators. Robert W. Meserve, of Boston, generously told me that he would support my candidacy. But, in January, 1969, I learned that I could stay on as Solicitor General, at least for a while. I then immediately called Mr. Meserve, gave him the news, and told him that I would support him if he would run for the office. Mr. Meserve became the President of the Association in 1972–73. I think it is rather unlikely that I would have been elected if I had ever run for the office.

39. For a discussion of the origins of the Institute, see N.E.H. Hull, "Restatement and Reform," 8 Law and History Review 55 (1990).

Friendly, Judge Charles E. Wyzanski, Jr., Judge John M. Wisdom, Judge Herbert Goodrich, and, more recently, Judge Ruth Bader Ginsburg, former Dean and Attorney General Edward H. Levi, Chief Justice Vincent L. McKusick, Norris Darrell, Roswell B. Perkins, Judge Patricia M. Wald, former Judge William H. Webster, Professor Charles Alan Wright, and the more recent directors, Herbert Wechsler and Geoffrey Hazard, among others. It has always been a rewarding intellectual and professional task to work with the various Reporters of the Institute, as the Council helped them to perfect their work.

In early 1961, shortly after the election of President Kennedy, the Law School faced something of a crisis because several members of its faculty were summoned to work with the Kennedy Administration in Washington. These included Professor Archibald Cox, who became Solicitor General of the United States, Professor Stanley S. Surrey, who because Assistant Secretary of the Treasury for Tax Policy, Professor Abrahm J. Chayes, who became Legal Adviser to the State Department, and Assistant Professor Stephen M. Schwebel, who became Assistant Legal Adviser in the State Department, in charge of United Nations Affairs. In addition, Professor Charles M. Haar soon thereafter because Assistant Secretary in the Department of Housing and Urban Development, and Professor John T. McNaughton was on leave of absence as General Counsel of the Department of Defense. Most of these departures came on short notice in January, and a considerable amount of time and effort was necessarily devoted to finding suitable persons, mostly younger lawyers in the Boston area, to provide temporary replacements. It was at this point that my friend, Dean Robert M. Drinan, S.J., then of the Boston College Law School, provided the appropriate *bons mots*, "Old deans never die, they just lose their faculties."

H. Civil Rights Commission

During the early summer of 1961, I received a telephone call from McGeorge Bundy, formerly Dean of the Faculty of Arts and Sciences at Harvard, and then Special Assistant to President Kennedy. He asked if I would accept appointment as a member of the United States Commission on Civil Rights. I did accept, and the President's nomination was confirmed by the Senate. I was sworn into office in St. Louis, at the annual meeting of the American Bar Association, in July 1961, by Justice Whittaker of the Supreme Court.

After the Association meeting ended, Harriet and I proceeded by automobile to East Lansing, Michigan, where a meeting of the Commission was scheduled. At that time, John A. Hannah, then President of Michigan State University, was Chairman of the Commission. The Commission had been organized in 1956 in President Eisenhower's administration. It was given power to hold hearings, and to subpoena witnesses, and to make reports to the President and to Congress. It had no enforcement powers of any sort, only the power to investigate and to report. Other members of the Commission at that time were Eugene Patterson, Editor of the Atlanta Constitution, Robert Storey, a lawyer from Dallas, Frankie M. Freeman, a lawyer in St. Louis, the Reverend Theodore M. Hesburgh, C.S.C., President of the University of Notre Dame, and Professor Robert S. Rankin of the University of North Carolina. The Commission had a staff, including an able and energetic Staff Director. At the first meeting which I attended, several important reports were approved, relating to voting, housing, employment, and law enforcement.[40]

During my tenure on the Commission, I participated in hearings in a number of cities, including San Francisco, Phoenix, Cleveland, Boston, Memphis, and Newark. This is not the place to write a history of the accomplishments and failures of the Civil Rights Commission in the 1960s.[41] On the whole, I think that it performed very well in its role of investigating and reporting to Congress, the President, and the public. It would not have achieved much without presidential leadership, but, fortunately, that came from President Johnson.

President Kennedy was friendly to the Commission, but he felt hemmed in by the political necessity of preserving the "solid South." [42] In early 1962, the Commission learned that a new

40. For a summary of the Commission's powers, see Hannah v. Larche, 363 U.S. 420 (1960).

41. This has been done in F.R. Dulles, The Civil Rights Commission, 1957–1965 (East Lansing, Michigan: 1968). See also H. Graham, The Civil Rights Era (New York: 1990).

42. This was evidenced, for example, when William Harold Cox was proposed for appointment as United States District Judge in the Southern District of Mississippi, at Jackson.

Cox was a long-time acquaintance and supporter of Senator James O. Eastland, and, I believe, they were roommates in law school. President Kennedy was very reluctant to make the nomination. However, Senator Eastland, who was then Chairman of the Senate Judiciary Committee, made it clear that no nominations for judicial appointment would be confirmed unless Cox was nominated. President Kennedy, having no

airport building was being built, with federal funds, in Jackson, Mississippi. The plans for this building called for separate waiting rooms, and separate eating and toilet facilities. The Commission sought an appointment with President Kennedy for the purpose of discussing this matter. Despite considerable effort, no such appointment could be arranged.

In January, 1963, President Kennedy held a large reception at the White House in honor of the Centennial of the Emancipation Proclamation, and the members of the Civil Rights Commission and their spouses were invited and included in the group photograph which was taken on that occasion. Shortly thereafter, however, the President and Attorney General Kennedy "applied pressure on the Civil Rights Commission to cancel planned hearings in Mississippi on segregationist terror." [43] The Commission yielded on this, but soon, against pressure, published a report on violence in Mississippi and urged the President to consider his authority to cut off federal funds allocated to the state.

When President Johnson succeeded to the presidency in November, 1963, the Civil Rights Commission waited a reasonable period, in order to give him an opportunity to familiarize himself with the many problems which confronted him. However, the Commission was anxious to meet with the new President, in order to learn his wishes, and to see what would be the most useful way to cooperate with him. Despite several efforts, no appointment could be arranged through the President's staff. The matter was discussed extensively at a Commission meeting in February 1964. Finally, I said that I had an idea that might be useful. I did not want to disclose it, but I said that I hoped that the members of the Commission would stay in Washington through the evening until I had a chance to report to them.

The Commission then took a recess, and I returned to my room at the Mayflower Hotel. I called Abe Fortas (with whom I had an appreciable acquaintance) on the telephone, and he courteously said that he could see me. I then went to his office on Nineteenth Street. [44] I outlined the problem to Fortas, and he seemed sympathetic and understanding. He said that he did not

real choice, nominated Cox, and he was confirmed and appointed, holding office for nearly twenty-five years.

43. T. Reeves, A Question of Character (New York: 1991) 349.

44. This office was in the building which was the residence of Justice and Mrs. Butler during the early 1930s. I had often been in the residence in those years, and it was interesting to return to it some thirty years later.

From left to right—In the front row—Mrs. Robert F. Kennedy; Vice President Johnson; Mrs. Johnson; President Kennedy; Mrs. Kennedy. In the second row—Erwin Griswold; Mrs. Griswold; Dr. Robert C. Weaver, Administrator, Housing and Home Finance Agency; Mrs. Weaver. Behind Mrs. Kennedy—Dr. Spottswood Robinson, III, dean of Howard University Law School. Reprinted with permission of the John F. Kennedy Library.

know what he could do, but that he would try. He suggested that I return to my hotel room, and said that he would report to me by the end of the afternoon. I gave him the telephone number, and room number at the Mayflower, and returned to wait there.

Within no more than fifteen or twenty minutes, the telephone rang. I thought it was probably Fortas calling me to report that he had been unsuccessful. I picked up the receiver and said "hello." I was startled when the voice said, with an intonation which was unmistakable, "This is Lyndon B. Johnson. I understand that the Civil Rights Commission would like to meet with me. That is fine. I would like to meet with the Commission. Would seven o'clock this evening be convenient?" I replied that I was sure that a meeting at seven would be convenient for the Commission, but asked if it would be quite convenient for the President. He assured me that this was a good time for him. I thanked him, and we hung up our receivers.

I then returned to the office of the Civil Rights Commission, and had some difficulty in locating all of the members. Eventually, though, I got the word to them, and we all went to the White House together, just before seven. Security arrangements were much less strict then than they are now, and we had no difficulty entering the west wing entrance. We were then taken into the Oval Office, where the President greeted us graciously. There is a small room off the oval office, with a couch in it, and the President led us into this room, where he lay down on the couch. Chairs for members of the Commission had already been installed.

We had a remarkable conference with the President. I wish that it had been transcribed. But there was no stenographer present, and I had no reason to think that it was recorded. The Commission was then led by John A. Hannah, then President of Michigan State University, with Father Theodore Hesburgh as the Vice Chairman. The President started by stressing his great appreciation for the work of the Commission, and his interest in cooperating with it. All of the members of the Commission participated, and the President seemed eager to hear their views. The discussion ranged over all the aspects of the problem, voting, housing, employment, and administration of justice. The Commission left much encouraged by the President's approach and attitude, and the President seemed to be genuinely interested in having the Commission's help as he faced the political problems which were inherent in his task.

Despite the attitude of the President, cooperation from the Department of Justice was not always eagerly advanced. They were active in the Civil Rights field, but they seemed to regard us as subordinates, and competitors. In particular, when the Commission decided in early 1965, to hold a hearing in Jackson, Mississippi, a representative of the Department attended the meeting and told the Commission in strong terms not to hold the hearing. We were advised that the Commission could not expect any protection from the Department of Justice if it did hold the hearing. The reason for this was that the Department of Justice had filed a number of cases in federal courts, in which it was seeking to obtain orders requiring the registration of named plaintiffs as voters. There were usually forty or fifty names in each case, and the total number of plaintiffs in all of the cases was not large enough to make a real dent in the problem. I suggested that the Department was proceeding retail—which was good, and I wished them success—but that we wanted to proceed wholesale, that is, to obtain changes in the law which would result in hundreds of thousands of registrations. This had no impact. After the department's representative left, the Commission voted unanimously to hold the hearing in Jackson, and since preliminary investigations by the staff had already been completed, the hearing was held in February, 1965, shortly after a number of church burnings in the Jackson area.

The first problem encountered related to hotel accommodations for the Commission and its staff. One member of the Commission, Mrs. Freeman, was black, and many members of the staff were black. We would not go any place where we were not all welcome. Finally, through intervention by one of the members of the Commission, we were advised that the Holiday Inn in Jackson would take all of us, and we made plans accordingly. There was apprehension that there might be serious opposition on our arrival, but nothing developed. Indeed, the whole question of accommodations went quite smoothly. Thus, we integrated the hotels of Jackson. When we left, all of the staff of the hotel lined up and shook our hands.

The next problem came with respect to a place for the hearings. Chairman Hannah went to see Judge Cox of the United States District Court in Jackson, and asked if we might use his courtroom, as we had done in other cities. This was abruptly refused. Arrangements were then made to use the auditorium in the Veterans Hospital, conveniently located near downtown Jackson, and the hearings were held there. Finally, it developed that the local television station, which had for several years refused any black participation in its programs, was fearful that its license might not be renewed. Apparently it received good advice, for we were told that it would broadcast the hearings from beginning to end. This proved to be a very important development. I was later told by people in Jackson that they had watched the hearings with close attention, and had learned much that they had not previously known.

A day or two before the hearings began, Harriet and I were driven in a Commission (rented) car, with a black staff member driving, to visit the site of a recently burned church, about fifteen miles to the north-east of Jackson. When we got about three miles from the church we noticed that we were being followed by three or four cars. We continued on our way with appreciable concern, and went to the site of the church. I will confess that we did not get out there, but observed the scene from the car. We then swung around and drove towards Jackson, visiting Tougaloo College on the way. Tougaloo was a well-regarded black college, and I wanted to talk with its President. Some weeks before, an East Indian student at Tougaloo had been beaten by a group of white people. However, during the course of the attack, it was learned that the student was from India. One of the attackers called out: "Don't beat him. He is not an American." This stopped the attack.

The hearing in Jackson lasted for several days covering a great many instances of abuse and misconduct. One of the problems related to voting. The Constitution of Mississippi at that time provided that a person who applied to register to vote was required "to read and interpret" a paragraph of the Constitution of Mississippi. The staff advised us that paragraphs of the constitution were printed on cards, and that the "easy paragraphs" were in the front of the box, and the "hard paragraphs," were in the back of the box. When a white applicant applied, he was given an "easy" card. When a black applicant applied, he received one of the "hard" cards.

During the hearings, a registrar from one of the Mississippi precincts was a witness, accompanied by his lawyer. When it came my turn to question him, I opened the box, and picked out one of the back cards. I handed it to him, and asked him to read and interpret it. The card said something to the effect that "The writ of quo warranto is abolished, and all ex post facto laws shall be invalid." The registrar had difficulty reading this, and when it came to interpreting it, he turned to his counsel, who was sitting beside him. I said that I had asked for his interpretation, not his counsel's. There was further talk between him and his counsel, and then the witness said: "I decline to answer." I said, "Is this on the ground that it will incriminate you?" He said "Yes." That terminated the questioning, but the point was made. This appeared on national television, and was the subject of comment in the news magazines.

There were many other pieces of evidence of this sort, including a considerable amount of testimony to the effect that local black people would never report any offenses to the Federal Bureau of Investigation, because they found that any complaint they might make was immediately reported to the local sheriff, often with unfortunate consequences to those who had made the report. Director J. Edgar Hoover said that he did not have enough manpower to deal with all the complaints, and that, accordingly, he had to operate in close relationship with the local police. Whatever the reason may have been, though, it was clear that the F.B.I. was not undertaking any effective enforcement of federal civil rights law in Mississippi—at least until after the Philadelphia crimes.

These matters are covered in a report of the Commission on Civil Rights entitled "Law Enforcement—A Report on Equal Protection in the South," published in late 1965. At the close of this report, I attached a separate statement in which I said:

> It is my earnest hope that this Report of the Commission on Civil Rights will focus the attention of thoughtful people everywhere on the realities of this problem, and that, especially, it will lead to an awakening of awareness and responsibility on the part of citizens and lawyers of the South. * * * Too long have we too casually accepted a system in this area which too often, sometimes even unconsciously and unintentionally, has in fact been grossly discriminatory. When southerners, and particularly southern lawyers, can accept and face this deplorable fact, and begin to work, openly and assiduously, to correct it, we can have real hope that this situation will change to the great benefit of the South and of the Nation.

An interesting episode relating to the Law School occurred in early 1965, though my efforts to make it amusing were not wholly successful. This related to the "stand-up" desk of Justice Holmes.

Justice Holmes died in 1935, leaving neither widow nor children. Under his will, his tangible property went to his nephew, Edward Jackson Holmes, LL.B. 1895. The younger Mr. Holmes died in 1950, leaving no children. His tangible property passed to his wife, Mary Stacy Holmes. Mrs. Holmes died in 1964, and the tangible property of Justice Holmes then passed to the nieces and nephews of Mrs. Edward Holmes, who, of course, had no direct family connection with Justice Holmes. Late in 1964, all the deans and heads of departments at Harvard had received a rather stern notification from the Secretary to the Harvard Corporation that they had no authority to accept any gift of tangible property.[45] Needless to say, this instruction came

---

45. Apparently, some gifts had been accepted, such as a collection of fancy glassware, which involved large expenses for shelving, and recurring expenditures for cleaning, and so on.

to my mind when I received, early in 1965, a telephone call from the executor of the estate of Mrs. Edward Holmes, asking if we would accept a gift of the Holmes stand-up desk. I was told that the desk was already on a truck, that it would be delivered to the Law School if I accepted it, and otherwise it would go someplace else. Despite my instructions from the Corporation, I said that we would accept the desk, and within an hour it had arrived.

I reported this action to the Harvard Corporation in a very obsequious letter, in which I said that I had to report that I had knowingly violated the instructions of the Corporation. Despite my known lack of authority, I had accepted a gift of tangible property. I added that I felt that I should report this for whatever action the Corporation thought it appropriate to take. I thought that this was mildly amusing, and I awaited the response that I might receive. It did not come for several weeks, when I received a very official communication, signed by the Secretary to the Corporation, and reading somewhat as follows: "Voted, at a meeting of President and Fellows of Harvard College, held in Cambridge on" a date stated in 1965 "to ratify the action of the Dean of the Law School in accepting a gift of a desk once owned by Justice Oliver Wendell Holmes Jr." There was no covering letter, and no rebuke for my effrontery for taking the law into my own hands.

The desk was first acquired, early in the nineteenth century, by Justice Holmes' grandfather, Judge Charles Jackson, who was a judge of the Supreme Judicial Court of Massachusetts. It then passed to Holmes' mother and then to his father. It came to the Justice in 1900 as indicated by a brass plate attached by the Justice when he received it. The desk is now located in the Dean's office, and is surely a leading item in the treasures of the Law School.

CHAPTER IX

Change of Venue

A. Return to the Solicitor General's Office

In the fall of 1967, I started my twenty-second year as Dean of the Harvard Law School. I made the usual address to the first-year students, and looked forward to the coming year. There were signs of developing student discontent, based primarily on the draft and the Viet Nam War. I knew that there might be problems, but I was not particularly concerned.

As I look back, I think that I was finding less exhilaration in the teaching of the Federal Tax course. In the thirty-three years since I first taught the course in 1934, the tax law had become far more technical and complicated. Although tax law is necessarily based on a statute, there were many "common law" type questions, such as those arising from assignments of income, in the income tax field, and those arising from trusts with various sorts of powers, in the estate tax field. In the early days, the statute was less than one hundred pages long and the income tax regulations, on which I placed much stress, were in a single, rather slight, volume. In my teaching, I put great emphasis on careful construction of the terms of the statute and the regulations. In later years, I was stopped many times by former students who told me that I had taught them the most important thing they learned in law school, and this was: "What does the statute say?"

By 1967 the statute was far more intricate and complex. The regulations filled two substantial volumes. I found myself lecturing more than I did before, and more than I should be doing then. With the complexity of the materials, it was much more difficult to get a good discussion started.

In the early part of September, 1967, we had a celebration in Cambridge, commemorating the Sesquicentennial of the founding of the Law School in 1817. A number of prominent speakers were invited, and on September 23, 1967, there was a big dinner. More than a thousand people were present, and copies of the History of the Harvard Law School by Professor Arthur E. Sutherland were distributed. This was entitled "The Law at Harvard—A History of Ideas and Men, 1817–1967." Earlier that day, at one of the sessions on the program of the celebration, I had delivered a paper called "Intellect and Spirit."[1] In this address, I observed that "Much of the lawyer's work is human relations, not based too closely on statutes or court decisions." I urged that "it is important that we make changes [in legal education] which will give greater recognition to the role of what I have called the spirit in the training of our law students."[2] And I added that "If all lawyers are imbued with a truly public approach, if every law school graduate is fully aware of what Justice Stone called 'the public duties which rest on the profession as a whole,'[3] then it will be relatively easy for lawyers to shift from one section of legal activity to another, to spend some time in private practice, then to occupy a public legal office, and then in due course to return to private law practice." And I concluded: "What I urge is that the spirit of our activities be more fully recognized as basic to the success and the essential validity of our work. * * * Without a full recognition of the role of the spirit in helping us to determine what we do and how we do it, we may fail in our task, perhaps without ever knowing why."[4]

As I spoke these words, I had no realization of how soon I would myself be changing my career.

Late in September, I received a telephone call from Ramsey Clark, then the Attorney General of the United States. He asked me if I would be willing to have my name on a list to be submitted to the President for consideration for appointment as Solicitor General of the United States. As I later told the faculty, "I took fifteen agonizing seconds, and said yes." This was indeed

---

1. 81 Harv.L.Rev. 293 (1967).

2. 81 Harv.L.Rev. at 304.

3. Stone, The Public Influence of the Bar, 48 Harv.L.Rev. 1, 11 (1934).

4. 81 Harv.L.Rev. at 306–307. I had previously presented somewhat similar views in a Tyrrell Williams Memorial Lecture at Washington University in St. Louis. See E. Griswold, "Law Schools and Human Relations," 1955 Wash. U. L.Q. 217.

the only Federal office I ever really wanted. On the 29th of
September, I was called again and advised that the nomination
had been made. I was told that I would be picked up by a
military plane at Hanscomb Field at seven o'clock the next
morning. I would be flown to Washington, where others would
join me, and then we would proceed to the Johnson Ranch in
Texas, where the announcement would be made. I was further
told, in very stern terms, that absolutely nothing should be said
about this to anyone. I said that I would have to tell my wife,
and was told that that would be all right, but that I must be sure
that she did not give the information to *anyone* else. I then said
that I would have to tell President Pusey of Harvard University.
I could not leave the University after thirty-three years there, and
have its President hear this news on the radio, or see it in the
newspapers. I was strongly advised against this, but I continued
my insistence that I really had no alternative.

An appointment was made to see President Pusey at his
residence that evening. He was very gracious about it, though he
seemed somewhat doubtful about my wisdom in making the
change. There was no leak.

My wife drove me to Hanscomb Field early on the morning
of September 30th, and, in a state of considerable excitement, I
arrived, along with others, at the Johnson Ranch before noon.
President Johnson was at the airfield, driving a small car. We
were immediately taken to a covered area where there was much
television equipment. Soon I found myself being introduced by
the President, with the announcement that he was nominating
me to be Solicitor General. Other announcements were made,
and then the television ceremony was over.

I was invited to have lunch with the family at the Johnson
ranch house. I sat on the President's right, with the black box
(which I assumed contained controls for use of nuclear weapons)
in front of him. Mrs. Johnson sat across the table, and other
members of the family were in between, including the President's
grandchild, then about one-year old.

It was a very friendly family meal. Mrs. Johnson kept the
conversation going, in a kind and interesting way. There was no
pomp or ceremony. After a while, the President took his grandson and held him on his knee. I tried to enter into the conversation, and was, I think, reasonably successful in participating, not
too much.

After the lunch, the President took me in to his study, or
office, on the ground floor of the ranch house, off the living
room. The telephone on the desk was directly connected with

The White House in Washington, and the President asked me to use it to advise my wife, which I gladly did. Then, the President talked to me at some length about the Department of Justice. He said that he thought it needed strengthening, and that he hoped that I could contribute to that. He talked about various persons in the Department, and seemed to be well aware of the principal officers. At that time, of course, I knew little about the current problems in the Department, or about those in the Solicitor General's office. I did tell the President about my background in that office, and said that I thought that it would enable me to recognize problems, and to deal with them.

Later in the afternoon, the President took several of us in his open car to see his birthplace. He did the driving, going very fast down the dirt road. I rather felt that he took pleasure in giving us a thrill, and in watching us hang on in the car.

We were then driven back to the airfield. We flew first to the Andrews Air Force Base in Washington, and then I, alone, was flown to the Logan Airport in Boston, arriving at about eight o'clock. I then went on to the Harvard Club in Boston, where I knew that a five-year reunion of the Class of 1962 was in progress. The news about my nomination had appeared in the papers and over the radio, and I was plied with many questions about my trip.

Over the next two weeks, I spent several days in Washington, primarily for the purpose of calling on members of the Senate Committee on the Judiciary, which would be holding a hearing on my nomination. There was nothing particularly eventful about these calls, except for the most important one. It was imperative, of course, that I call on the Chairman of the Judiciary Committee, Senator James O. Eastland, of Mississippi. I was really frightened at this prospect, and wondered whether I could successfully carry it off. I was sure that he would be aware of the hearings held by the Civil Rights Commission in Jackson, Mississippi, and probably he would know about my part in those hearings. I feared, too, that he might seek some sort of commitment from me on one issue or another. I was determined that I would make no commitment, but I was dubious as to whether I could maintain that position in a gracious and successful manner.

Actually, though, there were no problems. Senator Eastland was kindly and agreeable. He raised no questions, and the whole interview lasted only a few minutes. When the hearing was held, it was uneventful, and I was promptly confirmed.

In the following days, I had several telephone calls from Warren Christopher, the Deputy Attorney General. It was arranged that I would be sworn in on the morning of October 23rd, and that this would be done at the White House. I took Harriet to Washington, and my daughter Hope and her daughter Claudia, then eight years old, came for the occasion. My sister Jane Holmes came from Cleveland. I was sworn in by Chief Justice Earl Warren, while Harriet held the Bible. The White House photographer took a nice picture of the group immediately after the ceremony.

The family then had lunch at the Cosmos Club. After that, I proceeded to the Department of Justice, where I entered the Solicitor General's office, and found it in good order. There were a number of files on my desk, and I examined a few of them, noting that the duties involved, and even the forms, were exactly the same as they had been in the early 1930s. I found a few of the files which seemed to be entirely clear, and I duly endorsed "No Appeal" on them, and signed my name. Thus began my work as Solicitor General.

The staff was excellent, and it continued. Ralph Spritzer was the First Deputy Solicitor General. Daniel M. Friedman, a graduate of the Columbia Law School, was next in line. Mr. Spritzer resigned after a year, and went to teach at the University of Pennsylvania Law School. Mr. Friedman succeeded him as First Deputy, and served in that capacity for the remaining five years of my tenure. He was wise and able, experienced and energetic, supportive and loyal, and I was very fortunate to have his aid and guidance over those years.

The title of the Solicitor General was taken from the English practice, but the parallel goes no further. In England, the Solicitor General must be a member of Parliament, and he is a junior cabinet officer. Both he and the Attorney General frequently appear as the trial advocate in major cases in the British courts.

In the United States, we do not have a parliamentary government, and neither the Attorney General nor the Solicitor General is a member of Congress. The Attorney General is a member of the President's Cabinet, and often acts as an advisor to the President, and to other Cabinet officers. Until 1950, the Solicitor General was the second officer in the Department of Justice. In that year, the office of Deputy Attorney General was established, with the result that the Solicitor General became the third officer in the Department of Justice.[5]

---

5. For a number of years, from 1977 to 1987, there was an Associate Attorney General, who ranked third, thus downgrading the Solicitor General to the fourth officer during those years.

At swearing-in as Solicitor General. The White House—October 23, 1967. Left to right: Hope G. Murrow (daughter); Attorney General Ramsey Clark; Chief Justice Earl Warren; Harriet F. Griswold (wife); President Lyndon B. Johnson; ENG

The duties of the Solicitor General are unique, making his position, in the opinion of many, the best legal office in the executive branch of the government. The Solicitor General is nominated by the President, and confirmed by the Senate, thus making him a "political officer." Under the law establishing the office, which was enacted in 1870, he must be "learned in the law," and my commission (as do the commissions of all Solicitors General) contains that accolade. It also provides that the Solicitor General holds his office "during the pleasure of the President." This, too, makes it plain that the office is a "political one." Yet, by long tradition and practice, it is usually recognized as being essentially a professional position. Reverting to the English terminology, the Solicitor General is the chief barrister for the United States, its officers and agencies. He is subject to the control of the President and the Attorney General, but his professional judgment is widely respected, and is rarely interfered with. When there is interference, the Solicitor General has two options: he can (1) resign, or (2) see if he can find some way to work the problem out which will not require him to act in a way which he thinks is not appropriate.

The basic responsibility of the Solicitor General is to represent the United States, its officers and agencies in any litigation before the Supreme Court of the United States. Since the United States is a party in more than half the cases pending before the Court (including criminal cases), the Solicitor General cannot personally handle all of the cases. He has a small staff in his own office.[6] Much of the brief writing is done by lawyers in the various divisions of the Department of Justice, such as the Antitrust Division, the Criminal Division, the Tax Division, and so on. But all of the drafts of briefs come to the Solicitor General's office, where they are reviewed in detail by the Solicitor General's staff. Briefs on the merits are personally reviewed by the Solicitor General, and, in my day, before the volume got so great, all papers filed in the Supreme Court were personally reviewed by me.

In addition to brief writing, the Solicitor General is also responsible for all the oral arguments in government cases before the Supreme Court. In recent years, there have been seventy-five or more oral arguments in government cases each year. Obviously, the Solicitor General cannot handle all of these himself. I used to argue about one case a week, during the Court's sitting, or about fourteen cases during the year. The rest of the cases were assigned for argument by the Solicitor General. In

---

6. In my day, there were sixteen lawyers, plus the Solicitor General. I understand that the staff has now grown to about twenty-four lawyers, in addition to the Solicitor General.

recent years, most of these assignments have been made to members of the staff in the Solicitor General's office. In my earlier time with the government, from 1929 to 1934, the various Assistant Attorneys General had first choice of cases to argue from among those cases which came through their division. In recent years, though, they have felt themselves to be too busy, and have generally not welcomed oral argument assignments. On very rare occasions, the Attorney General may argue a case, as did Attorney General Clark[7] and Attorney General Griffin Bell.[8]

In addition to the briefing and argument of government cases before the Supreme Court, the Solicitor General has one other major responsibility. Under the regulations of the Department of Justice, *no* case which the government loses in *any* court can be appealed without the authority of the Solicitor General. This is the one place where there is a measure of coordination of the government's massive litigation within the United States, and occasionally in other countries. Without such control by the Solicitor General, there would be a tendency for each U.S. Attorney to appeal any case which is lost in his office. This would result in increased congestion in the appellate courts, and in annoyance on the part of appellate judges, who might be led to underestimate the government's arguments in its more important cases.[9] These duties, in my time, involved the making of some four thousand decisions a year. This works out to be something like fifteen or sixteen decisions a day. Many of these are very easy to make, and require only a small amount of time; and a sizeable number of them are extremely complex, involving difficult problems and many different points of view within the government.[10]

From time to time, it is urged that each agency should make its own decision about its cases in the Supreme Court. Needless to say, it seems to me to be important that this

---

7. In the case of Jones v. Alfred H. Mayer Co., 392 U.S. 409 (1968).

8. In the case of Tennessee Valley Authority v. Hill, 437 U.S. 153 (1978).

9. In addition to these two powers, the Solicitor General also determines whether a brief *amicus curiae* shall be filed on behalf of the government in any appellate court, and whether an application for rehearing *en banc* shall be filed where the government has lost a case in a United States Court of Appeals.

10. The number is apparently much the same today, although the cases continue to increase in complexity.

authority be centralized in the Solicitor General.[11] My experience was that if care is taken to see that every point of view has a full hearing, a decision can be made which will be accepted. Some agencies have especially strong feelings about this matter. In particular, it took both patience and some skill to work out problems with the Securities and Exchange Commission. With respect to arguments on the merits in cases coming from the National Labor Relations Board, I took the position that if the case really involved a broad question of "administrative law," [12] I would argue it, but if the question involved was one of "labor law," I would assign the argument to the General Counsel of the Labor Board.

B. THE JOHNSON ADMINISTRATION

Because of my previous experience in the office, and my close following of its work, particularly under Solicitors General Archibald Cox and Thurgood Marshall, I found no difficulty in working into the routine of the office. Indeed, as I have indicated, the nature of the work was quite unchanged from what it had been when I left the office more than thirty years before. I took pains in establishing relations with the several Assistant Attorneys General, and their senior staff.

One of my early assignments was to serve as a member of a Board to make reports about wiretapping. When I came back to the office, I found that the practice was that the Department must disclose the fact that there had been a wiretap, but that it need not disclose the nature of the information obtained if it certified that the information had no relation to the case in which the question was raised.[13] The Board to consider this

---

11. My views on this were quite fully stated in one of my last acts as Solicitor General. This was in testimony and a memorandum presented before a subcommittee of the House Committee on Interstate and Foreign Commerce on June 7, 1973. See Hearings on Securities Exchange Act Amendments of 1973, Part I, 93rd Congress, First Session (Serial No. 93–50) 272–296.

12. As was the situation in National Labor Relations Board v. Wyman–Gordon Co., 394 U.S. 759 (1969). See K. Davis, Administrative Law Treatise (2d ed. 1979) § 7:25.

13. This practice was invalidated by the decision of the Supreme Court in Kolod v. United States, 390 U.S. 136 (1968) (where I appeared against Edward Bennett Williams, who was counsel for the petitioners). The Court there held that it "could not accept the Department's *ex parte* determination of relevancy in lieu of such determination in an adversary proceeding." This, of course, ended the role of the Board in such cases.

question consisted of the Solicitor General, the Director of the Federal Bureau of Investigation, J. Edgar Hoover, and the head of the Criminal Division, then Fred M. Vinson, Jr. Mr. Hoover attended the first session of the Board after I became Solicitor General, but thereafter he sent a deputy. As a matter of fact, I was acquainted with Mr. Hoover, since we had both been young men together in the Department of Justice before he became a leading figure there.[14]

When I returned to the Department, I looked for a case to argue, and soon found an appropriate one. It was a tax case with fairly simple facts, which raised an uncomplicated question of statutory construction.[15]

My first case of considerable importance arose under the Selective Service law.[16] It was argued before the Supreme Court on January 24, 1968. The defendant, O'Brien, burned his draft card before a considerable crowd of people. He told the F.B.I. agents he had done this "because of his beliefs, knowing that he was violating federal law." The court of appeals judges held that the statute on which the case was based was unconstitutional under the First Amendment. A petition for certiorari to review this decision had been filed and granted before I became Solicitor General. I was concerned about the case, as I was about all draft cases, but I thought that a good argument could be made that the statute was constitutional. Indeed, I was always reminding the members of my staff that we were advocates and not judges. I said that there were nine judges down there the other side of the Capitol who were very well qualified, and that our basic function was to represent the United States, making the

---

14. In the early days after my return to the Department of Justice, I became quite notable among the other officers because I was the only one who called the Director of the F.B.I. by his middle name, "Edgar." I must confess that I did not do this until after he had called me "Erwin." Our relations were somewhat distant, but reasonably good. I never had reason to question the accuracy of any statement he made to me in the course of my work.

15. The case was United States v. Correll, 389 U.S. 299 (1967). The Internal Revenue Code provided that a taxpayer could deduct "travelling expenses incurred in business, while away from home." The regulations of the Treasury Department provided that the deduction for meals would be allowed only if the trip required sleep or rest. Relying on the long-continued nature of the regulation, the Court held that a salesman for a wholesale grocery company who left his home early in the morning and returned home in time for dinner could not deduct the cost of his breakfast and lunch while on the road.

16. United States v. O'Brien, 391 U.S. 367 (1968).

best argument that we felt could be made while being very careful to present the facts accurately and not to mislead the Court in any way with respect to the law. Of course, I said, there are some positions which we will not take, if there is no respectable basis for advancing them. As far as the *O'Brien* case was concerned, I felt that a respectable argument could be made.

However, there was one aspect of the *O'Brien* argument which I was not willing to make. It had been contended in support of the statute that carrying a draft card served an important governmental interest, because it provided evidence that the individual involved had complied with the law by registering for the draft. My own experience was that actually being in possession of a draft card was of no particular value to the government. The regulation requiring possession of a draft card contained no exceptions, but it would have been extremely unlikely that a court would hold that it had been violated if the respondent was not in possession of his card while he slept. I knew from my experience with law students that many of them did not carry their draft cards, though they would be able to produce them on short notice if that became relevant. I felt that the actual carrying of a draft card was not important, and that the government must face up to the question whether a statute was constitutional when it was clear that the card had been publicly destroyed for the purpose of expressing opposition to the Viet Nam war. So I presented the case as involving conduct, not speech, and thus not within the protection of the First Amendment. The Supreme Court, however, in an opinion written by Chief Justice Warren, affirmed the conviction, largely on the "possession" ground, saying that requiring possession of the draft card brought into play the principle that "a sufficiently important constitutional interest in regulating the non-speech element can justify incidental limitations on First Amendment freedoms." [17]

There was another case which came up in 1968 which caused me concern. This was *Flast v. Cohen*,[18] which raised the somewhat technical and elusive question of "standing" to maintain a suit in a federal court. In the suit, it was alleged that officers of the Department of Health, Education and Welfare (as it then was) had supplied funds to finance instruction in non-religious

17. 391 U.S. at 376. It is very hard to reconcile the decision in the O'Brien case with the recent decision in the Flag Burning case (United States v. Eichman, 110 S.Ct. 2404 (1990)), and, indeed, the Eichman case (see also Texas v. Johnson, 491 U.S. 397 (1989)) may well have overruled the O'Brien decision, though that was not explicitly done.

18. 392 U.S. 83 (1968).

subjects in religious schools, and to purchase textbooks for use in teaching these subjects. The plaintiffs filed suit seeking a declaration that the statute, as so applied, was unconstitutional under the First Amendment. They rested "their standing to maintain the action solely on their status as federal taxpayers." [19] The local court dismissed the suit for lack of standing, relying on the well-known decision of the Supreme Court in *Frothingham v. Mellon*,[20] where the Court had held that a federal taxpayer had so small and indefinite an interest in federal expenditures that he did not have standing to challenge the constitutionality of a federal spending statute.

The Supreme Court noted probable jurisdiction to review this decision. This was a matter of considerable surprise in view of the *Frothingham v. Mellon* precedent. It could only mean that there were members of the Court who were prepared to review the earlier case and, perhaps, to overrule or qualify it. I felt that a decision giving taxpayers standing to raise questions as to the validity of federal statutes would open the door to a flood of lawsuits, leading to uncertainty and delay in the application and enforcement of federal statutes, with resulting difficulties, substantial in number and consequences, in the administration of the federal government.

Consequently, I prepared a comprehensive brief and received much help from my colleagues in preparation for oral argument. Rather to my surprise, the Supreme Court held that the plaintiffs had standing to raise this question, with only Justice Harlan dissenting. The Supreme Court's decision rested on the special importance of the specific constitutional provision in the First Amendment denying Congress power to pass a law "respecting an establishment of religion."

As things have worked out, the decision in *Flast v. Cohen* has been rarely utilized, and the flood of cases in the lower courts which I anticipated has not materialized. Actually, after the plaintiffs' victory in *Flast*, they did not pursue the decision, and never obtained the declaratory judgment which they sought in their complaint.[21] The Supreme Court did follow the *Flast* case in one decision involving schools.[22] Otherwise, *Flast v. Cohen* has been often cited, particularly in the lower courts, but rarely

---

19. 392 U.S. at 85.

20. 262 U.S. 447 (1923).

21. See National Coalition for Public Education v. Califano, 446 F.Supp. 193, 195 (S.D.N.Y. 1978).

22. Meek v. Pittenger, 421 U.S. 349 (1975).

followed, and, in subsequent decisions, the Supreme Court has closely limited it.[23]

Justice Stewart and I, in several conversations, found it amusing to develop a list of what we called "phantom decisions of the Supreme Court"—that is, decisions which seemed to be important at the time they were decided, but which turned out to be of little enduring consequence. I felt that *Flast v. Cohen* should be on this list.[24] Of course it is an ever-growing list, and always subject to change. Hopefully, *United States v. Nixon*,[25] will have a permanent place on the list.

Another case which I argued before the Supreme Court in the spring of 1968 was *Maryland v. Wirtz*.[26] This involved the constitutionality of an amendment to the Fair Labor Standards Act, which made the wages and hours provisions of the Act applicable to schools and hospitals operated by "any state or political subdivision of a state." The Court sustained the validity of the statute, thus bringing a wide range of state employees within the protection of the Fair Labor Standards Act.

This general area presents a problem on which the Supreme Court has found great difficulty in coming to a clear resolution. In *National League of Cities v. Usery*,[27] the Court held that 1974 amendments to the Fair Labor Standards Act which extended the minimum wage and maximum hour provisions of the Act to state employees generally, were unconstitutional, and *Maryland v. Wirtz* was overruled. This was a five to four decision. Then, nine years later, in *Garcia v. San Antonio Metropolitan Transit Authority*,[28] another five to four decision, the *National League of Cities* case was overruled. The *Garcia* case involved employees of a transit system operated by a city. Although I did not

---

23. See Valley Forge Christian College v. Americans United for Separation of Church and State, 454 U.S. 464 (1982), and Bowen v. Kendrick, 487 U.S. 589 (1988).

24. Others on the list included Robinson v. California, 370 U.S. 660 (1962); Bivens v. Six Unknown Named Agents of the F.B.I., 403 U.S. 388 (1971) (see 456 F.2d 1339 (2d Cir. 1972), *on remand* (holding agents not liable if they acted in good faith); Kleindienst v. Mandel, 408 U.S. 753 (1972); United States v. Caldwell, decided in Branzburg v. Hayes, 408 U.S. 665 (1972).

25. 418 U.S. 683 (1974).

26. 392 U.S. 183 (1968). My opponent in the oral argument in this case was my friend, Professor Charles Alan Wright of the Law School at the University of Texas.

27. 426 U.S. 833 (1976).

28. 469 U.S. 528 (1985).

participate in these later cases, the line of decisions themselves illustrates how close some of the questions in federal-state relations are, and how difficult it is to define the limits of federal power when dealing with state or municipal governments. In the *Garcia* case, the Court spoke through Mr. Justice Blackmun, and relied heavily on the political system—that is the electorate—to protect the states.[29]

When I accepted President Johnson's appointment to be Solicitor General, in September 1967, I assumed that there would be a fair likelihood that my tenure would last at least until after the election in 1973, that is, that President Johnson would be reelected and that I might be able to serve through his new term. Consequently, I was considerably dismayed when, one evening, as Harriet and I were watching President Johnson's address on television, I heard him say at the end that he would neither seek nor would he accept a renomination for the office of the President.[30] At that point, it seemed to me to be quite likely that I would have a rather short tenure, and that I would be leaving the government in January 1969.[31] There was little that I could do, though, except continue to try to meet my responsibilities, and watch how the situation developed.

President Johnson's announcement came shortly after the assassination of the Rev. Martin Luther King, Jr., on March 20, 1968. This tragic event brought deep reactions all over the country. In Washington, there was wide-spread rioting and looting, and many fires were set. Indeed the smoke from the

---

29. For a discussion, see Field, "Garcia v. San Antonio Metropolitan Transit Authority: The Demise of a Misguided Doctrine," 99 Harv.L.Rev. 84 (1985).

30. I was greatly troubled by the Viet Nam war, and the considerable number of draft cases which came to the Solicitor General's office. I never understood why we were in Viet Nam so extensively, nor why our involvement there lasted so long. However, these were matters over which I had no control, though I was determined to deal thoughtfully and carefully with the questions which became my responsibility in cases before the Supreme Court.

For some reason which I cannot now explain, I was not aware of the extent to which the Viet Nam involvement had affected President Johnson's political situation. Thus, I was quite taken by surprise when I heard his announcement in his television speech.

31. There was a time, in the late fall of 1967, when I thought I might be leaving the office of Solicitor General after a tenure of only a few weeks. This is cryptically summarized in a book review which I wrote, which was published in 33 J. of L.Ed. 388, 390–391 (1983). However, I found a way to work that out which seemed to me to be justified.

Florida Avenue area drifted down to the Department of Justice Building, and I had to close the window in my office in order to keep the air breatheable.

Attorney General Ramsey Clark assembled the senior staff in his office and gave us various assignments. Mine was to sit in the Attorney General's office and to write down summaries of his part of any conversations he had with governors throughout the country. He did not want to record these conversations, nor did he want to tell a governor that some one was listening in. So I heard only the Attorney General's part of the conversation, but it was felt that this would provide a summary of each situation, and that, in particular, it would make a record, for the Attorney General's benefit, of any agreements that he might make, particularly with respect to the sending of aid which any Governor might request.

One of the members of the staff of the Criminal Division, Fred B. Ugast (later Chief Judge of the Superior Court of the District of Columbia) was assigned to go, with car and driver, as far as he felt he could into the affected area, and report what he could find. This was because the Attorney General was receiving great pressure, particularly from Capitol Hill, to "do something," with arrests and prosecutions particularly in mind. The plan was that Fred would report to me whatever he might find, and we would then report to the Attorney General. When Fred returned, he said that the only thing he could find that could be proved in court was that Stokely Carmichael had been seen walking down Fourteenth Street, with a large following crowd. He was waving a pistol in the air and was saying repeatedly, "Not yet, not yet." The gun was not concealed. It very likely was not registered, and this might have formed a basis for a prosecution. But all agreed that, under all the circumstances, it was not appropriate to recommend a prosecution for that offense at that time.

This was one of the two occasions when I stayed at the Department of Justice over night, using the small bedroom which former Attorney General William D. Mitchell had arranged as a part of the Solicitor General's suite (and in the Attorney General's suite, too) when the building was being designed in the early 1930s. It was not very comfortable.

In the fall of 1968, an interesting draft case came before the Supreme Court. The registrant involved had returned his draft card to his draft board. He was then found to be delinquent for failure to have the card in his possession. Because of this action, pursuant to the Selective Service regulations, his classification was changed to 1–A, and he was ordered to report for induction. He then brought a suit to restrain his induction. This was dismissed in the district court, and the dismissal was affirmed by the court of appeals.

When the petition came to my desk, it was accompanied by a draft of a brief in opposition. On examining the petition, I noted that the registrant was a full-time student at the Andover–Newton Theological School, in Massachusetts. I called the dean of that school, and asked whether the registrant was a student at the school, and whether he was a *bona-fide* full-time student. I was given a clear affirmative response to both questions. As a result, I changed the brief in opposition, and filed a short acquiescence, stating the facts, and calling attention to section 6(g) of the Selective Service Act of 1967, which provided that "students preparing for the ministry" in qualified schools "shall be exempt from training and service" under the Act. Thus, it seemed to me to be clear beyond question that the order to report for induction was invalid on its face, and the Supreme Court so held.[32]

Before filing my brief, I made an appointment, and went to call on General Hershey, the Director of the Selective Service System. My purpose was to bring the matter to his attention, with the hope that he would issue instructions to the draft board to revoke the induction order. General Hershey observed that he had never before been called on by anybody from the Department of Justice. However, he was virtually blind, and relied heavily on his staff. In response to my suggestion, he said that he had no authority to tell any draft board what to do. I pointed out that he had issued a regulation requiring registrants to be in possession of their draft cards, and providing further that anyone who violated the regulation was "delinquent" and subject to reclassification and immediate order for induction. His response was that it was up to the board to make its own interpretation of the regulation.

There was a General Counsel of the Selective Service System and General Hershey had him prepare a brief supporting the action of the draft board. His counsel sought to file this with the Clerk of the Supreme Court, but the Clerk refused to receive it. General Hershey then went to call on his friend, Chief Justice Warren, and, as reported to me, the Chief Justice said: "Of course you can file the brief," or words to that effect. The brief was then taken back to the Clerk's office, which handled it with consummate skill. The Clerk still refused to allow the brief to be filed, but he did allow the brief to be "lodged" in his office, and he so notified the members of the Court. I am told that some of them came to the Clerk's office to examine the brief.

---

32. Oestereich v. Selective Service Board, 393 U.S. 233 (1968).

In early December, 1968, shortly after the election of that year, there was an item in the Washington Post saying that Richard Kleindienst, of Phoenix, Arizona, would be the Solicitor General in the Nixon Administration. Kleindienst had been a student at the Harvard Law School, where he received his law degree in 1950. A little later in December, however, John Mitchell, the Attorney General designate, called me on the telephone and asked me if I would be willing to stay on as Solicitor General "for a while." I asked him what he meant by "a while," and he replied that it was indefinite, but probably through the spring term of the Supreme Court, which usually adjourned in June. I told him that I would be glad to do that. At about this time, Kleindienst was announced as the new Deputy Attorney General. I never knew who may have been influential in the decision to keep me on, but I have always supposed that Richard Kleindienst had a role in it.

C. The Nixon Administration

As a result, I was, for a day after the Nixon Administration came in on January 20, 1969, the Acting Attorney General, since I was the only presidentially appointed officer still functioning in the Department of Justice. President Nixon could nominate the new appointees only after his inauguration, and they could not be sworn in until they had been confirmed by the Senate. As far as I can recall, my only official act as Acting Attorney General was to appoint the new officers (including the Attorney General and the Deputy Attorney General) as special assistants to the Attorney General, so that they could receive salaries beginning on Inauguration Day. Attorney General Mitchell was sworn in the next day, and my brief tenure as head of the Department of Justice came promptly to a close. Within a few days, I met the new appointees. I was particularly impressed by Johnnie Walters, the Assistant Attorney General for the Tax Division, Richard McLaren, the Assistant Attorney General for the Antitrust Division, and William D. Ruckelshaus, the Assistant Attorney General for the Civil Division, as well as Richard Kleindienst, the new Deputy Attorney General. Nothing further was said about my tenure until December 1972, a month or so after the 1972 election. The four years after January 1969, were interesting, to say the least, but, for the most part, were fully occupied by the usual professional responsibilities of the Solicitor General's office.

Early in February, 1969, there was an episode which was perhaps more significant than I then understood. My secretary told me that "the White House" was on the telephone. The voice gave the name of one of the new high functionaries in the Nixon White House. I made no note at the time, and I cannot now recall just who it was. Without much introduction or explanation, he said: "The President wants you to take" a specified action in a named case. Rather pompously, I suppose, I replied: "It seems to me that any instruction like that should come to me through the Attorney General." I then walked down the corridor to the other corner of the building, and promptly saw Attorney General Mitchell. I told him what had happened. He looked up at the ceiling with a wry smile, and said: "Well, I will take care of that." That was the last that I heard of the matter.[33]

This experience probably served to protect me from a good deal of direct pressure during my time as Solicitor General in the Nixon Administration.[34] I have also heard, in later years, of occasions in which Attorney General Mitchell shielded me in several matters. Otherwise, in view of what we now know about the Nixon White House in those years, I could not have survived for four years in the Nixon Administration. The later developments about John Mitchell are a source of great concern to me. Whether he acted under instructions from President Nixon, and kept that to himself, I do not know. Except on such a ground, I cannot understand his failure to prevent the Watergate break-in, which, apparently, he could have blocked at its

---

33. Former Attorney General Kleindienst has put the matter very well. He wrote, with respect to Attorney General John Mitchell: "The most important feature of his tenure, however, was the shield he erected between Justice and the White House staff. Not every attorney general has such a relationship with his president that permits that beneficial condition.

"One of the most difficult situations an assistant attorney general or a bureau head can be confronted with is an end run around the attorney general by a member of the White House staff. The circumvention is more often than not born of a momentary crisis, poorly thought out, and inconsistent with the policy of the attorney general himself. Such interference, if permitted, can not only lead to mistakes with varying degrees of consequences, but also be detrimental to the morale of the department. * * * If the attorney general has the full confidence and respect of the president, he wins; if he does not, the White House staff wins. As the solicitor general Erwin Griswold and that old pro Henry Petersen of the criminal division can attest, Mitchell won the contest early on." R. Kleindienst, Justice (Ottawa, Illinois: 1985) 64.

34. I understood that some of the Assistant Attorneys General made regular calls at the White House to review cases and receive instructions. I never did so. I went there only when I was requested to come, and that happened on only two or three occasions.

inception.[35] All that I can say is that Mr. Mitchell was always fair and square with me. I never saw anything in our association in the Department of Justice which gave me concern about his integrity.

Generally speaking, the Attorney General left me alone. He understood that I wanted to act professionally, and he did not seek to interfere with that. On the other hand, I regarded it as part of my responsibility to be aware of political interests and implications and to try, as far as possible, to handle matters in such a way as to minimize political ramifications. In particular, I felt that if I took an action which might have political consequences, I ought to be sure that the Attorney General was informed. My relationship with Attorney General Mitchell, though not intimate, was always warm and cordial, and I had no reason from any contact with him to have reservations about his professional or ethical conduct.[36] I have always had great sympathy for him, and have wondered whether there were not some explanations for what he did as adviser to the President, and Chairman of the Committee to Reelect the President, which he felt that loyalty required him not to disclose.

One of the first cases which I argued in the Nixon Administration was *United States v. Montgomery Board of Education.*[37] This case involved an order by Judge Johnson in the district court in Montgomery County, Alabama relating to the local school board. It provided for faculty and staff desegregation and specified that the school board must move toward a goal whereby "in each school the ratio of white to Negro [faculty] is substantially the same as it is throughout the system." The Court of Appeals for the Fifth Circuit modified this order by striking out the provision for specific goals. During the Johnson Administra-

---

35. It is not inconceivable that he did issue orders against it, but was overruled by higher authority, and that he then felt that loyalty required him to make no further disclosure.

36. He consistently backed me up, as the following pages will show. My only reservations about him related to his judgment of people. Some of the Assistant Attorneys General he chose did not seem to me to be of the requisite caliber. And I felt that other persons he recommended for appointment were quite unqualified, such as John Dean whom he supported for the post of Counsel to the President, in the White House, and Judge Carswell, whom he supported for appointment as a Justice of the Supreme Court. Another whom he advanced for the Supreme Court post, Herschel Friday, of Arkansas, is a fine man of high character, but he did not seem to me to have other qualifications requisite for that demanding post.

37. 395 U.S. 225 (1969).

tion, I had authorized a petition for certiorari to review the decision of the Court of Appeals, and certiorari was granted on March 3, 1969, shortly after the new administration began.

I argued the case vigorously in the Supreme Court. As the Supreme Court quoted in its opinion,[38] I contended that "the District Court's order 'is designed as a *remedy for* past racial assignment. * * * We do not, in other words, argue here that racially balanced faculties are constitutionally or legally required.'" The Supreme Court, in a unanimous opinion written by Justice Black, reversed the decision of the court of appeals, and approved of Judge Johnson's order "as he wrote it." I have always regarded this as one of the most important decisions in the desegregation struggle. If there is any one thing that makes a school a "black school," it is an all-black (or nearly all-black) faculty—and *vice versa*. For some reason, though, the case has not been very often cited.

Late in the summer of 1969, there was a considerable flurry in the school desegregation area. Robert H. Finch, who had been close to President Nixon in California, and who had been mentioned for the office of Attorney General, was appointed Secretary of the Department of Health, Education, and Welfare (as it then was). I never knew the full story, but apparently he brought about a considerable change in the attitude of the education people in that Department.[39] As a result, the Department supported a "slow down" in the desegregation of the schools in Mississippi. This was supported by a decision of the Court of Appeals for the Fifth Circuit,[40] which was entered on July 3, 1969. Petitions for certiorari were soon filed, and promptly granted, on October 9, 1969, at which time the Court set the case for oral argument on October 23, 1969.[41]

I could not vigorously support the position of the United States, so I assigned the case for oral argument to the Assistant Attorney General for the Civil Rights Division, Jerris Leonard.[42]

---

38. 395 U.S. at 236.

39. For some details, see H. Dent, The Prodigal South Returns to Power (New York: 1978) 123–136. See also H. Graham, The Civil Rights Era (New York: 1990) 319–320.

40. See United States v. Hinds County School Board, 417 F.2d 852 (5th Cir. 1969).

41. 396 U.S. 802 (1969).

42. I did sign the memorandum brief because I felt that a respectable argument could be made for the government's new position. But I could not put my heart into the argument. On the whole, I think I took the correct position, but it was not an easy decision.

The case was argued on October 23rd, and it was decided on October 29, 1969.[43] In a *per curiam* decision, the Court held, without dissent, that "the Court of Appeals should have denied all motions for additional time." And it added: "Under explicit holdings of this Court the obligation of every school district is to terminate dual school systems at once and to operate now and hereafter only unitary schools."[44] Thus ended the period of "all deliberate speed."

A year or so later, another important school case came before the Court. This was *Swann v. Charlotte–Mecklenburg Board of Education.*[45] This case involved an order by Judge McMillan in the United States District Court for the Western District of North Carolina. The order provided for desegregation of the elementary schools in a large school district, including provisions for busing.[46]

I knew that this was an important case, and a delicate one. In preparing the Government's brief, I had my staff assemble speeches made by President Nixon over the past two or three years, dealing with busing, and "neighborhood schools." The position I endeavored to support was that Judge McMillan's order was valid if its purpose was to eliminate the consequences of prior discrimination, but that it could not be supported under the Constitution if its purpose was simply to establish racial quotas. Several passages from the President's speeches were then built into the brief, not as direct quotations. They were paraphrased to some extent, and no reference was made to the President. I wanted to be able to show, in case any question arose, that the brief was consistent with the President's stated position.

When the brief was in page proofs, I received a message from Attorney General Mitchell's office saying that he would like to see the proof. Of course, this was his privilege. Though it was an unusual request, I had no question about complying, and I took the brief to his office. About four hours later, I was summoned again to the Attorney General's office. I figured that

---

43. Alexander v. Holmes County Board of Education, 396 U.S. 19 (1969).

44. 396 U.S. at 20. It has been suggested that the Administration's effort "was bent on shifting the onus of forced busing from the presidency to the courts." H. Graham, The Civil Rights Era (New York: 1990) 320.

45. 402 U.S. 1 (1971).

46. Judge McMillan's decision in this case eventually cost him promotion to the Court of Appeals for the Fourth Circuit, an undeserved penalty for a careful and courageous decision.

this was about time enough to send the proof to the White House, and to have it returned. The Attorney General raised four questions, none of which was of major importance. On one of them, I thought that the point made was thoroughly sound, and I incorporated it into the brief. On two of the points, I agreed to relatively minor changes which the Attorney General found acceptable. The remaining point was a very small one, and the Attorney General said that I had been so cooperative that he saw no reason not to accept my language on this point.

So, the brief went to the printer, and was filed. In due course, I argued the case before the Court, urging the position indicated, and this was the view which was taken by the Court in an unanimous decision.[47]

Another series of Selective Service cases arose in the fall of 1969, and in later years.

One of the most publicized cases was *United States v. Spock*,[48] Among the defendants in this case were Dr. Benjamin Spock, a well-known and highly-publicized pediatrician, and Rev. William Sloan Coffin, Jr., then the chaplain at Yale University. The defendants had been charged under the Draft Act with conspiracy to "counsel, aid, and abet" draft registrants to "refuse and evade service in the Armed Forces of the United States." The jury found the defendants guilty. The district judge had submitted to the jury ten special questions, to be answered "Yes" or "No," in addition to the general issue of guilty or not guilty. On appeal, the court reversed the conviction, holding that putting to the jury "what was essentially a special verdict," amounted to "judicial pressure" from the court. It said: "There is no easier way to reach, and perhaps force, a verdict of guilty than to approach it step by step." [49] The court remanded the case to the district court for a new trial. Judge Coffin disagreed with the remand. He would have ordered a full reversal, with dismissal

---

47. The case is fully discussed in B. Schwartz, Swann's Way (New York: 1986). There is a reference to my argument at page 98 of this book. I did object in my argument to extensive busing—over twenty miles each way—of very small children. This was the essential issue involved in the case of School Board of Richmond v. State Board of Education, 412 U.S. 92 (1973), where the opposing counsel was William T. Coleman, Jr. The decision below there, which had rejected such extensive busing, was affirmed by an equally-divided Court.

See also Davis v. Board of School Commissioners of Mobile County, Alabama, 402 U.S. 33 (1971).

48. 416 F.2d 165 (1st Cir.1969).

49. 416 F.2d at 181, 182.

of the case, saying that "to apply conspiracy doctrine" in such cases is "not consistent with First Amendment principles." [50]

The case then came to my desk for determination whether the Government should seek review from the Supreme Court. It seemed clear to me that it was not in the Government's interest to file a petition for certiorari. It was quite likely that the case would be lost in the Supreme Court, and I felt that there was no benefit to the Government from another loss in the Supreme Court in a highly publicized case. I noted, though, that the majority of the court of appeals did not direct an acquittal; it had remanded the case to the district court for a new trial. The lead counsel for the defendants in the case was Arthur J. Goldberg, former Justice of the Supreme Court. I called him on the telephone, and told him that I had the case on my desk. After preliminary remarks, I said that it seemed to me that we should coordinate our actions. I would not file a petition for certiorari, if he would agree that no petition would be filed by his clients. He replied that he would agree to that, if I would agree that the Government would dismiss the case, and that there would be no new trial in the district court. I said, in response, that this was beyond my authority—the question of a new trial would be up to the Criminal Division in the Department of Justice. We then discussed the possibilities, but I was non-committal. The conversation ended with a clear agreement between me and former Justice Goldberg that neither side would file a petition for review in the Supreme Court.

After this conversation, I made a memorandum for the files summarizing the mutual agreement. I attached a copy of the memorandum to the chit on which I directed "no certiorari"; and I sent a copy of the memorandum to Mr. Peterson, the Assistant Attorney General in charge of the Criminal Division.

Shortly thereafter, Mr. Peterson came to my office. He was most insistent that I must have the agreement put into writing, signed by Mr. Goldberg. I said that I would not ask for an agreement in writing from Justice Goldberg. He had given me his word. There was no doubt about the undertaking by both sides, and Justice Goldberg's word was good enough for me.

No petition for certiorari was filed on behalf of the defendants; and the Criminal Division decided not to seek retrial in this case. Thus, the case does not appear in the pages of the Supreme Court Reports, where, in my view, it was likely that

---

50.   416 F. 2d at 184.

there might have been ringing opinions adverse to the Government.

Shortly thereafter, *Breen v. Selective Service Local Board*,[51] and *Gutknecht v. United States*,[52] came along at the same time, with similar facts in each case. The *Breen* case involved a registrant who had surrendered his draft card to a minister for the purpose of protesting the Viet Nam war. His draft board then declared him "delinquent" for failing to have the card in his possession and, at the same time, reclassified him 1-A, "Available For Military Service." He appealed this action to the Selective Service Appeal Board, and, at the same time, filed suit in the United States District Court seeking an injunction against induction into the Armed Forces. The registrant was a twenty-year old student, and contended that he was clearly qualified for a student deferment.

In the *Gutknecht* case, the registrant refused to be inducted, and was then convicted in a prosecution for willfully failing "to perform a duty required of him," under the Selective Service Act.

Since the *Gutknecht* case was a criminal case, it came through the Criminal Division in the Department of Justice. The *Breen* case, however, being a suit for an injunction, came through the Civil Division.

I indicated that I was about to "confess error" in both cases, based on the *Oestereich* decision.[53] This brought strong protests from Will Wilson, Assistant Attorney General for the Criminal Division, and William D. Ruckelshaus, Assistant Attorney General for the Civil Division. I argued with them for a while, but they did not yield. They said that it was our duty to support our client, which was the United States and its officers and agents. I replied that we were all in the Department of Justice, and subject to the control of the Attorney General. I told them that I would not regard it as in any way inappropriate if they took the matter to the Attorney General, who had the ultimate authority in the Department.

Accordingly, a conference was held in the Attorney General's office, attended by ten or twelve people, including the two Assistant Attorneys General, members of their staffs, and me, with one or two members of my staff. Attorney General Mitchell presided over the meeting. There was a full discussion, as a result of

---

51. 396 U.S. 460 (1970).

52. 396 U.S. 295 (1970).

53. Oestereich v. Selective Service System, 393 U.S. 233 (1968). See p. 264, above.

which it was agreed that the cases would be defended in the Supreme Court. It was further agreed that the brief would be signed by Attorney General Mitchell, and that my name would not appear on the brief. The questions were discussed on the merits, and professionally, and the meeting was entirely cordial. At the close of the meeting, Attorney General Mitchell asked me to stay, and I did so, wondering just what he might have in mind.

After the others had departed, Mr. Mitchell said: "Well, Dean, what I want to know is whether this is satisfactory to you." I responded: "Mr. Attorney General, that is not the question. The question is whether this is satisfactory to you. I do not want to embarrass you in any way. If you think that this is inappropriate, I will withdraw from the Department." [54] His response came quickly and clearly. He said: "Why in the world would you do a thing like that?" I replied that I did not want to do that, and that if the arrangement agreed upon was entirely satisfactory to him, it was entirely satisfactory to me.

I then returned to my office, and assigned the two cases to Bill Ruckelshaus for oral argument. He made an excellent argument, but the Court decided in favor of the two registrants. Although there were some divisions of opinion among the Justices as to the reasoning, there were no votes supporting the government's position. The Court held that there was no statutory basis for an induction order based solely on the ground that a registrant was not in possession of his draft card.

In a number of other draft cases, I felt that my responsibility required me to state my views to the Court. Of course, I had no power of decision in these cases. Only the Court could *decide*. But I was the advocate for the United States. I did not regard this as giving me a duty to present extreme arguments for the United States. On the contrary, I agreed with the quotation inscribed outside the Attorney General's office in the Department of Justice that "The United States wins its point whenever justice is done its citizens in the courts." Accordingly, when I concluded, on the law and the facts, that a decision of a court of appeals could not be fairly supported, it seemed to me that I should advise the Court of my view, particularly in a case involving the liberty of the defendant.

Several of these draft cases came to the Solicitor General's office after criminal trials in the Eastern District of Kentucky.

---

54. I never threatened to resign, and this is as close as I ever came to offering to resign. On several occasions, I considered the question of resigning, but always found a way to handle the situation. But a "threat" to resign always seemed to me to be inappropriate.

The district judge there always gave a five-year prison sentence in any draft case, and rather boasted about it. The question first came to my attention with respect to the case of *United States v. Griffin*,[55] where the defendant, a member of Jehovah's Witnesses, refused to perform civilian services at the order of his draft board, though he said he would obey such an order from the district judge. The judge imposed a five-year sentence. A majority of the court affirmed this sentence. Circuit Judge Wade McCree (afterwards Solicitor General) wrote a strong and persuasive dissent concluding that the imposition of the maximum possible five-year sentence in such a case "runs counter to enlightened conceptions of correction and can only undermine respect for our judicial system and its professed human values."

The Criminal Division was rather insistent that I should oppose certiorari in this case. However, I fully shared Judge McCree's concern, and I thought it appropriate to express to the Supreme Court my thoughts about the decision. In response, the Court vacated the decision, and remanded the case to the Sixth Circuit Court of Appeals.[56] Another case came from the same court, presenting very similar circumstances.[57] Following the Supreme Court's action in the *Griffin* case, the Sixth Circuit reversed the decision of the district judge, and entered an order directing him to place the defendant on probation on condition that he "perform civilian work" during "a period of twenty-four months."[58]

A somewhat different case, involving certain procedural irregularities, as well as the withdrawal of an occupational deferment after the registrant surrendered his draft card, was *Wallace v. United States*.[59] On remand, the Ninth Circuit reversed the decision[60] holding that this was required by "a proper concern for 'the integrity of the Selective Service System.'"[61]

Gathering these cases together may leave the impression that I spent much of my time in seeking to undermine the Selective

---

55. 434 F.2d 740 (6th Cir. 1970).

56. Griffin v. United States, 402 U.S. 970 (1971).

57. United States v. Daniels, 429 F.2d 1273 (6th Cir. 1970).

58. United States v. Daniels, 446 F.2d 967 (6th Cir. 1971).

59. 403 U.S. 902 (1971), *vacating* 435 F.2d 12 (9th Cir. 1970).

60. United States v. Wallace, 472 F.2d 1201 (9th Cir. 1973).

61. 472 F.2d at 1202. The internal quotation comes originally from Sicurella v. United States, 348 U.S. 385, 392 (1955).

Service System.[62]   However, the cases to which I have referred
are only a few out of many which came to the Solicitor General's
office in those years.   The whole Selective Service area troubled
me greatly.   I felt, though, that the basic political decision had
been made by the President, and by the Congress, particularly
when it passed the Tonkin Gulf Resolution, and when it made
appropriations for the support of military forces in Viet Nam.[63]
Within that basic policy decision, in the relatively few matters
where I had a professional responsibility, I felt it was my duty to
aid the Court to see that the Selective Service System was administered fairly and in accordance with the law.[64]

---

62.   My feeling of responsibility was by no means limited to Selective
Service cases.   For example, I took similar actions in at least two cases
where defendants were imprisoned by state authorities and held for
some time pending state prosecution.   Then the state decided not to
prosecute, and released the defendants to federal authorities for prosecution for related offenses.   After federal conviction, the federal courts
gave no credit for the time served on the state charges.   See Nelson v.
United States, 434 F.2d 748 (8th Cir. 1970), *vacated,* 402 U.S. 1006 (1971),
credit for state sentence given on remand, 445 F.2d 631 (8th Cir. 1971);
Gaines v. United States, 436 F.2d 1069 (2d Cir. 1971), *vacated,* 402 U.S.
1006 (1971), credit given on remand, 449 F.2d 143 (2d Cir. 1971).

63.   The best discussion of this sort of problem that I have seen is in
Herbert Wechsler's essay on "Some Issues for the Lawyer," in R. McIver,
Integrity and Compromise: Problems of Public and Private Conscience
(New York, 1957).   He there discusses his role in preparing the brief for
the Government in the case of Korematsu v. United States, 323 U.S. 214
(1944), where the internment of Japanese during World War II (which
Wechsler had opposed) was sustained.   He wrote, "Of course, I could
have resigned.   Of course, Mr. Biddle [then the Attorney General] could
have resigned."   But he points out that there is "a separation of functions, a distribution of responsibilities, with respect to problems of that
kind, and this is particularly recurrent in the legal profession.   *   *   *
[F]or the lawyer, dilemmas and compromises must be the stock in
trade."   McIver, *supra,* at 124.

As I have written elsewhere: "The answers are rarely easy.   It is hard
for some people to recognize and accept the fact that compromise, on
some basis, may be the only solution for some ethical problems.   It is
easy for the on-looker or critic to think of ethical questions as absolutes.
It is very much harder for the person actually confronted with the issue
at the time to resolve it."   Book Review, 33 J.Legal Ed. 388, 390 (1983).
See also E. Richardson, The Creative Balance (New York, 1976).

64.   My actions in these and other similar cases led to an invitation
from Leonard Garment to have lunch at the White House Mess with
General Hershey.   Of course, I accepted the invitation.   When I arrived,
though, the General was not there.   He had sent a representative, the
Chairman of the Selective Service Appeal Board.   Mr. Garment joined

In addition to the *O'Brien* case, to which reference has been made above, I also argued before the Supreme Court the case of *Welsh v. United States.*[65] In that case, the registrant sought exemption as a conscientious objector. The statute provided for such an exemption for "persons who by reason of religious training and belief," were conscientiously opposed to war in any form. And that term was defined in the statute as "belief in a relation to a Supreme Being involving duties superior to those arising from any human relation," but not including "essentially political, sociological, or philosophical views or a merely personal moral code."

In applying for exemption, the registrant said that he could not affirm or deny belief in a "Supreme Being" and he struck the words "by religious training and" from the application form. He stated that he had deep conscientious scruples against participating in wars. The Government's position in the case seemed arguable, and, moreover, this was a recurring question, and it was important to have a clear decision from the Supreme Court.

The Court, too, found the question difficult. Four members of the Court felt that the statute was "not limited to those whose opposition to war is prompted by orthodox or parochial religious beliefs." Justice Harlan concurred on the ground that the statutory provision limiting exemptions to "religious beliefs" was unconstitutional as an "establishment of religion." Justice White wrote a dissenting opinion in which Chief Justice Burger and Justice Stewart joined, and Justice Blackmun took no part in the consideration of the case.

A short while later, the case of Cassius Clay (otherwise known as Mohammed Ali) came before the Supreme Court.[66] That, too, involved a case of conscientious objection, but it turned largely on procedural grounds. The Department of Justice had written a letter to the Selective Service Appeal Board, which the Court found was ambiguous. As a result, the ground on which the Board had denied exemption could not be known.

––––––

With one important exception, I played very little role in connection with judicial appointments. Nor did I participate in

––––––

with us, and we had a pleasant conversation. That was the last I heard of the matter. It was obvious that complaint about me had been directed to the White House, and I admired the way in which Mr. Garment handled the situation.

65. 398 U.S. 333 (1970).

66. Clay v. United States, 403 U.S. 698 (1971).

the steps which preceded the resignation of Justice Fortas. Indeed, I learned about that event from the newspapers, including the call which Attorney General Mitchell made on Chief Justice Warren.[67] I was not consulted with respect to filling the vacancy caused by the Fortas resignation.

When the nomination of Clement Haynsworth was announced, I was much pleased. I knew Judge Haynsworth as a fellow member of the American Law Institute, and had high regard for him as a person and as a judge. Though his views were not "liberal," they were not unduly "conservative" either. I felt that he was able and fair-minded. Perhaps I was prejudiced by the fact that he was a graduate of the Harvard Law School, as were his father and grandfather. (He was a member of one of the only two three-generation groups of graduates of the School, as far as I was aware.) I was not asked to participate in supporting the nomination. I knew that my colleagues Assistant Attorneys General Johnnie Walters and William Rehnquist were working on it, and I occasionally talked with them about it.

At the beginning, there was no reason to think that there would be any difficulty about the nomination. The South was surely entitled to an appointment on the Supreme Court, and Haynsworth seemed to be an excellent choice. Difficulty then arose, and I talked, at his request, rather extensively with Senator Charles McC. Mathias of Maryland. In our conversation, I tried my best to support the nomination, but I was not successful in persuading him. Some of the difficulties presented in the public discussions were specious. In others, Judge Haynsworth had perhaps been careless with respect to stock ownership and purchase. But the amounts involved were small, and the opposition seemed to me to be overblown. In considerable measure, I think, this was a reaction to the Fortas resignation. Though it was rarely, if ever, expressed, the atmosphere was that "you Republicans did this to a Democratic justice, so we will show our strength by opposing a Republican nominee."[68]

I did have some correspondence with Judge Haynsworth, and after the Senate denied confirmation, I wrote to him urging him not to resign. I felt that he should follow the path set by Judge John J. Parker, also of the Fourth Circuit, after a similar experience in 1930. He replied to me on November 26, 1969, saying "I will remain on the Court in the hope that, as Judge

---

67. See L. Kalman, Abe Fortas (New Haven: 1990) 367–369.

68. The details of the struggle over the nomination of Judge Haynsworth are given, through friendly eyes, in J. Frank, Clement Haynsworth, The Senate and the Supreme Court (Charlottesville, Va.: 1991).

Parker did, I can make greater contributions to the law and the administration of justice after rejection by the Senate then I did before." This he did accomplish, and he and his wife (universally known as "Miss Dorothy") remained friends of ours until his death in 1989. Along the way, the Senate, with the concurrence of the House, expressed its apologies by designating the United States Court House in Greenville, South Carolina as the Clement F. Haynsworth, Jr. Court House.

After the Senate denied confirmation to Judge Haynsworth, the President nominated Judge G. Harrold Carswell to fill the vacancy. Judge Carswell had been United States Attorney in Florida, then a district judge until he was appointed to the Fifth Circuit Court of Appeals. He was a thoroughly undistinguished judge, and I was shocked by the nomination. I tried to keep my thoughts to myself, though I had a brief conversation with Attorney General Mitchell about it, after the nomination had been made.

In due course, the Carswell nomination was also rejected by the Senate, so the President had to make a third nomination. This time, he chose Harry A. Blackmun of the Eighth Circuit Court of Appeals, perhaps suggested to him by Chief Justice Burger. I thought highly of Blackmun, and knew him fairly well, both through Harvard Law School connections, and otherwise. When he came to Washington for his hearings before the Senate Judiciary Committee, I wanted to show my support. I got in touch with him, and asked to be allowed to be his escort at the hearings. I made no public statement, but I wanted to show my backing for him, and felt that this was a good way to do it. Justice Blackmun has expressed appreciation to me for this action, but it was really done for my own benefit. I wanted to show that this was a nomination that I could enthusiastically support.

Without any appreciable difficulty, the Blackmun nomination was confirmed by the Senate, and he took his seat early in 1970.

Two vacancies on the Supreme Court arose in 1971 when Justices Black and Harlan both died during the course of the summer. When this happened, I went to Attorney General Mitchell, referred to the previous vacancies, and said that I thought that I might be of help with respect to the two pending vacancies. I said that I was well acquainted with judges and lawyers throughout the country. I added that I undoubtedly had a Harvard Law School bias—not really a bias, but I was likely to have a wider acquaintance among Harvard Law School graduates than among graduates of other schools. I said that I would try to guard against this, but that he should take it into account.

Somewhat to my surprise, and to my pleasure, Mr. Mitchell seemed interested, and asked me to sit down and talk. He mentioned a number of names, and I made comments on them. Lewis F. Powell, Jr., of Virginia, was not among those listed, but I raised his name, and said that he would be very high on my list. Mr. Mitchell said "He won't accept it," to which I replied "How do you know he will not accept it?" Mr. Mitchell then said "We have made some inquiries, and have been told that he will not accept." [69] My response to this was: "You will never know whether Mr. Powell will accept nomination until the President talks to him, in person, or on the telephone, and tells him that he is about to send Powell's name to the Senate, and will do so unless Powell advises him that he would not accept appointment." I knew that Powell would never put himself in the position of seeking the nomination, or even of being one of several who were under consideration. But I thought that there was a chance that he would accept if he were told by the highest authority that he had been chosen, subject only to his acceptance.

I had no further conversations with Attorney General Mitchell. I never knew what happened after the conversations I did have. I like to think that I may have played some role in the eventual nomination of Justice Powell. If I did, I regard it as one of my most important public services.

A matter which I regarded as a "fun" problem kept recurring in the Solicitor General's office. This related to demonstrations in Lafayette Park, which is the area just across Pennsylvania Avenue, to the north of the White House. [70] There is a statue of Andrew Jackson on horseback in the center of the park. In the four corners are statutes of Lafayette, Kosciusko, von Steuben, and Rochambeau, with oval fountains in between. "The remainder of the park is covered by trees, shrubbery, and grass interspersed with walks 15 feet wide. At various intervals there are benches on the walks for public use." [71] The park is frequented

---

69. These inquiries may have been made at the time of the Fortas vacancy, perhaps after the nomination of Carswell was rejected by the Senate. It would be understandable that a lawyer of Powell's distinction would not wish to have his name advanced in this situation.

70. This section, dealing with Lafayette Park, owes much to an extensive memorandum which was prepared for me by Jeffery K. Beach, Esq., while he was a summer law clerk in the Jones Day office in 1989.

71. Quaker Action Group v. Hickel, 362 F.Supp. 1161, 1171 (D.D.C. 1973).

by tourists, and by Washingtonians seeking a moment of respite from the day's activities. In recent years, it has become widely used for speeches and demonstrations, and it has been said that "the use of parks for public assembling and airing of opinions is historical in our democratic system, and one of its cardinal values." [72] Although I fully share these values, I felt that they were not exclusive. There is a well-recognized qualification to the use of First Amendment rights in terms of "time, place, and manner," [73] and I felt that some consideration should be given to the use of the park for relaxation and enjoyment, as well as for viewing the White House, as a sort of national shrine. In the 1960s, and early 1970s, demonstrations became massive, with many thousands of persons assembled in the park, and hundreds on the sidewalk in front of the White House, making it impossible for the ordinary citizen to use the parks or enjoy one of the symbols of his government.[74]

In addition, it seemed to me that there were valid considerations with respect to the safety of the President and other occupants of the White House, and also matters of aesthetics that could be taken into consideration. When the question first came before me, I found that there was no published regulation dealing specifically with the use of the park and the White House sidewalk. The Department of the Interior, through the National Park Service, was charged with the management and maintenance of the National Park System, which included "Memorial-core" parks, of which Lafayette Park is one.[75] The early regulations, then made by the War Department, banned park uses that "did seriously mar [the park's] appearance or give pleasure to one class of users at the expense of another class." [76] By 1927, the regulations had been amended so as to prohibit the use of parks for "functions of all kinds," without a permit.[77] No stan-

---

72. Quaker Action Group v. Morton, 516 F.2d 717, 724 (D.C. Cir. 1975).

73. "Expression, whether oral or written, or symbolized by conduct, is subject to reasonable time, place, and manner restrictions." Clark v. Community for Creative Non–Violence, 468 U.S. 288, 293 (1984).

74. See H. Calvin, "The Concept of the Public Forum," 1965 Sup. Ct. Rev. 1.

75. See 16 U.S.C. 1, 1a–1, 3 (1982), and 36 Code Fed. Reg. § 7.96 (1989).

76. United States Army, War Department, Rules and Regulations for U.S. Parks and Reservations (1900) 6.

77. Office of Public Buildings and Public Parks of the National Capital, Park Regulations (1927).

dards were provided for the issuance of permits. However, after supervision was transferred to the National Park Service, regulations were issued which banned "public gatherings of any kind and the making of speeches of any kind * * * " in Lafayette Park.[78] This restriction was said to be justified on the ground that "the particular purpose to which the area is devoted makes its use for public gatherings contrary to the comfort, convenience, and interest of the general public." Public gatherings and speech-making could occur in other parks within the national capital area provided a permit was obtained, but nearly complete discretion was vested in the Superintendent of Park Services, and permits were rarely allowed.

It was at this time that I came into the picture. I advised the Park Service that it would be difficult to sustain the validity of their regulations as they then stood. I suggested that they should prepare "proposed regulations" providing a reasonable limit on the size of gatherings in the park and on the sidewalks, with carefully stated requirements for the granting of permits. I further suggested that they should then hold hearings with respect to the regulations, and should include in these hearings testimony from responsible government officers, such as the Washington police, and the Secret Service, regarding the risks involved in massive demonstrations in front of the White House.[79] Regulations were issued,[80] preceded by a statement by the then Secretary of the Interior, Walter Hickel, in which he said that the governmental interests considered in the development of the regulations included the maintenance of park values for enjoyment by future generations, public safety, and the good order of the community, use of park facilities for rest and recreation purposes, and a "paramount concern [regarding parks in the White House area] to protect the safety and security of the President [and] others occupying the Executive Mansion."[81] The regulations were published in final form in late 1970.[82]

Without appreciable delay, the district court for the District of Columbia held that the 100/500 person limitation on demon-

---

78. 15 Fed. Reg. 3521 (1950).

79. These proposed regulations were made. They appear in 35 Fed. Reg. 11485–93 (1970).

80. Permits would be denied if a group seeking a permit to demonstrate would have more than 100 persons on the White House sidewalk or 500 persons in Lafayette Park. Quaker Action Group v. Hickel, 421 F.2d 1111, 1114 (D.C.Cir. 1969).

81. 35 Fed. Reg. at 11489.

82. 35 Fed. Reg. 15393 (1970).

strations on the White House sidewalk and Lafayette Park respectively, were an unconstitutional limit on freedom of speech, assembly, and petition for a redress of grievances. The district court ordered the Park Service to increase the limit on the size of public gatherings to 750/3000 persons, respectively, and this was done.[83] On appeal, the court of appeals made the rather surprising statement that Lafayette Square "had room in the neighborhood of 40,000 to 50,000," and that regulations allowing gatherings of this size could adequately take care of considerations "like physical space or protection of shrubs."[84] It ordered the Park Service to promulgate regulations under which limits on the maximum number of participants in public gatherings on the White House sidewalk or in Lafayette Park could be waived; and it held that a *per se* ban on continuous public gatherings lasting beyond twenty-four hours or beyond seven consecutive days was unconstitutional.[85]

This decision came after my period of service in the Solicitor General's office had ended. I found it rather astounding, and felt that it did not adequately take into account other elements in the situation which deserved consideration. In the ensuing years, there were a number of further changes in the regulations. A suggestion that the strength of the White House fence should be increased—which would have required the building of a wall around the White House grounds—was rejected because it would create a "garrison-type" appearance, and because it would deprive visitors of a view of the White House.[86]

Further changes in the regulations were made from time to time. One of these prohibited sleeping in national parks outside designated camping areas.[87] A case involving the validity of this regulation, as applied to Lafayette Park, went to the Supreme Court where the regulation was upheld[88] as a reasonable time, place, and manner restriction,[89] thus breathing life into the grounds of my original interest in the problem. Since that

---

83. 38 Fed. Reg. 24218 (1973).

84. Quaker Action Group v. Morton, 516 F.2d 717, 733 (D.C. Cir. 1975).

85. Id. at 732, 734.

86. 40 Fed. Reg. 58563 (1975).

87. 47 Fed. Reg. 24299 (1982), codified at 36 Code Fed. Reg. § 50.19(e)(8).

88. Clark v. Community for Creative Non–Violence, 468 U.S. 288 (1984).

89. *Id.* at 297–298.

decision, the situation has been reasonably quiet. New regulations have been made, designed to limit the size and number of stationary signs in Lafayette Park. As the Park Service noted, "The presence of these items has produced a dump-like atmosphere in this historical and finely landscaped national park." [90]

This whole problem is a fine illustration of the difficulty involved in reconciling competing considerations involved in application of constitutional provisions—here, freedom of speech on the one side, and safety, aesthetics and the rights of non-demonstrating citizens on the other. Although my part in the resolution of these problems—in so far as they have been resolved—was small, I did get established a proper procedure for the consideration and formulation of regulations, so that these problems could be recognized and examined in an orderly and thoughtful manner. I find some satisfaction in the fact that there is, for the present, one clear result, namely, that though you can demonstrate extensively, you cannot sleep in Lafayette Park.

Another "fun" case which came along at this time was *Executive Jet Aviation, Inc. v. City of Cleveland.*[91] This case arose out of an airplane accident which occurred at the Lake Front Airport in Cleveland. The plane was on a flight to Burlington, Vermont. It was cleared for takeoff by a federal Air Traffic Controller. However, as it went down the runway and took off, it ran into a flock of seagulls. Some of the birds were ingested into the plane's jet engines, and this caused an almost complete loss of power. The plane veered, struck some objects on the ground, and then settled in Lake Erie beyond the end of the runway. There were no injuries to the crew, but the plane was a total loss.

The owner of the plane brought suit in the federal court in Ohio, under that court's admiralty jurisdiction. The real issue in the case was whether the government, on the one hand, or the insurance company for the owner of the plane, on the other, should pay for the loss. If the suit had been brought in the state court in Ohio, it would have been subject to the defense of contributory negligence. However, if the claim could be treated as an admiralty case, doctrines of comparative negligence would apply, and the plaintiff could recover, at least in part, even if its pilot had been negligent. Such a recovery would reduce the amount which would have to be paid by the company which had insured the aircraft.

90.   51 Fed. Reg. 7555, 7557 (1986).
91.   409 U.S. 249 (1972).

The claimed basis for admiralty jurisdiction was that the plane settled in navigable waters of Lake Erie. There was precedent for treating this as within admiralty jurisdiction, particularly in the case of *Weinstein v. Eastern Airlines, Inc.*[92] That case arose out of a crash at the Logan Airport in Boston, where the plane ended up in the waters of Boston Harbor. The *Weinstein* case had always seemed to me to be wrongly decided. Particularly with a land-based plane, making a trip between two points in the United States, my view was that there was no real maritime aspect to the matter, and that it made no difference whether a crash on a transcontinental flight, for example, occurred on land or in the Mississippi River. In preparing my brief in the *Executive Jet Aviation* case, I advanced this argument. However, when it came to the oral argument, I went further. I took the position that a plane not equipped to land in water was never a seagoing vessel, and that no accident involving such a plane should be treated as raising any question of admiralty jurisdiction, wherever it occurred.

The Supreme Court held that there was no admiralty jurisdiction in the case, and that the district court was correct in dismissing it, saying that the fact that an aircraft goes down in navigable waters or that the negligence causing its crash occurs while the plane is flying over such waters, is insufficient to confer federal admiralty jurisdiction. The Court went on to say that, in the absence of legislation to the contrary, admiralty jurisdiction would exist only when there is a significant relationship to traditional maritime activity. Thus, the Court overruled the *Eastern Airlines* case, and held that there would not be admiralty jurisdiction in the event of an accident to a plane in a flight between points within the continental United States. Whether there would be admiralty jurisdiction in a case involving flights which perform a function much the same as "traditional maritime activity," such as a trans-Atlantic flight, remains to be decided.[93]

---

92. 316 F.2d 758 (3d Cir. 1963).

93. The opinion in the Executive Jet Aviation case was written by Justice Stewart for an unanimous Court. Later in the year, after the decision, Justice Stewart told me that he had had more fun writing the opinion than in any other case during the Term. So it was mutual.

CHAPTER X

Special Problems and Summary

A. Selected Cases

1. Public Aid to Parochial Schools

Beginning in 1971, a number of matters arose which brought a measure of tension to the Solicitor General's office.[1] The first of these involved the case of *Lemon v. Kurtzman*,[2] where the issue was the constitutional validity of a Pennsylvania statute, passed in 1968, authorizing the State Superintendent of Public Instruction to " 'purchase' specified, 'secular educational services' from nonpublic schools." Under this arrangement, the state reimbursed nonpublic schools, including parochial schools, "for their actual expenditures for teachers' salaries, textbooks, and instructional materials," in non-sectarian subjects.[3] Senator Hugh Scott from Pennsylvania, who was soon up for reelection, was much interested in the case, and he sent materials to the White House which were passed on to me.

---

1. There was only one such event during my time in the Johnson Administration. In this matter, there was, in effect, a direction from the White House not to take an appeal in a matter in which I had already decided that an appeal should be taken. This was only a few weeks after I had entered the Solicitor General's office. I feared, for a while, that my tenure was going to be the shortest on record. However, the Government's position in the case was weak, at best, and I found that a similar question would soon be arising in other cases. Trying not to be too stiff, I withdrew the authorization for appeal.

I have alluded to the episode in a book review already referred to. See 33 J. of Legal Ed. 388, 390–391 (1983).

2. 403 U.S. 602 (1971).

3. 403 U.S. at 609.

At the request of Attorney General Mitchell, I went to the White House for a meeting with John Ehrlichman, and he said that I should file an *amicus* brief supporting the validity of the Pennsylvania statute. The Government was not a party to the case, and I knew that any effort by the Solicitor General to participate in the case on that side as *amicus curiae* would be immediately seen by the Court to be politically, and not professionally, motivated.

I returned to my office and discussed the matter with my first Deputy, Daniel Friedman. I told him that I did not see how I could file the brief, and that I was thinking seriously of resigning. Friedman left my office, but in a half hour or so he returned, and said, "I will file the brief if you are willing to have me do so." This was a most generous offer, for which I was most appreciative. It was typical of Mr. Friedman's strong support and generous spirit. So the brief was filed, signed "Daniel M. Friedman, Acting Solicitor General," with a footnote reading "For the Solicitor General, who is disqualified for personal reasons." In due course, the Court decided the case against the constitutionality of the payments.[4] While the case was pending, newspaper reporters came to me and asked me what were the reasons. I smiled and responded, "Well, they're personal." The reporters were kindly and did not press me further.

The story is told by William Safire, who was on the White House staff at the time. He has written:

> Through Colson, the President ordered John Mitchell to file an *amicus* brief in the *Lemon v. Kurtzman* case being argued before the Supreme Court, permitting State aid to private schools. Solicitor General Erwin W. [sic] Griswold point-blank refused to file such a brief himself, because he believed the President's position was unconstitutional. The President told his special counsel to make sure the Justice Department filed that brief. Colson leaned hard on Mitchell to do so, which the Attorney General did not in the least appreciate. Grudgingly, he filed the government's support of the principle of State aid to private schools, and was not surprised when the Supreme Court, including two Nixon appointees, struck down the principle, 8 to 0.[5]

---

4. Lemon v. Kurtzman, 403 U.S. 602 (1971).

5. W. Safire, Before the Fall (New York: 1975) 559. This is essentially accurate except that I think "point-blank" is rather strong. I always tried to present my position in reasonable and professional terms, and sought some sort of middle ground, if one could be found.

2. The I.T.T. Case

Late in the spring of 1971, an aspect of the International Telegraph and Telephone case came to my office. This was the question of an appeal from an order of the district court in Connecticut which had refused to forbid the merger of I.T.T. with the Grinnell Corporation, the maker, among other things, of fire sprinklers, and other fire protection devices.[6] The appeal was recommended by the Antitrust Division. This was reviewed by two members of my staff who recommended that the Government should appeal. After further consideration, including a hearing given to local Washington counsel for I.T.T., I approved the recommendation to appeal.

In an antitrust case, the procedure then in effect required that we file a "Jurisdictional Statement" within a limited time. A draft of the Jurisdictional Statement was reviewed by my deputy, Daniel Friedman, and I examined and approved this draft. It was sent to the printer about April 15, 1971, and proof was returned to the printing office on the morning of April 19 for final printing.

On the afternoon of April 19, 1971, I was asked to go to the office of Deputy Attorney General Kleindienst. When I arrived, I found that the matter under consideration was the I.T.T. case, and Assistant Attorney General Richard McLaren, of the Antitrust Division, was there. It was obvious that Kleindienst did not want the Jurisdictional Statement to be filed, but the reasons for this conclusion were left to inference.[7] At the time, I assumed that Kleindienst had received some communication from a member of the White House staff,[8] and felt that he must comply with it. There was a reference to a letter which Kleindienst had received from Lawrence Walsh, counsel for I.T.T., in which there was

---

6. United States v. International Telephone and Telegraph Co., 306 F.Supp. 766 (D. Conn. 1969): See also United States v. International Telephone & Telegraph Co., 349 F.Supp. 22 (D. Conn. 1972).

7. Attorney General Mitchell was disqualified in this case because his firm had represented I.T.T. Accordingly, Mr. Kleindienst was Acting Attorney General on the case.

8. Actually, as we now know, he had, a little earlier, received such an instruction from Ehrlichman, which he (Kleindienst) declined to accept. See New York Times, Nov. 1, 1973, p. 33; R. Kleindienst, Justice (Ottawa, Ill.: 1985) 90.

For a description of the activities of counsel for I.T.T. during this period, see P. Hoffman, Lions in the Street (New York: 1973) 184–188; Kleindienst, above, at 96.

mention of discussions with other government departments, and the need for further consideration.

I was disturbed, but understood Kleindienst's predicament. It was not until more than two years later, through publication of the Nixon tapes, that the general public, and I, knew that an order had come to Kleindienst from the President himself. He started the conversation by calling Kleindienst a vulgar name, and then said "Don't you understand the English language?"— followed by instructions to withdraw the appeal.[9] President Nixon treats this rather blandly in his memoirs. He says that his "own role in the ITT anti-trust matter consisted in one angry phone call to Dick Kleindienst." [10]

---

9. New York Times, October 30, 1973, pp. 1, 33. The text of the tape of the President's telephone call to Kleindienst is printed in Newsweek, July 29, 1974, pp. 36–37. The content and flavor of the President's order can be ascertained from the following extract which appears in Newsweek, above, p. 37.

PRESIDENT: The order is to leave the God damned thing alone. Now, I've said this, Dick, a number of times, and you fellows apparently don't get the me——, the message over there. I do not want McLaren to run around prosecuting people, raising hell about conglomerates, stirring things up at this point. Now you keep him the hell out of that. Is that clear?

KLEINDIENST: Well, Mr. President—

PRESIDENT: Or either he resigns. I'd rather have him out anyway. I don't like the son-of-a-bitch.

KLEINDIENST: The, the question then is—

PRESIDENT: The question, is, I know, that the jurisdiction—I know all the legal things, Dick, you don't have to spell out the legal—

KLEINDIENST: (Unintelligible) the appeal filed.

PRESIDENT: That's right.

KLEINDIENST: That brief has to be filed tomorrow.

PRESIDENT: That's right. Don't file the brief.

KLEINDIENST: Your order is not to file a brief?

PRESIDENT: Your—my order is to drop the God damn thing. Is that clear?

KLEINDIENST: (Laughs) Yeah, I understand that.

A transcript of the tapes made in the President's office much later gives further details. See R. Kleindienst, Justice (Ottawa, Ill.: 1985) 90–91.

10. R. Nixon, RN: The Memoirs of Richard Nixon (New York: 1978) 580.

These tapes were not made available until late 1973. Of course, I knew nothing about the background of Kleindienst's determination either at the time when it was communicated to me in March, 1971, or when I testified at the Kleindienst confirmation hearings in 1972.

After Kleindienst told us his wishes, there was discussion of the possibility of keeping the matter open for a while by getting an extension of time. Kleindienst approved of this and told me to seek an extension, though, as I pointed out, it required some extension of the court's rules. I then talked with my deputy, Daniel Friedman, and he prepared a draft of an application for an extension. We were required to state the grounds for seeking an extension, and we said that this was needed in order "to resolve differences of opinion within the Executive Branch of the Government." The extension of time was granted by Mr. Justice Harlan on April 20, 1971. By this time, the printed Jurisdictional Statement had come back from the Government Printing Office and I told the Solicitor General's docket office that, in accordance with the application for extension of time, it should be held, and not filed until further instructions.

During the week of May 10th, Kleindienst told me that he was hopeful.[11] On Monday afternoon, May 17th, Mr. McLaren told me that the Deputy Attorney General had cleared the Juris-

---

11. A statement was put out by the White House and printed in the Washington Post on January 8, 1974, which contained the following passage:

The Justice Department, On April 20, 1971, requested and was granted a delay in filing the appeal, which was due that day. On the following day, April 21, 1971, Mr. John N. Mitchell, the Attorney General, advised the President that in his judgment it was inadvisable for the President to order no appeal to the Supreme Court in the Grinnell case. The Attorney General reasoned that, as a personal matter, Mr. Erwin N. Griswold, Solicitor General of the United States, had prepared his brief for appeal and would resign were the appeal not to proceed.

The Attorney General further feared legislative repercussions if the matter were dropped entirely. Based upon the Attorney General's recommendations, the President reversed his decision of April 19, 1971, and authorized the Department of Justice to proceed with the case in accordance with its own determinations. He said that he did not care about I.T.T. as such, but that he wanted the Attorney General to see that his antitrust policy was carried out.

See also R. Nixon, RN: The Memoirs of Richard Nixon (New York: 1978) 581; W. Seymour, United States Attorney (1975) 63–67.

dictional Statement in the I.T.T. case for filing, and the statement was promptly filed.[12]

Over the summer, I heard that negotiations were proceeding for a settlement of the entire I.T.T. antitrust situation. This involved not only the *Grinnell* case, which was then before the Supreme Court, and was thus my responsibility, but also two other cases, one involving a merger with the Hartford Fire Insurance Company, which was pending in the district court in Connecticut, and the other involving the Canteen Corporation, which was pending in a district court in Illinois.

The settlement negotiations were handled for the Department of Justice by Mr. McLaren. They led to an agreement in the late summer of 1971. Under the settlement, the Government received a consent decree requiring complete divestment by I.T.T. of the Fire Protection Division of Grinnell. This amounted to one hundred percent of what the Government sought in the *Grinnell* case, and, as far as that case (which was my sole responsibility) was concerned, I saw no reason for not going through with the settlement. The total of divested assets exceeded one billion dollars, "the most extensive divestiture proceeding in the history of the Department of Justice."[13] Even President Nixon made mileage out of the I.T.T. case. In his Presidential Papers for 1972, he is recorded as saying: "In this Administration we moved on I.T.T. * * * effectively. We required the greatest divestiture in the history of the antitrust law."[14] Accordingly, I filed a notice of settlement with the Supreme Court, and the appeal taken in the *Grinnell* case was dismissed.[15]

I was not a party to any conversations between the President and Attorney General Mitchell, and was never told about them, except through the publication of this statement by the White House.

12. All Government briefs have the date indicated at the end, by month and year. When the I.T.T. Jurisdictional Statement was printed and returned to the Solicitor General's office, it bore the date "April, 1971". Since nearly a month had passed before we were authorized to file it, I obtained some stickers from the Government Printing Office, reading "May, 1971" and one of these was placed over the April date in each copy of the Jurisdictional Statement. This was done not only to indicate the correct filing date, but in order to show that what we filed in May was precisely what we had prepared in April, without any changes of any sort, other than this date.

13. R. Kleindienst, Justice (Ottawa, Ill.: 1985) 97.

14. See S. Ambrose, Nixon (New York: 1989) 505.

15. United States v. International Telephone & Telegraph Co., 404 U.S. 801 (1971). The full text of the Consent Decree appears in the

Later, in a suit brought by Ralph Nader, the district court in Connecticut refused to reopen the consent decree, and this was affirmed by the Supreme Court.[16] Although there was some controversy about the wisdom of the settlement, those who examined it carefully, including Archibald Cox,[17] thought that it was a good settlement, and that the Government obtained all the relief which it had any prospect of receiving through further court proceedings.

3. The "Pentagon Papers"

Undoubtedly the most spectacular case in which I appeared was the one involving the "Pentagon Papers."[18] This was the last case heard by Justices Black and Harlan and their opinions in the case were the last opinions they wrote. Both resigned during the ensuing summer, prior to the commencement of the 1971 Term, and died before the end of the year.

When I first heard about the Pentagon Papers, on Sunday, June 13, 1971, I was in Florida with my wife, where I had gone to speak at a meeting of the Florida Bar Association. The first installment of the Pentagon Papers was printed by the New York Times on that day. When I saw this, I said to my wife that this case would almost surely go to the Supreme Court. But I shrugged my shoulders, because I thought that it could not possibly get there for some time. It could not get to my office until the fall, I felt, so I need not be concerned about it now.[19]

We returned to Washington that afternoon, and I found a message that I should report to the Attorney General's office at once. When I arrived there, a number of Department lawyers were assembled, including the Attorney General, and Robert Mardian, the Assistant Attorney General for the National Security

---

opinion of the District Court for Connecticut in United States v. International Telephone & Telegraph Co., 349 F.Supp. 22 (D. Conn. 1972). The provisions of the consent decree providing for divestment of the Fire Protection Division of Grinnell are stated in 349 F.Supp. at 31, n.12, and 35, nn. 16 and 19.

16. Nader v. International Telephone & Telegraph Co., 410 U.S. 919 (1973).

17. See New York Times, October 31, 1973, p. 27. Cox so testified before the Senate in 1973, after his dismissal. See R. Kleindienst, Justice (Ottawa, Ill.: 1985) 189.

18. New York Times Co. v. United States, 403 U.S. 713 (1971).

19. In the following account of the Pentagon Papers case, I have drawn freely on a speech I gave at a meeting of law teachers. See E. Griswold, "Teaching Alone Is Not Enough," 25 J.Legal Ed. 251 (1973).

Division. I did not realize how far matters had proceeded, and I asked whether it was desirable to take any action with respect to the publication. If there was "any dirt" in the papers, it had all occurred in previous administrations, since the forty-seven volumes of the papers closed with the end of the Johnson Administration. I raised the question why the Nixon Administration should be concerned about this.[20] In addition, I wondered, in a preliminary way, whether the Government had "any ground to stand on." The general thrust of the First Amendment was against the Government's position, and there was no statute which undertook to give the Government authority to prevent publication of classified material even in national security cases.[21] I pointed out that the system of security classification was based on an Executive Order, and that no penalty had ever been provided by Congress for failure to comply with a classification under that order. Moreover, as far as I could see, the restraints established by the Order applied only to government employees, and thus were not applicable to the newspapers.

Actually, the whole imbroglio of the Pentagon Papers case was largely due to a broad misunderstanding, which could have been avoided if the courts had been willing to take the time to ascertain what was actually before them. This was not an unreasonable thing to do in view of the fact that the *Times* had held the papers for nearly three months before bringing them to publication. The Government had the Pentagon Papers, which contained some material which was important to the security of the United States. The Government had no reason to think that what the newspapers had was in any way different from "The Pentagon Papers," which the Government had compiled.

Over the years, it has slowly become apparent that, with relatively small exceptions, the newspapers did not have any of the material with which the Government was primarily con-

---

20. In L. Colodny and R. Gettlin, Silent Coup (New York: 1991) 112–113, it is plausibly suggested that Henry Kissinger, who "had been a consultant to the Kennedy and Johnson administrations" feared "that his own role in shaping Vietnam policy would be revealed," and that he "convinced Nixon that the publication was a grave threat to national security."

21. The Trading with the Enemy Act of 1917 did make it a crime for any person to give information to "the enemy," for the purpose of "injuring the United States." But it was hard to see how the New York Times or the Washington Post could be called "the enemy," and it could at least be claimed that the material was disclosed for the purpose of aiding the United States.

cerned.[22] If this had been known at the time, there might well have been no Pentagon Papers case. The case actually before the Court did not in fact present the security problems which the Government, with reason, feared it did.[23] But the only way the Government lawyers could find this out was through the allowance of a reasonable period of time to examine what the newspapers actually had. With the benefit of hindsight, it now seems clear that it would have been wise for the Court to do what the Second Circuit Court of Appeals did, namely, to allow time to determine what risks the case actually involved.[24]

The *New York Times* case was filed in the Federal District Court in New York on Tuesday, June 15th. I had no role in the trial since the Supreme Court was not yet involved. The responsible officers in New York were Assistant Attorney General Mardian, and the United States Attorney for the Southern District of New York, Whitney North Seymour, Jr. The district court refused to grant an injunction solely for the purpose of providing time in which to determine whether there was anything in the papers which, if published, would imperil national security.[25] That case went on appeal to the Second Circuit, where the court, on Monday, June 21, 1971, by a 5–3 vote, directed the issuance of a stay, and remanded the case to the District Court to ascertain what was in the papers held by the Times.

While these proceedings were being held in New York, copies of the materials were given to the Washington Post. I was told that "it had been determined" that we should do everything we could to prevent publication of the papers. I assumed that this meant the White House, and very likely the President, but no definite information was given about this. At that time, I knew

---

22. See p. 310, n. 37, below.

23. As Judge MacKinnon said in his dissenting opinion in the court of appeals: "It is unfortunate that this case comes to us on a blind record in which the actual documents in the possession of the newspapers are not before us." United States v. Washington Post Co., 446 F.2d 1327, 1329 (D.C. Cir. 1971).

24. This position was clearly stated by Chief Justice Burger and by Justices Harlan and Blackmun in their dissenting opinions in the Supreme Court. New York Times Co. v. United States, 403 U.S. at 748–763. Justice Harlan wrote that: "With all respect, I consider that the Court has been almost irresponsibly feverish in dealing with these cases." Id. at 753. As his last opinion, it is a monument to his wisdom.

25. The case in New York was presided over by Judge Murray Gurfein, sitting in his first case after appointment to the District Court bench.

nothing about the President's intense concern about "leaks."[26] Nor did I know that Henry Kissinger was then about to go to China on a very secret mission, and that there might be legitimate fears that the Chinese would be very cautious in their dealings with the United States if they felt that the United States could not "keep secrets."[27]

The Washington Post case was tried before Judge Gesell in the District Court in the District of Columbia on Monday and Tuesday, June 21 and 22. At the conclusion of the trial the court declined to enter an injunction against the publication of the papers by the Washington Post. An appeal to the United States Court of Appeals for the District of Columbia Circuit was immediately authorized, and the court set it down for hearing on Wednesday, June 23. I had assumed that Robert Mardian, the Assistant Attorney General for the National Security Division of the Department would argue the case in the Court of Appeals.

While the case was being tried, I felt more and more that it was a very unfortunate situation and that perhaps some way could be found to bring about an adjustment. I had met Mrs.

---

26. There is evidence that Nixon's concern was stimulated by strong reactions from Secretary Kissinger, who, according to Wicker, "was beside himself with rage and fear." This was not a "summer cloudburst. * * * Kissinger's anger was more like a hurricane." T. Wicker, One of Us (New York: 1991) 641. See also C. Colson, Born Again (Old Tappen, N.J.: 1976) 58–60. Daniel Ellsberg, who delivered the Pentagon Papers to the newspapers, had been an aide in Kissinger's Defense Policy Seminar at Harvard in the 1950s, as Haldeman observes, and had also been an aide to Kissinger in the White House. H. Haldeman, The Ends of Power (New York: 1978) 110. This especially annoyed Kissinger, who, according to Haldeman, "made charges against Ellsberg * * * that, in my [Haldeman's] opinion go beyond belief." (See also S. Hersh, The Price of Power (New York, 1983) 385.) Haldeman adds that "Nixon was as angry as his foreign affairs chief." Haldeman, above, at 110–111. The final result came when Kissinger said to the President that the publication of the country's diplomatic secrets "could destroy our ability to conduct foreign policy. * * * It shows you're a weakling, Mr. President." Haldeman, above, at 110. Further details are given in S. Hersh, The Price of Power (New York: 1983) 383–393; H. Klein, Making It Perfectly Clear (New York: 1980) 344–350.

Kissinger says, in his White House Years (Boston: 1979) 730: "I not only supported Nixon in his opposition to this wholesale theft and unauthorized disclosure: I encouraged him."

27. See Kissinger, White House Years (Boston: 1979) 730: "Our nightmare at that moment was that Peking might conclude our government was too unsteady, too harassed and too insecure to be a useful partner."

Graham, publisher of the Post, since she was the widow of Philip Graham, a member of the Harvard Law School Class of 1939, who had been a student of mine. After the case had gone to the Court of Appeals, on Wednesday, June 23, 1971, I called her on the telephone, and said that I thought that the case was regrettable and that it seemed to me that it ought to be possible to come to some sort of an agreement, or, at least, to minimize the controversy. She was very pleasant, but intimated that she was not informed as to details.

Mrs. Graham referred me to Benjamin Bradlee, the Executive Editor of the Post. Shortly thereafter, I talked with Mr. Bradlee, by telephone. I told him that there were certain items which caused the Government great concern, and I added that I did not think that the Post really wanted to publish those items, or needed to do so. He asked me what items I had in mind, and I referred him to several. In this conversation I relied on information given me by Mr. Mardian, and members of his staff, and by Whitney North Seymour, Jr., the United States Attorney who was in charge of the New York Times case before the Second Circuit in New York.

After a while, Mr. Bradlee called me back and said: "We don't have any of those items." This took me by surprise, and the only explanation I could think of was that only a portion of the papers had been delivered to the Post, and the papers they received did not include these items. I then said: "Well, please tell me what you do have, and I will tell you which ones give us concern." He responded: "Oh, no. We could not do that. That would disclose our source." This put me in a rather frustrating spot, since I already knew the source. I had seen J. Edgar Hoover at a meeting, and he told me that they knew that the source was Daniel Ellsberg. But he asked me not to disclose this to anyone, since they thought there were others who participated, and they did not want any disclosure while they were looking for these others. So, I could not tell Mr. Bradlee that I knew the source.

From this and other matters, a fact has slowly become apparent to me which has not been made clear in previous discussions of the Pentagon Papers case.[28] The papers which Ellsberg had, and which he gave to the New York Times, the Washington Post, the Boston Globe, and other newspapers, were

---

28. See S. Ungar, The Papers and the Papers (New York, 1983), for a generally accurate account of the case. See also D. Rudenstine, "The Pentagon Papers Case: Recovering Its Meaning Twenty Years Later," 12 Cardozo L.Rev. 1869 (1991); W. Seymour, United States Attorney (1975) 190–210.

not the same as the forty-seven volumes of Pentagon Papers of which a few sets were made, one of which was kept in the safe of the Secretary of Defense. This resulted from two factors. In the *first* place, Ellsberg, while he was an employee in the process of compiling and editing the Pentagon Papers, did not have access to all of the papers in their exact final form. And, *second*, we now know that Ellsberg deliberately withheld important items in the material he did have.[29]

Thus there was no clear way to raise precise issues. The newspapers had a set of copies which bore an appreciable resemblance to the Pentagon Papers, but were different in many ways. On the other hand, the Government had the Pentagon Papers, but had no way of knowing what the newspapers had. In this situation, any effort to come to an agreement was bound to fail, without disclosure by the newspapers which they did not feel was feasible.

On the Wednesday morning after Judge Gesell's decision, the Attorney General called me to his office, and said that he would like to have me argue the case in the Court of Appeals. I replied "Mr. Attorney General, I have never seen even the outside of the Pentagon Papers. I do not know what is in them, and I have given no real study to the applicable law." His response was: "Well, Dean, if you don't want to argue the case, I suppose I can get someone else." I then stood up straight and said: "Mr. Attorney General, if you want me to argue the case, I will do it."

On returning to my office, I called my wife on the telephone. I asked her to bring me a pair of black shoes, to replace the brown ones that I was wearing. I also asked her to bring a "quiet" tie which I could wear instead of the somewhat gaudy one I had on. And, finally, I asked her to put a little lunch in a paper bag, and bring these things to the Department of Justice. In due course, they arrived, while I worked feverishly on learning what I could about the facts and the law of the case, with the great assistance of my First Deputy, Daniel M. Friedman.

The case was heard by the full bench of the Court of Appeals on Wednesday afternoon. About a half hour before the argument, I left the department to walk to the Court of Appeals. I felt that the fresh air and the mild exercise of the walk might clear my thinking somewhat. When I got to the Court of Appeals, it was almost impossible to enter, since the corridors and the courtroom were thronged with reporters, with many photographers outside the door.

---

29. See p. 310, n. 37, below.

It is quite unusual for a Solicitor General to appear in one of the lower courts. When I finally got into the courtroom, one of the deputy clerks asked me: "Who is going to move your admission?" I replied that I had been admitted to practice before the Court of Appeals in about 1932. His response was that their records did not go back that far, and that he would act on my statement that I had been admitted.

I argued the case, in a rather feckless way, since I did not know much about it, and still had never seen even the outside of the Pentagon Papers. We now know (though I knew nothing about it at the time) that the Washington Post (presumably through their counsel) communicated with the court of appeals during its closed session following the argument. They agreed "not to publish 'very limited quotations from two documents which the *Post* did not deem to be of reportorial significance.' " [30]

One of the difficulties in reconstructing the events in connection with the Pentagon Papers is the fact that things happened so fast, and under such pressure, that it is very hard to know who in the government knew what, and when he knew it. While the *New York Times* case was in the District Court of New York, and in the Court of Appeals for the Second Circuit, the responsible officer of the Government was the United States Attorney, Whitney North Seymour, Jr. Similarly, Assistant Attorney General Robert Mardian was the responsible officer in the *Washington Post* case while it was in the lower courts, even though I was assigned to argue it in the Court of Appeals. In the ordinary case, which is usually pending in the Department of Justice for months, there is adequate opportunity for exchange of information. This opportunity was not available in the Pentagon Papers case simply because of the pell mell way in which the courts proceeded.

For example, there is a rumor, said to originate from a Supreme Court Law Clerk, that, after the case went to the Supreme Court, "an army general" delivered some papers to Chief Justice Burger, or (in another version) to the Clerk's office. I can only say that I never heard anything about such an event, and I feel fairly sure that, if I had known about it, I would have been concerned about it, and would not forget about it. It may

---

30. See S. Ungar, *supra*, at p. 203. See also McKinnon, J., dissenting from the denial of a preliminary injunction in United States v. Washington Post Co., 446 F.2d 1327, 1329 (U.S. App. D.C. 1971): "However, by agreement of the parties some of the documents will be protected. * * * I would not reward the theft of these documents by a complete declassification." I knew of no such agreement.

be that Assistant Attorney General Mardian knew about this (if it occurred) and simply did not have an opportunity to pass the word to me.

On Thursday, June 24th, we received word from the Clerk of the Court of Appeals that the court had affirmed Judge Gesell's decision, thus denying an injunction in the *Washington Post* case. My deputy, Daniel Friedman, and I discussed the situation. We felt that it was not decent for the New York Times, which had first published the papers, to be subject to an injunction, while the Washington Post was free to publish. Accordingly, we prepared an application to the Supreme Court for an order staying publication by the Washington Post until the *Post* case and the *Times* case could be heard together. While this application was being typed, I said to Friedman, "Let's add the following to the application." So, these two lines were put in: "If the Court wishes to treat this application as a petition for certiorari, we have no objection." This must be the shortest petition for certiorari in the history of the United States. It was filed in the early evening of Thursday, June 24th. The New York Times had filed a petition for certiorari about noon of the same day.

The next day, Friday, June 25th, at noon, Chief Justice Burger called me on the telephone. He said: "The Court has granted both petitions for certiorari. The case will be heard at 11:00 a.m. tomorrow, and briefs will be exchanged by both sides in the courtroom."

At this point, I arranged to have a set of the Pentagon Papers brought into my office. They were accompanied by an Army Staff Sergeant, with many decorations, who sat beside them. Shortly thereafter, my secretary came into the office. The sergeant pointed to her and said: "Who's she?" I replied, "She is my secretary." His response was "Is she cleared?" I replied that I did not know, but that she was my secretary, and I had to have her assistance. The Sergeant then said: "If she is not cleared, she cannot come in here."

I then confronted the United States Army, and said: "In this office, I am in charge. I am responsible for this case, and I cannot do my work without the aid of my secretary. Will you please leave, at once, and report to your superior whatever you feel that you should report." To my surprise, and relief, he did leave, and I had no further problem in that area.

In the meantime, I had made arrangements through Assistant Attorney General Mardian for three persons to come to my office that afternoon, each for a half-hour meeting. One was Vice Admiral Noel Naylor, director of the National Security

Agency. Another was William B. Macomber, Jr., Deputy Under Secretary of State for Administration (a graduate of the Harvard Law School), and the third was Lieutenant General Melvin Zais, director of operations for the Joint Chiefs of Staff. I asked each of these gentlemen to tell me what was really dangerous in the Pentagon Papers, and would cause appreciable harm to the interests or the security of the United States. I had a yellow pad in my hand, and I noted down the page references for their responses. I had in the back of my mind the thought that the publication of the plain text of any coded telegram would be serious, since it would provide information for breaking the code. Admiral Naylor laughed at this, and said: "That has not been true since about 1935." At that point, I felt that about half of my case, as I had analyzed it so far, went out the window. Admiral Naylor went on to say that there was a separate code for each message, that printing a plain text of a telegram would help to break the code for that message, and that, of course, was of no importance, since the plain text of the message was already available.

From these discussions, I picked out forty-one specific items and then undertook to study each of them as carefully as I could in the limited time available.

By this time, Daniel Friedman and I had agreed that he would write the "open brief" for the Government, while I would write the "secret brief." Mr. Friedman, as would be expected, produced a fine brief, showing a number of instances where prior restraint on publication had been granted. These included such matters as forbidding the use of wording like "Whites Only" in advertising for houses or employment, similar illustrations in labor law (where an employer cannot threaten to fire his employees if they join a labor union), and the whole area of copyright law. Knowing that the "open brief" would be well done, I was able to devote all of my time and thought to the "secret brief."

After examining the items which had been brought to my attention by my three visitors, I felt that there were only a few that had any chance of finding favor before the Supreme Court. I finally reduced these to eleven items, which I summarized in the closed brief. One of these items, on which I particularly relied, consisted of four volumes of the Papers, known as the "Negotiating Track." I devoted a full page to these materials in my closed or secret brief, with the conclusion that "The publication of this material is likely to close up channels of communication which might otherwise have some opportunity of facilitating the closing of the Vietnam War." In my oral argument, I laid particular emphasis on this material.

After finishing the dictation of the closed brief, at about three o'clock in the morning, I decided to go home. I felt that I should get at least some sleep before the argument was scheduled the following morning. My secretary stayed and completed the typing of the brief. Just before leaving, I recalled that the forty-seven volumes of the Pentagon Papers were in my office, and that the office was not secure. It quickly occurred to me, though, that the F.B.I. headquarters was just down the corridor from my office, and that I could get somebody from there to take charge of the papers. I reached for the Department of Justice telephone book, and was surprised to find that the F.B.I. telephone numbers were not included in the book. Eventually, a number was found, and very quickly an F.B.I. agent came and took charge of the papers. I arranged with him that the papers would be delivered to the Supreme Court at 10:30 the next morning, where I had them put on the counsel's table so that they might be available in case any question arose with respect to some particular item.

The next morning, I returned to the office at about eight o'clock. It was Saturday morning, and there is no general help available in the Department of Justice on Saturday. My secretary and I ran off copies of the thirteen legal sized pages of the brief on the new Xerox machine. In those days, they had no facility for collating, so we arranged chairs around the perimeter of my office. We then put the pile of copies, one page to a chair, and walked around the room assembling the copies, hoping that we got them in the proper order. We made about twenty copies altogether, and I assembled thirteen copies to take to the Court, ten to be filed with the Clerk's office, one for me, one for Alex Bickel, counsel for the New York Times, and one for William Glendon, counsel for the Washington Post. We had found a rubber stamp reading "Top Secret," and put its mark on the outside cover of each copy.

By this time, it was about nine-thirty on Saturday morning. Over the night, I had ruminated about the eleven items, and had finally come to the conclusion that our only chance of success was to waive objection to the printing of the great bulk of the material, but to seek an injunction as to the eleven items on which I had specifically relied. I realized that this was a great change in the position of the Government, and I came to the conclusion that I should inform Attorney General Mitchell. I knew that he had gone to Alabama to make a speech on Friday evening, and that he would not be returning to Washington until the wee hours of Saturday morning.

I thought that I ought to give him a decent time for rest. At about nine-thirty, however, I called him and said: "Mr. Attorney General, we have this Pentagon Papers case this morning." He said, "Yes, I know. It is a very important case. I wish you good luck." I then said: "There is something on which I think I should have your approval. I am taking the position that we waive objection to the publication of everything in the papers except eleven items. I have reviewed the papers as carefully as I can, and it is my view that the only ground we have to stand on where there is a chance of success is with respect to these eleven items." I can still hear his response: "Well, Dean, I do not see how I can approve that." At this point, I nearly collapsed. Here I was with the case scheduled for argument in a little more than an hour, and the brief I had prepared did not meet the approval of my superior. After a few seconds, though, Mr. Mitchell said: "I have never read the papers, and do not know what is in them. But you are in charge of the case, and if it is your view that that is the proper way to handle it, I am behind you." Of course, he was right. I should not have asked him to approve my action, since I knew that he was not familiar with the content of the papers. He was very generous in giving me his backing and support, and I appreciated the position he took.

I then proceeded to the Supreme Court with the thirteen copies of both briefs, the open brief and the secret brief, in my briefcase. When I got there, I found the Pentagon Papers already installed on counsel's table, and a different sergeant, with decorations, sitting beside them. I first put out ten copies of the brief, and the sergeant said: "What are you going to do with those?" I said: "I am going to file them with the Clerk of the Court, one for each Justice, and one for the Clerk's file." The response was: "Is the Clerk cleared?" I said that I did not know whether the Clerk was cleared or not, but that I did know my responsibility as counsel for the Government in the case, and that the only chance we had to get our views before the Court was to file the briefs with the Clerk. I then took the briefs to the Clerk's office where they were filed, in accordance with the rules of the Court. When I returned to the courtroom, I picked out two more copies. The sergeant said: "What are you going to do with them?" I said: "I am going to give one to Mr. Bickel, counsel for the New York Times, and one to Mr. Glendon, counsel for the Post." The response to this was: "That's treason, that is giving them to the enemy." However, I was not intimidated, and I handed the briefs to the two counsel, knowing that our only chance to communicate to the two newspapers the matters with respect to which we had real concern was through the material in these briefs.

At precisely eleven o'clock, the Court came in, and the Justices took their seats. I had filed a motion that a portion of the argument be held *in camera*, without the public present. The purpose of this was to give me the opportunity to discuss the details of at least some of the eleven items on which the brief relied. I was not surprised when this motion was denied, though it did restrict my presentation. I then addressed the Court.[31]

The argument was recorded, as all Supreme Court arguments are. Eventually, these recordings go to the National Archives, where they are available for scholarly and historical proposes. A friend of mine, Professor Paul R. Baier of the Law School of Louisiana State University, obtained a copy of this recording, and made it available to me. Every four or five years or so, I get this tape out and play it. It brings back interesting memories. Considering the difficulty of the case I had, and the inadequate knowledge I had of the actual facts, I feel that I did all right.[32]

Justices Black, Brennan and Douglas were especially hostile. Justice Black, interrupting Justice Marshall, said "Does not the First Amendment say 'no law' and do you not think that 'no law' means no law?" Justice Black included my response in his opinion, as showing how wrong I was. I must say, though, that it still seems to me that there was something to my answer. I said:

> Now, Mr. Justice [Black], your construction of * * * [the First Amendment] is well known, and I certainly respect it. You say that no law means no law, and that should be obvious. I can only say, Mr. Justice, that to me it is equally obvious "no law" does not mean "no law," and I would seek to persuade the Court that that is true. * * * [T]here are

31. S. Ungar, in The Papers and the Papers (New York: 1988), at p. 228, wrote: "Griswold somehow looked as if he belonged in the Supreme Court's red-draped courtroom. [He] seemed almost part of the furnishings that make up a great institution. Bickel sounded ceremonious, Griswold comfortably sonorous. The Solicitor General's voice rose and fell with natural, precise punctuation."

32. The full text of the oral arguments in the Pentagon Papers case is printed in the New York Times for Sunday, June 27, 1971, p.24, and in 71 Landmark Briefs and Arguments of the Supreme Court of the United States: Constitutional Law 213–261. Both of these contain a significant error. In response to a question from Justice Marshall as to whether "The Federal courts" should "be a censorship board," I said: "I do not know what the alternative is." The transcripts of the oral argument have "Justice Marshall" saying: "The First Amendment might be." Actually, it was Justice Black who interrupted, and this was the prelude to the material quoted in the following paragraph of the text, above.

other parts of the Constitution that grant powers and responsibilities to the Executive, and * * * the First Amendment
was not intended to make it impossible for the Executive to
function or to protect the security of the United States.[33]

My only criticism of myself about this is that I should have
said: "Yes, Mr. Justice, and the Constitution says 'Congress shall
make no law * * *' And *Congress* has made no law in this
case."

As is well known, the Supreme Court held that the publication by the two newspapers could not be enjoined. Three members of the Court (Black, Douglas, and Brennan, JJ.) held that
there could be no prior restraint in any case. Three Justices of
the Court (Marshall, Stewart, and White, JJ.) held that there
could be a prior restraint in some cases, but that there was not
sufficient ground for such an order in this case. And three
members of the Court (Burger, C.J., and Harlan and Blackmun,
JJ.) held that an injunction should be allowed in order to enable
the Court to have time to find out whether items presenting a
serious threat to security were involved.[34]

The Monday following the argument, I went to my office,
and found Mr. Glendon, counsel for the Washington Post, standing outside my door. I said: "Mr. Glendon, what brings you
here?" He said: "I have never seen a copy of your secret brief."
I replied: "Why, Mr. Glendon, I personally handed you a copy of
that brief in the courtroom last Saturday morning." His response was: "Yes, and as soon as the argument was over, that
security guard came up and took the brief away from me."

I then gave a copy of the secret brief to Mr. Glendon. He
said that it did not mean much to him unless he could see the
Pentagon Papers, and find out just which items we were concerned about. I then called J. Fred Buzhardt, Jr., General Counsel of the Defense Department. He was very courteous, and said
that he would be glad to make the Pentagon Papers available to
Mr. Glendon if he would come to the Pentagon. He added,
though, that since the material was classified, Mr. Glendon could
not make copies of any of the items, and could not take notes
about them. I communicated this to Mr. Glendon, and he then
went to the Defense Department. How much he was able to
remember about what he saw, I do not know.

---

33. New York Times Co. v. United States, 403 U.S. 713, 717–718
(1971).

34. The case is discussed in B. Schwartz, The Ascent of Pragmatism
(Reading, Mass.: 1990) 158–162. See also D. Rudenstine, in the article
cited at p. 300, n. 28, above.

Although the Court's decision went against us, I sometimes say, for my own amusement, that we won the Pentagon Papers case. I think that the Court reached a useful decision. As things have worked out, we now know that there was probably not adequate ground for an injunction in that case, in part because the newspapers did not have all of the Papers. A majority of the Court did not say that there can *never* be a prior restraint on publication. This means that the media have a great deal of freedom, as they should have. On the other hand, it means that there can be items where publication can be enjoined, like, to use an old example, the sailing dates of troop ships.[35] Thus, the net result is that the media have great freedom. On the other hand, as a result of this decision, they also have great responsibility, and are clearly reminded that they must act responsibly. The admonition that there are some times when publication can be subject to restraint is a useful reminder to the press that it has responsibility in the area as well as privileges.[36]

---

35. This is the sort of item to which Chief Justice Hughes referred in his opinion in Near v. Minnesota, 283 U.S. 697, 716 (1931). One could add another example now, namely, the movement of troops around Kuwait during the final stages of Operation Desert Storm.

36. An interesting development came nearly two years after the decision in the Pentagon Papers case. About the middle of May, 1973, the newspapers printed an affidavit by Egil Krogh, which was filed in the Ellsberg trial in Los Angeles. In this affidavit, Krogh said that copies of the Pentagon Papers had been delivered to "the Soviet Embassy" before the case was argued in the Supreme Court. (It is not clear whether this delivery was to the Soviet Embassy in Washington or to the Soviet Mission to the United Nations in New York.) See Washington Post, June 3, 1973; Los Angeles Times, June 3, 1973, p. IA–8. See also C. Colson, Born Again (Tappen, New Jersey: 1976) 58. (Inquiry made by another Department of Justice lawyer showed that some five thousand pages had been delivered to the Embassy on June 17, 1971, together with a letter signed "Friend." This information came to the F.B.I. on June 25, 1971, and was not received in the Department of Justice (outside the F.B.I.) until June 26, 1971.)

The Pentagon Papers case was argued on June 26, at 11:00 a.m. I had no knowledge of anything about this until the Krogh affidavit was printed in the newspapers, and no knowledge of the details outlined above until May 23, 1973. I was interviewed by members of the press on May 21, 1973, who felt it was improper for the Government to present the case to the Supreme Court if it knew at that time that the papers were already in the hands of the Soviets. After investigation, I advised them of the facts outlined above, and they appeared to be satisfied. I have never heard any other report of the episode, and have no knowledge beyond what I have set forth above.

As a matter of fact, neither the New York Times nor the Washington Post published any of the eleven items in the ensuing few weeks, very likely because they did not have them.[37] By that time, Senator Gravel of Alaska had introduced the Ellsberg version of the papers into a hearing of the Senate Post Office and Post Roads Committee, and they were published by the Unitarians in Boston. To the extent of that publication, there was no basis for objection to the further use of any of this published material, by the newspapers or by anyone else. As far as I know, though, none of the material which was "objectionable" from my point of view was ever published by anyone, including the newspapers, until several years later.

A few days after the decision in the Pentagon Papers case, Harriet and I, for some reason which was not clear to us, were invited to lunch at the White House, with a group of some thirty people. There was a receiving line, and we went through the line to shake hands with President Nixon. When I came up to the President, I said: "Well, Mr. President, we did not do so well in the Pentagon Papers case." The result left a vivid impression on me. The President froze, and seemed to glare, saying nothing. It was, to me, a wholly unnatural sort of reaction. I said nothing

---

37. On April 2, 1991, nearly twenty years after the Pentagon Papers case came before the Supreme Court, I was invited by the Kennedy School of Government, at Harvard, to participate in a conference on the Pentagon Papers. This was attended by a number of important press people, including A.M. Rosenthal, who had edited the Pentagon Papers for the New York Times, and Eugene Patterson, who performed the same function at the Washington Post. Another participant was Daniel Ellsberg, whom I had never met before. Ellsberg was, of course, the one who delivered the Papers to the newspapers.

At this meeting, I learned for the first time, from Mr. Ellsberg, that he had not delivered to the newspapers the "four volumes" which gave the details of the "negotiating track," through which the Government of the United States had sought to find a resolution for the Viet Nam controversy. As indicated above, it was these four volumes which gave me the greatest concern, for many of the persons involved were in communist countries, might have suffered there, and their further assistance would be eliminated. (The fact that these volumes were not delivered by Ellsberg was disclosed in S. Hersh, The Price of Power (New York, 1983) 321n, but I had not seen this item.)

I also learned, again for the first time, that the papers, as delivered by Mr. Ellsberg to the newspapers, had their footnotes eliminated, thus striking out information as to names, time and place of many of the events described. Mr. Ellsberg said that the reason he did this was to minimize the risks of harm which might come from his delivery of the papers.

more, and quickly moved on. I had, of course, underestimated the importance of the case to the President, as he saw it.

In the ensuing years, I have seen a few citations in books and scholarly articles to items in the published Pentagon Papers.[38] But I have never felt that any material in the published Pentagon Papers was of any appreciable significance for scholarly or historical purposes. As I look back over the period of twenty years which have followed that intense and emotional conflict, I find myself with two conclusions which seem to me to be reasonably clear.

First, the Second Circuit, and Chief Justice Burger, and Justices Harlan and Blackmun were correct in their view that a brief interim injunction was appropriate (a) in order to give the courts an opportunity to examine the papers, and have a rational basis for determining what risk, if any, they involved, and (b) to enable the parties to explore the differences between the papers which the newspapers wanted to publish, and the final Pentagon Papers which were (and are) a part of the government's files. After all, the New York Times had held the papers for nearly three months, during which period it engaged in extensive editorial activities. This was evidence enough that they did not contain information which required instant dissemination to the public. Moreover, courts of justice should surely act rationally, and, from my point of view, they do not do so when they do not have any real information about the facts in the case which they are deciding.

Moreover, if the parties had had an opportunity to explore their separate versions of the Pentagon Papers more carefully, they might have discovered that the papers which Ellsberg made available to the newspaper in fact contained no dangerous materials, and the government's case might have been withdrawn. As has been shown above in the discussion of the I.T.T. case, there were other occasions within that period when President Nixon reacted intensely to a particular situation, and then later, calmed down and came to a different conclusion.

Second, there is, in my mind, a serious problem about the conduct of the newspapers, a problem which they have never squarely faced, and, indeed, they have hardly, if at all, recognized that it exists and is real. It is clear that Daniel Ellsberg was in a fiduciary position with respect to the papers. He had been entrusted with them in a situation where he was under a legal

---

38. For example, see T. Reeves, A Question of Character (New York: 1991) 6, 467, 468, 489, 490 and elsewhere. All of these references relate to events in the Kennedy administration.

obligation to maintain confidence. He violated that obligation. This was a clear violation of fiduciary responsibility, what we lawyers call a "breach of trust." [39] The newspapers knew that his action in giving copies of the papers to them was a breach of trust. Thus, they were clearly, in legal terms, "participating in a breach of trust," and subject to the same restraints as Ellsberg was.

I recognize, of course, that this presents the situation rather starkly, and that this formulation can be called "legalistic." Nevertheless, it would be satisfying if the press recognized that there is a serious problem here, and that, whatever the justification may be, they were acting in concert with, and to facilitate the purposes of, a person who was clearly violating his fiduciary obligation. Instead, newspaper people continue to praise the Pentagon Papers case as the greatest decision since *Marbury v. Madison.* I can only say that I continue to hope that they will recognize their serious responsibility in appropriate cases, and that they will not feel that they are privileged to print anything which comes to hand, even though they know that they are encouraging a breach of trust. In my view, the Pentagon Papers decision is not a wide open gate. On the contrary, it still allows a barrier, though in a rather narrow class of cases.

In many ways, as things turned out, the whole Pentagon Papers episode was a tempest in a teapot. But it was a real tempest for a while, with long-range repercussions. In retrospect, I know of no harm which was caused by the publication of the Pentagon Papers.[40] In another sense, though, the Pentagon

---

39. Indeed, Ellsberg recognized this in his actions in withholding important parts of the papers, and in blocking out footnotes containing information as to names, dates and places.

40. I have so expressed myself in an Op Ed article which appeared in the Washington Post for February 15, 1989, and in a short Op Ed piece in the New York Times for June 30, 1991. Some comments about the article in the Post have somewhat overstated my position. There is an appreciable difference between a retrospective evaluation of an article, as to its consequences, and a prospective evaluation when you have no means of foreseeing what the consequences may be. I have no regrets about my representation of the United States in the Pentagon Papers case, though I do not think, as things turned out, that any measurable harm actually resulted from the publication by the newspapers of those portions of the Papers which they had.

Leslie H. Gelb, who was assigned by Secretary McNamara in 1967 to be in charge of compiling and editing the papers, has written that they

Papers episode was one of great importance in American history, for it was undoubtedly the root cause of the events which led to Watergate, the cover-up, and eventually to the resignation of President Nixon.

The Pentagon Papers case was decided on June 30, 1971. It was shortly thereafter that Egil Krogh came to the Western White House at San Clemente, on his return from a drug investigation in Viet Nam. It was at this meeting that President Nixon "authorized Krogh to put together a team of investigators, keeping it secret from the FBI and the CIA * * *" [41] This was the origin of "the plumbers," authorized by the President himself—so-called because their function was to stop leaks. From this action grew the Ellsberg break-in, the cover-up, and all of the subsequent tragic developments.[42] As Wicker says, without "the Pentagon Papers, there would have been no plumbers and no break-in at Dr. Lewis Fielding's office in Los Angeles. It was to a large extent for fear of exposure of that crime and other plumbers' activities that Nixon made his fatal decision to 'stonewall' and cover up the relatively unimportant Watergate break-in itself." [43]

After 1971, the number of instances of pressures from one agency or another continued, and this is a good place to summarize some of these events. The risk of doing so is that, by gathering these together, the question of "political pressure" may be unduly emphasized. Generally speaking the continuous and considerable volume of work in the Solicitor General's office was unaffected, and was handled—as I always tried to handle it

---

were "a vast, undigested mass of fragmentary truths," and that "I did not think then or now that the publication would compromise U.S. national security. They were 'history.'" L. Gelb, "The Story Behind the Pentagon Papers," New York Times, June 16, 1991, Section E, p. 17.

41. This meeting is described in T. Wicker, One of Us (New York: 1991) 645. Wicker described Krogh as "young, eager, patriotic, fervently admiring of Richard Nixon, deeply impressed by the term 'national security,' and in no doubt whatever that the President of the United States was empowered to protect it by any means necessary." Id. at 644–645.

42. Colson says: "Richard Nixon had simply blown his top. * * * Yet it was at that moment that the Nixon Presidency passed a crossroads of sorts." C. Colson, Born Again (Old Tappen, N.J.: 1976) 60.

43. T. Wicker, above, 662–663. See also Kissinger, White House Years (Boston: 1979) 730: "I was not aware of other steps later taken, the sordidness, puerility, and ineffectuality of which eventually led to the downfall of the Nixon Administration."

during my tenure—on a professional basis, with the effective support not only of my own staff but of the other divisions of the Department of Justice as well. I never initiated any discussions with the White House staff, and I only went there on two or three occasions, by invitation. I must have seemed very distant and aloof, and I came to feel more and more that it was desirable to keep things that way.

4. The Ellsberg Prosecution

In the summer of 1972, a prosecution was commenced in the federal court in Los Angeles against Daniel Ellsberg and David Russo, arising out of the distribution of the Pentagon Papers. After the jury was empaneled, it was disclosed that one of the counsel for the defendants had been overheard on an F.B.I. wiretap. The defense then moved for a dismissal, which might have been fatal to the prosecution since jeopardy had attached when the jury was selected and sworn. Justice Douglas granted a stay of the trial pending certiorari,[44] but the Supreme Court denied certiorari.[45] I handled this matter in the Supreme Court and thus became familiar with the nature of the surveillance. I do not feel free to disclose that now, but the conclusion of the District Judge that it was not relevant to the prosecution was, I think, entirely justified.[46] Nevertheless, this episode helped to crystallize my thinking about the desirability of a prosecution in the *Ellsberg* case. On August 28, 1972, I sent a five-page memorandum to Attorney General Kleindienst giving my tentative thoughts about the *Ellsberg-Russo* case, and concluding that "there is much to be said in favor of dropping the case." I never had any response, which did not surprise me. In the light of what we now know, I can well understand why Kleindienst did not think it would be fruitful to send my memorandum on to higher authority.

Throughout all of this (and the events recounted below), I was, of course, unaware of the extreme reaction within the White House about "leaks," "security," and related matters. Though I recognized that the higher levels of government were necessarily and appropriately "political," I assumed in my naive way that they were rational, and essentially honest. The disclosures which came in the ensuing years took me by surprise, and were

---

44. Russo v. Byrne, 409 U.S. 1219 (July 29, 1972).

45. Russo v. Byrne, 409 U.S. 1013 (Nov. 13, 1972).

46. The facts were fully disclosed to the Supreme Court before it denied certiorari.

very disturbing. To think that "my government," in which I served to the best of my ability, did such things, often with the approval of the President, has been a matter of deep concern. I can only say that I find some satisfaction in the occasions when I stood up against it. Under the circumstances that existed, as we now know them, I am surprised that I was tolerated so long. This must have been because of strong support I received from John Mitchell and from Richard Kleindienst, which, in my view, is much to their credit.

At about the same time, another matter arose, where the pressure came from another agency. A case was pending before the Supreme Court on a petition for certiorari.[47] The Securities and Exchange Commission was rightly much interested in the case, though the decision of the court of appeals had simply reversed a summary judgment, and remanded the case for a trial. Thus the record contained no developed facts. The S.E.C. urged my office to file an amicus brief supporting the grant of certiorari, but I thought that this was premature. The prospects of winning would be much improved, in my view, if the case went back for trial and a complete version of the facts was placed in the record.

The Chairman of the S.E.C., William J. Casey, then wrote a letter to Attorney General Kleindienst seeking review of my action. I prepared a memorandum for the Attorney General on August 30, 1972, summarizing my reasons. At a meeting with the Attorney General, he suggested that I invite Mr. Casey to lunch, and talk it over. That seemed to me to be a good idea, so I extended the invitation. No convenient lunch time could be found, so I suggested breakfast, which was arranged. Mr. Casey was my guest at the Cosmos Club. There was no meeting of the minds. In due course, the Supreme Court denied certiorari.[48] I am sure that Mr. Casey found me very obtuse and hard to deal with.

In late September, 1972 (shortly before the 1972 election), a very difficult problem arose. The case involved a suit by Ralph Nader against the Secretary of Agriculture challenging the amount of the milk subsidy for the fiscal year ending June 30, 1972. This had been fixed by Secretary Hardin in the spring of

---

47. The decision below was Harwell v. Growth Programs, Inc., 451 F.2d 240, 459 F.2d 461 (5th Cir. 1972).

48. National Association of Securities Dealers v. Harwell, 409 U.S. 876 (1972).

1971. It was charged that the Secretary's action in increasing the allowance was due to political influence. The issue decided by the Court of Appeals related to "mootness," which was not likely to appeal to the Supreme Court as a case for a grant of certiorari. I had been advised that John Dean, of the White House staff, was interested in the case, and wanted me to apply to the Supreme Court for a stay of the decision, so that depositions would not be taken.

I called John Dean on Thursday, September 28, 1972, and explained to him the difficulties about the case. I said that an application for a stay by us would be transparent, and would open the Government to immediate attack by the press. It would be widely contended, and widely believed, I suggested, that we had something to hide, and that we were moving desperately to cover up.[49] I observed that it would be better policy, and better politics, too, to let the case go back to the district court and take what steps we could there. That would be better, I urged, than for the government to take what would be seen as desperate moves to keep from having any depositions taken. Moreover, I suggested, the taking of the Secretary's deposition might serve to dispel some of the charges and innuendos which were then being bandied about.

Later on September 28th, the Deputy Attorney General came to my office. He had obviously heard from someone about the matter, though I never knew who that was. The Deputy said that he would not for a moment undertake to tell me what to do, but he was concerned. I never heard further from John Dean, and the time for seeking a further stay of mandate expired on October 1st. On Monday afternoon, October 2nd, I was "requested to file a petition. I said: "I simply can't file a petition," and I added that my only stock in trade was my professional integrity, and that my standing with the Court and my usefulness would be destroyed if I filed a petition in this case.

The Deputy then asked me to meet with Attorney General Kleindienst. After preliminary discussion, the Attorney General asked his secretary to get John Dean on the telephone. He advised Dean that a petition would not be filed, and that the

---

49. Little did I then realize the possible parallel between this matter and the problems growing out of the Watergate break-in. Indeed, we now know, from the Presidential tapes, that on September 15, 1972, the President called John Dean to his office "and told him 'to remember all the trouble' the President's foes had caused," and that "We'll have a chance to get back at them some day." T. Wicker, One of Us (New York, 1990) 4.

government would have to do the best it could in the district court.

Later that afternoon the Deputy Attorney General came to my office. He seemed quite pleased and relieved. In substance, he said that he felt I had done the right thing, and he was glad it came out as it did. As for Attorney General Kleindienst, he took the appropriate action promptly and firmly. He obviously did not relish it, but he did not waver.[50]

B. Final Events as S.G.

On November 8, 1972, all Presidential appointees in the executive branch were instructed (in an unsigned letter on White House stationery) to submit "a pro forma letter of resignation" within two days. I submitted mine on November 8th. On Monday, December 4th, Attorney General Kleindienst called on me at my office, and advised me that the President was accepting my resignation. Dick Kleindienst said that he had fought against this but had been unsuccessful. I have no doubt that he did; nor do I think there was anything that he could have done about it. Reference was made specifically to the milk case and to the Pennsylvania school case.

A few days later Kleindienst advised me that the President wanted to make the announcement on Friday, December 8th. The announcement was made by the Press Secretary, Mr. Ziegler. He said that I was retiring at the end of the current Term of the Supreme Court, and that Professor Robert H. Bork of the Yale University Law School would be my successor.

I never resented this action in any way. It was surely the President's privilege. My commission read that I held office "during the pleasure of the President," and he was free to act on any basis that seemed appropriate to him. I was surprised that it was also announced that he was appointing a Deputy Solicitor General. Not in recent times, I believe, had any subordinate officers in the Solicitor General's Office been named by the President. However, since that time, particularly in Republican

---

50. These paragraphs are based on a Memorandum for E.N.G. by E.N.G., written on October 3, 1972.

There is an intimation in S. Dash, Chief Counsel (New York, 1976) 229–230, that President Nixon had, on March 23, 1971, "reverse[d] his Secretary of Agriculture and increase[d] milk-price supports" and that this was "return payment for commitments by the milk producers to make massive campaign contribution." I had no information about this at the time, and have no basis for evaluating it now.

Administrations, it has become customary to have a so-called "political officer" assigned to the office.

In December, Roger Crampton, who was Assistant Attorney General for the Office of Legal Counsel, told me that while the milk case was pending, he had been asked to write an opinion that a petition for certiorari should be filed. He said he had looked at it, and had come to the conclusion "that it was perfectly clear" that I was right in my refusal to file a petition. I told him that I was sorry that he had become involved, as he, too, was one of those whose resignation was accepted, after only a few months in the Department. He then said that he had been told that he and I were not "malleable" enough. We both felt that this was a significant compliment.

Ehrlichman, in his memoirs,[51] has written that I was one of "the liberal, Ivy League clique who thought the Court was their own private playground." I can understand that, and from his outlook I must have been quite intolerable. The difference is subtle, but it has been well put by an experienced observer, Elliot Richardson. He has shown where the line should be drawn, a distinction which was quite beyond the comprehension of the White House staff of that time. He wrote that "it seems to me important to underscore the difference between the proper role of the political process in the shaping of legal *policies* and the perversion of the legal *process* by political pressure." [52]

Early in January, 1973, Professor Bork came to call at the Solicitor General's office. He was very friendly and agreeable, and we had no difficulty in working out arrangements during the first half of the year when he was obligated to teach at Yale Law School. I told him that there were matters—with political implications—on which he could work, on a part-time basis during the spring. This would be helpful to him when he came to the office on a full-time basis. These two matters were, first, the question of "impoundment" of funds by the President,[53] and, second, some very difficult and important questions arising with respect to the

---

51. J. Ehrlichman, Witness to Power (New York: 1982) 118.

52. E. Richardson, The Creative Balance (New York, 1976) 27. The italics are Mr. Richardson's.

53. In Train v. City of New York, 420 U.S. 35 (1975), and in Train v. Campaign Clean Water, Inc., 420 U.S. 36 (1974), both argued by Solicitor General Bork, the Court held that the executive had no power to impound the funds involved in those cases. See W. Middlekauff, "Twisting the President's Arm: The Impoundment Control Act as a Tool for Enforcing the Principle of Appropriation Expenditure," 100 Yale L.J. 209 (1990).

validity of wiretaps which had not been authorized by the Attorney General himself, or by an Assistant Attorney General specifically designated by the Attorney General, as required by the statute at that time.[54] I was glad to be relieved of immediate responsibility for these matters.

On leaving my office, soon to be his, Mr. Bork handed me a copy of his article which had recently appeared in the Indiana Law Journal.[55] He did this with some pride, I thought. I was, of course, interested, and I read the article. I was surprised, even startled, at some of the views expressed. They seemed to me to be an expression of past thinking which I felt that we had outgrown.[56]

There were a few events in the spring of 1973 which fit into the pattern of White House interest. In a school desegregation case in Montgomery County, Maryland, the district judge had entered an order requiring the busing of students. A stay of this order had been refused by the Fourth Circuit Court of Appeals, and there was pressure to seek a stay from the Supreme Court. Filing an application for a stay would have been in the teeth of the Supreme Court's decision in *Alexander v. Holmes County Board of Education.*[57] The Civil Rights Division in the Department of Justice was opposed to seeking such a stay, and it was clearly my view that there was no professionally sound reason for making such an application. Attorney General Kleindienst was obviously under pressure. He did not ask me to file the application for a stay, but he asked me whether he could file such an application in the Supreme Court and what my attitude would be towards his doing so. I responded that he was my superior

---

54. Omnibus Crime Control and Safe Streets Act of 1968, 82 Stat. 211–225, 18 U.S.C. §§ 2510–2520. This matter was resolved by the Supreme Court in United States v. Giordano, 416 U.S. 505 (1974), and United States v. Chavez, 416 U.S. 562 (1974), partly in favor of the Government, and partly adverse. Solicitor General Bork presented the argument for the Government in these cases.

55. R. Bork, "Neutral Principles and Some First Amendment Problems," 47 Indiana L.J. 1 (1971).

56. After reading Professor Bork's article, I sent it on to my deputy, Daniel M. Friedman, with a bucksheet which, as I have recently been reminded, said: "Try this!"

Louis Kohlmeier, a columnist in the Chicago Tribune for February 8, 1973, quoted "an Ivy League colleague" of Bork as saying: "Griswold is no flaming liberal, but Bork is far more conservative."

57. 396 U.S. 19 (1969). The case has been referred to at pp. 273–274, above.

and that he could do whatever he felt he should do. Accordingly, the application for a stay was filed with the Attorney General's signature. It was denied by the Court.

In February, 1973, considerable pressure was brought on me by representatives of the Vice President's office. This was with respect to the filing of an application for a stay, pending the filing of a petition for certiorari in a case involving claims of the Tesuque Indians.[58] I was reluctant to seek such a stay, since I had already decided that the case was not one in which certiorari should be applied for. As a result of this discussion, I wrote, with the assistance of Harry Sachse, a member of my staff who had a special interest in Indian matters, a long letter to the Secretary of the Interior explaining my understanding of the scope of the decision of the Tenth Circuit. My letter made it plain that the Government did not consider the Indian lands to be "public lands"—which was the basis of the Indians' concern.

Following the sending of this letter, there was a meeting in the office of the Assistant Attorney General for the Lands Division, including a representative from the White House, one from the Department of the Interior, and several members of the Indian Tribe. Mr. Sachse attended this meeting as my representative, and explained our position on the basis of my letter to the Secretary of the Interior. Mr. Sachse later advised me that the meeting had been a successful one, and that the Indians present seemed to be satisfied, although they felt that they would still have a problem in explaining the rather complex situation to their constituents. This was the kind of handling and negotiating in difficult matters which I enjoyed, and I am glad that it worked well in this case.

On April 30, 1973, Richard Kleindienst resigned as Attorney General to take effect on the qualification of his successor. I felt very sorry for him at this development, which seemed to me to be unfair. He had become Attorney General at a very difficult time—a much more difficult time than he or most other people realized. He had always been fair and honorable with me, and, like his predecessor John Mitchell, had frequently supported me and backed me up.

Richard Kleindienst was, and is, my friend, as well as a former student. He is probably responsible for my being retained as Solicitor General when the Nixon Administration took

---

58. The case was Davis v. Morton, 469 F.2d 593 (10th Cir. 1972). The concern for the Indians was not unwarranted, for the court of appeals had several times referred to land held in trust for the Indians as "federal lands."

office in January, 1979, and he became Deputy Attorney General. I worked with him closely for more than four years, including the period when he was Attorney General in 1972 and early 1973. I was present through his pain at the time his resignation was requested in April, 1973. I think he suffered more with less reason than any one else among those whose earnest efforts as conscientious government officers brought them in to the shadow of an amoral White House—one of the low points in our country's history. Kleindienst took no part in these actions. On the contrary, he refused to comply with instructions from the White House, more than once. And it was he who required the disclosure of the break-in of the Ellsberg psychiatrist.

Kleindienst was charged with failing to make full disclosure of all events relating to the I.T.T. case at his confirmation hearing before the Senate Judiciary Committee. He answered the questions that were put to him, about the settlement of the I.T.T. case. His difficulty arose because he did not make it completely clear that he was testifying about the *settlement* of the I.T.T. case, *after* he had brought about the filing of the appeal. He was not pressured as to the settlement, and his testimony, which he understood to be related to that distinct question, was accurate.[59] In the judgment of those who knew how staunchly Kleindienst had resisted White House pressure, Kleindienst should have been praised rather than prosecuted. Kleindienst was, however, charged by indictment for serious offenses. When it came to the time of trial, the prosecution dismissed the substantial charges, and he was allowed to plead guilty to a single misdemeanor charge. Some might think that this plea was, in effect, obtained by extortion. Apparently, that was the view of District Judge George H. Pratt, Jr., an experienced trial judge. He pronounced a short sentence, and suspended that.[60]

Kleindienst has written kind words about me.[61] I do not write what I have written here by way of return, but only out of a sense of duty. In my opinion, Richard Kleindienst made many difficult judgments, conscientiously and in the public interest. It was his misfortune to hold high office at the worst of times.

It was in the spring of 1973 that the break-in of Ellsberg's psychiatrist's office was revealed, at the direction of Attorney

59. S. Ambrose, Nixon (New York: 1989) 504, similarly fails to make the distinction between the *settlement* and the order that the *jurisdictional statement* should not be filed.

60. Cf. R. Ben–Veniste and G. Frampton, Jr., Stonewall—The Real Story of the Watergate Prosecution (New York, 1977) 377–380.

61. R. Kleindienst, Justice (Ottawa, Ill.: 1985) 108–109.

General Kleindienst. I cannot say that this was the sort of thing I had in mind when I wrote my memorandum to Kleindienst, in the late summer of 1972, suggesting that it would be wise to terminate the prosecution of Ellsberg. Never in my wildest speculation had it occurred to me that the Government of my country would be involved in such a squalid activity.

When the President announced a new investigation in April, 1973, I gave serious consideration to the matter of resigning forthwith, and perhaps I should have done so. However, my retirement had already been announced, to take effect only a few weeks in the future, and resignation under such circumstances might have seemed a rather weak sort of bravado. Moreover, I was much involved in cases then pending before the Supreme Court, and I had duties to the Court which seemed to me to counter an action which would, at best, have been only a rather empty gesture. As a result, I stayed in office until the conclusion of the Supreme Court's Term in June, 1973. During the last week of my tenure, the Court held a reception for me and Harriet, attended by all the Justices and their wives, and many friends. This was a very pleasant occasion for us, as well as a deeply appreciated honor. I remember it as the culmination of nearly six years of work as the head of the Solicitor General's office.

When the President announced the resignation of Richard Kleindienst, he also announced that Elliot Richardson would be the new Attorney General. Richardson had been a student of mine at the Harvard Law School shortly after World War II. He had been President of the Harvard Law Review, after military service.

During the course of the hearing on Richardson's nomination as Attorney General, questions arose before the Senate Judiciary Committee with respect to the handling of the investigation of offenses which might have been committed in the whole area which is now known as Watergate. It was proposed that there should be a special prosecutor, with independent authority to conduct these investigations. I urged on Elliot that this prosecutor should be "within" the Department of Justice, though given great independence, and this idea was given serious consideration by members of the Senate Judiciary Committee. I was concerned that there should not be an authority, essentially executive, which was floating around in space without being a part of any Department of the Government. The Senate committee seemed willing to have the Watergate special prosecutor "within" the Department of Justice, but was searching for a formula which would assure the prosecutor's independence. I suggested to Elliot the analogy of a tenured university professor, who is subject to removal, but only in rare cases.

This idea was further explored in subsequent conversations with Mr. Richardson. The formula for removal of a tenured professor at Harvard University is that he can be terminated only for "grave misconduct." I was reluctant to use these words, because I was sure that the press would immediately trace them back to the Harvard phrase, and would write snide pieces about how the Ivy League gets its fingers into every pie. I tried hard to come up with a different formulation, and found this very difficult. Finally, I suggested to Elliot that he might agree that the special prosecutor could be removed only for "extraordinary impropriety." I thought that both of these words were a little ponderous, but, though I tried hard, I could not come up with anything better. Finally, this formula was proposed to the Senate committee, and accepted by them. I thought that the idea was helpful, and I was glad that I could play a role, though a tiny one, in the process.

In due course, Professor Archibald Cox of the Harvard Law School was designated to be the Chief Watergate Prosecutor. Although I had little to do with this choice, Cox's name was on a list of several persons whom I suggested to Elliot Richardson, and I was pleased when he was chosen.

Both Cox and Richardson were sworn in early in May. Cox took his oath in my office, which had been his office when he was Solicitor General appointed by President Kennedy, from 1961 to 1965. It was perhaps unfortunate that a number of members of the Kennedy family attended his swearing in.

———

My final major action as Solicitor General was my appearance before the Subcommittee on Commerce and Finance of the Committee on Interstate and Foreign Commerce, of the House of Representatives, concerning a bill to amend the Securities and Exchange Act. One of the provisions of this bill [62] would have authorized the Securities and Exchange Commission "to conduct in its own name and through its own attorneys litigation * * * in the United States * * * Supreme Court." This was, of course, the consequence of my encounter with S.E.C. Chairman Casey, to which I have referred above.[63]

---

62. Section 101 of H.R. 5050, June 7, 1973.
63. See p. 315, above.

I started with the statement that "The Department of Justice strongly opposes this provision." I then surveyed the functions of the Solicitor General and undertook to state the reasons why control of government litigation in the Supreme Court by the Solicitor General was important. I next tried to show the problems which would arise if control of government litigation in the Supreme Court was divided. Finally, I discussed the arrangement for accommodation between the Solicitor General's office and other agencies of the government, with specific reference to the Securities and Exchange Commission. In preparing my statement, I relied heavily on a memorandum I had sent to Attorney General Richard Kleindienst in July, 1972, on "Fractionating Responsibility for the Government's Legal Affairs." The bill was not reported out by the Subcommittee, and things seem to have been reasonably quiet on this front in recent years.

———

The story of the "Saturday Night Massacre," when President Nixon ordered the discharge of Archibald Cox, and Attorney General Richardson resigned, and Deputy Attorney General Ruckelshaus either resigned or was discharged, are well known.[64] This was the event which, eventually, had more to do with the resignation of President Nixon than any other single item in the tangled web which he wove. The discharge of Archibald Cox was actually carried out by Solicitor General Robert Bork, in his capacity as Acting Attorney General, on Saturday, October 20, 1973. This was a little short of four months after my resignation as Solicitor General became effective. Though it is of no consequence whatever, I am personally sure that I would not have discharged Archibald Cox. I do not say this because I am so pure in heart. It is simply the consequence of two important factors which would have been controlling with me.

The *first* of these factors was that three of the individuals involved, Attorney General Elliot Richardson, Deputy Attorney General William Ruckelshaus, and Special Watergate Prosecutor Archibald Cox, were all students of mine. I knew them well, admired each one greatly, and had complete confidence in their integrity and judgment. I simply could not have discharged Cox after Ruckelshaus and Richardson had resigned or been discharged.

The *second* of these reasons was, as I have indicated above, that I had played a role in advising Elliot Richardson in connec-

———

64. This is perhaps best stated in Elliot Richardson's book, The Creative Balance (New York 1976) at 1–48.

tion with the selection of Cox, and particularly in suggesting the phrase which was used for the purpose of establishing the independence of the Special Prosecutor's office, namely, that the special prosecutor would not be dismissed except for "extraordinary impropriety." Having participated in this, I would have felt myself bound by the formula as much as Elliot Richardson did. And I was sure in my mind and heart that there was nothing to show that Cox had been guilty of "extraordinary impropriety." Of course, there were many things which I had not known, and much to be said now about the whole episode. But one thing has seemed clear to me from the beginning. I would not have discharged Cox, and I was sorry that Solicitor General and Acting Attorney General Bork did so.

C. The Role of the Solicitor General

What about the Solicitor General? What does the office do? What is its relation to other agencies of the government, including the Attorney General and the President?

My close contact with the Solicitor General's office has extended over nearly eleven years of my professional life. And I have followed the role of the office closely since I was first employed there on December 2, 1929, now more than sixty years ago. The Office of Solicitor General was established in 1870. Thus, this period covers more than half of the history of the Solicitor General's office in the United States.

I believe that I have set out above more about the actual work of the Solicitor General than has so far appeared elsewhere.[65] I have tried to describe some of the problems which occurred in my time in the office. In a "normal administration" these problems can be worked out, with a reasonable amount of give and take on both sides. Alas, the Nixon Administration, with its cover-up, enemies list, plumbers, break-ins, feeling of insecurity (however unwarranted at the start) was not "normal." With such a crew in charge, it is hard for me to see how I lasted as long as I did. In considerable measure, this was due to the firm support I received from the Attorneys General and Deputy Attorneys General under whom I served, and I am deeply grateful to them for that. They never talked to me about the pressures

---

65. L. Caplan, The Tenth Justice: The Solicitor General and the Rule of Law (N.Y. 1988) does deal with the office extensively, but it does not give much in the way of detail about the general run of cases. See also C. Fried, Order and Law: Arguing the Reagan Revolution (New York: 1991).

to which they were subjected, and only occasionally did any sign of it appear.

What I write here is my own conception of the responsibilities of the office, which I tried to follow over a period of nearly six years. I was fully aware that there are two sides to most any question, and I tried not to be merely mechanical or too rigid in my approach. For the most part, I have not reported here the occasional case where I yielded to "felt necessities" of the time. But I did try to be professional in my representation of my country's interests before the Supreme Court.

One thing was always clear to me: there can be no doubt that the office is a political office. The Solicitor General is nominated by the President, and confirmed by the Senate. He is currently the third ranking officer in the Department of Justice, coming after the Attorney General, and the Deputy Attorney General. His commission provides that he holds office "during the pleasure of the President." I have already alluded to the fact that under the statute establishing the office, the Solicitor General must be "learned in the law," [66] and there is no other office, I believe, which has such a requirement.

The Solicitor General is clearly in the Executive Branch of the Government, and no place else. He can be dismissed or retired by the President, as happened to me.[67] But the fact that he is in the Executive Branch and subordinate to the Attorney General and the President is not, to my mind, sufficient to define his role. His role is basically professional. He is an "officer of the Court" in a very real sense. For example, his name appears on the title page of the United States Reports along with the Attorney General, the Clerk of the Court, the Reporter of Decisions, the Marshall, and the Librarian. In carrying out his professional responsibilities, he has a clear duty to the Court. The essence of his assignment is to represent the interests of the United States before the Court in a way which is professionally responsible.

The duties of the office are not widely known, even by members of the bar. It is known that his basic work is the representation of the interests of the United States in briefs and oral arguments before the Supreme Court. But, he also has the responsibility of deciding whether any case lost by the United

---

66. Rev. Stat. § 347, now found in 28 U.S.C. § 505.

67. A recent Law Review Note labors the proposition that there is no basis for "a restriction on the President's ability to remove the Solicitor General." "Removability and the Rule of Law: The Independence of the Solicitor General," 57 Geo. Wash. L.Rev. 750, 777 (1989).

States in any court shall be appealed.[68] I find that many lawyers are unaware of this responsibility. Conferences with the Solicitor General on the question of appeal are rare, though it was my policy, and generally that of my predecessors and successors, I believe, to give a hearing on the question of appeal to any lawyer representing a client in the case. It is also ordinarily possible to have a hearing before the Solicitor General or a member of his staff on the question whether a petition for certiorari will be filed by the Government, or whether the Government will oppose or "acquiesce" in a petition filed against the Government.

It was surprising to me to find how frequently I was asked "What does the Solicitor General do?" I found that it was an informative response to say something like this: "I do what you think the Attorney General does." The Attorney General has a very responsible office. He advises the President, and gives political as well as legal advice. He carries on relations with the Congress, and particularly with the Senate in the highly political process of the nomination and confirmation of judges. He is responsible for a very large bureaucracy, including the Bureau of Prisons, the Immigration and Naturalization Service, the Federal Bureau of Investigation, and other agencies. He holds press conferences, and makes speeches. He has no time to be a lawyer. On the other hand, the Solicitor General does not engage in politics. When he makes speeches, they are usually to professional groups—like law schools, bar associations, and so on—on professional topics. His basic responsibility *is* to be a lawyer. He should, of course, endeavor to carry out his duties in such a way as to cause the Attorney General as little trouble as possible.

One way to approach the problem is to ask the question: who is the Solicitor General's client? It was clear to me that my client was the United States. I did not regard the President of the United States as my client, though he was my ultimate boss, and my tenure was at his will. The fact that the United States was my client became particularly relevant when the case under consideration came from one of the agencies of the Government, such as the Federal Trade Commission, the Securities and Exchange Commission, the Federal Communications Commission, the Comptroller of the Currency, and so on. One might say, in a

---

68. In addition, he has the responsibility to decide (1) whether a brief *amicus curiae* shall be filed in any case, and (2) whether a petition for rehearing *en banc* shall be filed in any court. These matters do not come up very often, but the approval of the Solicitor General is necessary to keep the lower courts from being flooded with applications of this sort, thus diminishing the impact of the occasional application which has substantial merit.

case involving the Interstate Commerce Commission, for example, that your client is the Commission, and that you should make the best argument you can for the position taken by the Commission. I never acceded to this view, and I do not believe that such a view has been taken by most other holders of the Solicitor General's office. This is particularly true in the matter of applications for writs of certiorari—that is, for review of a lower court decision by the Supreme Court—which are a very scarce commodity.

If each agency was left alone, the Court would be flooded by petitions filed by numerous agencies, more or less automatically, after losing any case. It is very important to the interests of the United States as a whole that such applications be carefully monitored and limited. In this way, the Supreme Court knows when it sees a petition with the Solicitor General's name on it that it has been carefully considered from a broad and professional point of view, and that an officer in whom, hopefully, they have confidence, believes that it is in the over-all interest of the Government, and worthy of the Court's consideration.

This is particularly true when several agencies have interests in the same case. I recall a case [69] involving rebroadcast of television programs where the Library of Congress (because of its Copyright Office), the Federal Communications Commission, and the Antitrust Division in the Department of Justice all had strong, but differing, views. I first assembled representatives of the three agencies in my office, and tried to get them to reach a common position. This was not successful, so I concluded that there was nothing for me to do but to present what I regarded as the "proper" view. The Supreme Court did not accept the argument which I advanced, but a few years later Congress amended the Communications Act so as to incorporate that position into the statutory law.[70]

The matter of the "independence" of the Solicitor General has been dealt with at some length in a recent book.[71] The author takes the position that some recent Solicitors General have been too "political," that is, that they have yielded too much to what they understood to be the views of the current administration. The author of the book is particularly critical of Solicitor General Charles Fried who, he says, "carried out" the policies

69. United States v. Southwestern Cable Co., 392 U.S. 157 (1968).

70. Act of Oct. 19, 1976, P.L. 94–553, 90 Stat. 2550, 17 U.S.C. § 111.

71. L. Caplan, The Tenth Justice: The Solicitor General and the Rule of Law (N.Y. 1988).

of Attorney General Meese and Assistant Attorney General Reynolds.[72]   And he quotes Bruce Fein, an attorney in the Department of Justice duringthe Reagan Administration, who told the author of the book that "My conception of the office of the Solicitor General is that it should be a foremost promoter of the policies of the President before the Court."[73]   I would not go so far. The Solicitor General holds a unique professional post, though, as I have said elsewhere, he is surely not "an ombudsman with a roving commission to do justice as he sees it."[74]

My own interpretation is that Fried did not yield to pressure. He stated his own views to the Court, which were indeed, generally consistent with the views of other officers of the Department of Justice. As an experienced reviewer of Caplan's book has said: "The general theme of Caplan's book—the politicization of the Solicitor General's office under Meese, Reynolds and Fried, and the substitution of a political agenda for the rule of law—does not withstand scrutiny."[75]

In my administration of the Solicitor General's office, I tried to be aware of the policies of the Attorney General and the White House, and to support them within wide limits. Among other things, I felt that it was my duty to see that the Attorney General was informed as to positions which I took. I did not think that he should have to face a press conference where he was asked: "Why did your Solicitor General take such and such an action," and have to reply: "I don't know, this is the first I have heard about that."

From time to time I adjusted my views, and, more frequently, my phraseology, to meet points made by my superiors. For example, it was possible, on some occasions, to narrow my argument so that it would not affect an administration policy. In the Nixon Administration, particularly, questions arose with respect to positions taken in the White House, since I was becoming more and more concerned about the people in office there below the President. If I had received a thoughtful direction or suggestion from the President, I would have gone very far to comply. But I never received any instructions directly from the

---

72. Caplan, above, at 80.

73. Caplan, above, at 80.

74. E. Griswold, "The Office of the Solicitor General—Representing the Interest of the United States before the Supreme Court," 34 Mo. L.Rev. 527 (1969).

75. Louis Fisher, Review of Caplan, The Tenth Justice, in 15 Law & Social Inquiry, 305, 319 (1990).

President, nor did I have any clear indication that the instructions made by others in the White House came with the President's authority.

The "independence" of the Solicitor General is a sort of ideal which cannot be fully met. As I have said, he is in fact, and inevitably, a political officer, subject to the President's control. But, in my view, he has, in the interests of his client, the United States, a special obligation to present his independent professional views to the Supreme Court. Calling him "The Tenth Justice" is a pleasant, but deceptive exaggeration. He is an advocate, but there are limits to what he will advocate, limits which are sometimes more restrictive than in the case of counsel representing a private client. The Solicitor General is obligated to recognize those limits, while pursuing his role as advocate as far as he can. If the President thinks that he is not sufficiently "political," he can always be removed. That is the inevitable professional hazard of the Solicitor General. It can on occasion be a tightrope, but the Solicitor General should keep his balance.

My experience was that most problems can be "worked out," and that finding a way to get some time for further consideration is often a help. For people who regard the Solicitor General as simply a "hired gun" for the administration, any showing of independence by the Solicitor General must be very aggravating. On the other hand, unless the Solicitor General maintains, in considerable measure, his ability to express his independent professional views, within the policies established by the Court, he will not have met the public responsibility of his office.

Former Solicitor General Charles Fried—a long time friend, and former colleague of mine at Harvard—has written a thoughtful book giving his views about the office in which he served from 1985 to 1989, in the Reagan Administration.[76] He takes a very different view of the Solicitor General's office from the one I have outlined above. In a chapter on "Loyalty," he writes that "the President not merely deserves to be, but can only be effectively served by officers whose minds, in the words of Franklin Roosevelt's letter to FTC Commissioner Humphrey, 'go along together' with his." Indeed, he goes so far as to say that "It is not at all a matter of guessing the President's mind—for he is unlikely to have one on the matter—but of constructing his leader's mind in a way that he will later embrace as his own."[77] This is

---

76. C. Fried, Order and Law: Arguing the Reagan Revolution (New York: 1991).

77. C. Fried, above, at 195.

surely the most "political" view of the Solicitor General's role that has yet appeared in print.

Here, as so often, there seem to me to be two sides to the question, and consideration can be given to certain distinctions. Some questions are truly "policy" matters. An instance from our history is President Franklin Roosevelt's decision to remove all Japanese from the West Coast in 1942. This was a purely political decision, with military overtones. It was clearly within the President's sphere of action in war-time. I have no doubt that it was the duty of every subordinate officer, including the Solicitor General, to support it—or resign.[78]

Then there is a significant related question. Even on an important matter, is the decision truly the President's—or is it one which has been made by subordinates of one sort or another, in the White House, sometimes influenced by members of Congress, or by outside lobbyists? Such decisions are ordinarily not motivated by a true consideration of the public interest. Perhaps such things occurred less frequently in the Reagan Administration than they did in the time of President Nixon.

Another distinction is between policy decisions and what may be called professional issues. The Solicitor General is the Government's chief barrister, its expert on the Supreme Court and its procedures, and he is appointed because of his ability and experience in that field. He should be heard on *professional* issues. Is the pending case a good one on which to risk the issue? One of the rules of the Solicitor General's office, based on much experience, is: Never risk an important question an a poor case. The Solicitor General's judgment is particularly important on such questions as whether a petition for certiorari should be filed. Should a stay be sought? Should the Solicitor General seek to appear as an *amicus curiae* in a case in which the Government is not a party? If the Court perceives such actions as being "political," its trust in the Solicitor General will be seriously minimized, his professional standing will be weakened, and his effectiveness will be impaired. As I have indicated, I was always backed up by my superiors in the Department of Justice.

Thus, as it seems to me, the problem is much more complicated—filled with nuances and questions of personality and judgment—than Mr. Fried indicates in his book. It is a very delicate balance, depending greatly on the good judgment of the various

---

78. This is the issue to which Herbert Wechsler refers in his chapter on "Some Issues for the Lawyer," in R. McIver, Integrity and Compromise: Problems of Public and Private Conscience (New York: 1957) 117–28. See also Book Review, in 33 J. of Legal Ed. 388 (1982).

persons participating in it.   In the final four-and-a-half years of my service as Solicitor General, I had no trouble within the Department of Justice—nothing like that described by Mr. Fried in his book.   My few difficulties came from subordinates in the White House,[79] who were clearly acting for "political," not "policy" purposes.   In such circumstances it seemed to me—and still does—to be my duty to do what I could to preserve the "independence" of the Solicitor General's office.   I had been appointed to a professional office, and I did my best to conduct it professionally, endeavoring all the time to be understanding, agreeable and accommodating, within the limits of high professional standards.

---

79.   There was only one exception, when the President intervened in the I.T.T. case.   I had no contact with him, and had no knowledge that he had personally intervened until many months later.   See pp. 293–294, above.

CHAPTER XI

Better Understanding with the Soviet Union

Over the years I have had a continuing interest in peace, better understanding among nations, and civil rights and human interests generally. I have been fortunate to be able to develop these interests, particularly with respect to some distant parts of the world—the Soviet Union and South Africa. In previous pages, I have recounted my efforts to acquire knowledge with respect to Soviet law at the Harvard Law School, and the early contacts which developed in that field. I have also referred to my trip to the Soviet Union in 1961, as a part of the Dartmouth Conference, where a substantial group of Americans and Soviets met for extended and constructive studies of the problems existing between the two countries.[1]

During the year which he was able to spend in the Soviet Union, Professor Harold J. Berman became well acquainted with Professor Boris S. Nikiforov, who was then with the Institute of State and Law of the Soviet Academy of Sciences. As a result, the Harvard Law School invited Professor Nikiforov to come to the School, and he came as a visitor in 1963. Professor Nikiforov and I had many talks together and became good friends. He also made a shorter visit to the School in 1966.

Thereafter, the Institute of United States and Canada Studies of the Academy of Sciences was established, and Professor Nikiforov became head of the law section there. In 1974, he invited Harriet and me to spend two weeks in the Soviet Union as the guests of that Institute. It was a strenuous but rewarding trip. We spent most of our time in Moscow, but also visited Leningrad and Kiev.

---

1. See pp. 210–211, above.

Professor Boris Nikiforov and E.N.G. Moscow, 1974

Professor Nikiforov arranged to have two young Russian lawyers assigned to us as aides, and one of them was with us at all meals, since we could not read the menus or talk to the waiters. One of these was Vasiliy Vlasihin, then about twenty-five years old, who was a graduate student at the Institute of U.S. and Canada Studies, training in American law. I was well impressed by him, and our contacts have continued ever since.

Vasiliy's English was excellent, though then not perfect. One of the difficulties arising from the vagaries of the English language can be illustrated by an exchange which occurred at one of our breakfasts. Vasiliy politely asked Harriet what she would like to have. She specified certain items, and then added "and toast." Vasiliy seemed surprised, and said "not toast for breakfast." At that time, there was a certain tendency on the part of the Russians to say that certain things, such as visits to a church, or to a building, could not be done. So Harriet responded, with emphasis, "Yes, I want toast." Whereupon, Vasiliy rose, picked up a glass of water from the table, and said: "To the friendship of the Soviet and American People." I felt rather sorry for Vasiliy,

Vasiliy Vlasihin and E.N.G.

From left—Anthony Sager, Executive Director of Lawyers' Alliance for Nuclear Arms Control; Adrian W. DeWind; John B. Rhinelander; E.N.G. At center—John Downs; Ambassador Vadim Sobakin; Sergei Plekhanov. Last two at right—Roger Fisher, Alan B. Sherr, President and Founder of Lawyers' Alliance.

since his English was quite good. "Toast," in the sense of bread browned by heat, is not known in Russia. Indeed, for the most part, they do not have sliced bread. It comes there in long loaves and pieces may be torn off by hand. When the Russians make toast for English or American visitors, they have to cut up a loaf, and hold the piece with a fork over a flame on the stove.

After my return to Washington, I was able to make arrangements so that Vasiliy Vlasihin could spend a year at the Harvard Law School. It was expected that he would come to Cambridge for the beginning of the term in September, 1976. However, the problems on the Soviet side were such that he could not depart until December, 1976, which put him out of synchronization with the School's program. Actually, he arrived in Cambridge during a snowstorm on Christmas Eve, 1976. There were no students at the School, no one to meet him, and no one to tell him where his

Left to right—E.N.G.; Chairman Terebilov of the Soviet Supreme Court; Shirley Hufstedler, former judge of the United States Court of Appeals for the Ninth Circuit and Secretary of Education—March, 1985

living quarters were located. Somehow or other he made it, and started his studies at Harvard in January, 1977.

Partly because of the timing situation, and partly because of his own wish, he enrolled as a "special student," and thus was not a candidate for a degree. He was, however, the first student from the Soviet Union since World War II, and, as far as I know, the first ever at the School. He attended classes regularly, and continued to improve his English. Various people were kind to him over the summer, including Mr. and Mrs. John P. Bracken of Pennsylvania. He also made a trip to the West Coast, where he visited with Seth and Shirley Hufstedler, of Los Angeles.[2]

2. Mr. Bracken was former chairman of the House of Delegates of the American Bar Association, and had met Vasiliy in Moscow. Seth Hufstedler was a President of the State Bar of California, and his wife, Shirley, was then a judge of the United States Court of Appeals for the

At the end of his stay at Harvard, in January 1978, Vasiliy came to Washington for several days. During this period, I helped him to see the sights of Washington. I took him to the Capitol, and to the Supreme Court building, where I introduced him to Chief Justice Burger. I also showed him around the Department of Justice, and introduced him to Attorney General Edward H. Levi during his final days in office.

After his return to the Soviet Union, Vasiliy continued his work in American law. He was an author with A.A. Mishin of a book on the Constitution of the United States, published (in Russian) in Moscow in 1985. This book set forth the full text of the United States Constitution, translated into Russian, followed by commentaries on each clause. I am not able to read it, but I have had a number of portions translated for me. In some cases, it seems to an American to be somewhat ideological. When I raised this question with Vasiliy, he responded: "Don't take that too seriously. It is our union card."

In later years, I gave a copy of this book to our Ambassador in Moscow. He said that it would be very helpful, since it was the first book published in modern times which made available to Russian readers the full text of the Constitution of the United States.

Vasiliy continued to deal with American law at the Institute of U.S. and Canada Studies. He also became active as an escort for various Soviet delegations who came to this country. As a result, I saw him from time to time, and followed his work quite closely. Any effort to engage in correspondence with Soviet citizens was then, and usually is now, quite unsuccessful. I used to write letters to Vasiliy and other Soviets whom I know, in which I carefully refrained from saying anything ideological, recognizing that the letters would probably be opened, and that any very specific discussion of current problems might lead to difficulties for the recipient of the letter. Very rarely, though, did any reply come back. The Soviets were thoroughly indoctrinated with the idea that any substantial contact with westerners was discouraged, and might affect their jobs and prospects for promotion.

While we were in Moscow in 1974, I was asked to give some lectures at the Institute of United States and Canada Studies. One of these came on the day of the announcement that President Ford had granted a pardon to ex-President Nixon. Before proceeding to the lecture hall, I went to the American Embassy and obtained a

---

Ninth Circuit. Vasiliy Vlasihin had acted as aide to all of these people when they visited Moscow in 1973.

copy of a press release issued in Washington about the event. I wanted to be sure that I had an accurate version of the facts, as I knew that I would be questioned about it. When I gave the lecture, there were nearly one hundred persons in the room. My lecture was, of course, in English, and there was no interpretation. I could not help thinking that it would be hard to put together one hundred persons in the United States to hear a lecture delivered in Russian. Language facility is a field in which we are very weak, and this is often a disadvantage.

After my lecture, there was a question period. I was immediately asked about the Nixon pardon, and particularly how there could be a pardon of an offense which had not yet been charged. I said that this presented no difficulty, at least under our law, and I referred to the widespread amnesty which was granted after the Civil War. Then, the next questioner arose and said: "Isn't this all just a part of a Wall Street takeover?" I was puzzled about this, and said that I did not understand. The questioner explained: "We liked Nixon. He brought about détente, which was a great relief to us. But, obviously, it did not please Wall Street or the military industrial complex, so they threw Nixon out—and brought in a Ford"—with a long pause—"from Michigan. And then what did they do? They brought in a *Rockefeller*"—with great emphasis—"from New York. What could be more obvious?"

I was really taken aback. There could hardly have been a clearer instance of misunderstanding, and its effect on thinking on Soviet–American questions. I replied that, yes, President Ford was from Michigan, but he had no connection with the Fords of Ford Motor Company. He was a well-known, long-time, and widely respected politician from Grand Rapids, which happened to be in Michigan. He had been in Congress for many years, and was not a wealthy man. As for Rockefeller, he *was* a grandson of John D. Rockefeller, the founder of the Standard Oil Company. He was a man of great wealth. But he had, for many years, been a politician. He had been the elected governor of New York, one of our great states, and was widely respected as a political figure, although there were, as is the case with most politicians, many persons who disagreed with him, or did not like him. I then added that it had never occurred to me—nor had I ever heard it said by anyone in the United States—that the recent events were "a Wall Street takeover," and that I did not believe that this was the case. The Ford and the Rockefeller appointments had occurred in accordance with our Constitution, and as a part of the democratic process. Whether I was successful in my explanation, I do not know, but I felt that I had at least planted some seeds for consideration by some thoughtful Soviets.

Early in 1983, I was asked by a Washington lawyer and friend, John B. Jones, Jr., whether I would be interested in joining an organization known as the Lawyers Alliance for Nuclear Arms Control—LANAC. (It is now called Lawyers Alliance for World Security—LAWS.) I asked for further information about LANAC in order to learn who the people were who were promoting it, but, especially, to see if "no first use" was part of its program. Although I recognized that the Soviets had made a public pledge of no first use, I did not have much confidence in that pledge. And, although I fervently hoped that my country would not engage in a first-use of nuclear weapons, I felt that the possibility that it might do so was an important element in our defense during that rather tense time of the cold war period.

My questions were soon answered, and I became a member of LANAC. It then developed that a joint conference was planned between delegates from LANAC and a corresponding group of Soviets. The Americans were all lawyers, and the Soviets were all what we would call lawyers. Of course, everyone in the Soviet system was a government employee, and the number of Soviets who "practice law" in our sense was very small, and without much influence on the government. The Soviet representatives at the conference were all middle echelon people, who were engaged in work similar to that done by many government lawyers in the United States—in the State Department, the Defense Department, the Environmental Protection Agency, and so on.

Our group went to Moscow early in July, 1983. It included the President of LANAC, Alan Sherr, and the Executive Director of LANAC, Anthony Sager. Among others in the delegation were Professors Roger Fisher and Abram Chayes, of the Harvard Law School, former Senator John Culver, Adrian DeWind, of New York, John Downs, former President of the Vermont Bar Association, and George Bunn. The arrangement was that the Soviets covered our expenses while we were in the Soviet Union, but we paid our own transportation costs to Russia, and back. We were put up at the Sovietskaia Hotel, a pre-World War I structure of high ceilings and some elegance.

Our meetings were held at the House of Friendship, which we had regarded as a relatively benign instrument of Soviet propaganda. Full simultaneous translation was provided, and, in the Russian fashion, an ample supply of bottles of various soft drinks was always on the table, together with cakes and other items, at the morning and afternoon breaks.

The meetings in 1983 were rather tense. There was strong feeling on both sides, and this was evident in the discussion

which, however, was always kept under control, and was generally constructive. At the time, the Soviets were very much concerned about the forthcoming installation of Pershing Missiles in
Europe, which they rightly regarded as a serious threat to them.
Much of the discussion turned on this question.

I regarded my role in the meeting as a rather broad one. I
was not an expert on arms control or on nuclear weapons
generally. I did feel, though, quite strongly, that no matter
what the experts might do, we would not make any real progress until we could develop an atmosphere of better understanding and of mutual trust. With this basic thought in mind,
I sat up very late one night writing a speech in which I tried to
advance this view.

The Russians had said early in the meeting that they had
great difficulty in negotiations with us because any agreement
reached had to be approved by a two-thirds vote in the Senate.
They said that in negotiations we urged them to give us more
because we would have to have it in order to obtain approval
from the Senate. Then, they said, we give you more, and the
Senate does not approve the treaty. Thus, they felt that they lost
their negotiating ground, and yet did not get a treaty. I undertook to give a brief explanation of our system, talking about
checks and balances, and said "there is no likelihood that these
constitutional elements will be changed. On the whole, the
people are happy with them and regard them—as they are intended—as safeguards of the rights of the people." I suggested that
"it would be useful if the Institute of U.S. and Canada Studies did
some extensive study on our constitutional limitations—on their
history, their origin [and] their operation over the years." I
added that "this should of course be wholly objective, not designed to show how bad or difficult we are, but designed to show
exactly what we are, so that you can take this into account in
negotiations and in entering into any agreements with us."

The sense of my speech was contained in several paragraphs
which I set out below in full.

The second fundamental problem is more difficult to
state but it is nonetheless real. We do not hate the Soviet
Union or its people. On the contrary, we rather admire
you—first, for your valiant role in the Great Patriotic War.
But we admire you, too, for many of your accomplishments. You have no unemployment, and we have not
satisfactorily solved that problem. You have less hooligan-
ism than we do. You are a more orderly people than we
are. To mention a small but irritating matter, I never see
graffiti in the U.S.S.R.

Griswold, Memoirs—12

But, here is the rub. Large numbers of our people are
seriously alarmed by you and your actions. And that, I
suggest, is something you should carefully take into account
in discussions of nuclear arms control. There are many
reasons for this. Some are old, but not forgotten: the Cuban
missile crisis and Czechoslovakia. Others are more recent,
actions in Africa, and by your Cuban ally in Angola. And
then Afghanistan. This goes back to one of your tenets—
your support of "wars of national liberation." I know that
this is firmly held. But I know, too, that you can change.
When I was here in 1961—at a Dartmouth Conference—we
were told very firmly that the U.S.S.R. would never allow
any sort of inspection. That, it was said, was a violation of
your sovereignty, and an affront to your dignity. But then
came satellites—where you were the leaders—and your position on inspection and verification has considerably modified.

Our political and economic systems are different. Each
has its merits. Why don't we live and let live? Why do you
press so hard to extend your system? Near here in Moscow
there is a large sign which reads "Communism will prevail."
That, coupled with "wars of national liberation" tends to
frighten many of us. Why don't you change it to "Communism is best," and let the marketplace determine in the
course of time?

Finally, let me suggest that this is in your own interest.
You are rightly concerned about our nuclear capacity, and
would like to see it limited, as we would, under proper
conditions. You are concerned about some of President
Reagan's statements, as I am. But I think you should give
serious thought to the suggestion made by Professor Bunn
that you share a great deal of the responsibility for President
Reagan's election in 1980, particularly by your actions in
Afghanistan. That frightened many people in our country
and led them to support the man they thought would make
the strongest President.

The United States is a very complex country and hard to
understand. It speaks with many voices, and it changes its
views with bewildering frequency. I urge upon you, though,
the importance of continuing your efforts to understand us
and why we act as we do. Some of the things we do that
trouble you are the result of external stimuli for which you
have some responsibility. If you recognize that fact, and
take it into account, it may prove to be the key which will
solve the problems of nuclear arms control. That is a lot to

ask, I know, but I do believe it is very much in your own interest.

For better or for worse, I remain an optimist. I believe we will resolve these problems. It is indeed the only way, and I am glad to have had the opportunity to participate in this thoughtful discussion.

The leader of the Russian delegation was Ambassador Vadim Sobakin. He had been a professor of international law, and also Permanent Representative of the U.S.S.R. to UNESCO. At the time of our meeting, he was also a consultant to the International Department of the Central Committee of the Communist Party. I think that, at the beginning, we tended to look on him as the "Commissar" whose role was to see that the discussions at our meeting did not get out of hand.

The tensions of the time, and the nature of the Soviet reaction is shown by what followed. I had endeavored to be conciliatory, and to share blame and to recognize our responsibility for misunderstandings with our Soviet friends. But Sobakin's response showed that I had badly failed in my endeavor. He said:

> You call on us to understand the United States. I ask *you* to understand the features of the Soviet Union. All countries who deal with you *do* take the factors Griswold mentioned into account, and sometimes we're sorry.
>
> United States is a great country, and elections are very important to you. But the year before elections all activity dies away, and once the new President is elected, activity is still asleep for the year afterwards. The world cannot wait for two years while this process goes on. Elections don't solve problems, and maybe they become more serious while the world has to wait.
>
> Often Americans and the western world don't want to understand us. You say that the Soviet Union must be "liberalized" before we can have normal relations. Who gives you such a right? Why do you have the right to amend and change the social order in the Soviet Union? You passed the Jackson Amendment [tying preferential trade benefits to human rights].

Then he added:

> Do we say we won't talk to the United States until racial discrimination is eliminated? The right to work is guaranteed in our constitution, which is not done in the United States, so should that affect normal relations?

You are concerned about our actions, and your mass media is responsible. * * * We can explain the motives of any action. I can explain Cuba, the Horn of Africa, Afghanistan and our attempt to deploy missiles in Cuba close to the United States. Now the United States is threatening to deploy missiles close to the Soviet Union, so do we threaten nuclear war?

Dean Griswold was concerned about our slogan "Communism will prevail." *Don't* take it that it will be imposed by force. We have confidence in historical determinism. Other countries will take that route. When they ask for help, we give it according to international law. We support national liberation movements. Resolutions of the United Nations General Assembly authorize help. It is a duty. When South Africa attacks Mozambique and Mozambique asks for help, we respond. Revolution is not exported from our side. Only when conditions are ripe in a country is social change possible.

When you choose a new president every four years, what about international obligations? Can a new administration decide what it wants to observe? Things that happen in an earlier administration can become invalid. How can we manage our affairs with that kind of a background?

United States actions trouble us. Czechoslovakia and Afghanistan are our neighbors. But what about the United States in Lebanon—at an earlier time and now? In connection with the Persian Gulf, how can that threaten the United States? How do we threaten the United States when we help our friends? Why does the United States claim to be a power with global interests? We don't claim such global interests and don't recognize the United States' global rights. The globe is not a sphere of rivalry.[3]

Thus it is obvious that my effort was not immediately successful. I do believe, though, that it opened the door through which we entered for a better understanding.

Actually, over the years, I have developed great respect for Mr. Sobakin, and we have become good friends. In addition to his other offices, Sobakin was Vice President of the Association of Soviet Lawyers, which provided the Soviet delegates at our meetings. I have no doubt now that it was in this capacity that

---

3. The quotation from Ambassador Sobakin's response comes from notes made by John H. Downs, of St. Johnsburg, Vermont, a member of the LANAC delegation.

he was designated as chairman of their group. In an interview given early in 1990 to John H. Downs, Mr. Sobakin said: "We Soviet lawyers believed that the time had come to start frank relations with our American counterparts, as opposed to formal meetings when we might get together, curse each other and part. What we had in mind was to establish the relations that would enable us * * * to try to prove that Soviets and Americans are able to communicate and to arrive at joint opinions."

In the same interview, he said:

As for the Americans, personally for me, I would like to underscore personally, and here I cannot help being subjective, Erwin Griswold has been the most valuable. I liked to describe him as "a peaceful conservative."

The first most memorable happening that I might recall is our showdown with Erwin Griswold that occurred in 1983, and you might recall it as well. Erwin started lecturing us. Quite candidly, I cannot stand being lectured, and I understand that you cannot stand it either. We have had many debates afterwards with my "best enemy" Erwin Griswold, but what kept me wondering was the naive conviction of Americans that their way of life is the best one and anyone who is trying to have it their own way are if not crazy, then at least somewhat not of this world—and in that sense Erwin is the best representative of the American people. You stubbornly fail to realize that there are other, different from yours, ideals, which doesn't make them any less humane or precious to people who abide by them. Those ideals are not defective, they are just different from yours. On the one hand this naive conviction always moves me, on the other it makes me indignant, but most of all it troubles me. Guided by that naive belief in the advantages of American system, of American values, the U.S. goes to Grenada and Panama, considering it nothing out of the ordinary. But others consider it as a total abnormality. For God's sake, try to understand that there are values that are not less humane, though they are not yours.

Thus that first showdown with Erwin was one of the most memorable happenings. But we managed to find an acceptable way out, which is a merit of our conferences. We keep on arguing, but we avoid fist-fights. We don't call each other bad names, rather we try to clear up issues.

Later in that first meeting in 1983, we were taken to Tbilisi in Soviet Georgia. We travelled in an Aeroflot plane, and had a gorgeous and spectacular view of the Caucasus Mountains. In

Tbilisi we met with Georgian lawyers and officials. On the evening of July 14, 1983, my seventy-ninth birthday, we were taken to the dacha of the Procurator General of Georgia, high in the hills above Tbilisi. It was a beautiful moonlit night, and the dinner was outdoors, with the long tables covered with innumerable bottles of many kinds of drinks. As is customary in the Soviet Union, there were many toasts. Vasiliy Vlasihin accompanied our party, and I was deeply touched when he rose and proposed a toast in honor of my birthday, saying that he regarded me as his "American father."

Shortly after our return to the United States, the disaster of the Korean Airlines Flight 003 occurred, and this greatly increased tension for a while.

The arrangement was that meetings would be held each year between the two groups, alternately between the two countries. Thus, the meeting in 1984 was held in the United States, at Airlie House in northern Virginia. Although the discussions were still intense, there was clearly better understanding at this meeting than at the meeting in Moscow in 1983. We knew each other, and there was an appreciable development of trust and confidence.

During one of the recesses at the 1984 meeting, I went up to Vadim Sobakin and said: "Vadim, you have mellowed." This was said in the presence of an interpreter, since Sobakin's English was limited. The interpreter spoke, and I saw that Vadim's face fell, with what could be called a scowl. So I asked the interpreter "What did you say?" He replied: "I used a word which means 'gone soft.'" That, of course, was not what I meant, and I could understand that Vadim was annoyed. I explained this to the interpreter and he called the other interpreter, and they had an extended discussion. As a result of this, the interpreter spoke again to Sobakin, and his face lit up. I again asked the interpreter what he had said, and he replied that he had used a word which means "become more flexible." And he added, we do not think that there is any word in Russian which corresponds exactly with the meaning of "mellowed" as you used it. But Sobakin smiled broadly, and seemed pleased. This is another instance of the difficulty of international communication, with different languages involved.

The gathering in 1985 was held in Moscow in the new International Trade Center, which had been sponsored by Armand Hammer. One of the matters discussed at this meeting was the phased-array radar at Krasnoyarsk. We had been briefed on this at the Defense Department prior to our departure from the United States. When we raised the question on the first day of the meeting, we were solemnly assured that there was no such thing. We said that we understood that there was, and thought that the matter ought to be discussed, since it appeared to be a violation of the A.B.M. Treaty.

The Soviets came back the next day, and said that they were now informed that there was such a structure, but they were not free to talk about it. We replied that the understanding at our meetings was that we would make agreed statements. If they were not free to talk about this, we would have to issue a statement in which we said that the question was raised but that the Soviet delegation advised us that they were not free to talk about it. We felt that that would be unfortunate. Then, they came back the third day and said that they were free to talk about it. As a result of this, we put together an agreed statement in which we said that this was a matter of considerable importance, and that the question whether the structure violated the A.B.M. Treaty should be the subject of full discussion between the two governments. As is well known, the Soviet Government later made public announcement about the huge structure, agreed that it violated the A.B.M. Treaty, and stated that it would be dismantled.

This is a nice example of the situation in the Soviet Union at that time. I believe that the Soviet delegates, or nearly all of them, were entirely honest when they told us on the first day that there was "no such thing." Information in the Soviet Union then was so highly compartmentalized that people generally did not know about such matters, even among the intellectuals and relatively high-level bureaucrats. When, following our first session, they reported what had happened, they were told that the phased-array radar did exist, but that it could not be discussed. Then, after the session on the second day, they reported that this would lead to embarrassment, and they were given freedom to discuss it. It could well be that Sobakin's influence with the Central Committee of the Communist Party led to this change in approach.

It was later in the same week that General Secretary Konstantin Chernenko died. At first there was no announcement, but we were soon given the information by Vadim Sobakin. That evening, we watched proceedings on the television, and so learned that Mikhail Gorbachev had been chosen as his successor. Our friends among the Soviet delegates seemed greatly pleased by this choice, and they advised us that there would be a substantial change in Soviet–American relations. Little did they—or we—see then how great those changes would be.

One of the important developments of this meeting in 1985 was the appearance of Sergei Plekhanov as one of the Soviet delegates. Mr. Plekhanov is an outstanding person, who has contributed much to the improvement of Soviet–American relations. He is not a lawyer, but is more like what we would call a "political scientist." He is now the Deputy Director of the Institute for U.S. and Canada Studies. He is also a speechwriter and adviser to President Gorbachev. Moreover, his English is perfect (all learned in the Soviet schools), and he frequently appears on television, shown in the United States, as the spokesman for the Soviet Union following an important international conference.

Plekhanov and I have become friends, and have developed great mutual trust. I feel sure that he takes as much satisfaction as I do in the greatly improved state of relations between the United States and the Soviet Union which has occurred in recent years.

In January, 1988, I participated in a completely separate discussion with Soviet representatives. This was held under the auspices of a church group in Holland, at the "de Burght" Conference Center at Brugh–Zeeland, Holland, not far from the Belgian border. The primary purpose of the meeting was to discuss freedom of religion in the Soviet Union, and there was a very impressive group of delegates from several countries, including Fedor M. Burlatsky and Alexander Sukharev, together with two priests of the Orthodox church, on the Russian side. Among the Americans present were several former Congressmen, Mrs. Rosalynn Carter, Rev. Theodore Hesburgh, Judge Abner Mikva, and Dr. S. Frederick Starr, President of Oberlin College. There were also delegates from Belgium, Czechoslovakia, France, Hungary, Italy, The Netherlands, Poland, Sweden, Switzerland, the United Kingdom, and West Germany.

The discussion was full and frank, on a number of topics. Perhaps the most interesting exchange was that between Fedor M. Burlatsky and Rosalynn Carter. Mr. Burlatsky spoke on "A Soviet View of Human Rights," and Mrs. Carter spoke on "An American View of Human Rights." The discussion showed a considerable difference in emphasis, and helped to highlight the problems which have arisen between the two countries.

In his presentation Mr. Burlatsky emphasized the right to employment, the right to housing, the right to education, and the right to health, pointing out that under the Soviet system all citizens were guaranteed housing and employment, and also education and health. He said that these things were far more important than freedom of speech, or absolute freedom of religion. He pointed out the problems of housing and employment in the United States, and how relatively little concern they give us, and how relatively little we do about them.

When Mrs. Carter spoke, she emphasized individual freedoms, like free speech and free press, protection against unlawful arrest and seizure of property, the "right to privacy," and so on. It was obvious that this made little impact on the Soviet delegates, who clearly felt that the freedoms they sought to protect were more important than those which we emphasized.

In the discussion following these remarks, I pointed out that the Soviets have no history or tradition of the freedoms we cherish. They have no "Freeborn" John Lilburne, nor William Penn, nor George Mason, nor Thomas Jefferson, and the other great figures who helped shape our convictions and practices in these areas. It was obvious that there was no meeting of the minds, each side feeling that its approach was the really important one in protecting human rights.

Later the discussion turned to freedom of religion. I suppose that the two Orthodox priests were included in the Soviet delegation to show how great their tolerance of religion really was. Here again the discussion was full and frank. However, several of the Soviets urged us not to press too hard. They said that there were important developments taking place in the Soviet Union and that it was more likely that they would achieve useful results if this was left to Soviet initiative and did not appear to be the result of outside pressure.

In March 1989, I attended another meeting in Holland as part of a very small group, including two delegates from the Soviet Union. This time, the subject for consideration was a draft of a proposed statute for "freedom of conscience." We went over this line by line, and urged that its title be changed to "freedom of religion." The principal Soviet delegate, Yuri Rosenbaum, of the Institute of State and Law, said that this was impossible, since the official view in the Soviet Union had been atheism, which was, as he said "no religion," and how could they adopt a statute providing for "freedom of religion," which he said would automatically exclude atheism. We tried to explain this on the ground that atheism is simply one form of religion, and that it would be protected as well as every other form, under a general guarantee of the freedom of religion. Mr. Rosenbaum seemed to be very skeptical about this.

In the fall of 1990 our papers carried a story that the Soviet Parliament had adopted a statute guaranteeing "freedom of religion." This occurred on October 8, 1990, and the text was published in Pravada on the following day.[4]

In 1988, the Soviets, sponsored by LANAC, came to the United States and visited several cities, including Boston, Philadelphia, Chicago, and San Francisco. By this time, the atmosphere had cleared considerably, and there were quite free and frank discussions among the delegates. However, the fact that the meetings were held for only a short time in each of a number of cities prevented the sort of comprehensive consideration and the statement of conclusions which had been characteristic of the previous meetings.

In October, 1989, there was a further LANAC meeting in Moscow, held in the "House of Friendship" as was the first meeting in 1983. The difference between the two meetings was startling. The tension had disappeared, and there was great freedom of discussion, with self-criticism on each side. It was really impressive to hear one of the Soviet delegates say, in open meeting, that "We must get rid of telephone justice."—meaning that they must eliminate the practice which occasionally occurred of a telephone call from party headquarters to the judges in a particular case, giving instructions as to how the case should be disposed of. We were also asked questions about crowd control, "the limitations of freedom of speech," and so on.

After several days in Moscow, the American delegates went by train to Minsk, in Byelorussia, where we were taken by a military bus, with escort, to an army establishment some thirty miles out of the city. There, we witnessed the destruction of nuclear launchers pursuant to the Treaty signed by President Reagan and Chairman Gorbachev on December 8, 1987.[5] We were, of course only unofficial observers. However, there were six United States Army officers present, including a Colonel. At the close of the session, we met, separately, with the Russian Colonel and the American Colonel. It was perfectly clear that neither of these military men wanted to have anything to do with a nuclear war.

---

4. A translation of the full text appears in the Current Digest of the Soviet Press, vol. 24, p.6. For a discussion of an earlier draft of the law, see Berman, Griswold and Newman, "Draft USSR Law on Freedom of Conscience, with Commentary," 3 Harv. Human Rts. J. 137 (1990).

5. This is the so-called INF Treaty, entitled Treaty between the U.S. and the U.S.S.R. "on the Elimination of Their Intermediate–Range and Shorter–Range Missiles." The full text is set forth in 45 Congressional Quarterly Weekly Report 3070 (1987), and in 27 Intl. Leg. Materials 90 (1988).

We then continued to Leningrad, where we had a series of meetings with citizen groups. They wanted us to tell them how to find suitable candidates for political office, and then, how to get them elected so that they could fill that office. It was an exciting challenge for them, and it was not easy for us to make constructive suggestions, particularly in view of our limited knowledge of the details of the Soviet situation.

Whether the LANAC activity had any influence in the development of events is hard to tell. As I sometimes have said, it was very likely only a "drop in the bucket." But you never get the bucket filled without accumulating drops, and each drop is important. We did make contact with upper middle level Soviet figures, and there is some indication that some of the matters which we discussed were known about and understood at fairly high levels. For example, in Mr. Gorbachev's New Year's Day Address in 1989, there were phrases which can be traced to discussions held in LANAC meetings in 1988. Sergei Plekhanov, who attended those meetings, has been something of a spokesman for the Soviet Union on international television, and has been a speech-writer for Mr. Gorbachev. Whether there was any connection here is unknown, and is not important. What is important is that there has been an almost unbelievable change in the atmosphere between the Soviet Union and the United States. Thousands of people, indeed millions of people, have contributed to this change, on both sides, and delegates to the LANAC meetings, both Soviet and American, have been among those who have contributed thought, ideas, and effort.

The meeting for 1990 was actually held in January, 1991. Again, there were sessions in several cities in the United States. I attended the meetings which were held in Washington.

The complete change in atmosphere which was apparent in Moscow in 1989 continued at the Washington sessions. The discussions were wide-ranging and friendly. Little concern was shown, on either side, with respect to the use of nuclear weapons between the United States and the Soviet Union. The primary concern was with respect to proliferation—the problems arising as the result of the spread of nuclear weapons to other countries. There was extensive discussion of problems within the Soviet Union. For example, the matter of the removal of Soviet troops from Poland presented difficulty to the Soviet delegates with respect to housing and employment for the troops, if they were brought back to the Soviet Union.

One consequence of the new developments, and the new atmosphere, was a change in the name and structure of LANAC. Instead of being called the Lawyers' Alliance for Nuclear Arms

Control, it is now the Lawyers' Alliance for World Security, or LAWS for short. The organizing group in Boston has turned over the leadership to a broader group, and the headquarters of LAWS is now located in Washington. I continue as a Vice Chairman of the Board of LAWS, and I am glad to work with others in helping to resolve the problems which are sure to continue, in one form or another, between the United States and the Soviet Union or whatever successor may develop to "the former Soviet Union."

CHAPTER XII

Practicing Law in Washington

⟳⟲

A. BECOMING A "WASHINGTON LAWYER"

Early in 1973, after my retirement had been announced by the Nixon Administration, I received a telephone call from H. Chapman Rose, a long-time friend, inviting me to have lunch with him and L. Welch Pogue. Rose had been for many years a partner in the Cleveland firm of Jones, Day, Cockley & Reavis, and Pogue was the managing partner of its Washington affiliate, known then as Reavis, Pogue, Neal & Rose.[1] I had had little contact with him in the intervening years. I was asked if I would be willing to join the firm as a partner when my service as Solicitor General was completed. My response was that I was much pleased to be asked, and definitely interested. At that time, though, some other proposals had been made to me, including one on behalf of a prominent Boston firm, which would mean returning to Massachusetts, and another to be the resident partner in London of a prominent New York firm. I asked if I might have time for further consideration, and this was kindly extended to me.

Later in the spring, I advised Messrs. Rose and Pogue that I would accept their proposal.[2]

---

1. Rose was a member of the Class of 1931 at the Harvard Law School, and he had been Under Secretary of the Treasury in the Eisenhower Administration. Pogue was a graduate of the Michigan Law School, who then received a graduate S.J.D. degree at the Harvard Law School in 1927. He had written an article which was published in the volume of the Harvard Law Review for which I was President. Pogue, "State Determination of State Law and the Judicial Code," 41 Harv.L. Rev. 612 (1928).

2. This meant, of course, that I could not participate as Solicitor General in any case involving the two related firms. However, no such potential conflict developed.

There were several factors that motivated this decision on my part. In the first place, Jones, Day was essentially a Cleveland law firm, and I had supposed in the early days that I would spend my life practicing law in Cleveland, as my father had done. A second factor was that perhaps half of the lawyers in Jones, Day were students of mine, or old friends with whom I had worked in American Bar Association or other activities. Finally, the firm offered me an opportunity to do appellate work, which I was qualified to do, and which I enjoyed. An overriding element was the wonder I had long had as to whether I really could have been "a lawyer." During my long period of academic work and government service, I was doing legal work, but it was not the same as being a lawyer working for clients, which I regarded as the great role of the legal profession. I have known good academics and fine lawyer public servants who would not have been successful in practice. I had long wanted reassurance as to whether I could make my way in practice, as my father did.

Now, thanks to the Jones, Day offer, and the opportunity it provided me, I know. It has added much to the fun, and has been very gratifying. Accordingly, at the age of sixty-nine, I became for virtually the first time a lawyer in private practice, starting as a partner, without the usual period of "associate" status. At the time, I assumed that this arrangement might last for four or five years. As things have worked out, I was a partner for sixteen and a half years, and have been called senior counsel since. These have proved to be interesting and stimulating years, with much work in practice, and much time made available for various sorts of "public service" activities.

People often ask me which part of my career I have liked best. My response has been that I have liked all parts equally, but that the succession has been ideal. I have greatly enjoyed my association with the other lawyers in Jones, Day and it has been a privilege to watch the growth and development of the firm in the intervening years. When I entered the firm, the only stipulation I made was that I should have "no administrative responsibilities." This restriction has been fully honored at all times. Thus, I have had an opportunity to watch developments, yet as an observer with no need to participate in the decisions.

When I came to the firm on July 1, 1973, the Washington Office was located at 1100 Connecticut Avenue, across the street from the Mayflower Hotel. It occupied two floors in a not very large building. At that time, there were about forty lawyers in the Washington office. Two other lawyers, James T. O'Hara, Jr. and Joseph S. Iannucci, also came to the firm on July 1, 1973, and it is obvious that the effort was to build up capacity in the field of taxation.[3]

The only adverse reaction I had when I came to the office was that the library was minuscule. I had the benefit of the Harvard Law School library for many years, and the library of the Department of Justice is excellent. I could well understand that a private law office could not maintain a very extensive library, and I thought to myself that this is simply one of the problems of private practice, and that I would have to make the best of it. In recent years, the Jones, Day library has been greatly strengthened, and there are excellent arrangements for interlibrary loans among the Washington law offices. I am much impressed, now, at how much can be provided so quickly by our office library.

For a few weeks, I was provided by the firm with a temporary secretary. Very shortly, though, Jeanette Moe arrived on the scene. She had had a period in the Foreign Service, being stationed in Trinidad and Tobago, and in Sierra Leone. I have been very fortunate that she has been with me ever since. She has proved to be extremely capable, as well as agreeable and helpful, and patient with my impatience. In recent years, when electronic equipment has taken over the law offices, she has kept up fully with developments, while I have not even tried to do so.[4]

On the day I came into the office, I was handed the papers in a Supreme Court case.[5] This came from the Cleveland office of

---

3. When my first partnership "draw" came, I found that I received two checks. Jones, Day, Cockley & Reavis in Cleveland and Reavis, Pogue, Neal & Rose in Washington, were actually separate firms, and I, along with the others who entered on July 1 were half-partners in each firm. This surprised me a bit, but made no difference to me. In due course, I learned that there were differences of view between some members of the Washington office and the Cleveland office. This eventually led to a break-up of the firm in 1979, with the dissenting members leaving to establish the firm of Crowell & Moring. Both firms have prospered. Though there was a measure of bad feeling at the time, this has long since dropped away. Crowell & Moring has been very successful in its field, and Jones, Day (by this time known as Jones, Day, Reavis & Pogue) has enjoyed an unprecedented period of growth and development.

4. Among other things, she has "keyed in" all of the manuscript for this book. One of the things that I do notice is the ease with which corrections and changes can now be made. In the old days of typewriting, a small change, a word or a letter, meant typing the whole page over again. Now it is made in a matter of seconds. This means, among other things, that one is free to make changes which, in the past, would have been left unmade.

5. Kewanee Oil Company v. Bicron Corp., 416 U.S. 470 (1974).

the firm, and involved a question of the Ohio law of trade secrets and its relation to the federal patent law. The petitioner's business involved the development of synthetic crystals, and it was able to produce crystals of greater size than its competitors. Employees of the petitioner, who had signed agreements not to disclose trade secrets, left, and began working in a competitor company, after which it was able to produce equally large crystals. Our client sought to enjoin these former employees from making use of the trade secrets, but lost in the Court of Appeals on the ground that Ohio trade secret law was pre-empted by federal patent law. My task was to prepare the brief on the merits in the Supreme Court, with the assistance of the lawyers in the Cleveland office who had previously worked on the case. Later, in January, 1974, I argued the case before the Supreme Court. The decision, which came down in May, was favorable to the petitioner, with two dissenting votes. This was, of course, a very gratifying entry for me into the field of private practice.

Shortly after coming to the office, I left for several weeks, pursuant to an arrangement which had been made while I was still Solicitor General. I went for three weeks as a visiting teacher at the Law School of the University of Illinois in Urbana–Champagne, Illinois.[6] I had visited this school while Albert J. Harno was in his long and productive period as dean. By 1973, the school had a fine new building, and I had a number of academic friends on its faculty. The arrangement was that I would give some lectures,[7] and participate in classes as might prove to be useful and agreeable to the teachers in charge of the classes. It was while I was at Illinois that Archibald Cox was discharged by President Nixon as Watergate Special Prosecutor, and I witnessed the "firestorm" there.

From the beginning, I was quite busy in the office. As was understood and planned, I spent a considerable portion of my

6. Before leaving for Illinois, I made a quick trip to Tallahassee, Florida, where I gave a talk at the dedication of the building which had been built there for the Florida Board of Bar Examiners. This has been published as "In Praise of Bar Examinations," 47 Fla. Bar J. 644 (1973). Before giving this talk, I was jokingly promised that if I gave it, I would be made a member of the Florida Bar. This has not yet happened.

7. Among other things, I gave a David C. Baum Memorial Lecture on Civil Liberties and Civil Rights. This was published as "The Supreme Court's Case Load: Civil Rights and Other Problems," 1973 U. of Ill. L. Forum 615.

Later, in 1974, I gave the Frank Irvine lecture at the Cornell Law School. This was published as "Rationing Justice—the Supreme Court's Caseload and What the Court Does Not Do," 60 Cornell L.Rev. 335 (1975).

time on "public service" activities, of one sort or another. I never came close to the so-called two thousand billable hours, but I did have billable hours in the range of twelve hundred per year, for most of my years in practice. Cases in the Supreme Court, were, of course, the highlight of my work. Much more time was spent on numerous unsuccessful petitions for certiorari—some of which I felt should have been granted. I also prepared a number of fairly elaborate opinions, including an interesting one on the liability of a public utility for losses from a nuclear energy catastrophe.

B. Commission to Investigate the Internal Activities of the C.I.A.

Early in January 1975, President Ford established a Commission to Investigate the Internal Activities of the Central Intelligence Agency. Vice President Nelson A. Rockefeller was appointed chairman of this committee. Other members included John T. Connor, former Secretary of Commerce, C. Douglas Dillon, former Ambassador to France and Under Secretary of State, Lane Kirkland, Secretary–Treasurer of the AFL–CIO, Lyman L. Lemnitzer, retired General in the Army and former Chairman of the Joint Chiefs of Staff, Ronald Reagan, former Governor of California, and Edgar F. Shannon, Jr., former President of the University of Virginia. I was asked to be a member of the Commission, and accepted.

This was a very interesting assignment. The Commission was quickly organized, and an excellent staff was put together. Hearings began in January, and were held regularly on Monday of each week for the following several months. This presented some problems for me, as I had long been committed to teach during the month of February at the University of Florida Law School, in Gainesville, Florida. This meant that I had to travel from Florida to Washington—with a change of planes in Atlanta—on every Sunday during that period, and then return to Florida late Monday evening, or on Tuesday morning. I had to leave my wife in Florida while I was gone, but we were able to work out the assistance which she needed in my absence.

At the meetings of the Commission, witnesses testified, and reports were made by the staff. A number of subjects were investigated, including mail intercepts by the CIA,[8] information

---

8. During the course of the hearings, the CIA made available to each member of the Commission the files which it had developed with respect to that member. In my file, I found copies of letters which I had written to Soviet citizens whom I had met when I went to the Soviet Union in 1961, as a member of the Dartmouth Conference. The letters were quite

collected on dissident Americans (this was known as Operation CHAOS), involvement of the CIA in improper activities for the White House, collection of foreign intelligence within the United States by the CIA, including foreign telephone call information, the testing of behavior-influencing drugs on unsuspecting subjects within the United States, the manufacture and the use of documents, indices, and files on American citizens, and various allegations respecting the assassination of President Kennedy. On the last of these items, the Commission concluded that there was no credible evidence of any CIA involvement.

The Commission seemed to me to be a remarkably fine one. The level of ability and of government experience was high. Unfortunately, ex-Governor Reagan made little contribution. He attended somewhat less than half the meetings of the Commission, and his participation—other than the anecdotes he told— was minimal.

The Report of the Commission was largely prepared by the staff,[9] in close consultation with the Commission. It was transmitted to the President on June 10, 1975. It is a careful and thorough summary and evaluation of the charges which were made with respect to activities of the CIA within the United States.[10] The report reached a number of conclusions and made a substantial number of recommendations, many of which have been carried out.

Despite the thoroughness of the report, I do not believe that it made a major impact, and it is not now widely remembered. This may have been due to the fact that shortly after President Ford established the Commission, a similar Commission was set up by Congress, under the leadership of Senator Frank Church of Idaho. This received wide publicity at the time, since most of its hearing sessions were open to the public, while those of the Rockefeller Commission were not publicized. The two reports covered essentially the same ground, and were not inconsistent in their conclusions. For a number of years, the reports, taken

---

harmless, but it made me sad to think that my government had opened my mail, without warrant, or any sort of probable cause.

9. Among the senior counsel on the staff were Ernest Gellhorn, then a professor at the University of Virginia Law School (he later was dean of the law school at Case Western Reserve University, and the managing partner of my law firm's office in Washington, and then in Los Angeles), and William W. Schwarzer, who later became a United States district judge in San Francisco, and director of the Federal Judicial Center in Washington.

10. Report to the President by the Commission on CIA Activities Within the United States (Government Printing Office, 1975).

together, had some moderating influence on the CIA, as far as domestic activities were concerned.

C. Investigation in Namibia

Perhaps the most interesting matter I dealt with in my practice, and in some ways the most successful, was brought to me by the Lutheran World Federation in New York, and, through them, with the Lutheran World Federation in Geneva, Switzerland.[11] At that time, thirty-one black Africans were held incommunicado in South West Africa, or Namibia. The assignment, essentially, was to go there and see what I could find out about these people. This matter came up late in 1975.

The first thing I had to do was to obtain a visa, since Namibia was then controlled by South Africa, and transportation was necessarily through Johannesburg. Fortunately, it had always been my policy to maintain reasonably good relations with the South African Ambassador, Roelof (Pik) Botha. There was some delay, and on several days I packed my bag in the morning only to learn during the day that the visa had not come through. Eventually, it did arrive. I flew first to Geneva to talk with my principal client. I travelled from New York, and then from Geneva to Johannesburg on the Swiss airline, and found it perhaps the most agreeable air travel I have ever experienced. I stayed a day in Geneva, and received many details about my mission, including a list of the names of the detained persons. I was also told about two Lutheran Bishops in Namibia. They had been advised of my coming, and I was instructed to get in touch with them.[12]

My flight from Geneva passed through Nairobi and Dar es Salaam, and arrived at Johannesburg at about 4:00 p.m. I was surprised when I was paged by a representative of the Foreign

11. This matter came to me on the recommendation of a Harvard Law School alumnus, H. Ober Hess, a prominent Lutheran layman who practices in Philadelphia.

12. A high proportion all of the people in Namibia, black and white, are Lutherans. This is because the area was first settled from Europe by Germans and by Finns, many of whom are Lutherans. Two Lutheran missions were established in what is now Namibia. These are about four hundred miles apart, but because of the nature of the country, there was little communication between them, except through Europe. One of the missions was established by Germans; the other was established by Finns. There was a Bishop heading the church in each of the two areas. There was no intermingling between the white Lutherans and the black Lutherans. The white Lutherans in South West Africa had mostly come from South Africa, and were affiliated with the Lutheran church in South Africa.

Office, who cleared my passport and baggage. He also asked me to call the former Ambassador, J.S.F. Botha, at his home in Pretoria. I eventually reached Mr. Botha, and told him that I would like to have an appointment to meet with Mr. Kruger, the Minister of Justice.

On the next day, a Sunday, I met with Mr. John Rees, the Director of the South African Council of Churches, who briefed me extensively. At one o'clock I took several of my South African friends to lunch at the Carleton hotel, where I was staying, and learned much from them. They told me that little had appeared in the local newspapers about the matter with which I was concerned. That evening, Mr. and Mrs. I. A. Maisels took me to supper, and gave me much information about Windhoek, the capital of South West Africa, and, in particular, about attorneys there. Judge Maisels had served for several years on the Supreme Court of Rhodesia (later Zimbabwe), after extended practice in Johannesburg.

On Monday, November 17th, I went to Pretoria and called on the American Ambassador and his political officer. The next morning, I called on Mr. Botha, who was very cordial and helpful. He advised me that my appointment with the Minister of Justice would be at two-thirty that afternoon. I had assumed that this meeting was simply a courtesy call, and that it would probably be over in ten minutes or so. Instead, it lasted for nearly two hours, and there was a broad interchange. In due course, I asked for permission to see the accused in Windhoek, and also to go to Ovamboland (on the Angolan border) to see Bishop Auala. (Mr. Kruger had never heard of Bishop Auala). Later in the meeting, Mr. Kruger said that I could see the accused, but that I would have to do it with a security officer present. I had hardly expected it would be otherwise, so I raised no objection. Mr. Kruger then said that he would not let me go to Ovamboland. Because of the military situation, permission to go there could only be given by the Minister of Defense, and he (Kruger) was sure it would not be given. However, Mr. Kruger said that he would see that Bishop Auala was brought to Windhoek. This gave me concern, because I feared that the Bishop would understandably be upset if he was approached by South African police who wanted to take him to Windhoek.

The whole problem arose because of the death of a Chief in Ovamboland. The South African police said he had been shot by members of the Southwest Africa Peoples Organization (SWAPO). People in SWAPO said the Chief had been murdered by the South African police. They said that he had formerly cooperated and had been useful to South African interests. But in due course, they said, the Chief had recognized "the winds of change." He had ceased to cooperate, and had become helpful to the SWAPO interests. It was for this reason, SWAPO adherents said, that the South Africans decided to do away with him.

I never knew what the actual facts were. There was no way that I could investigate the facts, and, in any event, they were not relevant to my inquiry. My role was to find out what I could about the present situation of the detained persons, and to help in the process of finding legal assistance for them.

In the course of my discussion with Mr. Kruger, I told him that I thought it was hard to justify the detention of so many people, incommunicado, for so long, now over three months. He said it was necessary because the investigation was still going on. I added, further, that it was impossible to arrange for counsel when there were no charges, and that he and I, as lawyers, knew that the defense needed time for investigation too.

Mr. Kruger advised me that there would be a trial, and that it would be held in Windhoek. He also said that the trial would start on Monday, December 1st. He went on to say, quite vigorously, that my coming had nothing to do with the fixing of the date of the trial.

Mr. Kruger then called in the head of the South African police, General Primsloo, and the head of security, General Geldenhuys. He explained the situation to them, and said that they would go to Windhoek with me. I immediately said that I did not want to go *with* them, since I did not want to create any impression on arriving in Windhoek that I was cooperating with them or that I was in their hands.

There was one flight a day from Johannesburg to Windhoek, and I took it on Wednesday morning, November 19, 1975. On arrival in Windhoek, I waited until the two South African police officers had left the plane, and then got off myself. Almost immediately I heard my name called on a loud speaker. As a result, I met Ralston H. Deffenbaugh, Jr, who had completed his second year at the Harvard Law School, and was spending a year in Windhoek as a missionary with the Lutheran Church. He told me that both of the Bishops were in Windhoek, and that one of them would make his car available to me, and had assigned Deffenbaugh to be my aide in Windhoek. He then took me to the Kalihari Sands Hotel, and then to the Evangelical Lutheran headquarters, where we had lunch, prepared by a Sister from Karlsruhe. Through them, I made contact with General Geldenhuys, who said that I could see the detained persons the next day, and that he would pick me up at my hotel.

That evening, I had an unusual experience, for I integrated the Kalihari Sands Hotel. For many years, the hotel was limited to "Europeans," that is to white persons. But the law had been changed effective on November 1, 1975. I asked Bishop Auala and Dr. deVries, the President of the Evangelical Lutheran Church, both non-Europeans, whether they would be willing to have dinner with me at the hotel. I said that I did not want to embarrass them in any way, and that I would fully understand if they felt that this was not desirable. Their immediate response was that they would be delighted to have dinner with me. They said that they had wanted to go there, but had not done so because they felt that it would be better if they went on invitation, rather than simply walking in themselves, and thus seeming to force themselves on the situation.

I was curious as to what might happen at the dinner, and the answer is that absolutely nothing out of the ordinary happened. I also invited Mr. Deffenbaugh and the four of us were shown to a table and nicely taken care of without any untoward reaction from anyone. Among other things, we talked about the attorneys I should arrange to represent the accused in the forthcoming trial.

On the next morning, November 20th, I went with General Geldenhuys, and a Colonel Schoon, to the Windhoek prison on the north side of the city near the African location called Katatura. On the way to the prison, I learned that I was to see all of the persons who might be charged, but that I would not see the persons who were detained as witnesses. When I protested this, and said that it was not in accordance with my understanding with the Minister of Justice, General Geldenhuys told me that he could "practically guarantee" that none of the persons I did not see would be charged. He also told me that I could complain by telephone to the Minister of Justice about my failure to see the other detainees, but I did not think that that would be worthwhile.

At the Windhoek prison, I saw four women detainees, whom I understood were nurses. All were young, in their early twenties. All were Ovamboes. None of them was on any list of names that I had seen.

All my interviews were through interpreters. As I talked with each person, I felt that I had to say that they should be careful, that government representatives were present, and that anything they might say could be used against them. This, of course, dampened their responses, but I did not feel that I could risk having them say things to me which might be used to injure them, where I could provide no sort of privilege. None of the women claimed any sort of abuse, but two of them did make specific requests with respect to their families.

After I had seen the four women, we went to the Windhoek police station, where I saw three men. They were dressed in simple, clean, civilian clothes. All appeared well, and showed no signs of physical abuse, from a merely visual examination while they were clothed. Of these three, two were on my list, but there was another whose name did not appear on any list which I had seen.

I advised all of the detainees I saw that Bishop Auala and Dr. deVries had asked me to tell them how concerned they were and to tell them that everything in their power was being done to be of assistance to them. I added that Bishop Auala and Dr. deVries would undertake to see that they had counsel.

That afternoon, I had a long interview with Dirk Mudge who was Chairman of the Constitutional Conference of South West Africa. Mr. Mudge made it plain that he is a third generation "Southwester." He said, most emphatically, that he was not a South African, and that he had no interest in South Africa except as it can help South West Africa. Mr. Mudge was very impressive—calm, quiet, thoughtful. He had worked very hard on the constitutional questions, seeking to bring people together.

That evening, Deffenbaugh and I went to the Daan Vilgoln Game Reserve, about twenty miles to the west of Windhoek. We saw a number of wild animals, mostly wildebeest, and there was a spectacular view of Windhoek in the distance to the east as the sun was setting behind us.

The next day, November 21, 1975, I went to the office of Lorentz & Bone, attorneys in Windhoek, where I met with Mr. John S. Kirkpatrick and his partner, Colin de Preez. In the first few minutes of our meeting, I was able to straighten out a misunderstanding which had developed, in another matter, between the firm and Dr. deVries. I then outlined the situation, told them of my meeting with the Minister of Justice in Pretoria, and of my meeting with some of the detained persons. I told them that I had no authority to retain attorneys, but that I was communicating at once with Dr. deVries and Bishop Auala. Mr. Kirkpatrick said, with no hesitation, that they would be prepared to take the representation if they were asked. We then discussed advocates who might be briefed by the Lorentz & Bone firm. When I left the attorneys' office, Deffenbaugh was waiting for me, and he took me at once to the Evangelical Lutheran Center where deVries and Auala were expecting my arrival. After discussion, it was agreed that Lorentz & Bone would be retained, and that the recommendation of that firm as to advocates would be followed.

On Saturday, November 22nd, I returned to Johannesburg, where I arrived late in the morning. I had lunch at the residence of Mr. and Mrs. Maisels, and then went to the Jan Smuts Airport, where I took off in the late afternoon. The plane arrived in Zurich the next morning. I quickly transferred to a plane which took me on to Geneva. It was Sunday, so I had a quiet day walking about the city, and enjoying the beautiful view across the lake. On Monday, November 24th, I reported to the Lutheran World Federation. The next day, I flew back to Washington.[13]

Much activity was crammed into this short trip, which appeared to be an appreciable success. Although there was uncertainty as to who had been detained, and how many, about ten were released shortly after my departure from South Africa, and ten more were released a little later. Eventually, seven persons were brought to trial, the four women whom I had seen, and the three men. The trial was not held at Windhoek. Instead it was held in Swakopmund, on the South Atlantic coast, a little over 100 miles west of Windhoek.

At the trial, the four women were convicted of having made small contributions—about $5 each—to SWAPO. Each received a five-year sentence, this being the minimum sentence under the Suppression of Communism Act. Of the three men, one was acquitted, and two were convicted, and received death sentences. The next stage of the matter was an appeal to the Appellate Division of the Supreme Court of South Africa, and my friend Issi Maisels was retained to present this case.

While the preparations were under way, it was discovered that, during the course of the trial, two employees of the attorneys, Lorentz & Bone, had been systematically making available to the South African police Xerox copies of statements made by witnesses, including some made by the defendants themselves. There had been suspicions about this during the course of the trial, because of the nature of some of the questions which were asked by the advocate for the State. (The information had been made available to the South African police, and they used it in preparing their advocate. There was no suggestion that the advocate knew the source of the information.)

The first problem was to get this into the record of the case. This required a special proceeding in the trial court, to supplement the record, and this was skillfully accomplished. With this material in the record, I felt that the prospects on appeal were good. I told my Lutheran World Federation clients that, though the South African courts had a harsh system to administer, I did not think that they would stand for this sort of conduct. With some research, I found a number of parallel instances in the United States cases, and I sent this material to Mr. Maisels.

---

13. Shortly after my return, I put together a letter to the Minister of Justice. This gives some further facts and details, and also presents some arguments which I hoped that he would consider. The full text of this letter is printed in Appendix A, at pp. 407–414, below.

However, he wisely felt that American authorities might not be very influential with the Appeals Court. Knowing that South African law was closely related to Scottish law, since both have Roman law origins, he found some Scottish decisions which were very helpful.

When the appeal was heard by the Appellate Division of the Supreme Court of South Africa, they unanimously reversed the decision because of the misconduct which had occurred in the trial.[14] I had feared that a decision of this sort would simply mean that the accused would be rearrested, and held for further trial, as so often happened under the South African law. However, the court, in a later order, held that, under the circumstances, a fair new trial would be impossible in view of the material already made available to the prosecution. Accordingly, the court not only reversed the judgments of the court below, but it also held that the charges should be dismissed, and that the accused should be released.

Thus ended an assignment which was, of course, of great interest to me. The net result, after a considerable amount of stress for the accused, was a complete victory. About one-third of the arrested people were released within a few days after my visit to South Africa. Another third were released a few weeks later. Eventually, as I have indicated, all of the accused who were put on trial were either acquitted, or the prosecutions were dismissed pursuant to the decision of the Appellate Division.

After an interval of six months or so, I wrote a letter to Chief Justice Rumpf of the Appellate Division, whom I had met at the time of the Treason Trial in 1958. I told him of my background participation in the case, and of my respect for the decision. In due course, I received a courteous, though non-committal response.

D. The Growth of Jones, Day—The "National Firm"

When I came into the firm in 1973, there were, as I have indicated, about forty lawyers in the Washington Office. The firm had originally started in Cleveland, and the Cleveland office had around one hundred and fifty lawyers at that time. There was a small office in Los Angeles with three lawyers in 1973. This office was located in Century Park, in west Los Angeles, and not downtown.

---

14. The decision is reported, in Afrikaans, in State v. Mushimba and others, [1977] 2 So. Afr. 829. An English translation of the Afrikaans is available in a separate volume using the same page designation.

The several offices grew in size, but not substantially. Although I knew little of the background, I became aware of some differences of opinion. There was, for example, some resistance in Washington to the opening and enlargement of the Los Angeles office.

Because I had stipulated that I should have no administrative responsibilities, and because I thought that my tenure was necessarily limited, I had little interest in the long-range problems of development, and I made few inquiries about these matters. I did know that a group in Washington were opposed to further development of the firm, while, on the other hand, the management of the firm, mostly located in Cleveland, were anxious to pursue their concept of "the national law firm."

The firm has always had a rather unique management structure. In the first place, Jones, Day, Cockley & Reavis (and its successor, Jones, Day, Reavis & Pogue) has always been a single firm (except for the dual firm situation in Washington), with all members of the firm, wherever located, contributing to and drawing from a single fund. Moreover, there has long been a "managing partner" who has wide authority over all decisions, including the opening of new offices, admission to the partnership, and partnership shares. He operates in association with a "partnership committee" and an advisory committee. This "one man rule" goes so far that the managing partner designates his own successor, though this must be confirmed by three-fifths of the advisory committee and two-thirds of the partnership committee. The "advisory committee," though nominated by the managing partner, must be confirmed by the partners. In practice, the managing partner gives close attention to the advice of these committees. As the firm has grown in size, each office has a managing partner, who reports to the "national managing partner." Somewhat to my surprise, this system appears to me to work extremely well. It has brought together a fine group of lawyers, who work together productively, and in harmony.

During my time, the managing partners (now called "national managing partner") have been John W. Reavis, Allen C. Holmes and Richard W. Pogue. All of these have been fine lawyers, of broad outlook, with apparently boundless energy, fine personalities, and good judgment.

On February 14, 1979, Allen Holmes, then the national managing partner, took steps to dissolve the separate partnership in Washington, pursuant to provisions in the partnership agreement. His purpose was to separate out the persons, all in Washington, who opposed geographical growth of the firm, and thus to set the stage for the further development of "the national law firm." Of course, this action (known at the time as the "Valentines Day

Massacre") stirred up a great deal of feeling, some of it rather bitter. There was a period when lawyers in Washington were given their choice of which group they would stay with. I took some time to get a better understanding of the situation. During this time an attractive proposal was made to me to join with the dissidents. However, after ten days or so, I sent around a memorandum saying that my choice would be to stay with Jones, Day.[15] This was, in considerable measure, for the same reasons that led me to accept the invitation to join the firm in the first place, namely that many of my former students and friends were in the firm, and because of my association with Cleveland. I felt, too, that the concept of the "national law firm" was a very interesting one, and I thought that it would be fun to watch the development during the time that was available to me.[16]

Eventually the situation quieted. Good judgment was used on both sides, and all issues were settled on a friendly basis. The dissident group established the firm of Crowell & Moring, and they have grown and prospered in the ensuing years. The Jones, Day lawyers found a new location at 1735 Eye Street, N.W., and the move there was completed in June, 1979. After the break-up, there were about forty lawyers in the Washington office of Jones, Day. I was told that my memorandum had been helpful in persuading a number of lawyers to stay with the firm. I have never doubted that I made the right choice.

Since that time, development of the firm has been steady and sound. The Los Angeles office became more solidly established. In due course, a Dallas office was opened, and an office in Austin, Texas came at about the same time, and an office in Columbus, Ohio was also opened. At about this time, the Los Angeles office was moved downtown, and a separate office was established in Irvine (Orange County), California.

In 1986, the long-established firm of Surrey & Morse joined with Jones, Day. As a result, a substantial office was opened in New York, together with offices in London, Paris and Riyadh, Saudi Arabia. After that, offices were opened in Chicago, and in Atlanta and Pittsburgh in the United States, and foreign offices were added in Geneva, Brussels, Frankfurt, Hong Kong, Taipei and Tokyo. This made a total of nineteen offices, of which ten are in the United States, and nine are in foreign countries, scattered quite widely over the northern half of the world.

---

15. A copy of this memorandum appears in Appendix B, at pp. 415–419, below.

16. The division of the firm is described, with understanding, in N. Lemann, "The Split—A True Story of Washington Lawyers," Washington Post Magazine, March 23, 1980, p. 18.

This growth has been much more than I anticipated, but it has been carefully planned and well-managed. It has been a particular source of satisfaction to me to see the development of the offices in other countries. My interest in this, of course, goes back to my part in the development of International Legal Studies at the Harvard Law School in the 1950s and 1960s. All of this, it seems to me, helps to bring the world closer together, and facilitates contacts and development between the different countries of the world. Much of the work done by the firm in the international field consists of advising American clients in planning and handling transactions which they may have in foreign countries. There is also a substantial amount of work in advising foreign clients with respect to their transactions in the United States.

During the period of eighteen years since I joined Jones, Day, there has been an enormous development in office machinery. When I came to the firm in 1973, there was one big Xerox machine in the Washington office. It did good work, but it did not collate pages, or do two-sided copying. Now we have many Xerox machines, and make too many copies. Eighteen years ago, we had many typewriters, and soon graduated to the IBM Selectric typewriters, and various models which made copies very rapidly. But they were typewriters, with much clatter. Now, the typewriter has almost disappeared.[17] With word processors it is quieter, and much easier to make corrections.

With respect to communications, the developments have been similarly spectacular. All of the offices of Jones, Day are inter-connected by telephone, as are the word processors. For quite a while, we had the telecopier, which is now known as Fax. Now we have electronic mail and interconnecting word processors, so that a draft of a brief made in my office can come off the printer in Dallas or Chicago at the same time it is produced here. All of this has, of course, contributed substantially to the development and to the smooth functioning of the "national law office." Together with electronic services like LEXIS and WESTLAW, it has also greatly increased the costs of providing legal services.

I found the general run of law practice in the office interesting, and usually stimulating. I enjoyed working with the other lawyers. I usually had an associate assigned to me on each matter, and I particularly liked the opportunity to work with

---

17. I still have one in my office which I use slowly, with one finger of each hand.

these younger lawyers, and to watch their growth and development. A number of them are now partners in the firm, playing leading roles in the firm's activities.

I also spent time interviewing applicants for positions, including those who were seeking opportunities as summer clerks. The summer clerkship was, of course, a rather new development. When I was a student in law school, the almost universal reaction of active practitioners was that a law student would be of no use in the office, and there was no thought that one might be hired during his law school days at an appreciable salary. On the contrary, law students were advised to use the summers in other kinds of work—to broaden their experience, or to get the benefits of travel. That was the course which I followed, and I think that this worked out very well.

The applicants from Harvard Law School were usually assigned an interview with me. This gave me an opportunity to keep informed about development at the School, and to learn about the work of the teachers whom I had helped to bring on the faculty. It was clear that summer clerks could make substantial contributions, if properly assigned. One of the summer clerks who worked with me was Raymond J. Wiacek, who was with us in the summer of 1974, after his first year at the Harvard Law School. I was then working on a case involving failure by a hospital to pay withholding taxes, resulting in an effort to collect the taxes from some of the trustees of the hospital. Ray very competently prepared for me abstracts of all of the cases—some two hundred in number at that time—which had involved this issue. For reasons too long and complicated to recount here, that case dragged on for sixteen years. In the process, Ray became an associate in the firm, and then a partner. He took on more and more responsibility for the case, and eventually, in 1990, obtained an unqualifiedly favorable disposition of the matter. I regretted that I had not been able to bring about this result, but I watched with interest and admiration as he successfully handled it in the later years.

My work involved a good deal of travel, most of it to nearby places like Philadelphia, New York, Boston, and Cleveland, but I occasionally made longer journeys. I attended the meetings of the American Bar Association, the American College of Trial Lawyers, and the Council of the American Law Institute. I also attended the meetings of the American Philosophical Society, and continued to preside at the two Continuing Legal Education programs undertaken each year by the Federal Tax Institute of New England, Inc. I argued cases in Philadelphia, New York,

Boston, Columbus, St. Paul, Denver, Carson City, New Orleans, and Richmond.[18]

———

Beginning in September, 1970, Harriet and I began going to a sylvan retreat at the very northern tip of New Hampshire. This is known as The Glen, in the town of Pittsburg, near the Canadian border. Our son Bill and his wife had found the place while they were travelling by automobile from Montreal to Boston. They immediately recognized its suitability for us, since it had a level entrance, and a few bedrooms on the ground floor in the main lodge. Thus, it was feasible for Harriet to get about without difficulty.

This was really a fishing lodge. Most of the guests spent their days on the First Connecticut Lake, and the nearby ponds and streams. I have never been interested in fishing. But there was quiet, and cool summer weather. Because of my interest in boundaries, I spent time walking along the international boundary between the United States and Canada, and made two "expeditions" to the source of Hall's Stream, which the Webster–Ashburton Treaty of 1844 established, quite erroneously, as the source of the Connecticut River. From the forty-fifth parallel, the boundary line goes north on Hall's Stream to its source, and then starts to follow "the highlands which separate the waters which flow into the Atlantic Ocean from those which flow into the St. Lawrence River." There is one place along the boundary where it passes close to a quiet pond, known as Boundary Pond. It can be reached by a relatively easy climb from the Canadian side.[19]

I did a certain amount of reading while we were at The Glen, including all of Jane Austen, during one summer, and the Brontës another summer. But I also "wasted" a good deal of time, doing jigsaw puzzles, and other relaxing things. I never had time to do anything like that while at work in Washington, or in Cambridge.

We usually drove from Washington to The Glen, a distance of about seven hundred miles. Of course we broke the journey, sometimes in Belmont, and in other years in various places in Connecticut and Vermont. I tried to find different routes for the

———

18. Through my career I have had at least one case in every Circuit of the United States Courts of Appeals, except the Eleventh Circuit. I did have cases, however, in the Fifth Circuit before the Eleventh Circuit was separated from it.

19. See pp. 24–25, 49–51, above.

trip, but the choice was rather limited without extending the distance and time unduly.

E. FURTHER TRAVELS

Interesting opportunities for travel continued. As I have already indicated, Harriet and I went to the Soviet Union in 1974 on the invitation of Professor Nikiforov. On this trip we met many people, and had an opportunity to build our understanding of the Soviet Union and its problems.

In 1979, we went to England, primarily to attend the meeting of the Association of Public Teachers of Law, which was held at the University of Warwick, near Coventry, that year. On our return to Cambridge in September, 1975, a very pleasant event occurred.

During the closing years of my tenure as dean at the Harvard Law School, two new buildings were built. One of these was Pound Hall, named after my distinguished predecessor, "my Dean," Roscoe Pound. The other was designated, at the time it was built, as the "Faculty Office Building." Much to my surprise, I was informed by Dean Albert M. Sacks late in the spring of 1975, that the Harvard Corporation had voted to redesignate this building as "Griswold Hall," and that there would be a ceremony to confirm this metamorphosis, which would take place in September. Accordingly, Harriet and I planned our trip to England so as to return to Cambridge just before the appointed day.

The weather was beautiful. There was a large gathering of friends, and several speakers.

I have never known who was basically responsible for this kindly action. I have assumed that Dean Sacks made the basic recommendation, but it may well be that President Derek C. Bok, who was my immediate successor as dean, played the crucial role. In any event, I am very grateful for this accolade.

In 1985, we attended the meeting of the American Bar Association in London, and saw again many of our old friends in England. This was followed by a motor trip which took us to Edinburgh, followed by another fascinating stay in the Lake District in Cumbria. In 1988, we went to Tokyo, where I participated in meetings of the United States/Japan Bilateral Session on A New Era in Legal and Economic Relations, sponsored by the Citizen Ambassador Program. Again we met several friends, including Professor Fujikura. There are now several hundred Japanese lawyers who have studied at the Harvard Law School.

Dedication of Griswold Hall, Harvard Law School, September, 1979.
Left to right: Dean Albert M. Sacks, President Derek C. Bok, E.N.G.

F. SUPREME COURT CASES—AND SOME OTHERS

In the office, the work continued. Altogether, I had eleven cases before the Supreme Court during these years. One of these was *United States Steel Corporation v. Multistate Tax Commission*,[20] involving the validity of the Multistate Tax Compact, which had never been ratified by Congress, as the Constitution seems to require.[21] This document, drafted in 1966, had been adopted by twenty-one states at the time of the litigation. It was called a Compact. It was surely, at least in form, an "Agreement" between the States. It looked like a compact, and had the effect of a compact. Yet the Supreme Court, in an opinion by Justice Brennan, held that the Compact was valid without the approval of Congress. The decision was five to two, with Justice White, joined by Justice Blackmun, dissenting. I know that "you can't win them all," but the loss of this case has been perhaps my greatest professional disappointment. I have never been able to see any ground to justify it, except perhaps the strained view that political considerations of federal-state relations warrant the conclusion that this multistate document, so clearly an agreement, is not an agreement within the Compact Clause.[22]

Later, in the same Term, I argued the case of *Federal Communications Commission v. National Citizens Committee for Broadcasting.*[23] The question there was the validity of regulations made by the Federal Communications Commission restricting "cross-ownership" of newspapers and television stations—that is, the ownership by the same organization of both a newspaper and a television station in the same community. The Supreme Court, in an opinion by Justice Marshall, without dissent, sustained the validity of the regulation, and at the same time, reversed the decision of the United States Court of Appeals for the District of Columbia Circuit which had held that the regula-

---

20. 434 U.S. 452 (1978).

21. Article I, Section 10, clause 3 of the Constitution provides: "No State shall, without the Consent of Congress, * * * enter into any Agreement or Compact with another State, or with a Foreign Power * * * ."

22. Later that same year, I successfully argued a somewhat complicated tax case, of no general consequence. Frank Lyon Co. v. United States, 435 U.S. 561 (1978). This led to a rather indignant article by my friend Professor Bernard Wolfman, indicating that I had "misled" the Supreme Court by some of the arguments I made. B. Wolfman, "The Supreme Court in the *Lyon's* Den," 66 Corn. L.Rev. 1975 (1981).

23. 436 U.S. 775 (1978).

tion *must* be applied retroactively, that is, it must bar "cross-ownership" in all cases, even where that had occurred in the very early days of broadcasting, and had been long-continued, and was in effect when the regulation was adopted.

A case which was both interesting and elusive to prepare and argue was *Loretto v. Teleprompter Manhattan CATV Corporation.*[24] This involved a New York statute which required a landlord to permit a cable television company to install its cable facilities upon his property. The case arose in New York City, where most of the residences were close together and the installation occupied portions of the roof and the side of row houses or apartment buildings. The question was whether the installation of this equipment constituted a "taking" of property for which "just compensation" is required under the Fifth and Fourteenth Amendments of the Constitution.

There are numerous cases in this area, and they are hard to reconcile. For example, "historical districts" can be established, and no compensation is required, though this seriously limits the power of the owner to use or to dispose of his property.[25] As the Supreme Court said in the *Loretto* case,[26] "the Court has often upheld substantial regulation of an owner's use of his own property where deemed necessary to promote the public interest." In preparing the brief for the case, we tried very hard to find cases where the Court had held that the occupation of an actual "segment" or "piece," small as it might be, had been sustained. We thought of mailboxes in an apartment house, but there the landlord always consents to the taking. At any rate, we lost the case, as the Court held that the laying of the wires constituted a "taking." In the long run, though, the decision did not prove to be of much importance. Following our loss in the Supreme Court, the case went to trial in the local courts in New York. The jury's function was to determine "just compensation," and it found that the damages sustained by the land owner were only nominal in amount.

My appellate work continued, not in overwhelming quantity, but I kept busy. I had a number of other cases in which I appeared before the Supreme Court.[27] One of these cases de-

---

24. 458 U.S. 419 (1982).

25. See, for example, Penn Central Transportation Co. v. New York City, 438 U.S. 104 (1978), involving Grand Central Station in New York.

26. 458 U.S. at 426.

27. These included Aaronson v. Quick Point Pencil Co., Inc., 440 U.S. 257 (1979), involving a question of patent royalties under a contract,

serves special mention. This is *Copperweld Corp. v. Independence Tube Corp.*[28] The question there was whether a corporation could "conspire" in an antitrust matter with its own wholly-owned subsidiary. The case is particularly interesting because the Court had held, principally in opinions by Justice Black, that an unreasonable restraint "may result as readily from a conspiracy among those who are affiliated or integrated under common ownership as from a conspiracy among those who are otherwise independent."[29] Similar statements were made in a series of other cases.[30] This was an imposing mass of authority to overcome, and there is no doubt that Justice Black would have fought vigorously to maintain his position if he had still been on the Court. However, the Court held that "the coordinated activity of a parent and its wholly-owned subsidiary must be found as that of a single enterprise for purposes of § 1 of the Sherman Act. A parent and its wholly-owned subsidiary have a complete unity of interest."[31] This decision left me with a feeling that I had participated in clarifying an area of the law which had long gone a bit astray because of Justice Black's powers of persuasion among his brethren.

———

Over the years, I had a number of cases in lower courts, both state and federal. Several of these were criminal cases, an area

———

after the patent application was rejected; Lewis v. BT Investment Managers, Inc., 447 U.S. 27 (1980), involving the power of Florida to keep an out-of-state investment management company from doing business in Florida; National Gerimedical Hospital v. Blue Cross, 452 U.S. 378 (1981), involving a question of the power, under the antitrust laws, of a local "health system agency" to bar construction of a hospital building; R.J. Reynolds Tobacco Co. v. Durham County, 479 U.S. 130 (1986), involving the power of a state to impose property taxes on tobacco stored in a "customs-bonded warehouse," and Rockford Life Ins. Co. v. Illinois Department of Revenue, 482 U.S. 182 (1987), where the question was whether the interest on bonds issued by the Government National Mortgage Association, a U.S. Government corporation, was subject to state taxation.

28. 467 U.S. 752 (1984).

29. United States v. Yellow Cab Co., 332 U.S. 218, 227 (1947).

30. See United States v. Griffith, 334 U.S. 100 (1948); Schine Chain Theatres, Inc. v. United States, 334 U.S. 110, 116 (1948); Kiefer-Stewart Co. v. Joseph E. Seagram & Sons, 340 U.S. 211 (1951); Timken Roller Bearing Co. v. United States, 341 U.S. 593, 598 (1951); Perma Life Mufflers, Inc. v. Int'l Parts Corp., 392 U.S. 134 (1968).

31. 467 U.S. at 771.

in which I had had some experience during my service in the Department of Justice. Some of these cases were handled on a *pro bono* basis, or partially so.

In *Calhoun v. United States,* the defendant had been convicted of armed robbery. On appeal, he contended that his conviction should be reversed because the counsel who had been assigned to represent him in the trial court had not given him effective assistance. The Chief Judge of the District of Columbia Court of Appeals (the local court, as distinguished from the federal court) at that time was Theodore R. Newman, Jr., a graduate of the Harvard Law School in the Class of 1958. Whether that had anything to do with it, I do not know, but I was assigned by the D.C. Court of Appeals to represent Calhoun on appeal.

My assistant in the matter was one of our young lawyers, Linda S. Gillespie—now Linda Stuntz.[32] We worked hard on the case, and developed a number of arguments which seemed to me to be worthy of presentation to the Court.[33] These included such things as violations of the defendant's privilege against self-incrimination in the course of the government prosecutor's argument to the jury, a "missing witness" argument, and eyewitness identification of the accused at the trial after the witnesses had been shown a line-up photograph immediately prior to their identification of the defendant.

I argued the case before the court of appeals, and lost. The court held that each of the matters referred to was error, but said that the defendant's counsel had made no objection, and that they were "not persuaded" that any of the erroneous actions "constituted plain error." [34]

I then filed a petition for certiorari in the Supreme Court, since there were some decisions holding that failure to file a petition constituted "inadequate assistance by counsel." While the petition was pending, and the defendant was in custody, he feigned illness, and was taken to a hospital. He was put in a room on the second floor, and was supposed to have a guard at all times. However, in the middle of the night, he went out through a window, climbed down a drainpipe, and disappeared.

---

32. She has since served as minority staff director for the Energy and Commerce Committee of the House of Representatives and as Deputy Assistant Secretary of the Department of Energy.

33. In the course of preparation we went to the District of Columbia jail to interview our client—an interesting experience.

34. (1980)—not reported.

At this time, it became my duty to advise the Supreme Court of this fact. I did so, and the Court denied certiorari.[35]

In 1982, Clifford Case, former Senator from New Jersey and an old friend of mine from Fund for the Republic days, came to see me in my office. He asked me if I would handle the appeal for Senator Harrison A. Williams, who had been convicted in one of the ABSCAM prosecutions. I agreed to do so, and spent a great deal of time on this matter over the next year or more.

The charge, in substance, was that the Senator had sold his services for the promise of a large sum of money to a man he understood to be an Arab sheik. The indictment also included counts charging bribery, conflict of interest, conspiracy, and other matters. The government's basic evidence consisted primarily of audio and video tapes surreptitiously recorded during an undercover operation. One of our young associates, Clare L. Shapiro, was assigned to work with me on this matter. This was a difficult case, and very much in the public eye. I was able, though, to maintain my usual practice of declining to talk with the press about any case in which I was acting as counsel.

When the Government first acted, it knew of no particular crime, or threat of crime, which it was seeking to uncover. Instead, the government made special arrangements with a district court, and obtained probation for one Melvin Weinberg, who has been characterized by a court of appeals judge as a "career swindler."[36] The FBI knew from experience of Weinberg's propensities since Weinberg had previously worked for the FBI as an informant. They let Weinberg "free-lance", with only general instructions from supervisors. They encouraged results at all costs by awarding bonuses based on the number and importance of persons convicted, and by shielding Weinberg from criticism when abuses were pointed out by attorneys in the Newark, New Jersey District Attorney's office.

The thing that bothered me the most about the situation was that, prior to the Government's use of Weinberg against him, Senator Williams was known to have had an alcohol problem.

---

35. Calhoun v. United States, 450 U.S. 924 (1981). Thereafter, the defendant was apprehended in Maryland, and charged with a murder there. He was convicted, and received a death sentence. However, that conviction was set aside by an appellate court. I have not been involved in any of the subsequent proceedings.

36. This phrase was used by Judge Sloviter in United States v. Jannotti, 673 F.2d 578, 581 (3d Cir.1982).

He had struggled with it, and had conquered it, to his credit. The record in the case showed that this fact was known to Weinberg. Indeed, Weinberg participated in the writing of a book about his activities, called "The Sting Man." In it, Senator Williams was described as "typical of many former alcoholics, warm wax waiting to be impressed."[37] It disturbed me greatly, and still does, that my government promoted this sort of activity, designed to take advantage of a man's weakness, and to promote a charge of crime where there would have been no basis for such a charge without the government's activities.

I argued the case before the Second Circuit Court of Appeals in New York on October 7, 1982. The court consisted of Chief Judge Friendly, presiding, and Judges Jon O. Newman and Amalya L. Kearse. The decision went against Senator Williams, unanimously, to my great regret.[38] I still believe, as Chief Judge Brown said in another case,[39] that, though this was not a case of entrapment, "its kinship to entrapment is not that the act of a government representative induced the commission of a crime. Rather, it is that the means used to make the case was essentially revolting to an orderly society." And he added, "there comes a time when enough is more than enough—it is too much. When that occurs, the law must condemn it as offensive whether the method used is refined or crude, subtle or spectacular."

Another case came to me through a former student who was a friend of a son of the defendant. The charge was the making of false statements under oath in a deposition, and the defendant had been convicted in the federal district court in Pittsburgh.

The charge was based on statements made by the defendant during a civil deposition. This testimony related to a contract which the defendant contended he had made with Conrail for the purchase of Penn Station in Pittsburgh. The essential basis of the charge was that the defendant had substituted certain pages in the contract.

After the trial, it developed that certain documents which had been excluded from evidence at the trial had been mistakenly taken to the jury room by a bailiff. The transcript of the deposition which was erroneously taken to the jury room, and seen by the jurors, had the defendant saying "and then finally, I

37. R.W. Green, The Sting Man: The Inside Story of ABSCAM (New York: 1981) 159.

38. United States v. Williams, 705 F.2d 603 (2d Cir.), cert. denied, 464 U.S. 1007 (1983).

39. Williamson v. United States, 311 F.2d 441, 445 (5th Cir.1962).

typed one up." This made it appear that the defendant admitted that he had created the typewritten inserts. However, the reporter who recorded the defendant's deposition signed an affidavit, given to an FBI agent, in which she said that there was an error "on page 71 at line 23. The 'I' should be corrected to 'he' typed" so that the deposition transcript should have read: "Finally, he typed one up."

The court of appeals held that it was error for the jury to have seen the erroneous transcript, particularly since it had been excluded from evidence, and it reversed the conviction of the defendant, and ordered him released pending a new trial. At this point, the defendant's son came to me and said that of course I would represent the defendant at the new trial. He was very complimentary about my work, and said that it was essential that I should try the case. I knew that it would be malpractice for me to undertake to try it. I have had no experience in trial courts, and, in any event, it would not be wise for a senior citizen from Washington to undertake to conduct a criminal trial in Pittsburgh. The son persisted. He said that I was letting them down. He said that I had undertaken to handle the case, and that I was now backing out on them. I finally told him that I would try to help them to find qualified counsel.

I then telephoned to a friend in Pittsburgh, and asked him to suggest to me some lawyers in Pittsburgh, in good standing, who had had substantial experience in local criminal defense practice. He gave me the names of several former assistant United States attorneys, and also the name of the president-elect of the Pittsburgh Bar Association. In due course, one of these lawyers was selected. The first thing that he did was to move to recuse the judge who had presided at the first trial, and had announced that he would preside at the new trial. The defendant's trial counsel apparently had enough background to lead to the judge's withdrawal. The new trial was then conducted, and resulted in acquittal. I was very much moved when the defendant, within fifteen minutes after the jury verdict was received, called me on the telephone and thanked me in fulsome terms for what I had done for him. I pointed out that the real work had been done by the attorney at the second trial. I was pleased, though, that he expressed his appreciation so clearly.

One afternoon in late 1986, I received a telephone call from a man who was held in a federal prison in Wisconsin. A good many such calls have come to me. They involve, of course, *pro bono* work, and one could build up a very large law office on such matters, if he could afford it. I usually try to give some general advice to the callers, find out what kind of representation they have had before, and indicate where I feel that they might get help. There was something about this man's voice, though, which attracted my attention. I asked him to tell me a little more about his case, and he responded by telling me that his conviction (for a series of bomb explosions at the Indianapolis racetrack) had been based on identification evidence given by witnesses who had previously been hypnotized. Indeed, they were not hypnotized by the FBI or other federal authority. That would have been forbidden by the rules of the FBI, unless there had been previous authorization from Washington. What had happened was that the FBI referred the witnesses to the state police. They carried out the hypnosis, and then reported the result to the FBI. It seemed to be a close analogy to the "silver platter" doctrine which had been repudiated by the Supreme Court.[40]

I told the man who called me to send me the papers, and said that I would consider it. If it turned out that his case would involve the use of post-hypnotic evidence in a substantial way, I said that it might be possible for me to handle it. When the papers came, I found that the testimony of witnesses after hypnosis was a major part of the identification evidence against the defendant. The case had already been decided by the Seventh Circuit Court of Appeals, which had affirmed the judgment of conviction.[41] Two associates worked with me on this matter, Michael J. Farley and Timothy R. Payne. In due course, we produced a substantial, and, I felt, a reasonably strong petition for certiorari, which was filed on February 27, 1987.

Most unfortunately, one of those unforeseeable events occurred just before we started to work on the petition. There was another case, *Rock v. Arkansas,*[42] in which the Supreme Court granted certiorari late in 1986. The *Rock* case involved a related but fundamentally different question, though it raised an issue of the use of post-hypnotic testimony. The difference was that in the *Rock* case, it was the defendant who had had himself hypnotized, and the Arkansas court held that he could not testify in his own defense.[43] This decision was, in due course, reversed by the United States Supreme Court in its decision in the *Rock* case.

---

40. See Elkins v. United States, 364 U.S. 206 (1960).

41. United States v. Kimberlin, 805 F.2d 210 (7th Cir. 1986), rehearing denied, January 9, 1987.

42. 288 Ark. 566, 708 S.W.2d 78 (1986).

43. The Arkansas Supreme Court had held that "the dangers of admitting this kind of testimony outweighed whatever probative value it may have," quoted in Rock v. Arkansas, 483 U.S. 44, 48 (1987).

The distinction between the *Rock* case and that in the *Kimberlin* case (where it was the *defendant* who was resisting the use of post-hypnotic testimony) seems to me to be obvious and substantial. Nevertheless, though the Supreme Court held the *Kimberlin* case until after it had announced its *Rock* decision, it then denied the *Kimberlin* petition.[44] This has bothered me, for it seems to me a rather clear example of the fortuitous nature of the Supreme Court's exercise of its certiorari jurisdiction. If the *Rock* case had not just arrived at the Court before the *Kimberlin* petition was filed, the Court might well have granted the *Kimberlin* petition. In any event, the precise issue involved in the *Rock* case was so different from that in the *Kimberlin* case (because the hypnotized evidence there was used *against* the defendant) that the *Kimberlin* case might well have merited review.

I have never met Kimberlin, though I have met his mother and sister. My only contact with Kimberlin has been by mail and telephone. He seems to me to be a very substantial and impressive person. There is some intimation that the person who committed the crimes was Kimberlin's older brother (now deceased), which could easily have led to a mis-identification. Kimberlin has had several other matters, relating to parole and other questions, and he has had substantial help from other lawyers in the Washington area. They have been able to shorten the time somewhat for his eligibility for parole.

There are two additional cases which merit reference. The first of these involved Michael T. Rose, who is now a State Senator in South Carolina. Mr. Rose is a graduate of the New York University Law School. He was also a reserve officer in the Air Force. In the latter capacity, he had attracted some resentment when he represented a number of Air Force cadets who had been subjected to charges at the Air Force Academy in Colorado. He sought admission to the Bar of Colorado, and was admitted there, but only after some controversy, not all of which was conducted in open hearings.

Thereafter, Mr. Rose applied for admission to the Bar of the Supreme Court of the United States. He was admitted there on March 8, 1982. Chief Justice Burger, joined by Justice O'Connor, wrote a dissenting memorandum.[45] Mr. Rose found himself in a very awkward position. He had been admitted to

---

44. Kimberlin v. United States, 483 U.S. 1023 (June 26, 1987).

45. The Memorandum Order in this matter was published in the Lawyers' Edition Supreme Court Reports. 71 L. Ed.2d 862 (1982).

practice before the Supreme Court, but two justices dissented from that decision, reciting various charges which had been made against Rose. This meant that when potential clients thought of retaining Rose, they found references to these charges in the Lawyers' Edition, and in the electronic services, like LEXIS and WESTLAW. He found that it was very difficult for him to get and retain clients.

I had never met Rose, nor had I heard of him. I do not know how he happened to come to me. He called me on the telephone, and I agreed to see him. I asked him to make a full statement of the situation, and to indicate what support he had for his position. When I examined the papers, I came to the conclusion that the charges made against him were not warranted. It was not clear to me what could be done since he had actually been admitted to the Bar of the Supreme Court. He was not in any sense seeking review of the action of the Court, but his problem arose because of the dissenting opinion in which two members of the Court had concurred.

I told Rose that I would try to see if I could help him, but I made it clear that I was not sure just what would be the best procedure. Obviously, this was a very delicate matter, which had to be handled very carefully. In the course of my consideration, I consulted former Dean Robert B. McKay of New York University Law School, and found that he knew Rose, and thought well of him.

In due course, a plan was developed, and Rose agreed to follow it. Under this plan, Rose resigned from the Bar of the Supreme Court, and, at the same time, filed a new Motion for Admission. I signed this motion as sponsor, and Dean McKay joined me in supporting the proposal. Attached to the application was an affidavit signed by Rose, together with an affidavit signed by a district judge in Colorado, who was a member of the Admissions Committee of the Colorado State Board of Law Examiners when Rose's case was pending there, and affidavits from two lawyers in Colorado who had personal knowledge of the facts.

We had planned to file these papers over the summer in 1986, so that they would come before the Court in its October Term in that year. However, in June 1986, Chief Justice Burger announced his retirement. It was important, of course, to have this matter before the Court while the Chief Justice was still a sitting member. Accordingly, we completed the final preparation of the papers, and filed them with the Clerk of the Supreme Court on June 26, 1986. On July 30, 1986, the Court granted the

new application for admission.[46]   Mr. Rose has now moved to
South Carolina, where he is active and effective in a number of
public activities.

A case which is fascinating to lawyers, and almost impossible
to explain to others, is *Freytag v. Commissioner*.[47]   Under Article
II of the Constitution, Congress may "vest the Appointment" of
inferior officers "in the President alone, in the Courts of Law, or
in the Heads of Departments."   Congress authorized the appointment of "special trial judges," with limited powers, by the Chief
Judge of the Tax Court of the United States.   The essential
question was whether the Tax Court was a court within the
Appointments Clause, in view of the fact that its judges did not
have life tenure and guaranteed salaries, as is required for judges
appointed under Article III, the Judicial Clause of the Constitution.

In the *Freytag* case, the Government contended that the Tax
Court was not a court of law, but that it was a "department," and
that the Chief Judge was the head of that department.   To many
of us, this seemed to be a highly artificial position.   To the judges
of the Tax Court, and to those who know the fine work which the
Tax Court has done over the years, it was a demeaning position.
Some judges of the Tax Court asked me to appear in the case as a
friend of the Court, presenting the view that the Tax Court is a
"court of law" within the appointments clause.   The Department
of Justice would not let me appear "on behalf of" the Tax Court
judges, saying that only the Department could represent an agency of the Government.   However, the Department did consent to
my appearance on my own behalf.

The total production by the Supreme Court on this matter
came to about 18,000 words.   Five Justices for the majority,
supported my position, and four Justices reached the conclusion
that the Tax Court is not a court of law, but is a "Department" in
the Executive Branch of the Government.

This is a field which was reasonably clear a long generation
ago, when I learned about it from Professor Felix Frankfurter.
It is unfortunate that, in recent years, the basic clarity of those
days has been dissolved by a number of verbose and complicated

---

46.   This appears as Matter of Admission of Michael T. Rose, 92 L. Ed.
2d 764 (1986), in the Lawyers' Edition.   Chief Justice Burger filed a
concurring opinion, in which Justice O'Connor joined.   In this opinion,
he said: "I concur in his admission.   Taken as a whole, the record
presented at this time demonstrates that the applicant is 'of good moral
and professional character.' "

47.   111 Sup.Ct. 2631, decided June 27, 1991.

opinions in several cases. In my view, the correct result was reached—though by the narrowest of margins—in the *Freytag* case, and I was glad that I had an opportunity to participate, and perhaps helped to bring about the decision supporting the status of the Tax Court.

G. Other Activities

During my period of law practice with Jones, Day, I spent an appreciable amount of my time in "public service" activities, of one sort or another. This was in accordance with the understanding when I came to the firm in 1973, although it is clear that the relative amount of this sort of "non-billable" work increased over the years.

I continued my work as a member of the Council of the American Law Institute, an association which I have highly valued over the years. Although I retired as an active member of the Board of Oberlin College on January 1, 1980, I have continued as an "honorary trustee," and have attended perhaps half of the meetings of the Board since that time. I have also continued to be active in the work of the Lawyers' Committee for Civil Rights Under Law, originally established by President Kennedy in 1963. Except for the period when I was Solicitor General, when I withdrew because of possible conflicts of interest, I have been continuously a member of that body for nearly thirty years.

I have also continued to be active in the American Bar Association, of which my membership is now in its sixtieth year. I was for twenty-seven years a member of the House of Delegates of the Association. I did not stand for reelection in 1985, however, after I had passed my eightieth birthday, because I felt that it was time for a younger person to take over. During the years 1971–1974, I was President of the American Bar Foundation. In 1978, I was greatly honored when the American Bar Association awarded me its Gold Medal for Distinguished Service to American Law.

In 1973, I was elected a Fellow of the American College of Trial Lawyers, and I have attended most of the meetings of that body since that time. In 1982, the College gave me its Samuel E. Gates Litigation Award.

In more recent years, I have been a trustee of the Southern African Legal Services and Legal Education Project, Inc. Most of the effort in the founding of this body was contributed by Lloyd Cutler of the firm of Wilmer, Cutler & Pickering in Washington. Its purpose is to raise funds in the United States in order to assist certain agencies in South Africa, particularly the Legal Resources

Centre, in which my friends Sydney and Felicia Kentridge have been active, and the Black Lawyers Association.

Finally, I may mention that I have been active in the Supreme Court Historical Society. I was for several years a trustee of that Society, and beginning in 1990, I undertook a term as Chairman of the Board of Trustees. My role was chiefly ornamental, as the basic work was done by the staff, and by the President, Justin A. Stanley of Chicago. He was succeeded by Leon Silberman, of New York. I participated in a number of gatherings on behalf of the Society, and was glad to be of assistance to Mr. Stanley in his successful effort to raise an endowment for the Society. Under his leadership, the membership of the Society increased substantially, and nearly $2,500,000 was raised for the Society's endowment.

I have also undertaken to act as the National Honorary Chairman of an effort to raise a large sum for the Harvard Law School. This has involved attending a number of gatherings, with an occasional short speech. It has been a pleasant assignment as it has given me opportunity to meet with many of my former students.

H.   Observations About Law Practice

The changes in our country during the twentieth century have been dramatic—just as they were during the nineteenth century. The population of the country has doubled since 1900. To those of us who remember the fairly early years of the century, many aspects of living are not now as attractive or as comfortable as they were then, even though the technological and economic progress has been great.

In the early years of the twentieth century, there were very few automobiles—and there were no paved roads outside the cities. Shortly after World War I, my father began to drive to his office in downtown Cleveland by automobile. I can remember his complaints that "it is hard to find a place to park." Parking was taken as expectable, almost a right of citizenship. After that came parking lots, and now huge underground garages in office buildings—and apartment houses. Millions of miles of paved roads, including the interstate highway system, have traversed the country in all directions, with resulting facility of travel—and sometimes gridlock.

In the early part of the twentieth century, the railroad system was well developed, with trains available to almost everywhere. Now passenger trains have nearly disappeared, and air transpor-

Supreme Court Historical Society dinner, January, 1991. Left to right—Mrs. Griswold, E.N.G., Justice David Souter.

tation has taken over. This leads to congestion at airports, and on the airways.

    We had the telephone when I was born, with calls placed by voice through "central," sometimes through instruments where you turned a crank. Shortly thereafter came the radio. Television did not become available to the general public until after World War II. More recently, we have had the electronic revolution, with enormous developments in communication and word processing. What will come next? Only time will tell, but there is no doubt that there will be further developments.

All of this has had a considerable impact on the legal profession, and on law offices. I grew up in a lawyer's family. My father's office was regarded as medium size. It had six or seven lawyers. There were a few "big firms" in Cleveland, with about twenty lawyers at that time.

There was very little "interstate" business, and when it did occur, it was usually handled in association with lawyers in the other state. There were very few firms across the country which had more than one office, and virtually none which had offices in more than one state. This was regarded as essentially an impossibility, since admission to practice was controlled by the states, and many of the states had strict limitations with respect to firm names, and maintaining an office in the state.

The total volume of law business was limited, and good openings for young lawyers were not easy to find. When I finished law school in 1928, I made the rounds of the New York law offices. I did receive a number of offers, but they were all at the fixed rate of $125 a month. There was no placement office then at Harvard Law School. All such matters were handled by Dean Roscoe Pound himself, utilizing his wide acquaintance throughout the American bar. Practically no member of my class at law school had a position at the time of our graduation. It was taken for granted that you would first take and pass the applicable state bar examination, and then knock on the doors of the law offices in the city of your choice and hope that some sort of an opening could be found. In many cases, these came with salaries of $75 or $100 a month—though, often, only desk space was available.

There was not a great deal of change until after the close of World War II. One of my first acts as Dean of the Harvard Law School in 1946–47 was to establish a placement office, with a recent gradate, Louis A. Toepfer, in charge. Salaries available remained relatively small until about 1967–68. At that time, some of the bigger New York offices began offering greatly increased salaries, sometimes as high as $15,000 a year. From then on, the scale went up by leaps and bounds, until it levelled off in the early 1990s. By this time, some of the beginning salaries in larger cities had reached $80,000 a year—so that beginning law clerks were being paid, in some cases, more than the judges in some of the courts where they would be practicing.

It is not very fruitful to discuss whether this has been a good or bad development. It is, indeed, the natural consequence of competition. At least two factors have brought about this change. In the first place, the general level of the economy of the country has greatly increased, while, at the same time, activities of governments at every level—local, state, and federal—have grown extensively. And the second reason is that the complexity of legal issues has steadily increased, sometimes enormously. All that one has to do is to compare the Internal Revenue Code of 1938, which had 184 pages, with the Code of 1989, which has 6,955 pages in fairly fine print. And whole new areas have developed, such as Environmental Protection, FIFRA (the Federal Insecticide, Fungicide and Rodenticide Act), the Equal Employment Opportunity Act, the Clean Air Act, and so on, which did not exist in the early two-thirds of the century.

It has been an interesting experience to live through this development, and to watch it at first hand, particularly during the past twenty years. Jones, Day, Reavis & Pogue (then known as Jones, Day, Cockley & Reavis) was a large firm when I became a partner in 1973. It had well over two hundred lawyers. It had originated in Cleveland, and most of the lawyers were in Cleveland. On January 1, 1991, the firm had a total of 1,223 lawyers, of whom 413 were partners. It also had 250 legal assistants, and a staff of 1,673 persons, for a total personnel of 3,212. Of these, 220 lawyers, including 77 partners, were in the Washington office. This development had occurred, of course, because the demand for services was there, and this was maintained by the capacity to deal with sophisticated problems on a first-class basis. It has been especially interesting to see the firm develop in many cities in this country, and, on an international basis, in eight or nine cities throughout the world. Some of this development has been facilitated by the great improvements in communications, with word processing interchange between the offices, fax communication on a national and international basis, and telephone communication between offices as easy as it is to call across the street.

All of this involves great expense. The firm's investment in electronic equipment is many millions of dollars. Its library expenses are considerable, in many offices as much as that required to maintain the library in a small law school. This, too, involves electronic equipment with access to LEXIS and WESTLAW, and other databases.

Such an office cannot be run effectively without extraordinary persons in the post of managing partner. This is clearly a matter of first importance since, from the beginning, Jones, Day has given the managing partner virtually complete control—subject to advice from committees, but the decisions are his. This responsibility has, during my association with the firm, been carried out with remarkable skill and effectiveness. The managing partners have been wise. They had the vision of "the national law firm," very early, and they took the steps, sometimes difficult, to bring this about. They consistently maintained the confidence of the members of the firm, and dissatisfaction among the partners has been minimal—I could almost say non-existent, apart from the break-up in Washington in 1979. Having dealt with the personalities involved in a law school faculty, I can only say that I have found this to be extraordinary and satisfying.

I would like to think that the expansion of the firm has reached a plateau, or, at least, that the firm would not expand further for a while. There is a point where the administrative problems will exceed the capacity of even the ablest managing partner. The development has already gone far beyond anything I would have thought possible when I joined the firm. At that time, I am sure that I would have said that a firm with 1,200 lawyers would be simply unbearable. But it has happened, I have watched it grow, and it has been a very interesting and satisfactory experience.

But there are problems, which are not easy to resolve. For one illustration, though the firm is superbly equipped to handle big matters, it is almost impossible for it to handle a small matter. I sometimes get telephone calls from friends, or from people who call in because they have heard my name. They may have a matter, of importance to them, which involves something of the order of $5,000. I have to tell them that we cannot handle it, though I try to recommend someone else, usually a recent law school graduate, who may be able to help them. For the fact is that, organized as it is, with the tremendous overhead it has, the firm cannot afford to take a matter which involves less than say, $50,000, and even on such a case the likelihood of a net loss to the firm is considerable. Thus, the big firm can, as a practical matter, handle only relatively big cases. Its only solace is that there are usually other lawyers available who can efficiently handle smaller cases.

Another consequence is the comparative pressure on the large firms. In order to attract first-class younger lawyers, the large firms have felt that they must pay extraordinarily high starting salaries. The way that they recover this, and sometimes more, is by charging high hourly rates for the work of these lawyers (which must cover not only their salaries, but also their proportion of the large overhead) and they must have a fairly rigid system of "billable hours." Sometimes the expected billable hours are said to be two thousand hours a year. This works out at forty hours a week for fifty weeks a year, with two weeks vacation, and no allowance for lunch time, reading time, visits to the dentist, home emergencies, and so on.[48] This gives me considerable concern.

The "billable hours" concept was originated by Reginald Heber Smith of the firm of Hale & Dorr in Boston in the 1920s. There is much to be said for it, if it is not applied too mechanically. Referring again to my father, I am sure that he kept no time sheet. When he completed a piece of legal work, he figured in a rough way how much time he had put in, took into account the benefit to the client, and the client's ability to pay, and came up with a figure which seemed to him to be appropriate under all of the circumstances. That was a rough and ready system, and his charges would have been much higher if he had followed the "billable hour" approach—and he might have lost some clients, too.

Where there is pressure, however guarded, to turn in billable hours, I have some feeling that there is a risk that, in some situations more hours will be devoted to a matter than are needed. Scheduling the work of the younger lawyers is an important task, requiring a partner's supervision. At some point, the young lawyer—and older ones, too—may find himself without much to do. Yet, he remains subject to the pressure to turn in billable hours. It is natural in such cases that he should pick up a job on which he has already worked, and see if he can make a further contribution by more extensive digging. He goes to the library, reexamines the encyclopedias and digests, finds and reads law review articles, and makes further memoranda. He might, of course, find something very important by such further research. It could be, too, that the additional time devoted, several hours, was not useful to the client. Yet, he, of course,

---

48. If the young lawyer's time is billed at $100 an hour, this means that his total billings would come to $200,000, if he was able to charge (and the firm was able to collect the charge) for the total of 2,000 hours. This seems like a large figure, but it should be reduced by at least ten percent for "charge-offs," uncollected bills, and so on. That leaves $180,000 a year actually collected. The office's overhead may come to half of this—including "training services," travel time, and other "billable hours" which are in fact unbillable. If the young lawyer's salary is $80,000, there are fringes which amount to twelve to fifteen percent—social security, health plans, and so on. This leaves very little "profit" to the firm from the young lawyer's services.

turns this in as billable hours, and so keeps up to schedule on his annual quota of two thousand hours.

I am not suggesting that the young lawyer is dishonest, or that he is engaged in a wholly "make-work" activity. My thought is only that if he is under pressure to see that all of his time is gainfully occupied, he may devote more time to a particular job than that job needs or merits.

Of course I favor the office's goal to provide truly first-class legal services. Perhaps, though, there should be a further goal of equal priority—to provide such services at the lowest possible cost within the quality goal. In the years I have been with Jones, Day, I have heard much talk about quality legal service, but I have heard less talk about lowest possible cost. There are many little ways in which costs are disregarded. Some of these costs are billed to clients. Others fall into the overhead of the firm. The younger lawyers are well trained on the electronic devices. They use LEXIS and WESTLAW, at appreciable cost to clients, when Shepherd's Citations is in the library, and, in some ways, easier to use, as well as cheaper. Many other examples could be given.

All in all, my experience with Jones, Day has been a thoroughly satisfactory one. I have enjoyed law practice, as I have enjoyed law teaching, and government service. They have all been fun. The firm has given me many opportunities, and it has been extremely kind to me, for which I am grateful. It provides a service of high-quality to its clients, a great many of which are American or foreign business corporations. I am fully aware of the fact that there are many other parties who need legal assistance, but, in a capitalist society, commercial corporations provide jobs and products which are essential to society. Good legal advice can do much to smooth out this process, to plan transactions so that they will not turn into disputes, to avoid transactions of doubtful character, and to resolve disputes without expensive litigation when they do occur.

CHAPTER XIII

The Legal Profession

Over all—and those words are important—I think well of the legal profession. Of course, my approach cannot help being influenced by my background and by my experience. I grew up in a lawyer's family, and often saw things that my father was doing which seemed to me to be good and useful. More than once, when I was young, he did not get home for dinner because he was taking care of some sort of an emergency involving a client, often a widow for whom he was a trustee under the will of a former client. And since those days, the law has brought me much satisfaction, through work that generally seemed to me to be useful, and often challenging, and because it brought me many public spirited and able friends.

I have often said that one of the fine things about being a member of the legal profession is the high caliber of people with whom one comes into contact—the faculty and students while I was myself a student, then in government service, followed by a third of a century in the academic world, where I met and worked with many fine people, students, faculty colleagues, alumni. Much of this time was, of course, centered at Harvard, but, as my activities broadened through work with the American Law Institute, the American Bar Association, and other groups, I came to know many fine and public spirited lawyers and law teachers on a broad basis, not only in this country, but in many foreign countries, too.

In appraising the legal profession it is important to keep in mind that it is divided into many groups, with different sorts of activities, and outlooks, capacities and responsibilities. There are, for example, trial lawyers (who, generally, get the most publicity), tax lawyers, constitutional lawyers, environmental lawyers, antitrust lawyers, patent lawyers (now often called "intellectual property" lawyers), corporate lawyers, communication lawyers, and so on. During my professional life there has been a great expansion in the statute law, bringing with it a massive increase in complexity. This has made inevitable an increase in specialization.

When I was a law student, most lawyers were generalists. A firm of fifteen or twenty lawyers was regarded as "large," though, in the great cities there were a few firms which were even larger. Most law firms had ten lawyers or less, and a high proportion of the total, perhaps as many as fifty percent of all lawyers, practiced as solo practitioners, sometimes sharing offices, but not clients, with two or three other lawyers. In such cases, the work for a lawyer who had gone through his apprenticeship and was reasonably established was fairly steady, but it involved small businesses, real estate transactions, wills, administration of estates, contract disputes, various aspects of family law—much the sort of thing that was then done by a solicitor in England.

From time to time, there would be a large corporate matter, and there would be an occasional tort case, including automobile accidents, slip-and-fall cases, and workmen's compensation matters. It was not until after World War II that the handling of automobile accident cases became a major activity of many law offices, and developed into a sort of separate industry. Along with the civil work, there were occasional criminal cases. But this was not well organized. Not until *Gideon v. Wainwright* [1] was decided in 1963 was there a right under the federal Constitution to representation in serious criminal cases. Indeed, the right to legal representation in the state courts even in capital cases did not appear until the Scottsboro case, *Powell v. Alabama*,[2] was decided in 1932.

In the 1920s, there were less than 150,000 lawyers in the country. In 1991, there were well over 700,000 lawyers, a rate of increase which is at least double the rate of population growth. As Geoffrey Hazard has pointed out: "Recruitment into the profession was affected by programs reaching out to racial minorities and women, whose assimilation into law practice became both a norm of public policy and a legal duty."[3] I am often told that "There are too many lawyers," and I reply, "That

---

1. 372 U.S. 335 (1963).

2. 287 U.S. 45 (1932).

3. Cf. G. Hazard, Jr., "The Future of Legal Ethics," 100 Yale L.J. 1239, fn.3, 1259 (1991).

may be true, but there are not enough good lawyers." This at least appears to be the verdict of the marketplace, because the top graduates of virtually all well-qualified law schools continue to be in demand for employment in law offices, and continue to make their way constructively in the legal profession and in public service, of many sorts.

There are two problems with which lawyers must constantly wrestle in carrying out the duties of their profession. As Dean Pound pointed out, lawyers are engaged in public service. In his words, "A profession is a group of men pursuing a learned art as a common calling in the spirit of public service no less a public service because incidentally it may be a means of livelihood."[4] The key words in this are: "public service". Whatever a lawyer is doing, he is trying to help someone, either a "person" or a public agency. He does this either by way of assisting his client to do something, or by way of providing defense against some sort of claim made against his client. In the process, the lawyer often uses public facilities providing a public service.

It does not detract from the professional nature of his calling that the lawyer is also engaged in making his living. He must charge for his services, or at least for a substantial portion of them, if he is to survive, to support himself and his family, and to do the other things which are expected of an active and responsible member of the community. If he charges too little, or takes on too much work without compensation, he cannot pay his bills. And if he charges too much, he is understandably the object of criticism and of resentment. Finding the appropriate balance in this area may present many difficulties.

Lawyers also encounter another problem. In other professions, such as the clergy, the objective is to do good, to uplift, to bring out the best aspects of the parishioners, and to help them understand their relation to the cosmos. Similarly with the doctor. He is always on the patient's side, and there is no human opponent. The doctor tries to bring about a cure, or to relieve pain, and is generally successful. As for the lawyer, though, if a client gets involved in a controversy, his lawyer does his best to help him. But, except in cases limited solely to pure advice, there is generally a lawyer on the other side, whose responsibility it is to advance the interests of an opposing client, and this often involves taking actions which seem harmful. Thus, the client may like his own lawyer, but he is likely to dislike the lawyer on the other side. And, in the nature of things, at least where litigation or controversy is involved, about half of the cases will

---

4.   R. Pound, Jurisprudence (St. Paul: 1959) Vol. 5, p. 301.

be lost. So, where the doctor wins a high proportion of his cases, the lawyer is much more likely to finish his work with an unsuccessful or only partially successful result.

Of course, much work done by lawyers does not directly involve matters of litigation or controversy. This is true of much general advice, or planning, or preparing wills and trusts, or work done in connection with real estate transactions, or tax returns, or other reports which have to be made to one or more agencies of government. Even in these cases, though, there is a problem, for the lawyer's task is to work through the technical requirements of "the law" or of "the government," and thus "the law" or "the government" may appear to the client to be the adversary. In this situation, the necessity for the lawyer's services may itself be a cause of resentment to the client. In short, a large part of the work of the lawyer is likely to involve tension on the part of the client, and this naturally leads the client, in some cases, to put the blame on the lawyer.

Many people, including a number of lawyers, are very critical of the legal profession.[5] For example, Professor Richard L. Abel, of the University of California at Los Angeles Law School, has written that lawyers, like members of other professions, use their status as members of a self-regulating profession primarily for their own benefit. He states that "[a]lthough professions portray self-regulation as a means of reducing client uncertainty, they deliberately draft ethical rules in vague and ambiguous language to preserve the indeterminacy that is a foundation of professional power."[6] This seems to me to be much too general and too sweeping.

An oft-repeated and rather worn-out complaint is that the prominent law schools only train lawyers to represent big corporations, whose interests are opposed to those of the common people. This is much too broad. Graduates of the larger schools can be found in many positions, all over the country. My law school roommate, Malcolm P. Mouat, spent his entire career, very usefully, as a "family solicitor" in Janesville, Wisconsin. Lawyers are, in fact, widely engaged in public service, in the judiciary, in every branch of the executive and administrative side of government, state and local, in charitable and other public service agencies often at modest compensation. Moreover, the complaint is misguided. Certainly business enterprise

---

5. See D. Bok, "A Flawed System of Law Practice and Training," 33 J. Legal Educ. 570 (1983).

6. R. Abel, American Lawyers (New York: 1989), reviewed by Professor Robert F. Drinan, S.J., 79 Geo. L.J. 388, 389 (1990).

is entitled to have appropriate representation under an adversarial system. And, in the long run, protecting business against unfair or improper claims works out to the advantage of the ordinary citizen. Indeed, that is the whole basis of "strict liability" in tort cases, which has swept the country over the past thirty years.[7] In the long run, corporations do not bear the burden of the losses which they incur in litigation. They inevitably raise prices. They have no alternative, if they are to stay in business. Thus, they eventually pass the costs on to the consumer.

The legal profession does, however, have many problems, of which several should be mentioned. These are: solicitation and legal advertising, self-regulation, legal aid for the poor, specialization, size of lawyers' incomes, and the approach that legal education should take to these and other problems. Let us look at some of these things.

Until a generation or so ago, the rules of the legal profession with respect to solicitation and advertising were those which had long been traditional. They were very strict. Solicitation and advertising were not allowed. There was an element of monopolization in this. Those who had been successful developed good reputations. As a result, clients, knowing little about the qualification of lawyers, came to them. It was undeniably difficult for the younger lawyer, the beginner, to attract clients, and thus to make his way in the legal profession, particularly in an era when more than half of the lawyers practiced as solo practitioners, or in very small firms. Under this regime, the law was a genteel profession, where, to an appreciable extent, those who had already established reputations found it relatively easy to capitalize on that fact. Of course, the "big" cases would have gone to the established firms, but there were many other lawyers who were well-qualified, and had few ways to make that known.

As an aid in meeting the needs of potential clients, many bar associations established "lawyer referral services," and many older lawyers found ways to steer work to younger lawyers whom they felt to be well-qualified.

In recent years, the Supreme Court, largely through the influence of Justice Black, has found a basis in the First Amendment to eliminate many restrictions on advertising. Even some of the big firms now sponsor television programs on educational stations, often without referring directly to their capacity as lawyers. There are also more blatant, advertisements on television and in the newspapers. Many firms put out newsletters in

---

7. See G. Priest, "The New Legal Structure of Risk Control," Daedalus, Fall 1990, p. 207.

the form of information for clients. In many ways, these provide helpful information as to current developments, and give a means of informing clients about potential legal problems which may not yet have come to their attention.

Although some of this is rather promotional, it does not seem to me that it has yet made any adverse impact on the profession or the way law is practiced. It is largely a result of greater competition within the legal profession. The aspect of it that gives me concern is that it is a part of a broader tendency. It brings pressure on lawyers to commercialize the profession. There is a good deal of feeling, particularly among the younger partners, that more should be done in the way of publicity.[8] This goes along with the view of some that charges should be increased to what the market will bear.

This seems to me to be unfortunate, with a considerable unprofessional tendency. I hope that in the years ahead, the profession will work out ways not only to provide the best possible legal service, but also to do so at the lowest cost consistent with quality work.

This leads to another, but closely related, problem. How should legal services be provided for the poor, for those who can pay only a small part of the costs for such services, and for those who cannot pay at all? This is a problem of long standing, on which much thought and effort have been expended. It is far from being fully resolved today, though much has been done, probably more than is generally recognized.

Some of the need is met by organizations which focus on particular areas of need. Probably the oldest of these is the NAACP Legal Defense and Education Fund. But there are many others devoted primarily to particular problems or issues: The Lawyers Committee for Civil Rights Under Law, the American Civil Liberties Union, the Sierra Club, the National Resources Defense Council, for example. And there are many other organizations, usually local, which provide legal services to particular categories of clients, such as women, the elderly, the handicapped, immigrants, the homeless, adoption services, and so on. More recently, a few law firms have been organized to provide legal services in "run of mine" cases on a more or less mass production basis, using standardized forms as much as possible. One of these, at least, known as "Hyatt Legal Services" has had a considerable degree of success, and has a large number of offices

---

8. When my firm's office occupied their building in Cleveland, it was jokingly suggested that a flashing neon sign should be installed at the roof line, reading "300 Lawyers—No Waiting".

in many cities and suburbs. Such organizations should, in my view, be encouraged. Not only do they make legal services available to a large number of people who need such services, but they also relieve the "old line" firms from obligations with respect to many cases which they cannot afford to handle on what, to continue the metaphor, is a "piece work" basis.

Many cities and states have established public defender offices, analogous to the local prosecutors. These are usually inadequately financed. Though very useful, they do not fully meet the need. For the past twenty years, there has been a federal Legal Services Corporation, which was set up to help to finance such services.[9] But this encountered the opposition of Governor Reagan in California, and he carried this opposition to Washington when he became President, and his narrow views have been largely pursued by President Bush. Under this negative leadership, the Board and the officers of the Legal Services Corporation have done much to reduce the effectiveness of that agency. But Congress has steadfastly refused to terminate the Corporation, and there is reason to hope that it can be vitalized, with great usefulness, in days to come.

In addition to these organized activities, a great deal of legal work is contributed by law firms throughout the country, far more than the general public is usually aware of. Sometimes, lawyers are assigned by a local court to handle a particular case, as I was on several occasions. In other matters, lawyers contribute their services in trying cases, and in writing briefs on appeal. For example, the State and Local Legal Center in Washington undertakes to act as a "Solicitor General" for state and local governments in cases pending before the Supreme Court. Their briefs, of first-rate quality, are usually written by lawyers in law offices, who contribute their services. The same is true for cases handled by the NAACP Legal Defense and Education Fund, and the Lawyers' Committee for Civil Rights Under Law.[10]

---

9. Louis F. Powell, Jr. of Richmond, Virginia, later a distinguished justice of the Supreme Court, was president of the American Bar Association at the time, and he did much to obtain the Association's support for the Legal Services Corporation.

10. These problems of the legal profession and legal representation are discussed with great insight by Robert McKay, in the 1990 Tyrrell Williams Memorial Lecture, "The Rise of the Justice Industry and the Decline of Legal Ethics," 68 Wash. U. L.Q. 829 (1990). See also G. Hazard, "Ethical Opportunity in the Practice of Law," 27 San Diego L.Rev. 127 (1990); A. Adams, "The Legal Profession: A Critical Evaluation," 14 Judicature 77 (1990).

Though the problems are very great, and the need never-ending, the legal profession does do much in carrying its share in meeting the needs of the public for legal services. There are now many law student clinics which handle a great variety of small cases, including minor criminal cases. There are legal aid offices, encouraged and sustained by the legal profession in nearly every city. In addition, in nearly every city, the local Bar Association maintains an active Lawyers Referral Service. And there are many organizations which have been established for meeting specialized needs. In the District of Columbia, for example, I have had contact—in addition to the organizations already mentioned—with the Council for Court Excellence, D.C. Law Students in Court, Legal Counsel for the Elderly, So Others May Eat, Friends of the Superior Court, and the Washington Legal Clinic for the Homeless.

This is not a complete list of local organizations; and it could be matched in every other city. In addition, there are a large number of other organizations served by the legal profession, with a national base, which work ably and vigorously to aid in improvement of the law.[11]

Meeting the general public need for greater access to legal services is not the responsibility of the legal profession alone. There should be greater public support in these areas. This is slow in coming, and that is understandable, in view of the demands from many other areas seeking public support, such as the need for health services. A very large part of the national resources now goes to pay for past wars. If we could only find a way to keep out of wars, the means for providing for many types of public need could eventually be readily found.

The most serious threat to the legal profession, it seems to me, comes from commercialism, and more thought should be given to the developing problems in that area. In the hope of stimulating such thought, I advance here some ideas, not at all as conclusions, but as matters which may be worthy of consideration in the further development of a truly great profession. Two

---

Judge Adams, in the article last cited, gives an interesting and significant set of figures: "In 1975, there were only four firms with over 200 lawyers in the United States * * * a recent survey reported well over 150 firms with more than 200 lawyers * * * ." 14 Judicature at 79.

11. These include the American Bar Association Fund for Justice and Education, American Bar Foundation, American Judicature Society, American Law Institute, Institute for Judicial Administration, Lawyers Alliance for World Security, National Center for State Courts, Natural Resources Defense Council, and World Peace Through Law Center.

particular aspects of the problem might be given special consideration.

The *first* is whether the "billable hours" concept results in a considerable increase in the amount of time devoted by lawyers to many legal matters, and thus serves to increase the costs along with lawyers' incomes. Although there is a measure of reason behind charges based on billable hours, it may be that it is applied too mechanically, especially when it is used like a time clock, to keep track of the hours, no matter what has been done, and then to determine a charge by multiplying a fixed hourly rate by the number of hours. It could be thought that this is an invitation for the application of Parkinson's Law, which states, it will be recalled, that "Work expands to fill the time allotted to it." And the converse of this, namely that "the amount of work completed is in inverse proportion to the number of people employed," may be particularly applicable to legal work in a large office. Some legal work is clearly worth the high hourly rates of leading lawyers. Not all of it is worth such rates, even when the time is expended by lawyers of great eminence. The answer that the hourly rate is an average may have some merit, but, perhaps, not enough.

Putting legal charges on a basis of numbers of hours times hourly rate has the merit of simplicity. Its limit seems to be what the market will bear. It may be that this approach to legal fees is impelled too much by an element of commercialism, and that it is not enough controlled by the fundamental vision of professionalism.

The *second* aspect of commercialism comes from the pressure which is now beginning to show itself that law offices should become "full service" business operations. Thus, there is appreciable pressure in some of the large offices that they should develop a number of affiliates or subsidiaries which would engage in financial operations, real estate brokerage, freight forwarding and shipping, management consulting, and perhaps even accounting, advertising, and other business services. The pressure for these things is essentially commercial, that is, to make more money, to provide convenient services—often through non-legal personnel—to customers rather than to clients, with the incidental effect of producing more business and larger incomes for the entrepreneurs. It reminds one of the conglomerate mergers which were so popular fifteen or twenty years ago, many of which did not turn out very well. Quite apart, though, from the economic merit of such arrangements, the risks that the legal professional will simply be swallowed up, and will no longer have a truly professional and suitably independent outlook and tradition, seems to me to be very great.[12]

What would happen if there were a general reduction of legal fees, either by modifying the mechanical application of the billable hours system, or by voluntarily limiting the operation of law firms to truly professional activities? Under such a system, charges would be based primarily on *quantum meruit*, that is, the value of the services produced for the clients and the results achieved, rather than by an aggregation of the hours of work allocated to the task—with varying degrees of efficiency.

There would surely be problems from any such a change in practice. Some lawyers, like other people, are very much interested in how much they make. As Dean Pound said, the legal profession is not the less a profession—like the medical profession—because it provides the means of making one's living. And making one's living should provide a reasonably comfortable sum for current expenses and a fund for emergencies and retirement. A firm choosing to proceed on a lower level of charges would have the satisfaction of professionalism. It might find that this helped to attract new clients; and it might even find ways to develop greater efficiency in its operations, with the consequence that lower gross fees would not seriously impair the net available for distribution to partners. This is not offered here as a conclusion, but as a suggestion for consideration and development. Of one thing, though, I am convinced: there are satisfactions derived from the purely professional practice of law which are surely worthy of full and careful consideration.

———

In considering problems of the legal profession—and, more broadly speaking, of the administration of justice—it is important to remember that these questions are chronic, that a vast amount of thought, time and effort is in fact devoted to them, that some progress is made, and that some of the problems are not susceptible to definitive solution. The law usually must speak in general terms. It is necessarily somewhat mechanical in operation. We have concluded, long ago, that it is better to have some standardization in the application of legal rules. The ideal of justice being distributed on an individualized basis by Haroun al Raschid,

———

12. In the 1980s, the American Bar Association had a very thoughtful Commission on Professionalism, under the chairmanship of Justin A. Stanley, of Chicago. See " * * * 'In the Spirit of Public Service:' A Blueprint for the Rekindling of Lawyer Professionalism," 112 Fed. Rules Dec. 243 (1986).

sitting under a tree, has long since been put away because of the disparities and discrimination inherent in that approach. Even the English chancellor, whose duty it was to "see that justice was done," found it necessary to develop some rules. As John Selden said, it would not work to have justice measured by "a Chancellor's Foot, what an uncertain measure would this be? One Chancellor has a long Foot, another a short Foot, a third an indifferent Foot. 'Tis the same thing in the Chancellor's Conscience." [13]

No matter how it is approached, the administration of justice is a difficult task. It can be thought to be a rather remarkable achievement that justice is administered as well as it is in a country of two hundred and fifty million people which seeks to proceed on democratic principles. In considerable measure, the problems are enhanced by "the anarchy in Congress, the conflicts between Congress and the other federal branches, the conflicts between the federal government and the states, and the divergences of interest between regions, ethnic groups, religious sects, and economic sectors in the nation at large." [14] And it should not be overlooked that many problems arise because large segments of the population do not insist on maintaining high standards—in judicial appointment, for example, in the election of legislators, and in the choosing of executive officers.

This book is focused on various aspects of the legal system as seen through the eyes of one lawyer who has labored in the legal vineyard, who has seen much of the effort which has been devoted in trying to find ways to bring about improvements, and has shared in the disappointment resulting from the failure to accomplish more.

One of the greatest voices for legal reform and improvement in the twentieth century was that of Roscoe Pound, who was born in Lincoln, Nebraska in 1870, two years after the founding of the city. In 1906, he was invited to address the American Bar Association at its annual meeting held in St. Paul, Minnesota. This meeting was held in the new State Capitol, designed by Cass Gilbert, who later designed the Woolworth Building in New York, and the majestic building of the Supreme Court of the United States in Washington. The title of Pound's address was "The Causes of Popular Dissatisfaction with the Administration of Justice." In it, with much scholarship and far-sighted analysis,

---

13. J. Seldon, Equity Table Talk (London 1869) 46, quoted in E. Gerhart, Quote It! (New York: 1969) 198.

14. G. Hazard, Jr., "The Future of Legal Ethics," 100 Yale L.J. 1239, 1280 (1991).

Pound issued perhaps the clearest call of the century for improvement in our justice system.

The American Bar Association then had about four thousand members. It was thus a relatively small body of generally conservative lawyers. There were about three hundred fifty persons in the audience which heard Pound's address, and the reaction was generally hostile. A motion to print the address and send it to all of the members of the Association was unsuccessful. The only contemporary printing of the address was in the Annual Report of the American Bar Association for 1906.[15]

Pound started his address by saying "Dissatisfaction with the administration of Justice is as old as law." And he concluded by saying that some of the causes for dissatisfaction with the administration of justice "inhere in all law and are the penalty we pay for uniformity; that some inhere in our political institutions and are the penalty we pay for local self-government and independence from bureaucratic control; that some * * * are the penalty we pay for freedom of thought and universal education." But, "too much of the current dissatisfaction," he said, "has a just origin in our judicial organization and procedure."[16] And he concluded that "with the passing of the doctrine that politics, too, is a mere game to be played for its own sake, we may look forward confidently to deliverance from the sporting theory of justice; we may look forward to a near future when our courts will be swift and certain agents of justice, whose decisions will be acquiesced in and respected by all."[17]

That hope has so far proved beyond realization. There have been great developments in the twentieth century. Some states have found better ways for the selection of judges. New rules of procedure, and of evidence, have been established for the federal courts, and these have been widely adopted by the states. The American Bar Association has worked hard and long on the development of better rules of legal ethics, and these have brought about substantial improvements, despite the counter-

---

15. At p. 400. The address has since been reprinted many times. Perhaps the most convenient place to locate it is 35 Fed. Rules Dec. 273 (1964). See also J. Wigmore, "Roscoe Pound's St. Paul Address of 1906; the Spark that Kindled the White Flame of Progress," 20 J.Am.Jud.Soc. 176 (1937); Roscoe Pound and Criminal Justice, S. Glueck ed. (Dobbs Ferry, N.Y.: 1965) 57.

16. 35 Fed. Rules Dec. at 273, 290.

17. Id. at 291.

vailing pressures which have come from other sources, including, to some extent, from the Supreme Court itself.[18]

As a result of the changes in the rules of procedure, the "sporting theory of justice" has been largely curtailed. Lawyers can now learn most of the facts on which their opponents rely, before going to trial. Thus, there is much less "surprise" than there used to be. Many think, though, that these rules have gone too far. With their provision for extensive interrogatories, and almost unlimited depositions, they have brought about a considerable increase in the cost of litigation, and have, in some types of cases, materially extended the delays which are inherent in litigation. Here, though, the defect may not be in the rules themselves, but in the abusive use of them, with depositions used to run up costs which the other side cannot afford, and taking much time, which adds to the delays of litigation, especially with the added influence of the "billable hours" system of fee-setting.

On such matters, it may be that the answer lies in greater control by the courts. But the courts are overwhelmed with cases. Most judges are badly over-worked, and have very little time available for supervision of matters which occur outside the courtroom.

One of the greatest sources of delay in civil cases is jury trial. This is simply a statement of fact. The use of juries is, of course, deep-seated in the psyche of the American people, and it is embedded in our constitutions, state and federal. Juries do have an appropriate role in criminal cases. To me, though, it is clear that they are not worth their cost in most civil cases. Juries have virtually disappeared from civil trials in most other English-speaking countries, except in libel cases. There is no doubt, though, that it would be extraordinarily difficult to achieve a similar development in the United States. People who complain about delays in the administration of justice should recognize that in this respect the difficulty is political, and not anything that the legal profession can do much about. There is now little prospect that the considered consensus required to bring about a change through the political process can be brought about in the foreseeable future. But it is not appropriate to blame that largely on the lawyers—even though many of them do oppose any change in the use of jury trials.

There is another area where the legal profession has responsibility, but is, as a practical matter, unable to proceed. This has

---

18. Cf. former Chief Justice Warren Burger, in a book review of W. Olson, The Litigation Explosion (New York: 1991), in New York Times Book Review, May 12, 1991, at p. 12.

to do with the whole field of tort liability, or reparation for injuries, on the highways, and in product liability. Here there could be sharp improvement through the enactment of laws which would more closely control the award of damages, particularly punitive damages. Although such damages were occasionally awarded in the Eighteenth and Nineteenth Centuries, they were in small amounts, usually in libel cases arising out of neighborly disputes, where an extra ten dollars on the verdict was upheld as "smart money." As applied today, though, "these laws are being extrapolated to places where they no longer apply." [19] The opposition to the enactment of state legislation which would better solve these problems comes primarily from trial lawyers, who, as a practical matter, through the votes of our fellow citizens, control most of the state legislatures in the country. Lawyers are not alone in suffering from "the distortion of reason by self interest." [20]

There are problems and difficulties in the American legal system. Citizens who are concerned with them should recognize the extraordinary obstacles which arise against bringing about action which would help to resolve them. Many of these are matters of general responsibility, not the responsibility of the legal profession alone. As we continue the effort to achieve improvement, we must at all times, keep in mind the clarion call which Roscoe Pound made in the early days of this century. As the century now moves towards its close, we should be making better progress then we are despite the daunting difficulties.

––––––––

The challenges to legal education are great, and are the constant concern of many talented and devoted law teachers. They have recently been thoughtfully discussed by Professor Thomas D. Morgan, in a Tucker Lecture at Washington and Lee University School of Law.[21] He feels, rightly in my view, that "Legal education's challenge is to fight off proposed changes in accreditation regulation designed to bully all law schools into emphasizing one or another vision of law school training over all others." [22] And he concludes:

––––––––

19. Bernstein, "Dread Singularities" (Book Review), New York Times Book Review, April, 25, 1982, p. 10.

20. Miller, The First Liberty (New York: 1986) 351.

21. T. Morgan, "A Defense of Legal Education in the 1990s," 48 Wash. & Lee L.Rev. 1 (1991). See also G. Hazard, Jr., "The Future of Legal Ethics," 100 Yale L.J. 1 (1991).

22. T. Morgan, above, at 14.

Legal education is far from perfect. It simultaneously must expand its horizons and focus its resources on tasks it can do best. But legal education can take great satisfaction in the fact that it provides something that a lawyer gets almost nowhere else in his or her professional life. It provides an overview of the many layers that make up the law and a vision of the best of what the law and lawyers can be. I for one believe that law firms are more in need of understanding what is going on in the law schools than the other way around.

Above all, in evaluating legal education, we should not forget the words said to have been written by an anonymous eighteenth century British schoolmaster:

> At school you are not engaged so much in acquiring knowledge as in making mental efforts under criticism. * * *
> You go to a great school not so much for knowledge as for arts or habits; for the art of expression, for the art of entering quickly into another person's thoughts, for the art of assuming at a moment's notice a new intellectual position, for the habit of submitting to censure and refutation, for the art of indicating assent or dissent in graduated terms, for the habit of regarding minute points of accuracy, for the art of working out what is possible in a given time, for taste, for discrimination, for mental courage and mental soberness.[23]

Being a lawyer during the exciting days of the twentieth century has been an exhilarating privilege. The work has been interesting, though in the memorable words of Justice Holmes in his Ninetieth Birthday Address "the work never is done." The challenge is always great. And the opportunities which the profession gives to make what one feels to be contributions to the better and fairer operation of our society are rewarding.

---

23. Quoted in Graetz and Whitebread, "Monrad Paulsen and the Idea of a University Law School," 67 Va.L.Rev. 445, 459 (1981).

Appendix A

(See pages 359–365)

December 4, 1975

Hon. James Kruger
Minister of Justice, etc.
Union Building
Pretoria, South Africa

Dear Mr. Minister,

First, I want to send you my thanks and appreciation for your courtesy to me when I called at your office on November 18, 1975. It was good of you to give me so much of your time, and I greatly appreciate both the opportunity to talk with you, and the arrangements which you made in response to my requests. I want to extend my thanks, too, to General Geldenhuys and to Colonel Schoon for the assistance they gave me. As a result, I was able to interview seven persons, four women at the Windhoek Prison and three men at the Windhoek City Jail. I also met and interviewed Pastors Ndjoba and Hiata, who were brought to Windhoek for the purpose, and I had a long and very interesting interview with Mr. Dirk Mudge. These last three interviews were in accordance with your request, and I found them very informative and helpful.

With respect to the interviews with detainees in Windhoek, I have the following observations.

General Geldenhuys expressed surprise that I interviewed the four women at the Windhoek Prison. He said that he did not think that they should be charged since their involvement was quite peripheral. He told me that he would recommend that they not be charged, and I hope that it has worked out that way.

There were five detained persons whom I was not allowed to interview. I was advised that they were held in Ovamboland, and that they had not been brought to Windhoek. My request to you had been that I be allowed to interview all of the detained persons, and I understood that this was the arrangement which you had authorized. When I expressed surprise to General Geldenhuys that I was not seeing these five, he told me that they were being held only as witnesses, and that he could "practically guarantee" that they would not be charged. I asked him what he meant by "practically guarantee," and he replied: "99.9%." I told

407

him that if he would make it 100%, I would not complain. Otherwise, I felt that the arrangement you had made that I should see all of the detainees had not been complied with. I hope that it has worked out that none of these five persons has been charged or will be charged. I did not understand that the arrangement which you made with me—that I should see the detainees—had any exception for persons held only as witnesses, and I was quite disappointed when I found that this was the situation while I was in Windhoek. However, if these five persons are not charged, then I would not want to say anything more. (There is an exception as to a minor charge against one person, which General Geldenhuys explained to me. If this charge is really treated as a minor charge, I would understand the situation. If, however, it is made a serious charge, then I would think that I should have seen the person involved.)

There is one matter in connection with the interviews to which I would like to make reference here. One of the detainees advised me that he was allowed no reading matter, though he was detained incommunicado for more than three months. General Geldenhuys confirmed this, although he said that the prisoners were allowed to read the Bible. He further said that they were allowed to have "study materials." I take it that this would be materials for correspondence courses, such as those provided by the University of South Africa. These would, presumably, take several weeks to arrange. This is difficult to work out when a person does not know how long he will be detained. Moreover, this would only be applicable to a person who was qualified for study. Thus, it is not a very feasible or workable arrangement in such cases.

I understand that there is a decision of the Appellate Division of the Supreme Court of South Africa which says that you are not required to furnish reading material to persons who are detained. I do not understand, though, that there is anything in the law which forbids you from making reading material available to detainees. I can understand why you might not want them to have current newspapers, though I do not think that the risk would really be very great. I wonder, though, why you cannot make available selected books and other items so that the detained persons can have some means of occupying their minds during a confinement which often extends over a long period of time. Simple humanity would seem to require this, and, though it is a relatively small part in the overall picture, the failure to allow any sort of reading material (other than the Bible and study materials) is very harsh, and makes a very bad impression in other countries. I suspect that a simple order or instruction from the Minister of Justice could quickly change this, and I would like to suggest for your consideration the desirability of issuing such an order.

In addition to the seven detained persons whom I saw, and the five persons I did not see (who are said to be detained only as witnesses), I was able to check over lists of names which I had put together from various sources, and which I showed to General Geldenhuys. From this, I was able to verify that there were seventeen persons who had been released, and two persons on the list who had not been arrested, because they were deported from South Africa. In this way, I accounted for a total of thirty-one persons, although the four women whom I saw at the Windhoek Prison had not been on any list that I had been able to put together. Out of the thirty-one persons, it appeared that only three would be charged—plus the possibility that the four women might be charged, and without counting the five persons who were said to be held only as witnesses. This, of course, is quite a different picture from the "thirty detainees" which is all the information that was available when I came to South Africa. May I respectfully suggest that your policy of making no announcement, with names, about arrests, and holding people incommunicado for a long period, and without charge, and of giving no publicity to releases from detention, causes quite widespread apprehension, both within South Africa and abroad. I cannot help saying, Mr. Minister, with great respect, that I wonder why you find it desirable to conduct this function with so great secrecy. I would like to urge upon you the desirability, in terms of good governmental administration, of a public announcement, as a routine matter, of all arrests, and that a similar announcement be made with respect to all releases from detention. General Geldenhuys advised me that this is done. However, I could not find that there was any information on these subjects available among well-informed private persons either in South Africa or in South West Africa.

One of the requests that I made to you was that I should see Bishop Auala. This worked out very satisfactorily, since Bishop Auala was on holiday, and was in Windhoek, when I arrived there. As a result, I was able to have several satisfactory conferences with Bishop Auala and with Dr. de Vries, who is the President of the Evangelical Lutheran Church in South West Africa. Much of the information I was able to provide was new to them, despite their wide contacts in their respective areas.

Now I would like to venture some observations for your consideration. As you know, I have a considerable acquaintance in South Africa, and I have travelled extensively in your country. I have endeavored to inform myself about the history of South Africa, and I have followed developments there quite closely over the past twenty-five years. I think I have some awareness of the problems of South Africa, and the extremely difficult problems with which you have to deal. I do not think that I take a doctrinaire approach to these problems. Of course, I see the questions through the eyes of an outsider, but this may not be wholly irrelevant to your consideration, since external reactions have an impact within South Africa, and it would seem to be in your interest to improve your image externally when this can be done without material adverse consequences within South Africa.

With this background, and mindful of the free exchange we had when you so courteously received me in your office in Pretoria, I would like to make these observations or suggestions for your consideration.

It is natural and understandable for you who are within South Africa, and are carrying the responsibilities of its government, to say that outsiders do not understand the problems, and that they are in no position to tell you how to run your country, particularly when they have a good many unresolved and intractable problems in their own countries. Yet, South Africa does not exist in isolation. It needs understanding and support from other countries, and from people of good will all over the world.

There is a danger, I think, that South Africa's methods in handling some of its problems may lead to self-inflicted wounds, which, in fact, do great harm to South Africa, and to its standing in the family of nations. If these matters could be looked at dispassionately, in terms of cost-benefit analysis, it might well be found that the cost to South Africa abroad may in fact greatly exceed any benefit which is obtained at home. Many parts of the world are now sensitive to individual human rights. Moreover, in terms of your standing abroad, it is important that justice not only be done, but that it be seen to be done. In some cases, some of your methods seem to the outside world to be inconsistent with proper standards for the protection of individual human rights. In other cases, it may be that what you are doing would meet such standards, but the way you handle the matters does not make this apparent to the outside world.

1. The occasion for my recent trip to South Africa provides an excellent illustration of this. As far as the outside world was informed, some thirty persons had been arrested. They were held incommunicado, and without charge, for a period of three

months or more. No information about them was available. They could not be visited by their Pastors or relatives. In such circumstances, it is understandable, I think, that there was great concern, and that many rumors arose about the treatment of those arrested persons. It may be that there was no foundation for these rumors, but the existence of the rumors was a fact, which was a direct consequence of the long detention, incommunicado, and without charge.

I do not say that this was illegal under your law. I have read the Terrorism Act, and I know the powers which it gives you, and the powers which it denies to your courts. One of the legacies which the South Africa Act, 1910, left to you was the principle of the sovereignty of Parliament. This principle works very well in the United Kingdom, where the Parliament acts with a great concern for the preservation of individual rights. I know that your Parliament felt that it was concerned with very special problems. Nevertheless, I suggest to you that the powers granted by the Terro sm Act are extraordinary, and that they cannot be reconciled w. ʌ proper standards of individual rights. I suggest to you, too, that the denial to the courts of any powers in the nature of habeas corpus is an understandable cause of concern to persons abroad who would like to be your friends.

Despite the powers given to you by statute, might it not be wise for you to adopt the policy that you would not hold anyone incommunicado and without charge. The mere existence of public information would do much to answer some of the concerns which are raised by your present practices.

I know that it is said that you have to hold persons incommunicado and without charge in order to carry out your investigations. I wonder if this is really true. As you know, I have had some eleven years of experience in this country as a prosecuting officer; and over the years I have dealt with some very important cases. Under our law, when a person is arrested, he cannot be held unless proper cause is shown. If it is said that this cannot be done in your country, because of the need to carry on the investigation, the concern immediately arises as to the nature of that investigation. What force or influence is brought to bear on the detainees in order to induce them to talk? I know that you told me that you give strict instructions against physical force or "the third degree." How far are other influences brought to bear—psychological pressures of one sort or another? Why is it necessary to hold persons for so long, even for investigation?

There is a feeling abroad that these mass arrests, followed by long detention, without charge, are designed to put (or at least have the effect of putting) terror in the hearts and minds of those detained, and of other persons who fear that they might be detained. How far is it in the real interest of South Africa to have these fears and concerns felt abroad as intensely as they are now felt?

The effect of this is heightened by the economic hardships involved. No provision is made for compensation for the persons who are arrested, even when they are later released without charge. No provision is made to take care of families who may be left penniless when their principal breadwinner is detained. All of this creates a deep feeling of injustice and, I suggest for your consideration, and with great respect, does much harm to the image and standing of South Africa abroad. I find myself sincerely wondering whether this is necessary or useful to you, and whether it would not be in your interest to ameliorate your practices in this area.

2. Your statutory provisions are extraordinary, and they are the cause of great concern abroad. I am referring particularly to the Suppression of Communism Act, and the Terrorism Act. Both of these seem to me to be masterpieces of statutory draftsmanship, reaching every conceivable area and angle, in the most draconian terms, but without adequate consideration of either proper standards of individual rights, or to the impact which these statutory provisions inevitably have abroad.

I will not go into the details of these provisions. I have already referred to the denial of habeas corpus powers to your courts, and to the extraordinary powers of arrest and detention which these statutes provide. I would like to suggest to you, however, that these statutory provisions grant you much broader powers than are necessary, and that their mere existence on your statute books does you grievous harm abroad.

3. In recent years, South Africa has changed many of its policies substantially. This is evidenced in its relation to the countries to the north, and in your plans with respect to South West Africa. It was only twenty years or so ago that South Africa endeavored to incorporate South West Africa as an integral part of its territory. Now it is your policy to provide independence for South West Africa, and I applaud the steps which you are taking, through the Constitutional Conference, to work out the method by which this can be best achieved.

In this situation, I would like to suggest to you that the time has come when you should take affirmative steps to amend the Suppression of Communism Act, and the Terrorism Act, so as to provide greater safeguards for individuals, and to bring these statutes more closely into line with standards held widely in the world community. This would include (1) the elimination of, or at least substantial restrictions on, the power to hold persons incommunicado and without charge, and (2) the restoration to your courts (whose integrity is not questioned) of appropriate habeas corpus powers. Appropriate statutory amendments might also include provisions against abuse, either physical or psychological, of arrested persons, with proper sanctions; and they might also provide for compensation for persons who are detained without being charged, and make some sort of provision for life-sustaining payments to the dependents of persons who are arrested, at least until they have been charged and convicted.

It will be a great day in the history of South Africa, I think, when James Kruger, Minister of Justice, stands up in the Parliament of South Africa and proposes substantial amendments to these statutes. There is no need, as far as I am concerned, to say that they were wrong when they are enacted. It can be said, however, that experience under them shows that they go further then is necessary, and that it is now appropriate to amend these statutes in order that they may provide basic standards for individual liberties. You could refer to the strong tradition of justice in South Africa, derived from both your Roman-Dutch and your English legal heritage. You could say that South Africa, despite all its problems, is strong enough to guarantee basic civil and human rights to all its citizens.

Such an action by the South African Parliament, on your recommendation, would have enormous impact abroad. There are many people abroad who want to be your friends, but who find that they are really not able to support you as far as these extraordinary statutes are concerned. I know that you need to defend your country against many and unique perils. I think, though, that you can do this successfully without departing as far as you have from ordinary and traditional legal norms. I urge upon you the importance and desirability of considering such a change. I know it would not solve all of your problems, but I am sure that it would have an enormous impact on your standing in the world scene.

This letter is offered in great good faith, and as an expression of appreciation to you for your great courtesy to me when I was recently in South Africa. I was fully aware of the great lengths to which you went in meeting my requests, and I was sensible of the honor which you paid me in seeing me at such length and in going so far to meet my requests. As far as my particular mission is concerned, I feel that things worked out quite well, though I am still concerned about the four women I met at Windhoek Prison, and the five persons, whom I did not meet, and who are detained as witnesses, with strong assurances that they will not be charged.

If, in addition, you could bring yourself to the conclusion that the time has come to ameliorate some of your legal practices, and to bring about changes in your statutory provisions, I am sure that the effect would be very beneficial to South Africa. I earnestly hope that you will give this careful consideration.

With best wishes, and my sincere thanks to you again for your courtesies to me,

Very truly yours,

Erwin N. Griswold

Appendix B

(See page 367)

February 23, 1979

To My Washington Partners and Associates

We have had a very difficult period. I have talked to many of you over the past several weeks, and have tried to learn all that I could about the situation.

My first objective was to try to do what I could to see if a way could be found to hold this office together. I worked to that end in Cleveland on January 22 and 23, and later here in Washington. As I talked with many people, various things seemed to unfold.

Early in my consideration of the problems, I became convinced that there had been extensive misunderstandings and misperceptions on both sides. I also became convinced that there was a fundamental problem which existed quite apart from these misunderstandings.

For quite a while, though, I thought that if we could get together with Cleveland participants, necessarily through representatives, the misunderstandings and misperceptions could be straightened out. With that fog cleared away, the fundamental problems would stand out clearly. They could then be wrestled with; and I had hopes that particularly in the light of the trauma of the past few weeks, they could be worked out, and a new and firm foundation laid for the continued existence and development of the firm.

I still think there are misunderstandings. In retrospect, I am not happy with the way the matter was handled. I am likewise satisfied that there is a fundamental problem. My present thought is that this problem is so deep-seated and of so long-standing that there is no prospect that it can be worked out, even if the misunderstandings were dispelled.

What is the fundamental problem?

Exploring this question is made difficult by some of the events of the past few weeks. It has been said, for example, that a "government contracts" practice is inconsistent with a "national law firm." Carrying this idea forward, it has been said that success in any specialty is inconsistent with a national law office. I do not believe that either of these things is true. Nor do I believe that such a view is in fact held by responsible partners in Cleveland.

Why, then, was this said? It has surely contributed to the difficulties which we have encountered.

Let us look at the situation. There is felt to be a very serious problem, of long-standing, which appears to be getting more difficult. No one wants to point a finger, or make *ad hominem* arguments. It is difficult to describe the fundamental problem in abstract terms. Everyone wants to treat the situation in a responsible way, as ladies and gentlemen should. Thus, "government contracts" became a euphemism for the real problem, particularly because much of that problem, though not all of it, is felt to be exemplified by partners practicing in the "government contracts" area.

Again, I say: what is the real underlying and fundamental problem? I see it, I feel it, I am convinced it exists, and has existed for a number of years. It is hard to articulate it. The best word that I have heard applied to it is that there is an excessive "parochialism" on the part of some members of the Washington office. Another way to put it would be to say that there is too much "inward looking" reaction to problems—as David Riesman has put it, "inner-direction." Some people are felt to look at problems in terms of the Washington office, without giving adequate recognition to the fact that if this office is to be part of a national law firm, and not just another "Washington law firm," the overall interests must be constantly considered, and must ordinarily be primary. There is nothing wrong with being a "Washington law firm," but that is not what this office has purported to be. It is not the way Cleveland regards us, or what Cleveland needs. And it is not what we should be, exclusively, if we are to be truly a part of a national law firm.

That is in pretty general terms. How can it be made concrete? Some things, I am told, go back many years. I only know directly about those things during the past six years.

It was in 1973 that "the Washington Tax Group" joined the office, thus providing a significant capacity in the tax field through people with special backgrounds and standing in that area. There was resistance in the Washington office to the establishment of the Washington Tax Group, particularly with respect to the concept of dual partnership, and that attitude has persisted to the present time. I am a member of the Washington Tax Group, and I am a dual partner. I must say that I thought that the dual partnership concept was an excellent one, and it was especially appealing to me. I do not think I would have had

any interest in joining a "Washington law firm." Since coming
here, I have not felt under any pressure myself, but I have been
aware of the continued resistance in some quarters to the dual
partnership concept. I have tried to conduct myself so as to
show that the concept is a good one for this firm, but I have been
aware of a resistance, of a sort of "paper curtain" drawn around
some of my dual partners. I have disliked this, and have hoped
that it would be cured by time. That has not happened. On the
contrary, it has, I think, tended to get worse.

There has been continued resistance to lateral entries. A
partner was brought in to handle Federal Power Commission
matters. He was very successful as a lawyer, but he was almost
literally frozen out here, and departed after nine months or so.
There have been some similar situations.

The most recent, of course, was the arrival of the "antitrust
group." This was strongly resisted by a number of Washington
partners. It was said that we should develop our own antitrust
capacity, and that we had the start of such a capacity. But that
was not what the Cleveland members of the national law office
wanted or needed. For the most part, antitrust business is of
large scale. You do not attract it by the start of an antitrust
capacity. Here, again, in part for the purpose of protecting the
Washington partners, the "antitrust group" was brought in on a
dual partnership basis. This, too, was resisted. The approach of
many of my Washington partners and friends was that this is a
Washington law office. It must be run entirely from Washington, and we must make all of the decisions in Washington. That
is understandable if this is a Washington law office. But this is
not a Washington law office, and never has been. Understandably to me, having simply a "Washington law office" in Washington does not meet the needs of my Cleveland partners.

Before leaving the specifics, I will refer to one other matter.
Various references have come to me about "a firm within a
firm." This is hard for me to accept within my concept of a
Washington law office. Indeed, this element in the problem may
be the real source of the suggestion that "government contracts"
is incompatible with a national law office.

When the situation becomes persistent and clear, it is not
inappropriate for Cleveland to say, it seems to me, that we can
proceed no longer on the basis which has developed over the past
several years.

For some time, I pursued the hope that the parochial or inner-
directed approach of some of my partners would be modified. I
have long been a teacher, and I thought for a while that I could
help to lead them to a wider concept and a greater willingness to

meet national needs. As I have talked with people, and have learned more about the developing facts over the past several years, I have come to the conclusion that some of my Washington partners and friends will not change their perceptions, and that there is no reasonable prospect that the fundamental issue can be resolved by maintaining the present office intact.

At this point, I want to make one thing quite clear. I do not think that there is anything improper about the parochial view which, it seems to me, is held by some of my partners and friends. I do not say that they are wrong. It may well be that it would be better for all concerned if we were like Wilmer, Cutler & Pickering or Covington & Burling. But then, of course, we could not be Jones, Day, Reavis & Pogue.

After a good deal of careful thought, I have come to the conclusion that I want to stay with the "national law office." That was the concept I had when I came here. It seems to me to be a sound concept for a few firms in this country, and I would like to see this firm be the leading firm in that group. I think it can be done, if the objective is not confounded by parochialism. I want to give the concept a further try.

What, then, is the Washington office of a national law firm? It is very hard to operate a national law firm, as our experience has shown. I think it can be done.

There should be a large measure of autonomy in the Washington office, and I think we have had that. We hire our own associates, make our own recommendations for advancing associates to partnership, undertake our own leases and obligations of that sort. On the other hand, we are not a small, completely cohesive, inner-directed group. We should freely make all decisions in terms of the needs of a national law office, viewed in a broad way, and we should make such decisions easily, and naturally, more than gracefully. This does not mean domination from Cleveland or from any other quarter. It does mean willing responsiveness to the expressed need of Cleveland or Los Angeles. It does mean a willing acceptance of fifty-fifty partners in appropriate situations. It does not mean simply taking orders. There should be full scope for discussion, interchange of views, and negotiations, and full confidence on both sides that reasonable positions taken in one city or the other will be acknowledged and efforts made to meet them.

Being the Washington office of a national law firm does *not* mean that it is inappropriate for the Washington office to engage in a Washington practice, or, as it is sometimes put, to be qualified in "Washington specialties." In no sense is the Washington office to be simply a service bureau of Cleveland and Los

Angeles. It should provide that service as needed. But Washington should be entirely free to develop its own practice, to have its own clients, and to engage in many areas of law practice which are of no particular concern to Cleveland or Los Angeles.

At one of our recent meetings, statements were made to the effect that "a Washington practice was not consistent with the needs of a national law office." I am assured by the highest authority that this does not represent the position of the Cleveland office. In due course, I am going to try to prepare a statement outlining my concept of the proper function of the Washington office of a national law firm. I have already outlined this in general terms, and have encountered no resistance. I have no doubt that it can be worked out, and I hope that it may be helpful in considering problems in the future.

Each one will, of course, have to make up his own mind. My purpose in this memorandum is to outline the processes by which I have come to a conclusion. If this is helpful to any others, I will be glad. I will, of course, be glad to talk with anyone about any aspect of the matter, as I have been doing over the past several weeks.

I am very sorry that these difficulties have arisen. I am, however, convinced that there have been real and growing problems over a period of years, and that these problems are legitimate problems on which reasonable minds may differ. They are not quite the problems outlined in some recent memoranda, but they are real. Reluctantly, I have come to the conclusion that they cannot be resolved within the present framework.

In some ways, the fifty-fifty partner problem can symbolize the underlying problem, though it goes deeper than that. As I have said, I like the fifty-fifty partner ideal, because it points in the direction of the unitary nature of the enterprise, and helps to keep our horizons broad. I have always regarded it as a step in the right direction. I have hoped that we would take the further step, and have a common pot. That seems to me to be the natural way to operate in a national law firm. I hope that we can keep moving in that direction. There will be problems and difficulties, but it seems to me to be a desirable objective.

Accordingly, for the reasons I have tried to indicate above, I am opting for the National Law Firm. That is the concept in which I believe. I am convinced that it can be made to work. I look forward to watching it recover from the present stress, and to help in that process if I can.

Erwin N. Griswold

*

Table of Cases

References are to Pages

Index

✝